JUN	2004
		JUN 09	
		JUL X X 2015	

Collected essays on
Italian language & literature
presented to

Kathleen Speight

edited by

Giovanni Aquilecchia
Stephen N. Cristea
Sheila Ralphs

Manchester University Press
Barnes & Noble Inc.

71- 2130

© 1971 MANCHESTER UNIVERSITY PRESS

Published by the University of Manchester at
THE UNIVERSITY PRESS
316-324 Oxford Road, Manchester M13 9NR

UK ISBN 0 7190 0450 0
(subscription copies 0 7190 0449 7)

U.S.A.

BARNES & NOBLE INC
105 Fifth Avenue, New York, N.Y. 10003

US ISBN 0 389 04135 1

Printed in Great Britain by
Butler & Tanner Ltd, Frome and London

Contents

v

Contents

The editors wish to thank all those
who have contributed so willingly
to this volume
Their gratitude is also due to the Press,
which has made publication possible,
and to Mrs Nancy Stålhammar
for her secretarial assistance

The editors deeply regret that
they are not able to include a contribution
from the late Professor Roberto Weiss,
who was among the first
to promise his participation

Contributors

All the contributors to this volume have been at some time during the course of Dr Kathleen Speight's long career either students of hers, or colleagues, or have had personal contact with her through her work and research in this country and abroad.

Sheila Ralphs
Senior Lecturer in Italian
University of Manchester

Cesare Segre
Professor of Romance Philology
University of Pavia

Alan Freedman
Lecturer in Italian
University of Edinburgh

M. F. M. Meiklejohn
Stevenson Professor of Italian
University of Glasgow

Cecil Grayson
Serena Professor of Italian
University of Oxford

Maria Corti
Professor of History of the Italian Language
University of Pavia

Carlo Dionisotti
formerly Professor of Italian
Bedford College, University of London

Giovanni Aquilecchia
Professor of Italian
Bedford College, University of London
formerly in the University of Manchester

Contributors

J. H. Whitfield
Serena Professor of Italian
University of Birmingham

Conor Fahy
Professor of Italian
Birkbeck College, University of London

Peter Armour
Lecturer in Italian
University of Sheffield

Felicity M. Firth
Lecturer in Italian
University of Bristol

Uberto Limentani
Professor of Italian
University of Cambridge

Beatrice Corrigan
Professor of Italian
Department of Italian and Hispanic Studies
University of Toronto

Stephen N. Cristea
Lecturer in Italian
University of Manchester

C. P. Brand
Professor of Italian
University of Edinburgh

T. Gwynfor Griffith
Professor of Italian
University of Hull

Paola de Angeli
Lecturer in Italian
University of Sheffield

Paola Seganti
Lecturer in Italian
University of Manchester

Introduction

This volume of essays edited by members of the Department of Italian Studies in the University of Manchester is offered to its reader, Dr Kathleen Speight, to mark her retirement from university teaching in 1970. It is intended as an expression of esteem and affection for one who has devoted her life to stimulating interest in Italian studies in Britain.

Miss Speight was the third student to graduate in Italian studies in the University of Manchester, having arrived there with the intention of taking a degree in Geography. It is rumoured that the change of subject was due to a collision with the lecturer in Italian, Signor Azeglio Valgimigli, which scattered his armful of books. It was while retrieving these that she had her first, rather unusual, but apparently irresistible, contact with Italian literature! After graduating under Professor Piero Rebora in 1926, she spent several years in secretarial work before returning to academic circles in 1932. She then worked for a year as Assistant in Italian at Manchester University under Professor Mario Praz, with whom, in 1933, she took her M.A. degree (the thesis was entitled *Spirito e motivi dei poeti crepuscolari*). This was followed by a stay of three years in Italy when Miss Speight taught English in the British Institute in Florence. While there she worked on a thesis on *La critica del romanzo italiano moderno*, which she discussed in 1936 with Professor Attilio Momigliano, and which gained her the title of Dott. Lett. of Florence University. Since then Florence has been very much her second home, to be visited for at least a month every year. Returning to England, Miss Speight went as Lector in Italian to Cambridge for two years, where she took her M.Litt. in 1938 with Professor E. R. Vincent with a thesis on *T. J. Mathias and his place in Anglo-Italian relations*. From Cambridge Miss Speight came back to Manchester to act as part-time Assistant Lecturer in the Department of Italian under Professor Walter Ll. Bullock. This period coincided with the years of the second world war, and she lectured in Liverpool as well as Manchester, commuting from her home in Southport. The task was not without its hazards, as she occasionally found herself on a train heading irretrievably for the wrong city! Despite these exacting official duties, she managed for two years to find time to care for three Spanish children, victims of their country's civil war. After the sudden death of Professor Bullock in 1944, Miss Speight was left in charge of the

Manchester Italian Department, of which she continued as acting head until the chair was filled in 1961. Under her guidance and care the Department grew and developed considerably, and played an increasingly important part in the work of the Faculty of Arts.

Many ex-students remember Miss Speight with affection and high regard. She is an inspiring teacher whose enthusiasm is infectious, and her profound knowledge of Italian literature is never allowed to smother a bubbling sense of humour. Her special love is for the 'golden age' of Italian writing, the fourteenth century, but her interests, like her teaching, cover the whole field of Italian culture. Younger members of staff have particular reason to be grateful to her for the way in which, with absolute unselfishness, she encouraged them in their work, often by sacrificing to them the subjects she most enjoyed teaching. Italian assistants in the Department always received a warm welcome and a helping hand whenever it was needed. Indeed, munificent hospitality is one of the salient traits by which Miss Speight is known, and festive days spent by both staff and students at her home in Southport have contributed greatly to the gaiety and amicability which she has helped to make a characteristic of the Department.

In addition to work within the University, Miss Speight has taken every possible opportunity to encourage the study of Italian in schools, and was for long an active member of the directing committee of the Society of Italian Studies in Britain. She has been chairman of the Manchester Medieval Society, and for twenty-five years has held the position of honorary secretary to the venerable Manchester Dante Society, founded in 1906. The Society began by devoting itself to the study of Dante, but slowly broadened its scope, and now brings together members both within and outside the University who have an interest in any aspect of Italian culture. On the occasion of the Society's golden jubilee in 1956, Miss Speight organised the festivities and the exhibition of the *Works of Dante* shown in the John Rylands Library, Manchester. This exhibition was afterwards borrowed by Nottingham University and the University of Toronto. Then in 1965, to celebrate the seventh centenary of Dante's birth, Miss Speight was responsible, in collaboration with the History of Art Department in Manchester, for arranging the exhibition *Dante and his Illustrators*, for which she compiled the descriptive catalogue. This exhibition was held at the Whitworth Art Gallery in Manchester, and was then shown at the Italian Institute in London and at the University of Warwick. Miss Speight wrote an account of the history of the Dante Society in the year following the jubilee, and what she says there about Signor Valgimigli's twenty-one years as secretary applies very much to herself:

'Few societies have had so loyal, enthusiastic and tireless an honorary secretary. He gave unstintingly and generously of his time, energy and thought to promote its interests. The Society was for him of first importance. *It stood for the two causes he had most at heart: Italian studies and the promotion of Anglo-Italian friendship.'*

Miss Speight has attended a number of international conferences in an official capacity, and was invited to spend two terms as Visiting Professor at the University of Toronto in 1966. Later in the same year, after the disastrous flood in Florence, she organised the collection of a considerable sum of money, both to help flood victims and to contribute towards the restoration of damaged works of art. She also exhorted the University of Manchester to give generous financial help. Her contacts with scholars in Italy and other countries have often led to their visiting Manchester and lecturing there. They were always welcomed most cordially, and frequently returned to the city and University where they had been made to feel so much at home.

Miss Speight's publications can be divided into two categories: those which were inspired by the necessity of providing students with reference and practical material, at a time when Italian was a comparatively new subject in British universities, and the critical and bibliographical essays. The former include a series of *Passages*, with notes and key, for translation into Italian and other languages, and the grammar *Teach yourself Italian*, her most popular work, of which there have been numerous editions. Although meant for beginners, this book reveals the author's extensive technical knowledge of the language, and has enabled many thousands to learn Italian 'without tears', and with much enjoyment. A dictionary to be issued by the same publisher is nearing completion. Included in her other publications are an excellent survey of the John Rylands Library Dante Collection, published in *The Bulletin of the John Rylands Library*, 1961, essays entitled 'Linguistic studies in Italy, 1939–45', and 'Italian novels of today', both in *Modern Languages*, a bibliography of Antonio Pucci's works in the *Journal of Documentation*, and articles on T. J. Mathias—'An English writer of Italian verse' in *Studies in Philology*, 1946—and on Pucci—'*Vox populi* in Antonio Pucci', published in the 1962 *festschrift* offered to Professor Vincent of Cambridge. She also contributed the selected bibliographical lists to *Italian Studies* for ten years, and prepared the Italian part of the programme for the Writers' Conference at the Edinburgh Festival in 1962. Also about this time Miss Speight conceived the plan of publishing a number of Italian texts in this country with an introduction, notes and vocabulary to facilitate their use by students of Italian at all levels. This series, published by Manchester University Press, has been extremely successful, the list of prospective volumes is constantly increasing, and those already issued are widely used in adult classes, schools and universities. Miss Speight, who will continue to act as general editor, herself contributed the second volume in 1963, Emilio de Marchi's

Il cappello del prete, and is now at work on another volume, Boccaccio's *Decameron*.

The Italian government, in 1961, awarded Dr Speight the Cross of Cavaliere Ufficiale della Repubblica Italiana. It was an honour which she richly deserved, for Miss Speight, inspired by a boundless love for Italy, has been a ceaselessly active and enthusiastic promoter of Italian studies in this country. Many of those at present teaching Italian in British schools and universities have either studied under Miss Speight at some time or taught alongside her. Many more have entered her orbit for a moment and have left it enriched. She is one of that select group of people who have made the study of Italian language and literature what it is today in this country.

We all wish her a very happy retirement.

Sheila Ralphs

Cesare Segre

Strutture romanzesche,
strutture novellistiche
e funzioni

I§§ 70-71 de *La mort le roi Artu*[1] costituiscono un episodio
fortemente unitario, quasi un racconto nel romanzo. I tratti
di mistero dell'inizio (l'elegante navicella che giunge inattesa
sotto la torre di re Artù) trasferiscono presto la curiosità del
lettore ad Artù e Galvano, che vi salgono, esploratori; s'effonde
poi una nota di pathos estatico, quando in un letto ben addobbato
appare ai due una bellissima fanciulla morta; al centro del racconto,
un altro elemento accattivante: una letterina appassionata che, sulla
falsariga appena percepibile delle norme epistolografiche, esprime
l'amore e la disperazione della donna, vittima d'un rifiuto da parte
del più nobile dei cavalieri, Lancillotto (più avanti, conclusione
canonica di queste storie tragiche, una tomba accoglie il cadavere
sotto una lapide che sintetizza la sua vicenda).

Gli elementi narrativi individuabili (dirò per semplicità funzioni,
anche se mi mantengo, per motivi che vedremo, a un livello di
schematizzazione meno spinto di quello richiesto per poter
parlare propriamente di funzioni) sono questi:

1. Arrivo d'una navicella misteriosa.
2. Artù e Galvano vi salgono.
3. Vi scoprono, su un letto, il cadavere d'una fanciulla.
4. Galvano trova una lettera e la porge al re.
5. Lettura e chiarimento della vicenda.

Eppure l'episodio non solo si collega col romanzo, ma ne costituisce
un punto nodale. Infatti la fanciulla giunta—ultimo viaggio—alla
corte di Artù è la damigella d'Escalot, morta d'amore per il rifiuto
di Lancillotto (perfetto amante di Ginevra, non poteva accettare
le sue profferte pur attraenti). Ma Ginevra aveva creduto Lancillotto infedele: prima perché Lancillotto, costretto da una promessa
imprudente, aveva portato in torneo l'insegna della damigella, poi
perché Galvano lo aveva detto innamorato di lei: donde l'ingiusta
condanna di Lancillotto, spinto dallo sdegno della regina a
lasciare la corte. A sua volta l'assenza di Lancillotto privava
Ginevra dell'unico valido paladino di fronte a Mador, che
l'accusava della morte del proprio fratello. L'arrivo della navicella
mette dunque in chiaro molte cose, preparando gli sviluppi
successivi.

L'episodio ha poi una funzione più sottile. La lettera della
damigella d'Escalot, dimostrando l'innocenza di Lancillotto
(rispetto alla regina), conferma indirettamente ad Artù la colpa di

Ginevra (verso di lui), di cui lo hanno da poco edotto Morgana e le pitture fatte dallo stesso Lancillotto prigioniero della maga (la *Salle aux images*). Così ciò che da Morgana gli è stato presentato crudamente come adulterio, lascia intravvedere ad Artù il suo lato eroico e cortese: diventa più nobile, ma più grave e ineluttabile. Per questo certamente l'autore fa che sia proprio Artù, e non Galvano, a leggere il messaggio della morta.

I nessi con la globalità della trama sono attuati mediante una serie di notizie e notazioni particolari: quando la navicella arriva, il re sta guardando pensoso verso la *riviere*, preoccupato per la minaccia che Mador fa pendere sulla regina; trovata la fanciulla, Galvano la riconosce come damigella d'Escalot, e ricorda al re la conversazione, con lui e con Ginevra, in cui l'aveva detta amante di Lancillotto: il re, che s'era mostrato incredulo alle rivelazioni di Galvano, medita (immaginiamo) sulle amare implicazioni del suo aver avuto ragione.

In questo quadro, la prima analisi delle funzioni risulta incompleta: altre se ne devono enucleare, e tutte vanno raggruppate come fasi d'una chiarificazione progressiva: in 1, 2, 3 c'è ancora un clima avventuroso[2] e astratto; dopo 3 diventa fondamentale una funzione 3bis (riconoscimento della fanciulla da parte di Galvano), che inserisce l'episodio nella trama complessiva, e perciò pone le altre funzioni sullo stesso piano narrativo del romanzo, specie la funzione 5, che testimonia alla regina e a tutti la fedeltà assoluta di Lancillotto, e che produce una funzione 5bis (pentimento della regina), presente infatti nell'episodio.

Anche se si passa a una recensione degli *attanti* (per dirla con Greimas), ci si accorge che il loro numero e i loro rapporti cambiano quando si passa dall'episodio all'assieme del romanzo. Nell'episodio ci sono tre *attanti* in presenza (Artù, Galvano e la damigella, che, anche morta, parla con la sua lettera) e uno assente (Lancillotto), della cui azione permangono i risultati (morte della damigella); nella cronologia interna, gli *attanti* si ordinano a coppie: Lancillotto-damigella (loro rapporti e conseguenze funeste) e Artù–Galvano, testimoni postumi della vicenda. Ma nel complesso della trama, la damigella non è che un *attante* secondario, con funzione di catalizzatore (amante non riamata) riguardo al triangolo Lancillotto-Ginevra (amanti riamati)–Artù (marito tradito): Artù, a differenza di Galvano, passa dal ruolo di testimone a quello di scopritore della propria onta.

Questi successivi esercizi di schematizzazione non sono gratuiti. Vi è infatti chi ha avvertito l'unitarietà dell'episodio e lo ha liberato dai particolari tonali e dalle funzioni che lo collegano col romanzo (3bis e 5bis). Parlo del compilatore a cui risale la novella 82 del *Novellino*.[3]

I rapporti della novella con *La mort le roi Artu* sono noti;[4] ma non s'è mai studiato il metodo con cui N ha utilizzato la sua fonte. Schematizzando N, si ottengono questi elementi (o funzioni):

1'. Amore infelice della damigella d'Escalot per Lancillotto.

2'. Disposizioni per l'apprestamento del letto-catafalco e della navicella e per la vestizione del cadavere.

3'. Compilazione della lettera.

4'. Morte della damigella.

5'. Esecuzione delle disposizioni.

6'. Viaggio del battello sino alla corte di Artù.

7'. Artù sale sul battello.

8'. Artù vi scopre il letto col cadavere.

9'. Ritrovamento della lettera.

10'. Testo della lettera come delucidazione dei fatti.

Si vede subito che le funzioni 6'–10' di N corrispondono alle funzioni 1'–5' dell'episodio della MA. Ma è interessante individuare il procedimento narrativo che ha prodotto in N le funzioni 1'–5'.

L'episodio della MA propone, s'è visto, una soluzione frazionata ai suoi misteri: la navicella è totalmente misteriosa; poi la morta viene identificata come damigella d'Escalot; infine la lettera spiega perché ella sia morta, e s'intende che s'è fatta imbarcare sulla navicella per portare il messaggio, anzi il reclamo, ad Artù e ai suoi cavalieri. Il procedimento è reso possibile dai legami con parti esterne all'episodio: già ai §§ 38–39 sono descritti la passione della damigella per Lancillotto, e il diniego di costui, con la conclusione: 'Tout en ceste maniere devisa la damoisele sa mort; si l'en avint tout issi comme ele dist; car ele morut sanz faille por l'amour de Lancelot, si com li contes le devisera ça en avant'; e al § 57 si sono dati altri e più patetici particolari, con la conclusione: 'Lors se parti la damoisele [...] et s'en vint a son lit et se cocha a tel eür que onques puis n'en leva, se morte non, si com l'estoire le devisera apertement'.

Il lettore della MA conserva dunque nella memoria delle valenze libere che l'episodio è in grado di saturare: l'attesa suscitata dalle formule 'si com li contes (l'estoire) le devisera ça en avant (tout apertement)' si placa con la lettura dell'episodio. Si noti però che l'ordine dei fatti, cronologico nelle premesse extra-episodio, diventa retrogrado all'interno dell'episodio: prima arriva la navicella, poi s'apprende la morte della damigella, infine si risale alle sue cause. E s'aggiunga che tra le funzioni extra-episodio (amore deluso e morte, chiamiamole *a* e *b*) e quelle dell'episodio, tre restano implicite, rese ovvie dalla conoscenza complessiva dei fatti: la compilazione della lettera (*c*), l'ordine d'essere imbarcata sulla navicella (*d*) e l'attuazione dell'ordine (*e*).

Tutti i cambiamenti apportati da N derivano da una decisione abbastanza naturale: quella di spiegare ai lettori chi fosse la damigella d'Escalot. Il compilatore ha insomma compreso che per ottenere una novella doveva eliminare sì i riferimenti al romanzo per lui superflui, ma doveva inglobare per contro nel contesto gli elementi che nella MA lo preparano. Salvo che, dicendo sin dall'inizio chi fosse la damigella d'Escalot, s'eliminava la possibilità d'una soluzione frazionata e d'un rigoroso ordinamento retrogrado dei fatti, come proposto dalla MA.

Così il compilatore di N allinea le funzioni *a*, *b* e, salito sullo scivolo dell'ordine cronologico, si sente nella necessità di esplicitare le funzioni implicite *c*, *d*, *e*; dopo di che prosegue con l'ordinamento originario. Così abbiamo le funzioni 1'–5' di N, corrispondenti ad *a–e* di MA, e le funzioni 6'–10' di N, corrispondenti ad 1–5 di MA. Le due serie sono speculari, e la seconda (6'–10') non fa che ripresentare in ordine retrogrado ciò che la prima (1'–5') ha esposto in ordine cronologico.

Non sto facendo un'ipotesi, ma descrivendo dei fatti. È senz'altro da riferire ai fatti (in particolare a una certa inesperienza del compilatore) se il nesso tra le funzioni 1'–5' e 6'–10' è rimasto imperfetto, e conclama inequivocabilmente la difficoltà della sutura. Alludo a queste frasi: 'E in questa borsa avea una lettera, ch'era de lo 'nfrascritto tenore. Ma imprima diciamo de ciò che va innanzi la lettera', dove il *ma imprima diciamo* e il *de lo 'nfrascritto tenore*, soddisfatto solo alla fine del racconto, denunciano le incertezze della ristrutturazione, come pure l'imperfetto *avea una lettera* (cioè la funzione 3'), posto in un tempo intermedio e ambiguo tra quello delle disposizioni date e quello del ritrovamento effettivo (la funzione 3' avrebbe anche potuto precedere la 2').

Anche più sensibili le conseguenze sugli *attanti*. Il 'sistema' Lancillotto–Ginevra–(Artù), con la damigella quale catalizzatore, lascia il posto a un 'sistema' Lancillotto-damigella, in cui è Ginevra ad avere la funzione secondaria d'impedire, inconsapevole, l'amore tra i due, e in cui ad Artù s'affida soltanto la funzione testimoniale (scoprire la fanciulla e la lettera). La mancanza di compromissione di Artù nella vicenda è ben indicata da due fatti: (1) Artù assorbe in sé le funzioni, solo mediatrici, di Galvano; (2) non è Artù a ritrovare la missiva né, tanto meno, a leggerla ansioso: egli la fa leggere ad altri (*fecela leggere*), atarassicamente.

Tuttavia, anche elaborato, il racconto serviva benissimo al compilatore. Egli è stato colpito dalla lettera, che lo richiamava da un lato alla moda degli esempi epistolari, dall'altro alla lirica amorosa: due correnti già venute a confluenza nei *dictamina* erotici.[5] La parte finale della lettera è scandita come la stanza d'una canzone: 'già nol seppi tanto pregare d'amore/ ch'elli avesse di me mercede./ E così, lassa!, sono morta/ per ben amare,/ come voi potete vedere'.

Però l'amor cortese, nel *Novellino*, è generalmente 'distanziato' in una prospettiva romanzesca o aristocratica. Qui il distanziamento romanzesco è potenziato con un tono di fiaba (che si sostituisce a quello avventuroso della fonte). Alla fiaba conferisce l'insistita preziosità del *décor*: ricca è la *navicella coperta d'un vermiglio sciamito*, ricco il letto, con *ricche e nobili coverture di seta*, ricche le *pietre preziose* che lo ornano, *ricca di molto oro e di molte pietre preziose* la *bella corona* di cui si fa cingere il capo la donna, *ricca* la *cintura* e la *borsa*. Ed è soprattutto fiabesco il viaggio della navicella *senza vele*, che il mare guida sino a Cammalot.

Che questi elementi siano pertinenti, ce lo dice il confronto con la MA. Qui l'aggettivo *riche* è usato più raramente e in frasi più lontane, sì da produrre al massimo una tonalità ambientale. Viceversa sono fittissime le enunciazioni in ordine alla bellezza della fanciulla: *moult avoit esté bele ... si bele damoisele ... trop bele riens ... la grant biauté ... la bele damoisele ... la bele damoisele ... une des plus beles damoiseles del monde*. Nulla di questo è rimasto in N. La bellezza della fanciulla ha infatti la funzione di rendere più eroico il diniego di Lancillotto: ciò che importa molto nella trama della MA, mentre è irrilevante in N, dove domina la fanciulla morta di *mal d'amore*, col suo disperato messaggio postumo.

Questo esempio di analisi, favorito dalla semplicità dei mezzi stilistici e strutturali impiegati dai due autori, suggerisce alcune deduzioni e generalizzazioni. Intanto, s'è avuta una riprova eloquente della diversità tra le leggi strutturali che reggono romanzo e novella: persino il poco sofisticato compilatore di N mostra di averne avuto coscienza. A loro volta queste leggi strutturali sono attualizzate in rapporto con premesse di gusto e finalità letterarie, così che un contenuto sostanzialmente identico ne subisce trasformazioni decisive. Di ciò si deve tenere ben conto studiando i rapporti d'un testo con le fonti: il grado di fedeltà di quello rispetto a queste è profondamente condizionato da tale ordine di forze.

Deduzioni di validità più ampia credo siano già sgorgate dall'analisi. Le funzioni narrative son venute a identificarsi con certi schemi portanti del racconto. Ma: (1) le funzioni sono state formulate in modo massimalistico (semplificarle ulteriormente sarebbe stato facile, ma avrebbe comportato l'eliminazione di differenze di schema caratterizzanti: gli elementi differenziali sono alla base di ogni analisi, linguistica o critica); (2) è risultata l'esistenza di funzioni implicite, la cui eventuale esplicitazione incide sullo statuto narrativo; (3) è apparsa la netta differenza di risultati ottenibili da un contenuto sostanzialmente simile mediante una diversa successione delle funzioni (effetti di sorpresa valorizzati o eliminati; effetti d'attesa stimolati o neutralizzati).

È anche riuscita evidente, mi pare, la rilevanza 'misurabile' di elementi definibili a prima vista come connotativi. Il tema della bellezza è un elemento importante nell'episodio della MA, in rapporto con la fedeltà adamantina di Lancillotto. N, attento solo all'amore infelice della damigella, lo ha eliminato, rendendo invece, da accidentali che erano, funzionali, gli spunti (connotativi nella MA) sulla ricchezza degli addobbi e delle vesti.

Infine è apparsa la complessità del sistema degli *attanti*: è qui forse che le differenze tra episodio e novella son risultate più decisive. Mi par chiaro che gli *attanti* non sono individuabili a una semplice inquisizione personale: il loro *status* risulta da un paradigma di rapporti e dal suo eventuale mutarsi lungo il tempo della narrazione. Così, mentre nel tempo breve di N essi entrano in uno schema semplice e statico, nell'episodio della MA sentono i contraccolpi delle loro precedenti vicende e in particolare dei loro precedenti rapporti di forza.

Il 'modello' che ci si impone, anche sulla base di dati abbastanza

semplici come quelli offertici dal nostro esempio, mostra dunque
che non basta ricostruire l'interazione fra il sistema degli *attanti*,
quello delle funzioni narrative e quello delle costanti stilistiche,
ma che un ruolo fondamentale è appunto svolto dal tempo, non
in quanto durata ma in quanto luogo di mutamenti nel sistema
stesso delle interazioni. Ogni mutamento intervenuto è relazionato
o contrapposto, dai personaggi come dai fruitori dell'opera, con
la memoria delle precedenti fasi: memoria che diventa condizione
irrenunciabile alla comprensibilità globale della diègesi.

Note

¹ *La mort le roi Artu*. *Roman du XIIIe siècle*, par J. Frappier (Genève–Paris,
Textes Littéraires Français, 1964³). Lo cito con la sigla MA.

² 'A poi que ge ne di que les aventures recommencent' esclama Galvano
alla vista del battello.

³ In *La prosa del Duecento*, a cura di C. Segre e M. Marti (Milano–Napoli
1959), pp. 868–869. Lo cito con la sigla N.

⁴ Vedi R. Besthorn, *Ursprung und Eigenart der älteren italienischen Novelle*
(Halle, 1935), pp. 111–112.

⁵ Alludo ad epistole come quelle contenute nella *Sommetta ad ammaestra-*
mento di comporre volgarmente lettere (*1284–1287*), edita da H. Wieruszowski nel
vol. II dell' *Archivio Italiano per la Storia della Pietà*, pp. 193–198, o come le due
lettere d'amore pubblicate da J. Ruggieri in *Archivum Romanicum*, XXIV
(1940), pp. 92–94.

Alan Freedman

Passages from the Divine Comedy in a fourteenth-century Hebrew manuscript

In an article published in 1915,[1] Carlo Bernheimer described for the first time a manuscript, then in the possession of the Biblioteche delle Scuole Israelitiche of Leghorn, containing a philosophical work in Hebrew by the fourteenth-century Jewish scholar Giuda Romano,[2] a cousin of the more famous Immanuel ha-Romi (the 'realistic' poet known in Italian as Manoello Giudeo). Giuda Romano was a contemporary of Dante's (he was twenty-nine years of age when Dante died), and a particularly interesting aspect of this work is that it contains four quotations from the *Divine Comedy*.[3] At the same time the quotations, which range in length from three to thirteen lines, are unusual in themselves in that their wording and linguistic characteristics are different in several respects from those of any generally accepted Dante text, and also in the fact that they are written in the Hebrew alphabet.

Bernheimer did not discuss the author or the philosophical content of his work in any great detail, being principally concerned to bring the work to the attention of the public and to establish its date; nor did he reproduce the full text of the Dante quotations, being content to quote only three lines because of the 'due strane varietà di lezione' which they contain. He was, indeed, more concerned with the text as evidence for friendship between Giuda's cousin Manoello and Dante.[4] Only recently has the text of the Dante passages been published in full.[5] In a much more searching study of the manuscript (now in the library of the Hebrew University of Jerusalem[6]) Joseph B. Sermoneta brings out the philosophical interest of the text, with its translations from the works of scholastic philosophers such as Egidio Romano, Thomas Aquinas, Albertus Magnus and Alexander of Alessandria. He shows how the passages selected by Giuda Romano for translation and comment are all chosen to illustrate specific philosophical 'quaestiones'; and among the authorities quoted, there appears one writer in 'volgare', Dante Alighieri. Giuda Romano, then, is concerned with Dante not so much as a poet but as a philosopher; hence each of the four passages quoted from the *Divine Comedy* is relevant to the specific problem Giuda is concerned with— respectively vows, divine emanation, the power of prayer to affect divine decrees and free will. Sermoneta also brings out the importance of the work as evidence for the early diffusion of the *Divine Comedy* (even amongst such a 'remote' audience as contemporary

Jewish readers), not to mention the way it is here being utilised as a philosophical text on a par with the more usual scholastic authorities. He also points out the interest of the work, written at a date probably close to that of Dante's major poem, for insight into the manuscript tradition of the *Divine Comedy*; and these Dante passages have in fact been taken into account in Petrocchi's recent critical edition.

Although Sermoneta is concerned principally with a discussion of Giuda Romano's philosophical interpretation of the quaestiones and of his attitude towards Dante, he nevertheless also examines the linguistic implications of the Dante quotations; for, unlike the Latin authors cited by Giuda Romano, which are all translated into Hebrew, the extracts from Dante, evidently intended for an Italian–Jewish readership, are quoted in the vernacular but transcribed in Hebrew characters, as has already been mentioned, the language differing considerably nevertheless, from any generally accepted Dante text, especially in its dialect characteristics. Hence Sermoneta, besides providing a complete transcription in the Latin alphabet of the four passages, includes a detailed section entitled *Grafia* and a similar section entitled *Caratteristiche dialettali*.

Since the actual text, as will become evident below, is of particular relevance, I reproduce here, for the convenience of the reader, the four quotations as interpreted and transcribed into Latin characters by Sermoneta:

> Il cielo li nostri movementi inizia,
> non dico tutti, ma posto ke il dica,
> dato v'è el senno a bene ed a malizia
> e libero volere...
>   (*Purgatorio* XVI, 73–76)

> ...Cristiani a mover gravi
> Non siati como è penno ad onni...
> ...penseti ke onne acqua ve lavi.
> Aveti el novo e'l vecchio T...amento
> e'l pastor de la kesia ke ve guida
> quis... ...asta al vostro salvamento.
> Se mala cupe...s... altro ve guida,
> ommeni siati e non pecora e...
> si ke'l Jodeo de voi tra voi non rida,
> Non faiti... l'agnello ke lascia e latte

de la soa matre senpice e lasci...
e con si stesso el soo voler commatte.
Così Beatrici a mi comi io scrivo;

(*Paradiso* V, 73–85)

Ciò ke no more e ciò ke po' moriri
non è se no sprennor de quilla idea
ke partorisce, amanno, el nostro sire.

(*Paradiso* XIII, 52–54)

E quil ke segue 'n e la circonferenza
de ke ragiono per lo carco soperno,
morte nunziò per vera penetenza:
ora conosce ke 'l jodizio eterno
non se trasmuta quanno degno preco
faa crastino là jiò de l'odierno.

(*Paradiso* XX, 49–54)

Sermoneta draws on the concept of a 'Judaeo–Italian koine' as
the principal explanation for the linguistic peculiarities of the
quotations, seeing in them 'una *traduzione* in dialetto giudeo-
italiano, piuttosto che una *trascrizione* in caratteri ebraici'. And he
continues: 'Infatti, osservando attentamente il testo tramandatoci
da Rabbì Jehudàh, mi sembra conveniente supporre che egli
traducesse i versi della *Commedia* in dialetto giudeo-italiano sì da
renderli orecchiabili al pubblico che leggeva i suoi lavori.'
Furthermore, he adds that this dialect was 'come è noto... [una]
vera e propria koiné'. It is with this interpretation of the language
of the text that I wish to take issue here; for it represents the most
recent manifestation of a body of opinion which tends to see in
any unusual features of Italian texts written in Hebrew characters,
evidence for the existence of a peculiar Jewish dialect of Italian
in the Middle Ages, a dialect, so it is claimed, widely used by Jews
from different parts of Italy and thus constituting a 'koiné giudeo-
italiana'.

In the following discussion I shall, scholastic fashion, first try
to show why Sermoneta's linguistic interpretation of the above
passages cannot be accepted, and then I shall try to show what
these passages really represent.

In the first place, the characteristics, not to mention the
chronological and geographical range of the 'Judaeo–Italian
koine' have never been clearly established. The concept was

developed by Umberto Cassuto in a number of articles concerned with Italian texts in Hebrew characters, but especially in his study of the unique thirteenth-century elegy *La iente de Sion plange e lutta*, the long introduction to which contains an attempt to trace the history of the vernacular of the Jews in Italy in the Middle Ages. There can be no doubt that the text there presented constitutes a masterly critical edition of what is the most original and notable Italian text in Hebrew characters known.[7] Cassuto considers the language of the *Elegia*, of which he gives a scrupulous and accurate analysis, to be a Judaeo–Italian dialect. The linguistic affinities between this *Elegia* published by Cassuto and Giuda Romano's quotations from Dante have therefore been taken by Sermoneta, quite understandably, as proof that the latter are written in Judaeo–Italian koine.

Yet even in a comparatively long and complete poem, such as the *Elegia*, there is very little that can be found to support the idea that there is anything specifically Jewish about the dialectal characteristics of the language. Indeed at one point Cassuto himself, without seemingly being aware of the inherent inconsistency of his argument, states: 'Gli elementi specificamente giudaici nel dialetto dell'elegia sono scarsi'.[8] At times, the preconception seems almost to outweigh the evidence in Cassuto's thought, resulting in such contradictory conclusions as: 'Quanto al lessico, sembra che di proposito l'autore, volendo scrivere in volgare, abbia evitato di adoperare vocaboli schiettamente ebraici (al l'infuori di nomi propri come *Sion, Israel*, del resto presso a poco eguali anche in italiano), sebbene tali vocaboli non dovessero certo mancare nel dialetto da lui parlato'; whereas he says elsewhere that the author intentionally 'scrisse nel dialetto parlato dal popolo'. Further discussion of the language of the *Elegia* would be inappropriate here as we are only concerned with it as far as it is relevant to the Dante quotations; suffice it to say that Cassuto's attribution of the dialect type to the 'sezione marchigiano-umbro-romanesca' which both Migliorini and Contini accept without demur, seems to be all the classification necessary; there is no justification for having recourse to a specifically Jewish dialect of Italian.

Similarly, the evidence provided by other Italian texts in Hebrew characters[9] for the existence of a widely used, specifically Judaeo–Italian koine amongst Jews of different parts of Italy in the late Middle Ages is extremely inconclusive—but this again is a problem requiring extensive discussion inappropriate here.[10]

Thus it is very much open to question whether the language of the *Elegia* can be taken to represent a Judaeo–Italian koine and can therefore be taken as a standard of comparison. However, even if we were to accept it as such, there are three further reasons for thinking that the Dante passages do not represent a deliberate attempt to make a translation into a Jewish dialect of Italian.

In the first place, if one interprets the Dante fragments without the presupposition that the language is a Judaeo–Italian koine, i.e. if in transcribing the text from its Hebrew garb into the normal Latin alphabet one interprets it 'objectively', then the physiognomy of the language appears much less idiosyncratic, less dialectal than in Sermoneta's transcription—i.e. it looks less like Judaeo–Italian koine and more like Dante. For example, in his analysis of the language of the Dante excerpts, Sermoneta gives as the forms of the demonstrative adjective, *quisto, quilla*, which coincides with those of the *Elegia*. But it is difficult to see how these forms are derived from *this* text and not simply from a preoccupation with the koine. Demonstrative adjectives occur only three times in the excerpts; the first in *Par.* XX, 49 is written *equel* (transcribed by the editor as 'E quil'); the second in *Par.* XIII, 53, written *quela* (but transcribed 'quilla'); the third in *Par.* V, 78, where the MS is indicated as defective and where there are no vowel points—hence the word could be read equally as *quis...* or *ques...* ; and there are a number of further anomalies of this kind in the transcription, varying considerably in importance, but which generally tend to emphasise unjustifiably the apparent dialectal peculiarity of the language.[11] This is not to say that the text contains no genuine dialect features; but one must beware of reading them into the text where they do not exist just as much as one should be wary of interpreting a genuine linguistic feature as a slip of the pen.

In the second place, there are important differences between the linguistic characteristics of the *Elegia* and those of the Dante passages. For example, the definite article, a very indicative element of the language, occurs in the brief text of the Dante quotations in the following forms: twice as *el* and once each as *il, lo, l', 'l*; whereas *el* or *il* never occurs in the *Elegia*, where the form *lo* is constant in this long poem except for one instance of *lu*.

Thirdly, the genuine dialectal features which are present in the language of the text (pointed out by Sermoneta, and attributed to the koine) are found in non-Jewish mediaeval texts of Roman origin, such as the anonymous *Vita di Cola di Rienzo*. For example, Sermoneta cites 'Preposizioni e particelle pronominali: *de, ve'*—but these occur regularly in the *Vita*,[12] e.g. *de Roma, Pregove, ve trova*; 'conservazione della *j* iniziale: *Jodeo, jodizio*'[13]—this is regular in the *Vita*, e.g. *iudicava, Iubileo, iente*; 'I nessi *nd, mb, mn* danno sempre: *nn, e mm*' and Sermoneta cites as examples *amanno, commatte, onni* or *onne*—in the *Vita* we find *secunna, palomma*, etc.[14]

It is doubtful then at the very least, that the linguistic character of the Dante quotations can be attributed to their having been translated into or adapted to a Judaeo–Italian koine. Indeed, this assumption seems to leave Sermoneta himself in considerable perplexity when he attempts to envisage the exact process whereby the text has been transformed from Dante's version to the one we find in this manuscript. This perplexity stems from a false assumption, i.e. that the MS in question represents more or less faithfully what Giuda Romano wrote;[15] whereas on the contrary, the closer one examines the MS, the more evident it becomes that this is a copy and not a very good one at that, for it contains errors which cannot be ascribed to the author. The most conclusive evidence that we are dealing with a copy which has undergone considerable alteration from the original is afforded by the point which Sermoneta, with good reason, considers to be one of the most perplexing in the MS. Referring to the quotation of *Par.* XX, 51, he says, 'Non so spiegarmi la lezione "nunziò", al posto di "indugiò".' Indeed it would be difficult to explain how Giuda Romano could have written 'morte nunziò per vera penitenza' for 'morte indugiò per vera penitenza', which gives an almost opposite meaning, if he understood, as Sermoneta has skilfully demonstrated he did, the full significance of Dante's text. Clearly this is not what he originally wrote, but the work of one or more copyists; for, if we take into account the problems involved in copying an Italian text written in Hebrew characters, we can indeed trace a connection between the presumable original 'morte indugiò' and the 'morte nunziò' of the MS. First let us consider the nature of the scribal problem involved.

Giuda Romano was a learned scholar and was well acquainted with works not only in Hebrew, the normal literary language for an Italian Jew in the Middle Ages, but also with a wide range of Latin writers, as Sermoneta has illustrated, and evidently with Italian literature too if he was able to select so expertly passages to suit his purpose from the *Divine Comedy*. On the other hand, we cannot assume that the scribes copying his text were acquainted with any other literary medium than Hebrew, at least as far as writing was concerned. When they came across short passages of Italian they may well have had some difficulty in interpreting them correctly. The task would be rendered more difficult by the fact that the original quotations were almost certainly written in unpointed Hebrew characters (i.e. without a precise indication of the vowels involved) for to judge from their inaccuracy in this MS, the vowel points must be considered a later addition of scribes accustomed to pointing normal Hebrew but not Italian in Hebrew characters. The difficulty of the task can only have been aggravated by the fact that the extracts concerned are some of the more difficult doctrinal passages from the *Purgatorio* and *Paradiso*, quoted out of context. Moreover, the language of these contains some unfamiliar enough expressions even when written quite unambiguously in its normal alphabet.[16] In other words, faced with a somewhat ambivalent text in Hebrew characters, whose language was clearly Italian, but whose exact import was self-evident only to the author himself or to someone who knew Dante's text well, the scribes have made a number of errors in copying.

Bearing in mind this probable discrepancy between the author's abilities and intentions on the one hand and those of the scribe on the other, let us now return to the problem of *nunziò*. Assuming that Giuda Romano intended to represent in Hebrew characters something equivalent to *morte'nduçiò*, he might well have written the second word something like this:

נדוציאו

This might well have been misread as:

נונציאו

i.e. *nunziò*,[17] by a scribe trying to make sense of a difficult passage which was probably rendered even more obscure by the absence of vowel points. The crucial point is that the *nunziò* in the Jerusalem MS is the result of one, or possibly a series of copyist's errors. Once it is clear that we are dealing with a rather untrustworthy copy, a number of the peculiarities of the text can be seen as mistakes and not as a conscious attempt to conform to a certain dialect type. For instance, the spelling רָאטֹו for *dato* (*Purg.* XVI, 75) is inexplicable unless one assumes that the consonants are correct but the pointing is erroneous. And what are we to make of לְאָסוֹאָה? for *la soa* (*Par.* V, 83) except that the vowels are chaotic, whereas the consonants unexceptionable? Without the pointing it would read quite clearly *la soa* or *la sua*, using a system of orthography to be found in a number of Italian texts in Hebrew characters. In the *Par.* XX, 49–54 passage alone, consisting of only thirty-nine words, there are at least eight scribal errors.[18]

Apart from the fact that we do not have the Dante quotations in the form Giuda Romano wrote them, because this is a copy remote from the original, another factor to consider in order to account for the linguistic traits of the text is the effect the scribes' vernacular has had on the copy. The author of the work was Roman and the copy under discussion was owned by a Roman notable about the years 1329–1331,[19] so there is no sound reason to look beyond Rome for the ambience in which the work was copied. In fact none of the linguistic features of the text need lead us to suppose that we have here anything other than a partially 'Romanised' copy of a Tuscan original. This process of dialectal adaptation by scribes, which is evident in the MS, is not at all unusual in mediaeval Italian texts.[20] The results of this process may be seen in the features mentioned above; the forms *de*, *ve*; the assimilations in *quanno*, *sprennor*, *amanno*, *commatte*; probably conservation of *yod* in *jodizio*, *jiò* ('giù'), *Jodeo* (unless the double *yodh* should be read ǧ-); also, the preference for atonic or intertonic *e* rather than *i* in *penetenza*, *movementi*, *omeni*; and the unvoiced plosive in *matre* (cf. *matre*, *patre* in the *Vita di Cola di Rienzo*), which, of course, like all the other features mentioned, is not exclusive to Rome.

A further point worth considering is that although, on the one hand, we can be certain that Giuda Romano did not write his own errors, such as *nunziò* for *indugiò* or *faa* for *fa*, we cannot be equally certain about these genuine dialect traits. It is possible that the process of Romanisation, especially where it affects the consonants, started with the author.[21] But this is unlikely if a glossary of philosophical and grammatical expressions contained in the British Museum MS (Additional 27179) is indeed his. For here we find the Tuscan and Latin *-nd-* rather than the Roman assimilation *-nn-*, in terms of the type *mondo spirituale* and *mondo circolario*.[22]

We do not know what kind of text of the *Commedia* Giuda Romano was familiar with; but some of the features of his quotations must be attributed to his source and not to his Roman copyists, as can be seen from comparison with Petrocchi's apparatus[23] where we find, for example, *homeni, sciati, iudeo, faite, semprice* (*Par.* V, 80–83) and of particular interest, *sprendor* (*Par.* XIII, 53).

To sum up: the Dante quotations embodied in Giuda Romano's Hebrew philosophical treatise do not represent at all accurately the original text of either Dante or Romano. The text has been corrupted by being copied by uncomprehending scribes whose vernacular must have been close or identical to the *romanesco* of the fourteenth century, but whose writing habits were formed on normal Hebrew texts. They have therefore had some difficulty in understanding short passages of Italian (especially when these are difficult doctrinal passages of the *Purgatorio* or *Paradiso*, containing a number of unfamiliar expressions) when written in a Hebrew text which probably contained no vowel points. They have not only made some mistakes in copying the consonantal original, but have added vowel points, in a rather 'amateurish' fashion, to facilitate reading of the Italian text and have tended to superimpose dialect characteristics of a Roman type on the original. The modifications to the text, then, have been due in part to scribal misunderstandings and in part to a process of local adaptation of the original dialect character of the text during the copying process.

These factors are sufficient to account for all the peculiar features to be found in the Dante quotations. The latter show no sign of having been translated into a specifically Judaeo–Italian koine and cannot be considered as evidence that such a koine existed.

Notes

[1] 'Una trascrizione ebraica dalla Divina Commedia sugli inizi del sec. XIV', in *GSLI*, LXVI (1915) pp. 122–127.

[2] Yehudàh ben Moshèh ben Daniel, also known as Leone or Lionello Romano, or as Leone de Ser Daniel, or as Rabbi Yehudàh ha-Filosof. He was

born in 1292 and died after 1330. He lived and worked principally in Rome, but spent some time at the court of Robert of Naples. He is best known for translations from Latin into Hebrew by which he sought to make Christian scientific literature available to the Jews. For bibliography see n. 5 on p. 24 of the article by Sermoneta quoted in note 5 below.

[3] The passages quoted by Giuda Romano are: *Purg.* XVI, 73–76; *Par.* V, 73–85; *Par.* XIII, 52–54; *Par.* XX, 49–54.

[4] Sermoneta (see below) rather harshly, but not without some justification, summarises Bernheimer's arguments thus: 'Jehudàh aveva trascritto brani della *Commedia*, Jehudàh era cugino di Immanuele, *ergo* Immanuele conosceva Dante. Sillogismo di una rara spassosità!' On the whole question, see U. Cassuto, *Dante e Manoello* (Florence 1921).

[5] J. B. Sermoneta, 'Una trascrizione in caratteri ebraici di alcuni brani filosofici della Commedia', in *Romanica et Occidentalia: Études dediées à la mémoire de Hiram Peri (Pflaum)* (Jerusalem 1963), pp. 23–42.

[6] MS Hebr. 616, quarto.

[7] 'Un'antichissima elegia in dialetto giudeo–italiano' in *AGI*, XXII–XXIII (1929) pp. 349–408 (= *Silloge Ascoli*, Turin 1929). See also 'Agli albori della letteratura italiana: il più antico testo poetico in dialetto giudeo-italiano' in *Rassegna Mensile di Israel*, XII (1937) pp. 102–112. The *Elegia* had previously been published by E. S. Artom, 'Un'antica poesia di autore ebreo' in *Rivista Israelitica*, X (1913–15) pp. 90–99, but in a much less complete edition, i.e. without an attempt to transcribe the text into Latin characters and based on only one MS.

[8] These elements seem to be limited to what Cassuto seeks to show is a specifically Jewish use of a handful of terms such as *scola, taupina, patto*.

[9] Most of the other Italian texts in Hebrew characters are translations (especially biblical or liturgical) or aids to translation (such as biblical glossaries). For an idea of the range of these texts recourse must be had to the following works: C. Roth, 'Essai de bibliographie du judéo-italien' (which lists over forty MSS and printed works) in *Rev. des Ét. Juives*, LXXX (1925) pp. 63–65; and U. Cassuto, 'Bibliografia delle traduzioni giudeo-italiane della Bibbia' (containing fifty-six items, only in part overlapping Roth's bibliography) in *Festschrift A. Kaminka* (Vienna 1937), pp. 129–141.

[10] See in particular the conclusions of M. Berenblut in *A Comparative Study of Judaeo–Italian Translations of Isaiah* (New York 1949).

[11] In *Purg.* XVI, 74, the Hebrew text does not justify *i* in *il*; nor is there any good reason for writing *ke* for *che* hence 'posto che 'l dica' would be a better reading. Similarly the Hebrew text indicates: in *Par.* V, 'movere' (73), 'si che al* Jodeo' (81) 'volere'(84), not to mention errors (?) which have been corrected 'non *paiati*' (82), 'e *co* con si stesso *e* el soo' (84). On the other hand why not 'che lascia *el* latte' (82) if one can read the *omeni* of the Hebrew text as 'ommeni' (80)? In *Par.* XIII: 'morire' (note 'sire' in 54), 'sprennore de quella idea.' In *Par.* XX: 'E quel che... cerconferenza,' 'fa crastino' (why *faa* yet not *veraa*, *penetenzaa*, for which there is as much justification?).

[12] The examples are all taken from pp. 12–15 of *Vita di Cola di Rienzo di anonimo romano* ed. F. Cusin (Florence 1943).

[13] This, however, is not at all self-evident from the system of transcription

used in the Hebrew text, for the symbol used (double *yodh*) could equally well represent *ǧ*. Indeed Sermoneta himself, without comment, transcribes it as such in the word *ragiono* (*Par.* XX, 50). It is evident that the reading *jodizio* rather than *giodizio* derives not from internal evidence but from a conviction that the language has the same features as that of the *Elegia*. The *j*- rather than *ǧ*- would seem preferable, nevertheless, but on the grounds of comparison with the *Vita*; and then of course it can carry no weight as evidence for the koine.

¹⁴ The development MN > *nn* can hardly be considered a valid dialect characteristic, being common to pretty well the whole Italian peninsula including, of course, the literary language (*colonna, autunno, donna,* etc.).

¹⁵ E.g. 'Rabbi Jehudàh, avendo corredato, come vedemmo, la sua trascrizione di segni vocalici…'

¹⁶ Especially *Par.* XX, 49–51, 54.

¹⁷ This transformation probably took place in more than one stage. Several possible ways in which the second and third letters of the word (*daleth* and *waw*) could be misread (hence becoming *waw* and *nun*) suggest themselves. However, what is significant is to see the physical resemblance between the two words, assuming the original was written in either an Italian cursive or rabbinic hand of the fourteenth century. C. Bernheimer's *Paleografia ebraica* (Florence 1924), is very helpful in this respect, but even more so the examination of Italian MSS of the fourteenth century.

¹⁸ Here, of course, I am not considering as errors such features as *aman*[*n*]*o* for Dante's *amando*, etc. However, there are words like *vera, penetenza, fa, la, odierno*, incorrectly pointed *veraa, penetenzaa, paa* (i.e. with *daghesh* indicating *p* not *f*), *laa, odeerno*. Strangely, Sermoneta transcribes these as *vera, penetenza*, etc., but *faa* (as I have mentioned above), without any explanation. Moreover, he attempts to explain the scribe's aberrations as a system which includes a special sign to indicate 'una sillaba muta'. This is ingenious but highly improbable; for in the first place it would have to be considered a special invention of this scribe, as it is unknown elsewhere as far as I am aware, and in the second place the reader would need a microscope to distinguish it from the common vowel sign *qamez*. Surely this is simply a *qamez* written in the wrong place?

¹⁹ C. Bernheimer, 'Una trascrizione', p. 126.

²⁰ 'tale fenomeno è un dato di fatto indiscutibile, di carattere generale e si può dire necessario, che vale dunque per i canzonieri come per ogni manoscritto di ogni genere di prose e di poesia; per il Notaio come per la *Divina Commedia*; per i codici siciliani come per quelli di qualsiasi regione; per i copisti toscani come per quelli siciliani, o pugliesi, o del resto d'Italia…' Moreover: 'tra le cosiddette traduzioni siciliane di testi toscani fatte nel secolo decimoquarto, l'una o l'altra non sarà affatto una traduzione, nel proprio senso di questo vocabolo, ma il risultato di un progressivǒ, involontario, quasi spontaneo travestimento in siciliano del testo originariamente toscano.' E. G. Parodi, *Lingua e letteratura*, Venice 1957, p. 168.)

²¹ In this respect, it should be borne in mind that the Dante text could not in any case be *copied* in the ordinary sense—nor in writing it in Hebrew characters would it be normal to *transliterate* it. The text would have to be read or

pronounced and the *sounds* represented in Hebrew characters. Thus, although Giuda Romano was evidently accustomed to reading and writing *mondo* he might well pronounce it in the Roman fashion, *monno*, and this might well induce him (or his amanuensis) to represent it thus in Hebrew characters.

22 Unpublished, as far as I know. However, J. Elbogen gave an account of this work based on two MSS in Parma (without knowing of the B. M. copy) in 'Ein hebräisch-italienisches Glossar philosophischer Ausdrücke' in *Festschrift A. Berliner* (Frankfurt 1903), pp. 65–75. In three columns he gives the Hebrew term, the Italian gloss (in Hebrew characters) and his transcription of the latter. His transcriptions are somewhat 'Italianising' in nineteenth-century fashion (whereas Sermoneta's tend to be 'dialectalising'). Hence features such as *retolica* (all three MSS), *retondo, arismetica* are transcribed *retorica, rotondo, aritmetica* and even *conč[o]sia consa* as *conciossiaché*, etc. The significant point here is that in this fairly extensive glossary (about 220 expressions) there is no evidence of the Romanised phonology present in the Dante extracts.

23 G. Petrocchi (ed.) *La Commedia secondo l'Antica Vulgata* (Milan 1965), vols. 3 and 4, *passim*.

M. F. M. Meiklejohn

The identity of Dante's Matelda

One of the figures in the *Divine Comedy* of Dante who has excited most discussion is that of Matelda, first presented, as we know, in canto XXVIII of the *Purgatorio* as

> una donna soletta che si gìa
> cantando e scegliendo fior da fiore
> ond' era pinta tutta la sua via.

Dante has now passed through the seven circles of Purgatory, is purged from sin and has arrived in the Garden of Eden, the earthly paradise. Matelda acts as his guide there, plunges him in the waters of Lethe and Eunoe (so that he may forget sin and remember goodness) and finally hands over her charge to the care of Beatrice. But why does Dante name her Matelda? And is she based on a historical personage and, if so, which?

Two things may be taken for granted. The first is that Matelda represents the perfection of earthly life, *quel dolce pome*, and of life on earth both spiritual and temporal, the *beatitudo huius vitae* of the *Monarchia*.

The second is that she was in life a person who really existed, for such is the poet's practice with his symbolical figures. Liberty, Human Reason and Divine Revelation are not presented merely as shadowy abstract personages, but are Cato, Virgil and Beatrice. There are many Matildas, but which has Dante chosen? Matilda, Countess of Tuscany, might be ruled out on account of the bequest of her domains to the Papacy, which increased the temporal power of the Church, if we were sure that Dante knew of this.[1] In view of Dante's political theories he is not likely to have made her the perfection of anything, if he did. Two German nuns, Mechtildis von Hackeborn and Mechtildis von Magdeburg, may also be dismissed, since they might represent perfection of the contemplative life, but never of the active, even though it is a coincidence that the former, in her *Liber Specialis Gratiae*, describes seven terraces of purification. An alluring theory is that Matelda was 'an early friend of Beatrice, a Florentine girl whose premature demise is mourned in the *Vita Nova* VIII, sonnets III and IV.'[2] This identification is attractive, since in the Earthly Paradise, with its springlike background and the meeting at last with Beatrice, there is much of the atmosphere of Dante's youth. But where is the evidence which shows that the unfortunate young woman might have borne this name? Is there any mention in Florentine archives of a Matelda dying about the right date? It is finally possible that the name Matelda might be a mistake, since she is named only once in the poem (*Purgatorio* XXXIII, 119).

Another possible identity of Matelda is so obvious that it is astonishing that nobody, it appears, has pointed it out: this is Saint Matilda (895–968). 'Matilda was the wife of the German King, Henry the Fowler, and mother of, among others, Emperor Otto I and the Saint Bruno who was archbishop of Cologne. She was a widow for thirty-two years, during which she suffered ill-treatment from Otto, provoked by her favouring of another son, Henry called 'the Quarrelsome'. But Henry too showed himself ungrateful to her. Both complained among other things of their mother's liberality to the poor and to the Church. She bore with them patiently, and died with a great reputation for goodness among the people.'[3]

There you have it: an empress and a saint, and the mother of a saint and an emperor. What person could more suitably personify the perfection of the spiritual and active life, especially when we consider Dante's conception of the Pope and Emperor being equal, 'due soli', not the 'sun and moon' of Innocent III. Moreover Otto, in Dante's view, would be a 'genuine' emperor, not an absentee German prince, for he ruled in Italy like Charlemagne and the Hohenstaufen, and was crowned in Rome, in 961. The co-operation of Church and State was, moreover, the corner-stone of his policy. Dante may also have known that Otto III took up residence on the Aventine in order to celebrate the Millennium in the city of Popes and Caesars.

The identification of Dante's Matelda with the Saint and Empress must of course depend on the possibilities of his having had knowledge of the latter, but it would be extraordinary if a man of his breadth of learning did not know something of a historical saint. He certainly knew of her son Otto, as is shown by the *Monarchia*. Possible written sources are also numerous, as can be seen in Pertz's *Monumenta Historiae Germanicae*, where are, apart from writings about Otto the Great, two lives of Matilda and one of Saint Bruno the Less. Dante is likely to have read everything that was available to him and an example of the breadth of his reading is shown by his quoting Justinian in the *Vita Nova* —'nomina sunt consequentia rerum.'

Matilda does not figure in the *Legenda Aurea* and Liutprand of
Cremona, whom Dante is likely to have read, is strangely reticent
about her in his panegyric of Otto, the *Antapodosis*, perhaps
because, the book being propaganda, he is anxious to conceal the
emperor's differences with his mother. Dante seems unlikely to
have known the *Vita Antiquior* of Saint Matilda, written at
Nordhausen and dedicated to Otto II, but he might possibly have
read the *Vita Mahtildis Reginae*, written by order of Henry II,
though the *Monumenta* do not cite any Italian manuscript of this.
Ruotger's *Vita Brunonis* is another possibility.

We can be certain, however, that one work dealing with the
Empress Matilda was known in Italy in Dante's time: this is
Widukind's *Res Gestae Saxonicae* (*Monumenta* III, pp. 408–467), of
which there existed a manuscript at Monte Cassino, written in
Beneventan script about 1200. Here we can read two passages
about the Saint:

> Genuit quoque ei et alios filios clara et nobilissima ac singularis
> prudentiae regina, nomine Mahtilda, primogenitum mundi amorem,
> nomine Oddonem, secundum patris nomine insignitum, virum fortem
> et industrium Heinricum, tertium quoque nomine Brunonem, quem
> pontificis summi ac ducis magni vidimus officium gerentem.

And:

> Cuius [i.e. the Emperor's] mater licet peregrina, nobili tamen erat
> genere procreata. Hic cum audisset, aegrotare coepisse matrem impera-
> toris, mirae sanctitatis feminam, nomine Mahtildam, dumque eius
> expectat funus, proprio funere ipsius funus procedit. De cuius laude si
> aliquid dicere cupimus, deficimus, quia omne argumentum ingenioli
> nostri superat virtus tantae feminae. Quis enim digne possit explicare
> eius vigilantiam erga cultum divinum? Omnis nox omnibus modis et
> omni genere cellulam suam divinorum carminum melodia inplebat.
> Erat enim ei cellula ecclesiae proxima, in qua modice requiescebat; de
> qua omnibus noctibus consurgens intrat ecclesiam, nichilominus
> cantoribus et cantricibus intra cellulam et pro foribus et in via tri-
> formiter constitutis, qui divinam clementiam laudarent atque bene-
> dicerent. Ipsa intra ecclesiam in vigiliis et orationibus perseverans,
> missarum sollempnia expectabat. Deinde infirmos ubicumque audivit,
> in vicino visitavit, necessaria praebuit, deinde pauperibus manum
> porrexit, deinde hospites, qui semper aderant, cum omni largitate
> suscepit; neminem sine afflatu blando dimisit, nullum fere sine munu-
> sculis vel necessariis adiumentis vacuum reliquit. Saepe viatoribus,
> quos longius de cellula prospexit, necessaria transmisit. Talia opera

licet valde humiliter diebus ac noctibus exerceret, tamen nichil de honore regio minuebat et sicut scriptum est, quamvis sederet tamquam regina circumstante populo, semper et ubique erat moerentium consolatrix. Domesticos omnes famulos et ancillas variis artibus, litteris quoque instituit; nam et ipsa litteras novit, quas post mortem regis lucide satis didicit. Ergo si omnes virtutes eius velim narrare, hora deficeret: facundia Homeri vel Maronis michi si adesset, non sufficeret. Igitur plena dierum, plena omni honore, plena operibus bonis et elemosinis, cunctis divitiis regalibus distributis servis Dei et ancillis et pauperibus, secundo Idus Martias animam Christo reddidit...

and perhaps, after that, was appointed guardian of the Garden of Eden.

It will doubtless be objected that there is a difference between the venerable devout Saint and the gay youthful figure in *Purgatorio*,

> qual era
> Proserpina nel tempo che perdette
> la madre lei, ed ella primavera.

but it is not the physical appearance of the two characters which we must consider, but their symbolic meaning. Saint Matilda, with her knowledge of the affairs of the great, with her active benevolence and her unremitting piety, typifies the same as does Dante's young woman—active and contemplative life in their perfection. There is, of course, no positive proof that the Empress is the one after whom Dante's Matilda was named, but she fulfils the symbolic requirements and unless a fifth Matilda is disinterred she seems the most probable archetype.

Notes

[1] See B. Nardi, *Nel Mondo di Dante*, pp. 275–284 (Rome 1944).
[2] C. H. Grandgent's edition of the *Divine Comedy* (Boston 1933).
[3] D. Attwater, *The Penguin Dictionary of Saints* (London 1965).

Acknowledgement

I would like to thank Professor G. Aquilecchia for suggested amendments to the text.

Cecil Grayson

Four love-letters attributed
to Alberti

I N his edition of Alberti's *Opere volgari* Anicio Bonucci
included four 'epistole amatorie' which begin as follows:

   A. 'Io v'ho scritto ora più lettere, vero e caro e solo mio
     signore'.
   B. 'Se a me fosse licito, valorosa ed accorta mia donna'.
   C. 'Ritrovandomi, nobilissima e cara madonna, già gran
     tempo'.
   D. 'Nobilissima e valorosa madonna. Non potendo io'.[1]

Their attribution to Alberti has not gone unchallenged. Vittorio
Rossi implied doubts about *C* and *D*; Girolamo Mancini directly
questioned the authenticity of the same two letters.[2] In order to
determine whether some or all of them should enter the corpus
of Alberti's Italian works, it is necessary to examine their creden-
tials. The results of such an examination not only help to solve
this particular question, but also throw some light on the possible
author of the 'rifacimento' of Alberti's *Deifira*.

For the text of letter *A* Bonucci used two MSS of the Biblioteca
Nazionale, Florence: Magl. VII. Var. 376, and Magl. VIII. 33.[3]
In the first of these—a fifteenth-century miscellany of prose and
verse—the letter occurs, without title or name of author, immediately after Alberti's *Deifira*, or rather that version of the *Deifira*
contaminated with passages from the *Lettera a M. Pino de' Rossi*
and *Fiammetta* which persuaded Bonucci that Alberti and not
Boccaccio wrote these last two works.[4] The MS contains no other
work by or connected with Alberti, and here the version of the
Deifira bears the title: *Romanzo di Pulidoro e Filomeno*, and has no
name of an author.[5] In the other MS used by Bonucci (Magl. VIII,
33) letter *A* occurs at the beginning of the first part of the collection along with other letters and various orations and poems, all
of which have nothing to do with Alberti; it is unattributed and
has the title: *Epistola mandata da uno fervente amante a una gentile
giovane dove lui si duole d'una seconda lettera a llei mandatogli che non
l'acietta come la prima e in fine molto gli si racomanda.* The second part
of the collection, on the other hand, is entirely made up of
works by Alberti, in the midst of which figures his *Deifira* in
the uncontaminated form and without trace of any appended
letter.[6]

The conditions in which letter *A* figures in those two MSS are
hardly such as to warrant attributing its authorship to Alberti.

Suspicion is further deepened by its appearance, in circumstances not unlike those of Magl. VII. Var. 376, in another Florentine MS, where, however, it is claimed as the work of a certain Antonio di ser Guido de' Magnoli. This MS, II.IX.108 of the Biblioteca Nazionale, is a fifteenth-century collection of amorous works written and annotated throughout apparently in the hand of this same Antonio.[7] It opens with Alberti's *Deifira* in the version contaminated with Boccaccio and bearing neither title nor name of author. This text is preceded by a coloured illustration of a blindfolded woman sitting in a boat on the water with a tree at each side of the small picture. Above and around this picture its author, Antonio di ser Guido, has written an explanation of why he has represented his lady in this way. Half a page after the end of the text of this *Deifira* there follows letter *A*, and in the space between them we read, still in the same hand, the following explanation:

Lettera fatta e mandata per me Antonio di ser Ghuido de' Magnoli a una mia 'mança, la quale à nome Ginevra, dolendomi chome ne la filicità avea riceuto chon grande amore e letere e 'nbasciate, di poi per lei mi venne una ruina che io stetti due mesi ch'io non vi voli andare per buona chagione, di più che, terminata la mia ruina, né letera né inbasciate non volea udire richordare; il perché io gli fo questo libretto chon tutte queste chose che ci sono scritte perché tutte sono achadute alla materia nostra; ciò e un altro più adorno e chon molti sonetti e cierti versi e due morali ch'io gli fe' e poi gliele mandai, assai m'ebono a giovare, ché pure degnia a sua posta parlarmi, e alle volte chon buono amore, e sempre diciendomi: mai non mi inghanare né abandonare per alchuno, diciendomi: questo amore vienne da me, e anche so le pene ch'ai sostenuto per me; il tuo amore non merita io sia la dea della crudeltà.

This statement would seem to leave no doubt as to the authorship of the letter; it also sows the first seed of suspicion that perhaps this same Antonio may have been responsible for the 'rifacimento' of Alberti's *Deifira*. Not all the MSS of this contaminated version contain also letter *A* as a kind of adjunct; but it is true to say that, with the sole exception of Magl. VIII. 33 (in which it occurs in a non-Albertian context and remote from *Deifira*) this letter does not figure in any MS except along with the contaminated version of *Deifira*.[8] This seems a rather striking coincidence. Yet, if all these circumstances indicate that letter *A* is not by Alberti, how sure can we be of the claims of this Antonio

di ser Guido, and who was he anyway? Let us take the questions
in that order.

Looking further at his MS (II.IX.108) our initial confidence
somewhat diminishes. Following the letter *A* is a sonnet
beginning: 'De', nonn esser Gianson s'i' son Medea', which
is accompanied by this note of Antonio:

> Sonetto fatto per me Antonio di ser Ghuido de' Magnioli andando
> con cierti chompagni dove era una mia 'mança; ella non volea venire
> dov'io fussi e fe' così più volte sì ch'io le fe' questo sonetto il quale
> partorì in vitoria, ma pocho bastò ch'ella si ritornò nella sua crudeltà.

This sonnet is ascribed in some MSS to the Veronese poetess
Amedea degli Aleardi, and has been published as her work on
more than one occasion.[9] The attribution was challenged by
Sabbadini in 1911, since when no one seems to have pursued the
matter further.[10] I have not carried out a thorough research into
the MSS containing this sonnet.[11] It is sufficient for present purposes to be aware that the authorship of this sonnet, which
Antonio claims as his, is by no means certain, and indeed up to
the present has been commonly attributed to someone else.

After the sonnet there follows a long poem in 'terza rima'
beginning: 'Nel tempo che riducie il charro d'oro', which is
preceded by a long and circumstantial note:

> Versi fatti per me Antonio di ser Ghuido de' Magnioli per vedere
> s'io potea rivochare una mia 'mança, la quale mi tene e tiene in força e
> in chatene d'amore avendol'io ripresa d'alchuno suo fallo; ond'io per
> questi versi gli mostro quelo aviene della ingratitudine, richordandogli
> molti amanti e inamorati ed i molti che morirono per amore e di non
> seghuitare l'amore chon giusta e bella maniera, e lla vendetta che si
> seghuita chontro a choloro che sotto ombra d'angiole inghannano,
> richordandogli molte storie diletose e piacevole e tutte sentençe ch'i'
> le sapese rachontare, per la qual chosa io l'o rinovata dove ogi dimora
> a parlarle e di grata indimanda [?] perché quando era in chasa sua sempre
> stava in grandissima quistione in mala vita.

Our difficulty in accepting Antonio's word is here even more
acute, for the long 'capitolo' he says he composed is elsewhere
(though not in the same version) authoritatively ascribed to
Francesco Malecarni, who, according to contemporary sources,
presented it at the 'Certame Coronario' of 1441.[12] It is admittedly
not a little puzzling how a vision poem about love came to be

submitted for a competition on the theme of friendship.[13] Yet can we on the basis of Antonio di ser Guido's note, and in the face of a respectable and long accepted tradition which assigns the poem to Malecarni, change the attribution? Or, more simply, who borrowed whose poem? Francesco from Antonio for the 'Certame', or Antonio from Francesco to impress his mistress? A closer look at the text suggests the second as the more likely answer. In the Malecarni version, first published by Bonucci and then more accurately by Wesselofsky,[14] the poet goes out for a morning walk to hear the birds and console his grief in love in some solitary spot; here he has a vision of the tormented lovers of antiquity and of the romances—a Dantesque catalogue appropriately ending with Francesca da Rimini (and two unnamed lovers, for whom see below). There then appears

> Il cortese Ferrando Valentino
> Il cui nome in Italia è tanto chiaro:
> E parea che dicesse: 'De, meschino,
> Merita questo il tuo fedele amore,
> Ch'un vil prete ti mandi a tal destino?'
> I' non lo conoscea in su quel furore,
> Se non che Ganimede alto mi disse:
> 'Venios assi, che Dius vos doni onore'.
> Quella parola sì 'l cor mi traffisse
> Che presto al collo al padre mi gittai,
> E poco vi mancò ch'i' non finisse.
> E incominciò: 'Francesco, tu che fai
> Fra questa turba mesta sconsolata?
> La fiamma ch'i' vo' dir, non morì mai?'
> 'Dimmi, diss'io, chi è questa brigata?
> Qual vendetta gli chiama a tanto strazio?'
> E' disse: 'Ell'è la turba inamorata'.

Up to this point, in spite of numerous minor variants, Antonio di ser Guido's version is substantially the same, except that the last two tercets quoted above become:

> E mi disse: 'O Antonio tu che fai
> fra questa turba mesta e sconsolata?
> La fiamma di ciestell no morì mai?
> I' rispuosi di no, perché 'n brigata
> fra questa gente corro a talle strazio.
> E disse egli, è la turba inamorata.

Furthermore Antonio has written the following gloss beside the name of Ferrando Valentino: 'Messer Valentino è uno studiante chatalano il quale achade che nello orto di ciestelli intervenne cierte chosse chon lui per la quale chosa io il nomino perch'acade alla materia e tu G. entenderai'; adding also: 'Ghanimede è uno figliuolo di messer Valentino'.

Wesselofsky is possibly right when he refers us for Ferrando Valentino to Vespasiano da Bisticci's *Vite*, though it is far from clear why this eminent ecclesiastic and counsellor of Alfonso of Aragon should be made to play the role he has in Malecarni's 'trionfo'.[15] Something has radically changed in Antonio's version, if his Ferrando is a 'studiante catalano' with a son called Ganimede. In the Malecarni version the party witnesses in the rest of the poem a love-hunt based on Boccaccio's tale of Nastagio degli Onesti (*Decameron*, V, 8), in which Ferrando attempts to intervene in favour of the lady and is reproved by the 'queen' for interfering with the course of justice. Here are the dogs at work:

> Afferar vidi li spiatati denti,
> E 'l magnanimo e franco Catelano
> Disse: 'Dè, sieno i giorni e' cieli spenti!'
> E 'l pulito pugnal si recò in mano
> Correndo contra a' can, se non ch'un grido
> Venne, che 'ntronò l'aire e 'l piano.

The 'cavaliere' explains his case, the 'queen' restrains Ferrando who falls on his knees asking forgiveness, and the chase and slaughter follow their course. Antonio di ser Guido sees things differently. It is he who tries to interfere:

> E forar vidi li spiatati denti,
> Ma 'l magnanimo, 'Antonio', disse, 'va piano'.
> Po' dissi: 'Or sono i giorni e' cieli spenti!'
> E 'l pulito coltello mi recai in mano, etc.

It is he who hears the huntsman's tale and kneels before the 'queen'.

This exchange of roles constitutes the most conspicuous difference between the two versions, though there are many other minor variations affecting the location and other details.[16] It is perhaps impossible at present without a complete review of all the MS sources of this poem, to assess the minor differences correctly.[17] The impression given by the comparison illustrated above, taken together with the minor variants and some errors in Antonio's version,[18] suggest that he was probably not the original author, but a plagiarist who appropriated Malecarni's poem, adapted it to his own needs and purposes and claimed it as his own work with suitable (for him) circumstantial explanations and glosses in order to further his suit with his Ginevra.

This conclusion is reinforced by the probability that he also 'borrowed' the sonnet of Amedea Aleardi (or *chi per lei*). It seems far more likely that Antonio de' Magnoli borrowed from them than vice versa; for in the latter case one would have to assume a kind of conspiracy on the part of two quite unconnected poets to steal the products of an otherwise unknown versifier. The case seems particularly clear for Malecarni, who after all produced his 'trionfo' at the Certame in 1441 *in public*. I deliberately say 'produced at', because I suspect it was not specially written for that occasion, but may have been composed some time before, and perhaps the Certame seemed to him an appropriate occasion to give it an airing and a chance for the prize. This suspicion would help in part to explain one of Antonio's glosses to his copy. In the catalogue of lovers, after Francesca da Rimini and before the appearance of Ferrando, there is an allusion to an unnamed pair, which Wesselofsky did not attempt to explain:

> Poi venien due col volto sì nascoso
> ch'i' non conobbi, ma molti gridaro:
> 'Anime, Idio del ciel vi dia riposo!'

Beside this tercet Antonio de' Magnoli wrote: 'La marchesana e 'l figliuolo morirono per amore, ma perché il sangue apena è rasciuto non gli nomino a nome'. The allusion (whether or not intended in Malecarni's version) must be to the fate of Ugo and Parisina d'Este as a relatively recent event. They were executed in 1425.[19] How long can one go before such an event ceases to be recent and not explicitly mentionable? As far as the death of Niccolò III (1441)? The question may be important for dating Antonio's version and glosses, providing, that is, one excludes the possibility that this is just a device of his for claiming and antedating 'his' poem. I would not regard it as conclusive evidence that Antonio was the original author, but rather as an indication that Malecarni's poem was possibly about in the

36   *Cecil Grayson*

1430's before the 'Certame', and that Antonio's version also belongs to those years.

If I am right in my assessment of the evidence and in my conclusion that Antonio de' Magnoli borrowed other people's work *and claimed it* as his own, we might also doubt his claims to letter *A*, which he could similarly have appropriated from someone else. Even so, such a hypothesis would add nothing to the evidence for supposing that someone else was Alberti. More important, perhaps, is the consideration that it might give more weight to the suggestion already made, that Antonio di ser Guido was responsible for the interpolations in Alberti's *Deifira*; for, if he could borrow and adapt a sonnet and a 'capitolo' from other poets, he might well have done the same with Alberti's work. If this cannot at present be definitely proved, one thing seems clear: that the MS evidence is inadequate for supposing that letter *A* was written by Alberti. At the same time, this letter, whoever wrote it, seems to have some connection with *Deifira*, not simply in the sense that it accompanies this text in its contaminated version in several MSS, but because it reads like a letter written by the love-sick Filomeno (i.e. the Pallimacro of Alberti's version), who, rejected by his Deifira, proposes to depart into exile. In other words, it may be seen as a kind of epistolary appendix to *Deifira*. The fact that it is never associated with the authentic Albertian version, taken together with the circumstances described above, suggest strongly that someone other than Alberti was responsible for that appendix, and that someone, possibly, was Antonio di ser Guido de' Magnoli.

'Chi era costui?' Speaking negatively first, I think we can absolutely exclude his identification with the well known fifteenth-century Florentine poet Antonio di Guido, who 'si presentò al pubblico in S. Martino giovanissimo, circa il 1437', and died in 1486. Though he was evidently a 'nobile viro', we do not know his family name; he is consistently referred to as 'maestro Antonio di Guido' or 'da Firenze' or 'canta in panca'. Despite some contemporary slurs on his moral character (which Flamini attempts to remove), this Antonio has never been suspected or accused of plagiarism from fellow-poets of his age. A fair number of his poems survive, and he was praised, among others, by Poliziano.[20] By contrast our Antonio di ser Guido de' Magnoli appears ostentatiously conscious of his full name (in a determined effort perhaps to distinguish himself from other Antonio di Guido?), and, as far as I have discovered, is represented as a poet only by the two compositions he claims in the MS we have examined.[21] The family of the de' Magnoli in Florence seems to have belonged to the 'Sesto di Porta di Domo' in the fourteenth century, or Santa Maria Novella, Unicorno, in the fifteenth century, but I have so far been unable to find an Antonio or Guido in the archives of those areas or the genealogies of the family.[22] It is possible that a letter dated 23 September 1431 and signed 'Antonio di ser Ghuido', was written by our Antonio, and there are some slight indications in its content which might support the identification.[23] It might well fit also for date, and serve too further to distinguish him from the poet Antonio di Guido who was 'giovanissimo' in 1437. Alberti's *Deifira* was probably written in the late 'twenties or early 'thirties,[24] and, as I have suggested, Malecarni might well have composed his 'trionfo' some time before he presented it at the 'Certame' of 1441. Taking all these facts into consideration, together with the gloss concerning Ugo and Parisina d'Este, I am inclined to place Antonio di ser Guido de' Magnoli's activities in MS II.IX.108 somewhere in the 'thirties, and to believe that they were intended for private consumption. Further examination of the MS tradition of *Deifira* may show whether his 'copy' is in fact at the base of the contaminated version; and others may be able to throw more light on his identity. In the meantime there are some grounds for believing Antonio to be the author of letter *A*, and none at all for attributing it to Alberti.

The problems surrounding letters *B*, *C* and *D* are fortunately less complex. Bonucci did not indicate his source for these, but it must have been MS Pal. 212 of the Biblioteca Nazionale, Florence.[25] This contains: ff. 1*r*–12*r*: *Deifira*, attributed to Alberti and in the authentic text; ff. 12*r*–*v*: letter *B* without title or attribution; ff. 13*r*–15*v*: Alberti's *Mirzia*, followed by the dedicatory letter and proem of his *Ecatonfilea*, both attributed to Alberti; ff. 16–18 are blank; ff. 19*r*–21*v* contain letters *C* and *D* without title or attribution and transcribed by a different hand from that of ff. 1–15. We have here, therefore, a MS which, apart from the letters *B*, *C* and *D*, contains only known works by, and here attributed to, Alberti. It would not be improbable in consequence that the letters were also written by him—assuming, that is, that the two copyists of the MS had in mind to make a collection of Alberti's amorous works. This assumption appears valid for the first part of the MS, and to suggest that at least letter *B*, between *Deifira* and *Mirzia*, could be Alberti's work. But at f. 15*v* the continuity of the MS breaks down after the transcription of the dedication and proem of *Ecatonfilea*. The three blank leaves (16–18) would have been inadequate for the text of that work. Serious doubt arises, in consequence, whether this interruption and change of hand also imply a change of programme and therefore of authorship of the works copied.

At this point it is worth examining the contents and styles of the letters. Letter *B* is a short epistle in relatively simple style, that could be a sort of appendix to *Deifira* in the sense in which, as we suggested, letter *A* might appear; that is, as a letter written by the rejected lover on his proposed departure into exile. It reads as follows:[26]

Se a me fosse licito, valerosa ed accorta mia donna, palesemente cridare e piangere in questa mia crudele partita, siate certa che li stridi di Vulcano né de Cariddi, né li gridi della dolorosa Dido, foro mai sì grandi, che li mei non fossero molto maiori. Ma cognosco veramente, speranza dell'anima mia, la quale se notrica per voi ne lo amoroso foco, che 'l cridare e piangere è più presto da animo feminile che verile. Resta solo, unico mio bene, fra me stesso condolermi con grave pene, e lamentareme de la iniqua e perfida fortuna e crudel mio destino che me ha condotto, non possendo scusarla. Ve supplico, regina del mio cuore, che non ve adirate de questa mia partita, ma pregate Dio che me riduca alla vostra grazia, ché senza la quale al mondo non voria stare.

> Fa che non manchi l'amorosa voglia,
> el ben voler, el desiderio antico.
> Considera quel ch'io dico,
> ninfa mia bella, e pace del mio cuore.
> Abbi mercé al mïo gran dolore.
> Vidi fortuna a quel che m'ha condutto.
> Qual serà mio redutto
> se non la morte a gli aspri martiri?
> Poi che mi convïen[e] pur partire,
> superna Diana, stella de orïente,
> fa che 'l caro servente
> Abbi nel petto con devoto cuore.

Letters *C* and *D*, on the other hand, are much longer and more fulsome and passionate in their protest of love and desire for recompense. They do not imply that the writer has been definitely rejected, but only that he has not received the returns of love he believes he deserves. Their position in this MS, removed from any proximity to *Deifira*, does not suggest they are linked with this work. Unlike *B*, which is comparatively simple and direct in style, *C* and *D* read like exercises in florid Boccaccesque amorous prose.[27] It is not impossible that they were inspired by something like the situation of Pallimacro in *Deifira* before his final crisis of love that forms the subject of that work; but this is so general a possible connection as to have no value in establishing a link between the letters and *Deifira*. Furthermore, in this MS, they contain many northern Italian forms (such as *fati*, second person, plural, present; *inzenochiato*; *quellui*) that seem unlikely to represent the language of Alberti.

In all these circumstances I am inclined to accept *B* as probably Alberti's work, as a letter of departure from Pallimacro to Deifira, added as a postscript or appendix to the tale of his woes told in the dialogue of the work that bears her name. On the analogy of this, I suspect that whoever did the 'rifacimento' of *Deifira*, contaminating it with Boccaccio (and I believe this might have been Antonio di ser Guido), also had the idea of adding, or substituting for *B*, a more eloquent letter, viz. *A*, as a fittingly Boccaccesque tailpiece. As for *C* and *D*, the case is far more doubtful, and until and unless further evidence for the attribution comes to light, I believe they should not enter the canon of Alberti's works. They may have been prompted by the example and spirit of his *Deifira*, but appear to belong to someone far more committed to the imitation of Boccaccio than Alberti ever was.

Notes

[1] L. B. Alberti, *Opere volgari*, ed. A. Bonucci, vol. III (Florence 1845), pp. 411–417 (letter *A*); vol. V (1849), pp. 325–333 (letters *B*, *C* and *D*).

[2] V. Rossi, reviewing V. Cian, *Le rime di B. Cavassico* (Bologna 1893–4), in *G.S.L.I.*, XXVI (1895) pp. 214–222, refers to letter *A* apparently without questioning its attribution, then says of *B* that Bonucci included it in his edition, 'non credo a torto', adding that *C* and *D* may also be read in Bonucci (p. 218). Cf. Cian, *op. cit.*, pp. lxxviii–lxxx, where letter *B* is reproduced with some extracts from *C* and *D* in the context of an outline from the thirteenth century onwards of the tradition of 'Epistole amorose in verso ed in prosa'. G. Mancini, *Vita di L. B. Alberti*, second edition (Florence 1911), p. 75, note 2: 'Questa (he means *B*) può credersi dell'Alberti, ma le altre due (he refers to *C* and *D*)...dubito che gli appartengano'.

[3] *Ed. cit.*, vol. III, p. 411.

[4] *Ibid.*, vol. III, pp. 347–361. Mancini, *op. cit.*, pp. 75–76, disposes of this strange thesis, and shows that the contaminated version (with speakers Polidoro and Filomeno) published by Bonucci and represented in six Florentine MSS, is distinct from the authentic text (with speakers Pallimacro and Filarco) found in three other Florentine MSS and in various editions of the fifteenth and sixteenth centuries. Indeed one might now add that no printed edition besides Bonucci's follows the contaminated version, and that this is in fact represented in a minority of the known MSS of the work. I believe Mancini is correct in supposing that Alberti could not have been responsible for the interpolations, which apart from other considerations, are clumsily inserted and, as Mancini observed, do not fit the context for style and content. Mancini, p. 76, n. 5, takes Bonucci to task for 'una imperdonabile e maliziosa licenza'; he could also have accused him of using only four Florentine MSS of the contaminated version for his text, whilst knowing others properly attributed to Alberti and without the Boccaccio passages. For further information concerning the MSS see below, note 8.

[5] For a description of the contents of the MS see Mazzatinti, *Inventari*, vol. XIII (Forlì 1905–6), pp. 83–86. In brief they are: *Geta e Birria* (1–33), anon. stanze, canzonette, sonnets (some by Petrarch), a frottola of Jacopo del Bientina, and other anon. poems (34–71), the 'romanzo' (73–107), and various anon. ballate, stanze, sonnets (108–124).

[6] For a description of this MS see my edition of Alberti, *Opere volgari*, vol. II (Bari 1966), pp. 448–449. Note that in this MS the letter begins: 'Io v'o scritto ora *due* lettere...' (ff. 1–3); and *cf.* the title it bears, cited above in the text. The second half of the MS containing works by Alberti occupies ff. 22–65, with *Deifira* in ff. 40–50.

[7] See Mazzatinti, *Inventari, cit.*, vol. XI, p. 283.

[8] To my knowledge at present there are seven MSS containing the contaminated version, of which three also have the letter *A*, viz. the two Florentine MSS (Magl. VII. 376 and II.IX.108) and MS Ital. XI. 27 of the Marciana. On the other hand, there are sixteen MSS of *Deifira* without Boccaccio interpolations; none of these, except Magl. VIII. 33 in the circumstances described, contains this letter. I reserve details of the MSS and their relationships for vol. III of my edition of the *Opere volgari*.

[9] G. Biadego, 'Un sonetto di Medea Aleardi poetessa veronese del sec. XV', in *Propugnatore*, vol. XIII, pt. II (1880), pp. 255–256; G. Pacchioni, *Un codice inedito della Bibl. Estense: un poeta e una poetessa petrarcheschi* [i.e. Gio. Nogarola and Medea Aleardi], (Modena 1907). I take this information from *G.S.L.I.*, vol. LI (1908), p. 476, as I have been unable so far to see this publication. Information about Amedea seems scarce; she would appear to have flourished in the early years of the fifteenth century, judging from indications in the article by Sabbadini, cited in next note.

[10] R. Sabbadini, 'Versi latini di Gian Nicola Salerno' in *G.S.L.I.*, vol. LVIII (1911), pp. 358–366. Salerno, like Malpigli, addressed poems to Amedea, and wrote at least one 'in persona di Amedea Aleardi', apparently in the first decade of the fifteenth century. Referring to the sonnet 'Deh non esser Jason...', Sabbadini writes: 'Ma io non credo che il sonetto sia suo.

Primieramente esso porta nei codici il nome di altri autori; secondariamente la Aleardi non si chiamava Medea, bensì Amedea, come provano le didascalie del Salerno e del Malpigli; in terzo luogo chi esamini il sonetto, vedrà che l'autrice potrebbe essere con egual diritto denominata Arianna e Didone. Si tratta di un esercizio poetico e nulla più; e il nome di Medea del primo verso diede la spinta ad attribuire il componimento alla Amedea'. As far as I can discover, this has remained chronologically the last word on the attribution.
[11] Biadego gave the text from a MS at Udine, Pacchioni from cod. Estense X.B.14 (*cf. G.S.L.I.*, vol. XXII, 1893, p. 319), in both of which it is presumably ascribed to Amedea (but see notes 9 and 10 above). The sonnet is ascribed to Antonio in cod. Laur. LXXXIX, inf. 44, c. 165*r*, with minor variants in comparison with cod. II.IX.108. I do not know who the 'altri autori' are in Sabbadini's statement cited above, n. 10. Antonio's version has seventeen lines compared with Biadego's text of sixteen. The major difference is in the last lines, which I give as a sample:
Amedea (Biadego), v. 12 ff.

> Cara speranza, amor, chi mi ti ha tolto?
> Se non vieni a por fine al mio dolore,
> Io haggio al bianco collo il lazo avolto
> Per puor con una morte fine a mille,
> Ne non mi mancharà l'ardir di phille.

Antonio (II.IX.108), v. 12 ff.

		cod. Laur.
Charo mio .G. amor chi mi t'a tolto?		.S'.
Chome no mi vien tu a vedere?		De come
Ch'io ò gia intorno al cholo i'lacio avolto		
E ollo su racholto		
E vo fare una morte e non ben mille		
E non mi mancherà l'ardir di fille.		

Antonio's line 12, with the abbreviation .G. (in Laur. ..*S'*.), remains enigmatic; metrically it should represent a monosyllable. This, together with the lack of a syllable in line 13 (supplied in Laur.), does not inspire confidence in Antonio's authorship.
[12] F. Flamini, *La lirica toscana del Rinascimento anteriore ai tempi del Magnifico* (Pisa 1891), pp. 27–31 and 685; A. Altamura, *Il certame coronario* (Naples 1952), p. 20. See also V. Rossi, *Il Quattrocento* (Milan 1945), p. 114.
[13] Flamini, *op. cit.*, p. 27: 'scelse un ingegnoso espediente per isbizzarire lontano da una incommoda trattazione filosofica'; Rossi, *op. cit.*, p. 114: 'a Fr. di Bonanno Malecarni piacque sgattaiolare di fra le strettoie del tema e descrivere... un trionfo d'amore'.
[14] *Opere volgari*, ed. Bonucci, *cit.*, vol. I, pp. cxcv–cciv; A. Wesselofsky, *Novella della figlia del Re di Dacia* (Pisa 1866), pp. xcv–cv. Bonucci does not indicate his MS source, but it was probably Laur. XC, inf. 38 (*cf. loc. cit.*, p. clxviii); Wesselofsky based his text on Magl. VII. 1145, compared with Ricc. 1091 and 1142, and Laur. XC, inf. 38, but indicated very few variants. According to Flamini, *op. cit.*, p. 685, all these MSS attribute the poem to

Malecarni; in three others it is anonymous; in Laur. LXXXIX, inf. 44, where
it immediately precedes the sonnet *Deh non esser Gianson* (see note 11 above) it
is ascribed to Antonio de' Magnoli, and presents with some slight variations
the same text as that of MS II.IX.108.

¹⁵ Wesselofsky, *op. cit.*, p. xcvi. *Cf.* Vespasiano, *Vite di uomini illustri del sec.*
XV, ed. P. D'Ancona and E. Aeschlimann (Milan 1951), pp. 523–527; this
life is more about Alfonso than Ferrando, but it explains why the poem could
say 'il cui nome in Italia è tanto chiaro'.

¹⁶ Here are some examples:

	Malecarni	*Antonio de' Magnoli*
v. 15	per gir *ad una costa* ove si sale	*in un giardino*
v. 18	...per udir qualche verso	
	D'alcuno vago ugelletto tal fiata	*D'alcuna donçeletta*
v. 20	...senti' da traverso	
	un concento d'augelli inamorati.	*alcuni che ben parreno...*
	Anzi...	*E certo...*
v. 45	Circundato *da selve* a ogni mano	*da alori*
v. 49	E un *corrente fiume gli* fa mura	*pantan d'un fiume vi*
v. 128	*Sanson,* che'l capo in grembo alla nimica	*Orbo*
	Tenne...	
v. 184	E io che non mi posso veder sazio	
	Né trovo altro diletto che 'nparare	*del mio signor che mi fa consumare*
v. 193	*Vedrai tutte quelle che straziando*	*Tu vedrai quelle che saramentando*
	I lor amanti, tenner tanto a bada	*A lor amanti inganna e tiene a bada.*
v. 244–5	I' fu suggietto a questa donna e schiavo	
	E più del suo servir che di Dio ero.	*Come se' tu che più che di Dio ero.*
v. 254	Allor mi *strinse* lo spirito pravo	*mosse*

¹⁷ As noted above (n. 14) Wesselofsky gives very few variants from the
MSS he used—two to be exact. One of these appears in the Magnoli version in
II.IX.108 and Laur. LXXXIX, inf. 44: in tercet 48 (Wesselofsky, p. ci):

> Medea dicea: Puniscasi il gran torto
> Qual usò già lo spiatato Giansonne,
> Onde l'un figlio e l'altro vide morto.

Ricc. 1091 (like the two MSS of Antonio's version) reads in the last line: Che
mangiò il cor de' figli per conforto.

¹⁸ A poet copying his own verses might be expected not to produce the
following readings, which look like errors:

Antonio (II.IX.108)	*Cf. Malecarni (Wesselofsky)*
v. 79 Eravi la sbandita pudicizia	Qui v'era la corrotta pudicizia
che *falsifen* col toro scellerata	Che *Pasif fe'* col toro scellerata
v. 123 E Adriana, che morì amando	
Quando *il cor di lieo a llei*	Quando *dal lito incontro le*
pervenne	pervenne
v. 276 ...a' cani	
Lo diè *ancor me ne viene un errore*	...*che ancor me ne vien un terrore*

I should add that the same readings occur in the other MS which attributes the poem to Antonio (Laur. LXXXIX, inf. 44). On the other hand, it cannot be said that Wesselofsky's text of Malecarni leaves one entirely satisfied; but this does not affect Antonio's 'errors' in 'his' poem.

[19] Ugo d'Este, Niccolò's son, and his stepmother Parisina were beheaded for adultery in March 1425, according to the *Diario Ferrarese* in *Rer. Ital. Script.*, xxiv, Pt. vii, in May of that year, according to G. Manini Ferranti, *Compendio della storia... di Ferrara*, t. III (Ferrara 1808), p. 24.

[20] For the information we possess about this Antonio, some of which I have briefly summarised here, see Flamini, *op. cit.*, pp. 162–174 and 639–643.

[21] That is, MS II.IX.108 and the same two poems in the related MS Laur. LXXXIX, inf. 44. A search in the two volumes of P. O. Kristeller's *Iter Italicum* provides no items for Antonio de' Magnoli, though there are several entries under Antonio di Guido, most of them for the Florentine 'Maestro Antonio' and some for one or more of the same name in the late fifteenth and early sixteenth centuries.

[22] Ildefonso di S. Luigi, *Delizie degli eruditi toscani* (Firenze 1770–86), contains various references (vol. 7, 159; vol. 8, 81; vol. 11, 128) to the de' Magnoli family and some members of the early fourteenth century 'del Sesto di Porta di Domo'. L. Passerini, *Genealogia delle famiglie nobili*, in Carte Passerini, Bibl. Nazionale, Florence, 189/27, gives a family tree from the fifteenth to the eighteenth centuries, but no Guido or Antonio are to be found in it; one entry for 1457 regarding a Tommaso di Piero di Tommaso comes from 'S. Maria Nov[a] Unico[o]'. Search among archival documents some years ago failed to bring to light any certain information on Antonio or ser Guido de' Magnoli; the nearest possible indication I found in Arch. di St., Tratte 39, *Descrizione dell'età dei cittadini Fiorentini*, c. 81, Unicorno: 'Antonio di Guido di Giuntino a dì 29 dic. 1399'. This could very well be our man, but without the family name one cannot be sure.

[23] Arch. di St., Florence, Med. a. princ., A III, c. 356. The letter written from Ponte d'Era to Averardo de' Medici 'chomissario del comune di firenze in campo', concerns supplies and contains references to 'la venuta qui di ghuido d'arezo' and the arrival of a letter from 'Betto di Signorino'; it also alludes twice to a lady with the initial *G* ('e prima avisando la nostra G'; 'et diceva avver auto letera da G'). This last feature might suggest a link with Antonio de' Magnoli's 'mança' (see above, pp. 2 and 5). The major difficulty in making a certain identification is that while the hands are very similar, certain letters are not alike (particularly *b, d, e* and *l*). These differences might be accounted for by the more cursive nature of the epistolary

hand, but they are too characteristic to be overlooked, and the solution to this question must await further search. I am very grateful to Dr John Woodhouse for examining these documents again on my behalf in an attempt to resolve this problem.

[24] The *Vita anonima* of Alberti (in *Op. volg.*, ed. Bonucci, *cit.*, vol. I, p. xciv) dates *Deifira* about the same time as the *De comodis literarum atque incomodis* and before *De familia*, bks. I–III (*cf.* Alberti L.B. in *Dizionario biografico degli italiani* vol. I, Rome, 1960).

[25] For a description of the MS see Gentile, *I codici Paletini*, vol. I (Rome 1889), pp. 266–267; f. 17*v* bears the date 1459. *Cf.* also G. Mancini, *Vita, cit.*, pp. 75–77, in notes, though I believe, with Gentile, he is incorrect (p. 76, n. 4) in saying that the corrections to this MS are in Alberti's hand.

[26] I give the text as it appears in the MS, with minor necessary corrections to the verse. *Cf.* Bonucci's ed., *cit.*, vol. V, pp. 325–326.

[27] I give some excerpts as examples. From C:
'Nobilissima e graziosa madonna, regina e imperatrice del mio misero e dolente core, quantumque io credesse che sopra degl'inamorati lo amor dominasse ed avesse imperio grandissimo e forze, mai cretti che in lui fosse tanto podere e forza che contra el voler di chi si sia, lui podesse ligare e sciogliere altrui como li piace. E quanto io vi dico, che essendo io ignorante incauto de la vostra ligiadria e ineffabil belleza, alla quale io credo non si trova simile, subito con uno solo sguardo fui ligato e preso; e credendomi di tal vista godere m'è intrevenuto como alla luçola, che di nocte vola nel foco; e così mi ritruovo pien d'affanni, martiri e guai, e in tal modo ardere nel foco d'amore che ormai poco più mi rista excetto la morte' (*Cf.* Bonucci's ed. *cit.*, vol. V, p. 327).
From *D*:
'Ma benché essendo io giloso e timido de l'onore vostro, in cotal modo mi sia lontanato, mai la dolce memoria delle vostre divine e angeliche belleze, del vostro soavissimo e mellifluo parlare, mai né dì né notte, dovunque io me fosse, non m'è uscito del cuore, però che non d'altro alimento o vero cibo sì me nutrisce e pasce, e senza voi non steria in vita un giorno. E certo, io non so qual sì indurato cuor di sasso e crudo avesse udito li mei lamenti e guai, si fusse continuto di piangere, e non se fusse mosso a tenereza e a pietade' (*Cf. ed. cit.*, vol. V, p. 332).

Maria Corti

Ma quando è nato
Iacobo Sannazaro?

P aolo Giovio, che soleva schizzare nelle sue lettere penetranti ritratti di contemporanei, ci descrive il Sannazaro come uomo dalla natura aristocratica, che dosava le parole soprattutto se dovevano essere di elogio e si circondava di una elegante atmosfera di riserbo;[1] in questa luce mi pare si spieghi la maniera indiretta e allusiva a cui il poeta ricorre ogni qual volta viene a mettere sulla pagina se stesso, il suo passato, le sue cose, quindi anche la sua nascita. Eccolo dirci ripetutamente di essere venuto al mondo, felice coincidenza, nel giorno dedicato a San Nazaro, il 28 luglio,[2] ma tacerci l'anno; o meglio evocarlo in modo vago e insieme suggestivo. Vago perché l'anno non è indicato, suggestivo perché è detto quel tanto che consente di collegare daccapo la sua nascita a una personalità sontuosa, non più un santo ma un grande re, Alfonso il Magnanimo: 'Vegno a me adunque, il quale in quegli estremi anni che la recolenda memoria del vittorioso Re Alfonso di Aragona passò da le cose mortali a più tranquilli secoli, sotto infelice prodigio di comete, di terremoto, di pestilenzia, di sanguinose battaglie nato et in povertà, o vero, secondo i savii, in modesta fortuna nudrito, sì come la mia stella e i fati volsono, appena avea otto anni forniti, che le forze di Amore a sentire incominciai', prosa VII, 9.[3] Orbene, Alfonso d'Aragona morì il 27 giugno 1458. È opinabile che al Sannazaro sarebbe piaciuto poter scrivere che era nato contemporaneamente nel giorno in cui si festeggiava il suo santo protettore e nell'anno in cui il mare della vita aragonese si era richiuso sopra un grande re; ma non poteva. Perciò non scrisse 'nell'estremo anno', ma ripiegò sull'espressione più comprensiva di tempo: 'in quegli estremi anni'. Poiché non mi risulta attestato l'uso dello stilema 'estremi anni' nel senso di 'lontani anni', bensì soltanto di 'ultimi anni',[4] con un supplemento di modelli petrarcheschi (*per l'estreme giornate di sua vita*, XVI, 6; *venne a salvarmi in su li estremi giorni*, CCCLXVI, 32; *Poi che l'ultimo giorno e l'ore estreme/ spogliar di lei questa vita presente*, CCXCV, 5–6), dal brano dell'*Arcadia* si può ricavare un dato elastico, ma ugualmente significativo: nascita di poco anteriore al 1458, anno della morte del re. Ancora a un clima di grandiosità, oltre che a un *topos* letterario, riporta 'l'infelice prodigio di comete, di terremoto, di pestilenzia, di sanguinose battaglie'; il terremoto è senza dubbio quello famoso del 1456 di cui ci dà notizie Angelo di Costanzo nella *Istoria del Regno di Napoli*,[5] vol.

terzo, libro XIX, p. 176: esso colpì molte città e 'castella' del Reame, distrusse in Napoli l'arcivescovado e la chiesa di San Pietro Martire, fece quarantamila vittime; la peste è quella del 1457-1458, che infieriva ancora a Napoli alla morte di Alfonso, tanto che baroni e ambasciatori si riunirono per riconoscere l'erede Ferrante a Capua e non nella capitale, come ci informa il Pontano nel *De bello neapolitano*, libro I, p. 254*v*.[6] Le 'sanguinose battaglie' si riferiscono al periodo 1460-1462, cioè alla guerra fra Ferrante I e il pretendente duca Giovanni d'Angiò alleato ai baroni ribelli: il colpo d'occhio storico del poeta investe quindi il drammatico periodo della sua nascita e prima infanzia ('nato et in povertà ... nudrito'), un arco di tempo accidentato che si presta a funzionare da mirabile sfondo per una narrazione di poetiche infelicità, non certo da indicatore di una esatta data di nascita.

A questo punto della riflessione ci imbattiamo, come quasi sempre allorché ci si occupa di cose napoletane, nelle proposte di Erasmo Percopo, figura di studioso che sempre colpisce per il fiuto tartufesco, che gli fa scovare e dissotterrare preziosi documenti, ma insieme per quel pizzico di fantasia deformante che interviene all'atto della loro interpretazione. Nel caso specifico, i documenti portati alla luce dal Percopo sono due e fra loro in contraddizione. Nel primo, *Atti del R. Fisco con li magnifici Giacomo e Marcantonio Sannazzaro*, ove si rinvengono le deposizioni dei testimoni presso la R. Corte della Summaria del 1501,[7] il Percopo trovò alcune notizie interessanti, su cui si tornerà più oltre, ma nulla che a parer suo lo autorizzasse a modificare la data di nascita del poeta offerta dalla tradizione e già presente nella cinquecentesca *Vita* del Sannazaro scritta da G. B. Crispo (Roma, Zannetti, 1593), cioè il 28 luglio 1458. Tale data infatti si incontra nella sua *Vita di Jacobo Sannazaro* (*op. cit.*, pp. 16-17). Rinvenuto nel 1900 all'Archivio Cassinese un documento del 3 maggio 1474 sulla rinuncia dei Sannazaro a una terra presso Mondragone, nel quale il Sannazaro risulta diciottenne, il Percopo nell'articolo *Per la giovanezza del Sannazaro*, contenente in appendice il documento,[8] sposta la data di nascita del poeta al 28 luglio 1456; a dire il vero un po' precipitosamente, perché in effetti nel documento Iacobo è detto *maior annis decem et octo*, mentre Marco Antonio risulta *maior annis decem et minor quartodecimo*; orbene, se Iacobo fosse nato il 28 luglio del 1456, al 3 maggio del 1474 non avrebbe avuto più di diciotto anni, ma gli sarebbero mancati ancora tre mesi a compierli. Comunque, la nuova data fu accolta dal Carrara ed entrò nelle successive storie letterarie. A questo punto, riconosciuta la contraddizione fra i due documenti, si deve dedurre: (1) che almeno uno dei due contiene notizie erronee; (2) che per uscire dal circolo vizioso bisogna partire da altre testimonianze, estranee ai due documenti e tali da presentarsi o in sé decisamente più attendibili o almeno in accordo con uno dei due documenti.

Al dato sopra esposto, cioè la dichiarazione del poeta di essere nato negli ultimi anni della vita di Alfonso, perciò prima del 1458, va accostato un secondo ricavabile dall'epigrafe mortuaria posta sulla tomba del poeta a Mergellina: *vixit an. LXXII, obiit MDXXX*. Già il Percopo nella *Vita* cit. (p. 94) affiancò alla prima delle due testimonianze dell'epigrafe (*vixit an. LXXII*) quelle di Paolo Giovio, per cui il poeta visse *annos septuaginta duos*, del Crispo, di Angelo di Costanzo, del Capaccio, tutte concordanti; quanto alla data MDXXX, è importantissima l'annotazione diaristica del cardinale Gerolamo Seripando: *1530, Die 24 aprilis Actius Sincerus moritur*.[9] Conferma offre (e già lo vide il Colangelo, *op. cit.*, p. 93, n. 1) l'edizione delle Rime del Sannazaro, datata al novembre 1530, uscita in Napoli presso Sultzbach, dove l'elenco di correzioni agli errori tipografici è preceduto da un avviso 'Ai lettori' in cui si informa che la morte del poeta è stata in parte causa del permanere degli errori stessi. Torniamo al Percopo. Poiché al tempo in cui stese la *Vita* egli credeva il Sannazaro nato il 28 luglio 1458, fu portato dal confronto delle date di nascita e di morte a postillare che il 24 aprile del 1530 al poeta mancavano in effetti ancora tre mesi e quattro giorni ai settantadue anni; a questo punto cosa ci si aspetterebbe? Che egli rimettesse in discussione la presunta data di nascita; e invece no, con una curiosa propria logica deformante egli considera in errore tutti i contemporanei, tutti quanti distratti nel non far caso a quei tre mesi e quattro giorni. Più tardi, allorché la data di nascita fu da lui spostata al 1456, epigrafe ed attestazioni contemporanee si vanificarono, scomparvero senza traccia dal suo discorso. Ma l'epigrafe c'è, le attestazioni del Giovio, del Seripando ecc. ci sono. Per di più, se si rileggono i *Codicilli* testamentari, stesi dal Sannazaro il 29 settembre 1529 alla presenza del notaio Sebastiano Canoro di Napoli, che visitò il poeta *iacentem in lecto, infirmum corpore sanum tamen mente* nella sua casa in *Plathea Sancte Marie de Gratea civitatis Neapolis*, documento cui il notaio tolse i sigilli alla presenza di un giudice e di vari testimoni il 18 agosto 1530, e che si trova edito in appendice all'opera citata del Colangelo (pp. 232–244), noi veniamo a sapere che fra gli esecutori testamentari, incaricati di erigere la tomba del poeta, ci sono il fratello Marco Antonio e Cassandra Marchese (p. 241), che l'età del Sannazaro dovevano ben conoscere; e la Marchese, morta quasi novantenne nel 1569, era ancora ben viva quando l'epigrafe fu scolpita.[10]

A conclusione del discorso mi sembra necessario avanzare la proposta che si consideri data di nascita del Sannazaro il 28 luglio 1457; solo con tale data il poeta poteva avere 72 anni il 24 aprile del 1530 e insieme essere nato negli 'estremi anni' della vita di re Alfonso; *qualsiasi altra data* mette in contraddizione due testimonianze per noi sicuramente attendibili.

È ora il caso, alla luce di questa conclusione, di ritornare ai documenti d'archivio presi in esame dal Percopo. In primo luogo interessa il grosso insieme di incartamenti che ha per oggetto la lite condotta a singhiozzo dal 1500 al 1517 fra il Regio Fisco e i fratelli Sannazaro a proposito dell'*Alumiera de Agnano*, cioè della miniera di allume situata nei monti di Agnano e portata in dote a Iacobo Sannazaro, nonno del poeta, dalla moglie Cicella de Anna, allumiera di cui i Sannazaro, per natura poco abili in affari, non curarono più lo sfruttamento. Polarizza l'attenzione uno dei documenti, in volgare, edito per intero dal Cestari (*op. cit.*, pp. 26–32) da cui risulta che il 10 maggio 1465 Ferrante I e Guglielmo Lo Monaco, 'suo Bombardiere', stipularono un contratto, firmato da Antonello de Petruciis, per lo sfruttamento del l'allumiera a danno della vedova di Cola Sannazaro, madre del poeta, e degli eredi fanciulli, ignorando addirittura il loro diritto di proprietà su quella terra, o meglio fingendo di ignorarlo.[11] Dal documento inoltre risulta che, al momento del contratto, Guglielmo Lo Monaco già da tre anni lavorava ad organizzare il funzionamento della miniera: cap. 1, '... lo dicto M. Gulielmo con grandissima fatica e dispese lui e tucta la sua famiglia ezioè mogliere e figliolo e genero ja sonno tre anni ha facto una lumera vicino al lago de Agnano e reductala in termine che con lo ajutorio de Dio e mediante la fatica e la sollicitudine del dicto M. Guliermo epsa lumera per tucto lo mese de Magio sera in ordine in la manera de sopto contenuta cioè de VII fornace da cuocere le petre de fare alume e de una casa de fabrica longa vinte canne con septe caldare da bullire alume ...' ecc. (p. 26). Dunque, già dal 1462 il Lo Monaco si era appropriato della miniera in abbandono; questa data ci dice qualcosa. Il Lo Monaco, 'cavaliere e gubernatore de l'artigliaria' della Maestà del Re, aveva combattuto in difesa di Ferrante la guerra contro il duca Giovanni d'Angiò, chiamato dai baroni del regno a contrastare l'elezione a sovrano dello stesso Ferrante: come è noto, Giovanni d'Angiò sbarcò alle foci del Volturno nell'autunno del 1459, sconfisse Ferrante presso Sarno il 7 luglio 1460, fu a sua volta definitivamente sconfitto dall'aragonese in Puglia, a Troia, il 18 luglio 1462 per merito soprattutto dell'artiglieria del re, che permise l'occupazione dei castelli della Puglia, i quali al re *iter reddebant infestius*.[12] Dopo questa battaglia la maggior parte dei baroni si arrese e Ferrante ebbe solo scontri minori con i residui della resistenza sino alla definitiva pace firmata nel settembre 1463. Dunque, dopo l'agosto 1462 il Lo Monaco, libero da grossi impegni militari e oggetto di gratitudine da parte del re, per la cui vittoria si era prodigato come 'gubernatore de l'artigliaria', poteva iniziare la programmazione di quel grosso affare che si rivelò lo sfruttamento dell'allumiera di Agnano; è molto probabile che a questo astuto affarista la geniale idea sia stata suggerita da alcune particolari circostanze: proprio nel 1462 lo Stato della Chiesa aveva iniziato lo sfruttamento dell'allumiera della Tolfa presso Civitavecchia (Cestari, *op. cit.*, pp. 67–68) e il re Ferrante aspirava a sua volta al possesso delle allumiere di Ischia, che nell'inverno 1462–63 sottrasse al ribelle Torelles, dandole poi in affitto a mercanti veneziani (Nunziante, *op. cit.*, XXIII, p. 153, n. 4). Di fronte all'insediamento del Lo Monaco nella terra dei Sannazaro il re Ferrante chiuse un occhio: i sovrani, si sa, hanno un modo tutto speciale di beneficare, tolgono da una parte e passano all'altra; per di più c'era la prospettiva di uno sfruttamento a due, re e suddito fedele. Ma naturalmente il re poté chiudere un occhio in quanto Cola Sannazaro, padre del poeta, li aveva chiusi tutti e due; morto, dicono le deposizioni del 1501, a Napoli 'al tempo della guerra del duca Johanne' (notizia già portata alla luce dal Brognoligo in una nota alla *Vita* del Percopo, n. 1, p. 17). La vedova, in tutt'altre faccende affaccendata e assai inesperta nelle cose pratiche, lasciò fare. Orbene uno dei testimoni al processo del 1501, Filio de Anna (si ricordi che la nonna del Sannazaro, proprietaria dell'allumiera, era Cicella de Anna), depose che alla morte del padre Iacobo aveva quattro anni e il fratello Marco

Antonio sei mesi, non erano cioè in età da opporsi a un'usurpazione; un altro testimonio, Iacobo Scannasorice, confermò che Iacobo realmente 'non era più de quattro anni' e Marcantonio 'in sei o sette mise', con l'aggiunta di un particolare realistico: essendo vicino di casa dei Sannazaro, quando gli portavano il bimbo e lui lo accarezzava 'ipso Marco Antonio lo chiamava *tata*', cioè papà secondo le parlate meridionali.[13]

Vediamo di collegare fra loro i dati: il Lo Monaco occupa la terra dei Sannazaro nel 1462 e può farlo in quanto il padre dei 'pupilli' è morto; da ciò consegue che, se la sua morte ha avuto luogo, come affermano i testimoni, al tempo della guerra del duca Giovanni, egli deve essere morto fra il 1460 e la prima metà del 1462; un prezioso testo, lo *Istrumento tra Giacomo Sannazaro ed i Padri detti i Servi di Maria per l'erezione del loro monistero a Mergellina*,[14] ci tramanda giorno e mese della morte: 7 ottobre. Orbene, se Iacobo nacque, come crediamo di aver dimostrato, il 28 luglio 1457, egli compì i quattro anni nel luglio 1461: i conti tornano. Non tornano per nulla se, invece, si segue la cronologia del documento cassinese, in base al quale il Percopo arbitrariamente fissò come data di nascita il 1456. Non tornano in primo luogo perché, secondo quel documento, il Sannazaro dovrebbe essere nato nel luglio 1455, condizione necessaria perché avesse più di diciotto anni il 3 maggio del 1474; ma se portiamo la data di nascita al 1455, andiamo contro tutte le testimonianze esistenti (i quattro anni alla morte del padre, i settantadue nel 1530). E non basta: il documento cassinese falsa la differenza di età fra i due fratelli: Iacobo sarebbe *maior annis decem et octo*, Marco Antonio *maior annis decem et minor quartodecimo*: cioè fra i due fratelli ci sarebbero cinque anni e mezzo di differenza, invece di tre e mezzo. In altre parole: Marco Antonio ha qui un'età che si accorda con le deposizioni dell'altro documento, Iacobo ha due anni in più, sottratti i quali si reintegra la data di nascita 1457, sopra dimostrata come l'unica possibile. Ma perché un simile errore nel documento? La lettura dello stesso convince che non si tratta di un errore, ma di una deformazione della verità precisamente calcolata: con quel sorprendente documento la madre del poeta, che non figura certo come un modello di donna d'affari, rinuncia in favore dei monaci benedettini del Convento di Sant'Anna degli Acquaviva ai suoi diritti su un terreno nelle vicinanze di Mondragone, terreno riguardo al quale il marito in vita avrebbe litigato coi monaci per la loro appropriazione indebita, indi avrebbe incassato dagli stessi la somma di dodici ducati di carlini d'argento; di cui però, guarda caso, i monaci non possiedono quietanza né alcun altro documento scritto. E c'è di più, un ultimo tocco, una quasi esilarante postilla; se qualcuno in avvenire trasgredisse a detta rinuncia e gli venisse in mente di vantare diritti, dovrebbe per prima cosa pagare cinquanta once di carlini d'argento per il fastidio dato ai monaci. È chiaro che, per una così stupefacente rinuncia, ai monaci e al loro notaio faceva molto comodo che almeno uno dei due eredi risultasse maggiorenne e firmante in proprio accanto alla madre (*et ipse Jacobus suo proprio nomine*). Al poeta adulto non resterà che il diritto di rimpiangere le belle terre dalla sua famiglia possedute in quel di Sinuessa (Mondragone), nei campi Falerni e nei monti Massici; rimpianto che dalla VII prosa dell'*Arcadia* rimbalza alle posteriori Elegie latine (*Te foecunda tenent saxosi rura Petrini,/ rura olim proavis facta superba meis,/ et sinuessanas spectas, mea gaudia, Nymphas,/ quique novo semper sulfure fumat ager. Eleg. I, I, vv. 1-4*).

A lettura ultimata di questo documento e soprattutto della giungla di atti del processo fra i Sannazaro e il Fisco (1500-1517), disperato tentativo di riparare a distanza di anni a un cumulo di storditezze familiari, si ha l'impressione di comunicare più da vicino col Sannazaro, di capire quel sordo lamento scandito per tutta la sua opera, il ricordo della terra sempre offeso dalle ombre provocatorie dell'ingiustizia, donde la nostalgia a petto gonfio. Partiti in cerca di una data, si è giunti a cogliere le radici di uno stato d'animo; sorprese della ricerca. E se, in fondo, queste radici sono molto più importanti di una data, tuttavia anche le date giuste a qualcosa servono sempre.

Notes

[1] Paolo Giovio, *Lettere*, a cura di G. G. Ferrero, in *Pauli Iovii Opera*, I, II (Roma, Istituto Poligrafico dello Stato, 1956); I, lett. 60, alle pp. 174-178.

[2] *Cf. Elegiae*, II, II vv. 3-4; *Hymnus ad divum Nazarium, Epigr.* LVIII, vv. 21-26 (in *Poeti latini del Quattrocento*, a cura di Fr. Arnaldi, L. Gualdo Rosa, L. Monti Sabia, Milano, Ricciardi, 1964, pp. 1134; 1164); già Erasmo Percopo nella *Vita di Jacobo Sannazaro*, edita postuma a cura di G. Brognoligo (Napoli, Società Napol. di Storia Patria, 1931), cita (p. 16) *Epigr.* II, XXXVII.

[3] Si cita da Iacobo Sannazaro, *Opere volgari*, a cura di A. Mauro (Bari, Laterza, 1961).

⁴ *Cf.* il Tommaseo Bellini, dove sono registrati per *estremo* tre valori semantici: ultimo, grandissimo o gravissimo, eccessivo.

⁵ Milano, Società Tipografica dei Classici Italiani, 1805, vol. 3.

⁶ In *J. J. Pontani Opera*, Venetiis in aedibus Aldi et Andreae soceri, mense Aprili MDXIX.

⁷ *Cf.* G. Cestari, *Anecdoti istorici sulle alumiere delli monti Leucogei* (Napoli 1790), dove i documenti del processo sono in parte riprodotti, in parte riassunti. Poiché il fondo dei 'Processi antichi' dell'Archivio di Stato di Napoli ha subito notevoli perdite in seguito all'ultima guerra, le ricerche eseguite nei 'Processi della Summaria' superstiti hanno dato esito negativo riguardo ai documenti in questione, impedendomi qualsiasi riscontro diretto.

⁸ In *Miscellanea di studi critici edita in onore di A. Graf* (Bergamo, 1st v. Arti Grafiche, 1903), pp. 775–788.

⁹ Già citata dal Colangelo, *op. cit.*, p. 93.

¹⁰ Sulla costruzione della tomba del Sannazaro, suoi autori e data, *cf.* B. Croce, *La chiesetta di Jacopo Sannazaro*, in *Storie e leggende napoletane*, seconda edizione (Bari, Laterza, 1923), pp. 197–219.

¹¹ Sotto le seguenti righe si legge che Ferrante I e il Lo Monaco sapevano benissimo di fare i propri affari in casa d'altri: 'Item si per caso fosse alcuna persona la quale o per instromento o per privilegio autentico mostrasse la montagna donde se piglia la petra de l'Alume esser sua ch'*eo casu* la predicta M. sia tenuta accordare la dicta tal persona et epso M. Guliermo habia da contribuire in la mità de quillo se pagasse per tal accordo. Placet R. Majestati' (cap. 10 del documento di contratto edito da Cestari, *op. cit.*, p. 29).

¹² Pontano, *De bello neapol.*, *cit.*, libro IV, p. 293v. Sullo svolgimento della guerra, *cf.* E. Nunziante, 'I primi anni di Ferdinando d'Aragona e l'invasione di Giovanni d'Angiò' in *Arch. Stor. per le Province Napoletane*, XVII (1892), pp. 299–357, 564–586; XVIII (1893), pp. 3–40, 205–246, 411–462, 561–620; XIX (1894), pp. 37–96, 300–353, 553–658; XX (1895), pp. 206–264, 442–516 (scontro presso Sarno e sconfitta di Ferrante I); XXI (1896), pp. 265–289, 494–532 (alla fine del 1461 Ferrante ha riconquistato gran parte dell'Abruzzo e la Calabria, ridotta fedele la Terra di Lavoro); XXII (1897), pp. 47–64, 204–240 (ripresa della guerra nella primavera del 1462, battaglia di Troia); XXIII (1898), pp. 144–210. *Cf.* anche A. Ratti, 'Quarantadue lettere originali di Pio II relative alla guerra per la successione nel reame di Napoli (1460–1463)' in *Miscellanea di Studi e Docum. offerta al Congresso storico internaz. dalla Società Lombarda* (Milano, Cogliati, 1903), pp. 75–107.

¹³ Per queste testimonianze, *cf.* Cestari, *op. cit.*, pp. 5; 33–43. Percopo, *Vita, cit.*, p. 18.

¹⁴ Datato 25 dicembre 1529, edito dal Colangelo, *op. cit.*, pp. 201–231; a p. 213 si legge che il Sannazaro richiede l'impegno da parte dei frati di recitare messe in quattro anniversari: 29 novembre per il 'Serenissimo Federico', 7 ottobre per suo padre, 28 luglio per sua madre e 'a quel giorno che passerà da questa vita per esso'.

Carlo Dionisotti

Appunti sui capitoli
di Machiavelli

Fondamentale è stato ed è il contributo inglese agli studi su Machiavelli. Non parrà dunque inopportuno che, volendo rendere omaggio, debito omaggio e non ricambio, a Kathleen Speight, benemerita italianista inglese, uno studioso italiano si volga all'opera di Machiavelli. Né parrà inopportuno che prudentemente si limiti a considerare testi di secondaria importanza. È d'altra parte noto che tutto o quasi tutto quel che di Machiavelli ci resta appartiene alla piena maturità di lui ed è perciò, in varia misura, importante. Ci restano di Machiavelli cinque capitoli, un dei quali, 'Poscia che a l'ombra sotto questo alloro', è dagli editori qualificato pastorale e conseguentemente, e a ragione, distinto e disgiunto dagli altri. Nella recente e buona edizione delle *Opere letterarie* di Machiavelli a cura di L. Blasucci, Milano 1964, p. 347, si legge in proposito la seguente nota introduttiva: 'Si ritiene che in questo capitolo, sotto la stilizzazione bucolica e attraverso il personaggio del pastore Iacinto, il Machiavelli inneggi a Giuliano o a Lorenzo dei Medici, per attirarne la benevolenza... Se così fosse, la composizione cadrebbe tra il 1513 (liberazione del Machiavelli dal carcere e suo desiderio, già espresso in lettere di quest'anno, di essere impiegato dai Medici) e il 1519 (morte di Lorenzo; Giuliano era morto nel '16)'. Come si vede, il Blasucci riferisce le ipotesi dei precedenti studiosi, ma non le fa proprie e insomma non mostra di considerarle soddisfacenti. In realtà, dei due studiosi ai quali il Blasucci rinvia, Tommasini e Gigli, il primo, che di gran lunga è il più autorevole, aveva ipoteticamente riconosciuto nel pastore Iacinto del capitolo Lorenzo de'Medici, non Giuliano, che sarebbe stata, ed è, identificazione assurda. Perché Iacinto è un giovincello, colmo fin dalla nascita di celesti virtù, ma ancora ai primi passi di una carriera che *farà*, come è detto al v. 51, non che abbia già fatto, la sua gloria manifesta. E subito dopo il poeta, se così può chiamarsi l'autore del capitolo, precisa che 'tutt'i pastor che 'n queste selve stanno', cioè secondo l'ipotesi i cittadini di Firenze, hanno rimesso nelle mani di lui ogni loro differenza, cioè lo hanno riconosciuto superiore, 'sanza riguardo a l'età iuvenile'. È chiaro che si può identificare Iacinto col ventenne Lorenzo, non certo con Giuliano che, quando tornò a Firenze nel 1512, aveva 33 anni. L'identificazione con Lorenzo non è soltanto possibile: è probabile. Ma in tanto è probabile in quanto il capitolo sia stato composto nei primi anni della restaurazione medicea, prima che

Lorenzo diventasse Duca d'Urbino, cioè principe. Perché, se anche la precisa allusione nel v. 97 ai 'privati panni' del bimbo Iacinto beneficato dagli Dei, cioè al fatto che non era nato principe, restasse pur sempre giustificata, perché veridica, non è credibile che l'autore del capitolo se la lasciasse scappar di bocca quando ormai il vizio d'origine era sanato. E naturalmente resta fermo l'argomento già addotto dell'età giovanile, per cui bisogna pensare al momento in cui Lorenzo–Iacinto faceva i suoi primi passi nel governo di Firenze e in cui ancora faceva spicco la sproporzione fra il ruolo e l'età. Tanto può bastare per la data e per l'interpretazione del testo. Ma, detto ciò, bisogna anche affrettarsi a dir chiaro che questo capitolo pastorale poco somiglia e di troppo è inferiore a qualsiasi altra scrittura di Machiavelli a noi nota. Che sia di Machiavelli è possibile, perché un grande uomo può accidentalmente rivelarsi men che uomo e far vergogna a se stesso, ma non è probabile. E non può considerarsi probabile sulla sola base di una tradizione manoscritta accettata a occhi chiusi. Non insisterò su questo punto, non potendo riesaminare coi miei occhi quella tradizione. E appena accennerò alla difficoltà ovvia di attribuire un così abbietto e smaccato panegirico di Lorenzo de' Medici a un uomo che nei suoi rapporti con quella famiglia e coi potenti in genere non ci risulta essere sceso mai a così basso livello. Ma non posso fare a meno di rilevare che lingua e stile di quel capitolo non sono di Machiavelli, e che, per fare un solo preciso rilievo, non si può attribuire a lui fino a contraria prova un *pianti* per piante in rima sul bel principio (v. 5). E aggiungerò, saltando alla chiusa e a un altro ordine di argomenti, che Machiavelli non poteva offrire a Iacinto–Lorenzo il suo armento (vv. 115–117). Perché purtroppo non aveva armento: tordi sì poteva offrire il vero Machiavelli a Giuliano, accompagnandoli con un sonetto degno di lui, e tordi magri come lui, ma pecore, sia pur povere, il povero Machiavelli non n'aveva da offrire. E non è il caso di appigliarsi alla vaghezza della finzione pastorale. Perché in tanto questa finzione era di moda allora, in quanto essa era presa sul serio. E Machiavelli era più di ogni altro incline a prendere sul serio ogni sua finzione, qualunque essa fosse.

Gli altri capitoli di Machiavelli, d'una cristallina autenticità, sono a prima vista caratterizzati e accomunati dal fatto, non comune, che in fronte a ciascuno figura la dedica, o meglio l'indirizzo, d'un amico dell'autore. Comune anche è il tema morale: l'ingratitudine, la fortuna, l'ambizione, l'occasione. Quando però si passi al testo, salta agli occhi che l'ultimo, di soli 22 versi, sta a sé di contro agli altri tre, che si estendono rispettivamente per 187, 193 e ancora 187 versi. L'ultimo sta a sé anche per il buon motivo che non è, come gli altri, composizione originale di Machiavelli: è una semplice, benché libera e a suo modo, cioè al modo di Machiavelli, originalissima, versione in volgare di un epigramma latino. Ci si può chiedere se Machiavelli pensasse di includere questo epigramma in un componimento più ampio sullo stesso tema, a lui caro, dell'occasione. Ma è domanda oziosa, perché non si appoggia su alcun indizio o prova, e perché l'epigramma sta bene così com'è. Notevole è che la dedica al Nerli, che sta in fronte all'epigramma, non è richiamata nel testo, come invece è sempre richiamata quella degli altri capitoli. Insomma per la sua natura di volgarizzamento, per la sua struttura e mole, l'epigramma sta a sé e non può essere messo sullo stesso piano degli altri capitoli. Poiché la forma metrica è stata addotta come prova che di un capitolo si tratta, preciserò che, traducendo dal latino, Machiavelli doveva usare, come tutti allora usavano, la terza rima, non esistendo in volgare altra forma metrica che meglio corrispondesse al distico elegiaco. Né dal testo né dalla tradizione risultano elementi che consentano una qualunque ipotesi circa la data del volgarizzamento. Non sappiamo quando cominciassero i rapporti amichevoli di Machiavelli col Nerli: non necessariamente colle riunioni degli Orti Oricellari. Sappiamo per contro che durarono fino all'ultimo. Dirò che l'idea stessa di volgarizzare un epigramma di Ausonio e di dedicare il breve volgarizzamento a un amico, quasi a provare la validità della lingua moderna a competere con l'antica, mi fa pensare a una data tarda. Certo, nella sprezzatura stilistica e nel movimento drammatico rapido e incalzante dell'epigramma, non è traccia di quella prolissità e approssimazione, cui Machiavelli indulgeva quando ancora si illudeva di essere poeta.

Restano e fanno gruppo i tre capitoli veri e propri, dedicati a Giovanni Folchi, a G. B. Soderini e a Luigi Guicciardini. Prima di considerarli, come vanno considerati, insieme, bisogna sgombrare il terreno da alcune particolari questioni, inutilmente e stranamente rimaste aperte sulla data e interpretazione di ciascun capitolo.

Ci si può sbrigare del primo in poche parole, perché in esso dedica e contesto non hanno mai consentito alcun dubbio che Machiavelli scrivesse quando ancora era segretario, e però dopo il 1507, quando cioè già sapeva che il gran capitano Consalvo poteva servire di fresco esempio della ingratitudine dei principi. Sarà però il caso di precisare che questo accenno alla disgrazia di Consalvo esclude il 1507 e il 1512, perché Machiavelli scrivendo sapeva non soltanto che Consalvo aveva dovuto lasciare l'Italia, ma anche che, tornato in Spagna, non aveva ricevuto nuovi incarichi e favori proporzionati ai suoi meriti e insomma s'era trovato a dover vivere ivi sospetto al suo re, e d'altra parte perché Machiavelli segretario era troppo ben informato per non sapere che nel 1512 di Consalvo si parlava come di un possibile comandante delle forze della Lega Santa in Italia. Resta dunque un periodo di quattro anni, entro cui cercare la probabile data di composizione del capitolo. Risulta che Machiavelli s'indusse a scrivere, perché morso dal dente dell'invidia (v. 2), e di fatto sappiamo che proprio in quegli anni, fino al 1509 incluso, egli ebbe a soffrire e temere per la scoperta ostilità di quelli che a Firenze lo consideravano il *mannerino* del Gonfaloniere. Onde il Tommasini, che da pari suo discusse la questione e chiarì l'importanza del capitolo nei rispetti dell'analogo, e però sostanzialmente diverso atteggiamento assunto da Machiavelli nei *Discorsi* di fronte all'ingratitudine popolare, pensò che Machiavelli scrivesse il capitolo ai primi del 1510, subito dopo la fallita manovra dei suoi avversari per privarlo della carica. Se dovessimo o potessimo credere alla sentenza del Benedetto, editore e interprete delle *Operette satiriche* di Machiavelli (Torino 1920, p. 124n.), secondo il quale 'lo stile di tutto il capitolo sa d'improvvisazione', ci converrebbe pensare, come il Tommasini ha fatto, a uno stimolo immediato e forte per la composizione del capitolo. Ma è chiaro per chiunque legga il testo spregiudicatamente, e però con discrezione storica e col dovuto rispetto, che quella sentenza non sta in piedi. Già una improvvisazione di 187 versi sarebbe stata eccezionale allora per un improvvisatore di mestiere, come Serafino Aquilano, fosse stato ancora vivo. Il capitolo di Machiavelli è composizione meditata dello stesso uomo che avrebbe scritto di lì a qualche anno i *Discorsi*. Ed è composizione che, movendo dal caso personale, da una persecuzione sofferta e che ancora dura, non dà però luogo, come ci aspetteremmo, ad alcuna apologia. Machiavelli comincia dicendo che gli è di conforto la poesia, prosegue spiegando, senza più alcun riferimento ai casi suoi, come l'ingratitudine sempre abbia operato e operi nella storia e nella vita politica, e rifacendosi al tema iniziale, conclude che 'ciascun fuggir le corti e stati debbe'. Inizio e chiusa dunque danno rilievo a quel motivo dell'evasione letteraria dalla fallacia e miseria del vivere politico che era così insistente nella tradizione umanistica e che curiosamente lo stesso Machiavelli, a suo dispetto e per sua gloria, in qualche modo partecipava e partecipò per tutta la vita. Insomma il testo del capitolo senza dubbio presuppone il motivo personale di una persecuzione sofferta e in atto, non però, necessariamente, una fresca vittoria contro quella persecuzione. Il motivo dell'evasione letteraria e l'ampio, industrioso sviluppo teorico del tema senza alcun riferimento personale sembrano piuttosto intesi a confermare l'immagine che Machiavelli già aveva proposto di sé colla stampa del suo *Decennale*, come di un uomo che, fedelmente servendo nell'impiego politico, non era però servo a qualunque costo dell'impiego, di una meschina e fatua ambizione, come gli avversari supponevano: aveva altre frecce al suo arco, altri e più alti e disinteressati pensieri in mente. Pertanto direi che la data proposta dal Tommasini sia possibile piuttosto che probabile. A una data anteriore mi fa pensare l'inizio del capitolo, diverso affatto da quello degli altri due, e in cui mi pare evidente che Machiavelli, facendo di nuovo appello alla poesia, si richiami alla prova già fornita nel *Decennale* (onde il v. 5: 'Non sì ch'io speri averne *altra* corona') e si preoccupi di precisare i limiti modesti della sua ambizione poetica. Conseguentemente penso che fra la stampa del *Decennale* e questo capitolo Machiavelli non avesse scritto in poesia null'altro e che però l'intervallo fra i due testi fosse abbastanza breve perché, iniziando il secondo, egli potesse richiamarsi al primo. Penserei dunque piuttosto al 1508 che al 1510. Ma non è che la differenza importi molto a questo punto. Importa che il capitolo sia riconosciuto come il primo impegnativo, nient'affatto improvvisato esperimento poetico di Machiavelli dopo il *Decennale*.

Come il secondo capitolo di Machiavelli sulla Fortuna, dedicato a G. B. Soderini, abbia potuto fin qui essere pacificamente attribuito 'all'indomani della caduta di Pier Soderini e del ritorno dei Medici in Firenze', resta per me inspiegabile. D'una ipotesi si tratta che subito, prima ancora di un esame del testo, appare improbabile. Dopo la disgrazia dei Soderini e sua, Machiavelli non aveva motivo di ripudiare, né avrebbe potuto, anche volendo, gli stretti rapporti suoi con quella famiglia. Ma naturalmente aveva buoni motivi per evitare che i Medici e i loro aderenti sospettassero di lui più di quanto già mostravano di fare. Una qualunque testimonianza pubblica di solidarietà con gli esuli Soderini avrebbe tolto a Machiavelli ogni speranza di poter essere adoperato, come egli si ostinava a sperare, dai nuovi padroni. Di fatto sappiamo quanto egli si preoccupasse, da quel galantuomo che era e sempre fu, dell'imbarazzo in cui si sarebbe trovato, andando a Roma, se far visita o no al card. Soderini. Supporre che in tali condizioni, a ufo, solo per 'inviare un conforto ai vecchi amici, filosofeggiando sul comune disastro', come opina il già citato editore delle *Operette satiriche*, L. F. Benedetto (p. 140), Machiavelli componesse e divulgasse un capitolone di più che 200 versi, e a questo modo si preparasse la via per dedicare a Giuliano de' Medici il *Principe*, è ipotesi assurda e non discutibile. Né si può addurre, a riscontro di un testo poetico evidentemente fatto per essere divulgato, la minuta dei *Ghiribizzi scritti in Raugia al Soderino*, che in quella forma certo non uscirono mai dallo scrittoio di Machiavelli e che in qualunque forma non poterono uscirne se non per il tramite di una segretissima corrispondenza. Se mai, bisognerebbe pensare per il capitolo a una data molto più tarda, quando si era ormai alleviato il rigore contro gli esuli e quando d'altra parte Machiavelli non avesse più motivo di sperare d'essere impiegato dai Medici. Ma sarebbe sempre un'ipotesi improbabile. Resta a vedere, per togliere ogni dubbio, il testo del capitolo. Non pare che gli interpreti, disposti ad ammettere che Machiavelli nel 1512–13 imprudentemente si rivolgesse in pubblico a un Soderini, si siano stupiti del fatto che nel capitolo 'nessuna allusione imprudente richiama direttamente alla memoria i casi recenti di Firenze, le recenti sventure dei Soderini'. È chiaro che qui la prudenza è troppa, e non si giustifica più né umanamente né, trattandosi di poesia, retoricamente. Tanto più è chiaro, perché le recenti sventure dei Soderini erano sventure dello stesso Machiavelli. In realtà il capitolo si dimostra scritto prima delle sventure, le quali perciò appunto non figurano. Altrimenti non si spiega l'affermazione iniziale che il Soderini non può né deve temere d'altre ferite che dei colpi della Fortuna. Segno che ancora non era stato colpito. E temere può e deve, perché, aggiunge Machiavelli elogiando l'amico, la Fortuna 'spesso si suole oppor con maggior forza dove più forza vede aver natura'. È un pericolo futuro, che incombe su chi è forte. Non si parla di forza impegnata a sostenere un colpo già inferto e sofferto. Intanto, prosegue baldanzosamente Machiavelli, la diva crudele rivolga 'ver di me gli occhi sua feroci e legga quel ch'or di lei e del suo regno canto'. Dunque la Fortuna non si era ancora degnata di gettare gli occhi su di lui Machiavelli, cioè di colpirlo, e perciò appunto Machiavelli, che dantescamente vuole dimostrarsi alla Fortuna, come vuole, presto, lancia la sua sfida, insieme augurandosi che per rappresaglia essa colpisca lui prima e piuttosto che l'amico Soderini. Né la chiara lettera di questo proemio è infirmata da quel che segue: nessun cenno mai che il Soderini o Machiavelli siano stati o siano vittime della Fortuna. La conclusione pessimistica del capitolo consuona perfettamente con quella del capitolo precedente. Poiché di fortuna politica si tratta, e non d'altra, la lezione della storia qui è che 'pochi sono e' felici e que' son morti prima che la lor ruota indietro torni o che voltando al basso ne li porti', come là era che per la forza dell'Ingratitudine, buona ministra anch'essa della Fortuna, 'ciascun fuggir le corti e stati debbe'. Dunque il capitolo al Soderini è sicuramente anteriore al 1512 e probabilmente non lontano dal capitolo al Folchi. Non ha importanza per la cronologia, ma per altro verso, come si vedrà, importa la dedica. Con mirabile accordo, se ho ben visto, gli editori un dopo l'altro ripetono che il dedicatario del capitolo, G. B. Soderini, era fratello del Gonfaloniere. Donde abbiano ricavato la notizia non so, ma non mi pare temerario il sospetto che abbiano, o il primo della fila abbia, scambiato Giovan Battista con Giovan Vittorio, che questo sì era fratello di Piero. Certo è che la fonte ovvia, oltre la quale non mi sono curato di andare, e cioè il Litta, non registra fra i figli di Tommaso alcun Giovan Battista, ma registra e illustra Giovan Battista figlio di Paolo Antonio e pertanto nipote del Gonfaloniere Piero, nato nel 1484. Questo, fino a contraria prova, credo sia il dedicatario del capitolo di Machiavelli: ancora giovane, sui venticinque anni, al tempo della dedica, così come ancor giovane era, politicamente alle prime armi, il dedicatario del terzo capitolo, Luigi Guicciardini. A differenza del secondo capitolo, cui soltanto *ex silentio*, come si è visto, possiamo assegnare una data approssimativa, il terzo capitolo, dedicato a

Luigi Guicciardini, ci porta con frequenti, precise allusioni nel bel mezzo della scena politica contemporanea. Subito all'inizio Machiavelli allude a 'questo caso ch'a Siena è seguito', specificando al v. 124 che si era trattato di una fraterna lite, ovviamente fra membri della famiglia Petrucci, predominante a Siena. Al solito il Tommasini aveva visto benissimo che doveva trattarsi di una lite fra Borghese e Alfonso Petrucci scoppiata nel 1509, e non di una più tarda lite, del 1516, 'perché le condizioni politiche d'Italia descritte nel capitolo rispondon meglio al vero, supponendole di quello anzi che di questo anno'. In italiano, si sa, non esiste la figura retorica dell'*understatement*. Formulato a quel modo, il motivo addotto dal Tommasini parve debole. La data tarda piacque e prevalse, e solo recentemente è stata a malincuore rimessa in questione, non perché sia stata riconosciuta, come avrebbe dovuto essere, storicamente e politicamente insostenibile, ma perché sono state riconosciute valide alcune ovvie consonanze fra il capitolo e le lettere scritte da Machiavelli durante la sua missione a Verona nel 1509. Bisogna dunque anzi tutto chiarire che i sostenitori della data tarda, saltando di piè pari le condizioni politiche d'Italia descritte nel capitolo, non hanno però creduto di potersi sottrarre al dovere di spiegare in qualche modo l'accenno che nella chiusa Machiavelli fa al suo timore che la guerra, di cui egli è stato ed è spettatore in terra altrui, stia per estendersi alla Toscana e produrre ivi le stesse rovine. E per spiegare questo accenno conclusivo e però messo da Machiavelli in tutta evidenza, quale mirabile ipotesi hanno escogitato? Questa: che nel 1516 Machiavelli, nelle condizioni in cui era venuto a trovarsi, costretto com'era a fare i conti, a Firenze e a Roma, coi nuovi padroni, avendo in mano per quelli, con o senza la dedica a Lorenzo, il manoscritto del *Principe*, in quel bel modo alludesse all'imminente guerra di Urbino, cioè alla guerra mossa con le armi del Papa e di Firenze per assicurare di fatto a Lorenzo de' Medici un sia pur piccolo principato. Inutile insistere a dimostrare l'assurdità non soltanto politica, ma anche storica, di una tale ipotesi, rilevando che se in prosieguo di tempo la conquista del ducato di Urbino si rivelò precaria e tanto più difficile del previsto a essere mantenuta e consolidata, senza di che non si spiega il trapasso dal *Principe* ai *Discorsi*, nel 1516, avendo Francesco I dato via libera al Papa in quel settore, la conquista di Urbino doveva prospettarsi a chiunque, Machiavelli incluso, come una facile impresa, non

certo, né allora né poi, come una guerra che rischiasse di mettere
a ferro e fuoco la Toscana e Firenze in ispecie. Alla peggio,
avrebbe messo a ferro e fuoco il territorio urbinate. Ma quel che
Machiavelli nella chiusa del capitolo prevedeva e temeva, non era
l'altrui dolore, era il dolore dei suoi: non del Veneto o dell'Urbinate
o d'altra parte d'Italia, ma della Toscana e di Firenze. Dunque
l'attribuzione del capitolo al 1516, non richiesta dall'accenno a
Siena nei versi iniziali, è esclusa dalla previsione di una guerra in
Toscana nei versi finali. Aggiungerò per buona derrata che, pur
volendo chiudere gli occhi a quel che sta in mezzo fra inizio e
chiusa, cioè alla sostanza stessa del capitolo, e giocando a
indovinare, la dedica a Luigi Guicciardini sarebbe stata sufficente
a mettere sull'avviso. Perché certamente nel 1516 il Guicciardini
non era più lo stesso uomo del 1509, e perché probabilmente
diversi affatto erano i rapporti fra lui e Machiavelli. Nel 1509 era
il figlio di Piero e nulla più, e Machiavelli segretario e tanto più
avanti negli anni poteva rivolgersi a lui famigliarmente, secondo
il costume fiorentino. Nel 1516 messer Luigi era il capo della
famiglia, di quella famiglia, e se anche i Medici non ne facessero
troppo conto e gli preferissero il minor fratello Francesco, e
anche proprio per questo, non era più uomo cui Machiavelli
reietto e sospetto si potesse rivolgere in pubblico allo stesso
modo. Di fatto neppure più si ha notizia di rapporti privati fra i
due, e se anche si debba accogliere con riserva la testimonianza
del Busini che nell'*Asino* Machiavelli avesse preso di mira Luigi
Guicciardini, certo è che il silenzio su di lui nel carteggio col
fratello Francesco fa pensare che la cordialità di rapporti cui si
ispirano le lettere del 1509 e il capitolo, fosse in seguito venuta
meno. Ma, ripeto, tutto ciò può servire per chi giochi a indovinare.
Più economico, oltre che doveroso, è leggere il testo e spiegarlo.
Machiavelli dunque descrive e giustifica le vittorie delle armi
francesi in Italia, che hanno successivamente provocato la rovina
del Regno di Napoli, del Ducato di Milano e della Repubblica di
Venezia (vv. 67-69). Il paragone in termini politici e militari, che
giustificando Machiavelli istituisce, è esclusivamente tra Francia
e Italia. Dopo la decisiva vittoria di Agnadello, Machiavelli poteva
anche prescindere dalla sconfitta del Garigliano e da un paragone
tra Francia e Spagna. Ma non avrebbe potuto prescinderne più
dopo Ravenna, e se si fosse trovato a scrivere più tardi ancora,
dopo Marignano, è chiaro che il paragone non si sarebbe più

posto, in termini militari, tra Francia e Italia. È inoltre chiaro che
nel capitolo Machiavelli considera *disfatto* lo stato di S.
Marco, come prima erano stati quelli di Napoli e di Milano. Scriveva
dunque ancora sotto l'impressione della disfatta di Agnadello e
delle sue immediate conseguenze, prima della riscossa veneziana.
Finalmente, nei vv. 124–126, Machiavelli invita l'amico a non
preoccuparsi di Siena e a voltar gli occhi 'a questa parte, fra
queste genti attonite e smarrite'. Quale parte e quali genti?
Evidentemente quella in cui e quelle fra cui Machiavelli si trova.
E prosegue invitando a rivolgere gli occhi *in qua*, non soltanto
l'amico, ma chiunque 'veder vuole l'*altrui* fatiche, e riguardi se
ancora cotanta crudeltà mai vidde il sole'. Segue nei versi 133–159,
la lunga, particolareggiata, orrida descrizione della strage e
devastazione che Machiavelli vede intorno a sé. Ma dove diamine
siamo? Non certo in Toscana. Strage e desolazione sono quelle
per cui 'San Marco a le sue spese, e forse invano, tardi conosce
come li bisogna tener la spada e non il libro in mano'. Sono
dunque, e Machiavelli è mentre scrive, nell'ex-dominio di Venezia
dilaniato dalle armi vittoriose dei nemici. Onde, concludendo,
Machiavelli può volgersi col pensiero e col timore alla patria
lontana, ai monti di Toscana. Insomma quel che si legge nel
capitolo addita con assoluta chiarezza il soggiorno di Machiavelli
a Verona nel 1509, l'impressione vivissima che egli allora ebbe,
come le sue lettere dimostrano, dallo spettacolo per lui nuovo di
una guerra che atrocemente e minutamente si esercitava ai danni
della popolazione civile. Perché la grandezza dell'uomo sta anche
in ciò che, quanto era incline, fin troppo incline, alla violenza nel
pensiero e nella lingua, tanto era sensibile e pronto a commuoversi
di fronte alla violenza reale, alle vittime umili e ignare, alla pura
e semplice umanità offesa.

I tre capitoli dunque sono cronologicamente vicini. La data
precisa del terzo fa pensare che in rapporto e prossimità con essa
vada ristretto il margine d'incertezza al quale ci costringevano i
soli elementi interni del primo e più ancora del secondo. Resta a
considerarli e compararli per quel che di fatto e anzi tutto sono,
cioè per la loro struttura letteraria. Su questo punto non mi
sembra che gli studiosi abbiano insistito a sufficienza. Conseguentemente vedo che essi danno per ovvio, senza naturalmente
appulcrare alcun riscontro o argomento, quel che non è per nulla
ovvio. Scrive ad esempio il Benedetto nella sua citata edizione

delle *Operette satiriche*, p. 122, che Machiavelli si servì 'del capitolo, genere già molto in voga a quei tempi, sorta di *sermo* oraziano più aperto alle notazioni logiche che alle emozioni potenti e ai puri fantasmi'. Lasciamo stare le emozioni e le fantasime. Io mi contenterei che mi venissero segnalati, non dirò una mezza dozzina di capitoli, ma tre soli, ch'è un bel numero, quanti son quelli di Machiavelli, in cui sia riconoscibile quella sorta di *sermo* oraziano, che secondo il Benedetto era genere già molto in voga a quei tempi. In realtà, se in aggiunta ai tre di Machiavelli saltassero fuori i tre da me richiesti, dovremmo affrettarci a riaprire la discussione, che andrà in ogni modo riaperta, sulle origini di quel capitolo di stampo oraziano che sotto il nome di satira ottenne, grazie all'Ariosto, pieno diritto di cittadinanza nella poesia cinquecentesca, mentre a picco andavano, sopraffatte e spregiate dalle nuove generazioni, tutte l'altre forme di capitoli, che quelle sì erano state in gran voga fino ai primi anni del Cinquecento, e a segnalare il loro naufragio insorgeva la parodia del capitolo faceto, bernesco. Insomma un esame letterario, ossia innanzi tutto tecnico, pedantesco, dei capitoli di Machiavelli s'impone, perché, quand'anche non avessimo per la loro stesura altro termine *ante quem* che la morte dell'autore nel 1527, e a maggior ragione sapendoli composti prima del 1512, prima che l'Ariosto cominciasse a scrivere le sue *Satire*, essi capitoli s'inseriscono di giusta misura in un periodo o momento che segna una svolta decisiva nella storia di quella forma di poesia.

Cominciando dalla struttura materiale, quantitativa, subito colpisce il fatto che, come già s'è visto, il primo e il terzo hanno lo stesso numero di versi, 187, il secondo 193, due sole terzine in più. Se anche non sapessimo che i tre capitoli sono cronologicamente vicini, l'esatta corrispondenza nel numero dei versi fra il primo e il terzo e la minima differenza in più del secondo basterebbero all'ipotesi di una stesura condotta secondo un disegno unico. Perché i dati quantitativi risultanti non possono essere attribuiti al caso. A differenza di altri componimenti, il capitolo in terza rima si prestava a tagli diversissimi, in parte corrispondenti alla diversità dei generi, amoroso, pastorale, encomiastico, morale, cui esso pure si prestava. Fra le rime di Lorenzo il Magnifico, i cinque capitoli spirituali sono brevi, da un massimo di 70 versi (I) a un minimo di 19 (V); per contro l'unico capitolo morale ('dove eccito ed esorto me medesimo') conta 157 versi e quello, pur unico nel suo genere, consolatorio a G. F. Ventura per la morte della figlia, 144 versi. A Firenze, particolare non trascurabile per Machiavelli, il capitolo amoroso ebbe scarsa fortuna, e come l'esempio stesso di Lorenzo dimostra, alla terza rima, normalmente usata in componimenti narrativi o didattici, erano preferiti altri metri per componimenti di più breve respiro. Non esistono capitoli fra le rime autentiche del Poliziano; i due che si leggono fra le apocrife, per la morte di Lorenzo e per l'avvento di Piero, contano rispettivamente 118 e 115 versi. L'esule Giuliano de' Medici, frequentando negli ultimi anni del Quattrocento le corti e i circoli aristocratici dell'Italia settentrionale, subito si addestrò a comporre capitoli amorosi, secondo la nuova moda ivi dominante. I quattro compresi fra le sue rime (ed. Fatini, I, XXXIX, XLIV, LIV) contano rispettivamente 70, 58, 58, 40 versi. A Firenze la nuova moda del capitolo e in genere della lirica cortigiana fu introdotta, per quanto sappiamo, da Francesco Cei, ben noto a Machiavelli. I *Sonecti, capituli, canzone, sextine, stanze et strambocti composti per lo excellentissimo Francescho Cei ciptadino fiorentino in laude di Clitia* apparvero per i tipi del Giunta nel 1503. Fra i capitoli del Cei, che insieme agli strambotti annunciano già nel titolo il carattere cortigiano della raccolta, è in primo luogo compresa una lunga egloga drammatica, cioè a dialogo. Gli altri sette capitoli veri e propri, tutti amorosi, contano rispettivamente 73, 91, 202, 148, 52, 208 e 76 versi, buon esempio della estrema varietà di taglio che il genere consentiva. Sarebbe facile allargare l'inchiesta alla poesia cortigiana non toscana di quell'età, in cui maggiore fu la fortuna del capitolo. Basti rinviare alle rime dell'Ariosto, dove figurano 26 capitoli (escludendo dal numero l'incompiuto poema o poemetto in terza rima su Obizzo d'Este), che si estendono da un massimo di 118 a un minimo di 22 versi, e alla recente edizione delle rime di Niccolò da Correggio a cura di A. Tissoni Benvenuti, dove figurano 44 capitoli d'ogni tipo, che si estendono da un massimo di 253 a un minimo di 37 versi. Per il loro numero, superiore a quello di ogni altra importante raccolta coeva (38 sono i capitoli di Panfilo Sasso), questi capitoli di Niccolò da Correggio consentono anche, nella estrema varietà quantitativa del genere, una stima approssimativa della lunghezza media. Risulta che sette capitoli soli, su 44, superano i 150 versi. Si può dunque asserire che la misura prescelta da Machiavelli, pur non essendo eccezionale, non era allora comune: era più ampia, e però verosimilmente più ambiziosa, della misura normale. Resta che di una scelta si trattò, coerentemente imposta ai tre capitoli. E senza dubbio, nella scelta del taglio, Machiavelli fu guidato dalla scelta qualitativa del genere, del capitolo cioè morale. Che questa scelta fosse ovvia per un uomo del suo stampo, non occorre dire. Caratteristico di Machiavelli è lo scarto, che pur nei suoi esperimenti letterari occasionali e minori egli fece e mantenne sempre, della tradizione lirica amorosa di ascendenza petrarchesca predominante nell'età sua. Ma con ciò si spiega l'aspetto negativo della scelta, che del resto, come già si è visto, caratterizza non soltanto Machiavelli, ma anche, generalmente, i poeti fiorentini fioriti subito prima di lui e con lui, quasi tutti restii ad accogliere la tradizione lirica petrarchesca. A spiegare l'aspetto positivo della scelta, non basta la vocazione teoretica e discorsiva di Machiavelli né il suo prepotente interesse per le questioni politiche e morali, perché è chiaro che egli avrebbe potuto, come di fatto poté, obbedire alla sua naturale vocazione scrivendo tutt'altro che capitoli in terza rima. Scegliendo questa forma del capitolo morale, egli si rifece a una tradizione senza dubbio antica e tenace, ma che nell'età sua, nonostante l'enorme fortuna del capitolo, e forse proprio per questo, risulta esile. Fra i già citati 44 capitoli di Niccolò da Correggio, ad es., due soli (368 e 371) possono considerarsi morali. È probabile che l'adattabilità del capitolo a tant'altri generi, elegiaco, epistolare, pastorale, encomiastico, confortatorio, sollecitasse a nuovi esperimenti piuttosto che a insistere sulle forme originarie. E si spiega che fra queste forme originarie il capitolo spirituale prevalesse su quello morale per la sua connotazione più precisa e per il suo facile impiego conclusivo anche da parte di chi petrarchescamente volesse far mostra di essere giunto o di voler giungere in porto dopo i giovanili errori amorosi. Insomma il quadro della poesia volgare quattrocentesca fino all'età di Machiavelli rivela sì distintamente una sempre maggiore apertura all'influsso della poesia latina, ma all'insegna dell'antico maestro Ovidio e degli elegiaci da un lato, del Virgilio bucolico dall'altro. L'influsso di Orazio lirico e satiro, scarso nella letteratura umanistica di quell'età, è pressoché nullo nella poesia volgare. Distintamente è però riconoscibile nella letteratura umanistica, e finalmente anche in una stretta zona della letteratura volgare, l'influsso della satira latina nella sua forma più retorica e violenta, di Giovenale e un poco anche di Persio, commentato a Firenze da Bartolomeo Fonzio. Non è da escludere, e può forse ritenersi probabile che Machiavelli segretario avesse notizia della singolare opera poetica, apparsa a Bologna nel 1495, d'un suo collega veneziano, Antonio Vinciguerra, che per le sue missioni diplomatiche e per le sue relazioni umanistiche aveva acquistato larga rinomanza, anche a Firenze. In quest'opera del Vinciguerra, ispirata dai poeti satirici latini, il capitolo in terza rima per la prima volta riappariva esclusivamente e di proposito usato per la discussione di argomenti morali, di una morale attinente piuttosto all'esperienza politica e civile che a quella religiosa. E in quest'uso il capitolo acquistava un taglio inconsueto per la sua ampiezza, toccando i 300 versi, e però anche, nei quattro capitoli dedicati alla questione del matrimonio e del celibato, restringendosi a 180, che è all'incirca la misura prescelta da Machiavelli. Sui meriti e demeriti di questa opera del Vincinguerra studiosi autorevolissimi, come il Della Torre e il Cian, si sono pronunciati in modo opposto, e la questione è rimasta aperta. Non è il caso di occuparsene qui se non in quanto di una questione si tratta che, come già ho detto, non può essere ignorata dallo studioso dci capitoli di Miachavelli. È chiaro che un albero genealogico della satira italiana in terza rima, nel quale Vinciguerra figuri padre di Ariosto, non è neppur discutibile. È anche chiaro che non si può far paragone del Vinciguerra in termini di abilità poetica, non dirò coll'Ariosto delle *Satire*, ma neppure col Machiavelli dei capitoli. La questione è altra: si tratta di spiegare come e perché non soltanto l'Ariosto, che in giovinezza aveva accolto la tradizione lirica petrarchesca di moda a Ferrara, ma anche Machiavelli che a quella tradizione, da buon fiorentino della vecchia guardia, era rimasto sordo, un dopo l'altro s'impegnassero a ricavare dal capitolo in terza rima un genere di poesia discorsiva, morale e finalmente satirica, che ancora non aveva una tradizione ben definita nella letteratura volgare e che insomma non era normale nell'età loro. Volendo spiegare ciò, non si può prescindere dai pochi documenti che ci restano, quali che essi siano, di un impegno analogo nell'età stessa. Fra questi documenti senza dubbio spiccano le satire in terza rima del Vinciguerra, che una qualche fortuna editoriale ebbero in quegli anni e che erano opera di un uomo largamente noto in Italia per titoli letterari e diplomatici, tale insomma da

attirare l'attenzione del pubblico e a maggior ragione dei colleghi.
Fra le satire del Vinciguerra una è indirizzata all'amico e
maestro padovano Giovanni Caldiera per consolarlo in occasione
della morte di una figlia. Come già si è visto, un analogo capitolo
consolatorio si trova fra le rime di Lorenzo il Magnifico, e altri
esempi si potrebbero addurre. Importa qui il fatto, non comune,
che il capitolo sia esplicitamente dedicato a un amico. Le prime
due satire del Vinciguerra sono declamazioni personali 'contra
falsum et imperitum vulgi iudicium' e 'contra vitia capitalia', ma
in fine appaiono con un sonetto dedicate al patrizio veneto
Bernardo Bembo. E a un altro patrizio veneto, Marco Zorzi,
appaiono dedicati i due capitoli del Vinciguerra sul tema
'utrum deceat sapientem ducere uxorem an in coelibatu vivere'.
Importano queste dediche perché, se anche patrizi veneti come il
Bembo e lo Zorzi non potessero dal suddito veneto Vinciguerra
essere considerati amici alla stessa stregua del dottore padovano
Caldiera, essi però non erano principi, non esercitavano su di lui
un potere personale, e però potevano essere amichevoli inter-
locutori suoi nella repubblica delle lettere. Di contro al sonetto,
che fin dalle sue origini dugentesche sempre era stato ed era
normale strumento di corrispondenza letteraria fra eguali, il
capitolo in terza rima ancora era di norma dedicato o alla persona,
donna o uomo, che per motivi amorosi, encomiastici, consolatori,
fosse argomento del capitolo stesso, o, come ogni altro componimento letterario, a un principe o patrono, benevolo e generoso
ascoltatore nel miglior dei casi, ma d'un' altra razza, non certo
semplice e amichevole interlocutore. Per i motivi già detti,
neppure le dediche del Vinciguerra sono esempi del tutto con-
vincenti di un nuovo indirizzo, come non sono altri esempi che
potrebbero addursi del Tebaldeo e di Marcello Filosseno, il quale
dedicò a patrizi veneti e a un gran signore friulano, Iacopo di
Porcia, che anche faceva professione di scrittore, alcuni dei suoi
Capitoli senili d'argomento morale. Ma questi esempi numerati e
dubbi non sono trascurabili perché indicano che nell'aria era
l'invito a una forma nuova dell'epistola in terza rima, diversa da
quella di stampo ovidiano che tanto successo aveva avuto e
ancora aveva nella poesia volgare. Caratteristico dei capitoli di
Machiavelli, come, subito dopo, delle satire dell'Ariosto, è
proprio il fatto che essi si presentino come lettere poetiche
indirizzate su un tema morale ad amici, coi quali il poeta discute,

perché il tema è di comune interesse. Non voglio dir con questo, Dio mi guardi, che i capitoli di Machiavelli e le satire dell'Ariosto siano *eiusdem farinae*. Dico che hanno tratti comuni che devono essere tenuti in conto. Anche dico e ripeto che questi tratti sono eccezionali: non hanno facile né preciso riscontro nella letteratura di quell'età, insomma rappresentano un indirizzo nuovo, di una poesia discorsiva e famigliare, non più sermocinante dal pulpito, come era ancora quella del Vinciguerra. Finalmente dico e ripeto che i tre capitoli di Machiavelli, se anche possano e debbano essere un per uno e per singoli tratti liberamente interpretati a riscontro delle opere maggiori e più tarde, anche però debbono essere in prima istanza considerati come opera letterariamente organica, posteriore al *Decennale* e anteriore al forzato ritiro di Machiavelli dalla vita pubblica. È un importante, se anche breve e interrotto, sviluppo della vocazione letteraria di Machiavelli. Nei capitoli, non nel *Decennale* o in altra scrittura di quel periodo, è riconoscibile già il maestro, a suo agio fra i giovani, degli Orti Oricellari.

Giovanni Aquilecchia

'*La favola* Mandragola
si chiama'

Tra le tante e notevoli precisazioni fatte riguardo alla storia e al testo della commedia dall'illustre biografo di Machiavelli, Roberto Ridolfi, non ritengo di secondaria importanza quelle concernenti il titolo, anche se elaborate solo in margine alla sua persuasiva definizione cronologica, editoriale e tipografica delle prime stampe, oltre che al suo fondamentale ritrovamento dell'unico manoscritto noto. Quanto alle prime stampe, la definizione cronologica, topica e tipografica (quest'ultima fin dove possibile) risulta ormai la seguente: (i) *Comedia di Callimaco e di Lucrezia* (Firenze, tipografo sconosciuto, 1518); (ii) *Comedia di Callimaco e di Lucrezia* (Venezia, Alessandro Bindoni, 1522); (iii) *Comedia facetissima intitolata Mandragola e recitata in Firenze* (Roma, Calvo, 1524); dopo la terza edizione il titolo esterno *Mandragola* si manterrà costantemente, a cominciare dalla quarta cesenate di Girolamo Soncino (1526), fino ed oltre l'edizione critica dello stesso Ridolfi (1965), basata sul testo della prima fiorentina integrato con lezioni desunte dall'unico manoscritto superstite. Il quale manoscritto (Laurenziano Rediano 129, cc. 110r-131r), non autografo, datato 1519, s'intitola, al di sopra del prologo, *Commedia fatta per Niccolò Machiavegli*.[1]

Quale fosse nell'intenzione dell'autore il titolo della commedia è da lui stesso esplicitamente detto con il verso 34 del *Prologo*: 'La favola *Mandragola* si chiama'.[2] Quanto al titolo esterno della prima (e seconda) stampa giova ripetere quel che ne ebbe a dire il Ridolfi: 'Un indizio che l'edizione non fu promossa dall'autore e che forse egli la vide soltanto a cose fatte, ci sembra il titolo impresso in fronte alla commedia: *Commedia di Callimaco e di Lucrezia*; un titolo che fa troppo sfacciatamente ai cozzi col titolo scritto nel prologo... A me pare che il Machiavelli, se ci avesse avuto le mani lui, o avrebbe messo nel frontespizio il titolo dichiarato nel prologo, come era ragionevole, o, se mai, quello da lui adoprato costantemente per indicare la commedia quando carteggiava con gli amici, nel 1520 con Battista della Palla e nel 1525 col Guicciardini: *Messer Nicia*. E si capisce. Dei due personaggi sui quali la sua mano si era indugiata di più quello era il solo, con tutta la sua sciocchezza, simpatico...; né fa perciò maraviglia che *Messer Nicia* fosse per lui come un sottotitolo della commedia, mentre quel titolo di *Callimaco e Lucrezia* non si vede donde né come sia potuto venir fuori'.[3] Quanto al titolo della terza stampa,

nulla di meglio che ricorrere alla perspicua e persuasiva spiegazione dello stesso Ridolfi: 'Come la prima e la seconda, la terza
edizione, quella che io ritengo collegata a una rappresentazione
fatta in Roma al principio del papato di Clemente VII, nel
carnevale del 1524, non portava neppure essa il nome dell'autore:
però, a differenza dell'edizione veneta del 1522, recava finalmente
in fronte il titolo vero, quello indicato nel prologo: *Comedia...
intitolata Mandragola*. Da ciò... mi sembra poter dedurre che il
Machiavelli, il quale dovette essere anche quella volta in corrispondenza con chi aveva cura della rappresentazione..., mentre
non credette di fare altre correzioni al testo della commedia, fece
però questa del titolo.'[4] Deduzione logica, che si rapporta alla già
notata discrepanza tra il titolo enunciato dal Machiavelli stesso
nel *Prologo* e la definizione esterna fornita dalle prime due stampe.
È da ritenere valida tale deduzione, anche se nel carteggio il
titolo di *Mandragola* non compare una sola volta pur nelle ricorrenti menzioni della commedia e del suo personaggio più comico
—oltre che, una volta, del frate—: 'ho parlato della vostra commedia' (Battista della Palla a N.M., 26 aprile 1520); 'A Santa
Maria in Porticu feci la imbasciata del suo *Calandro*, et vostro
Messer Nicia' (*ibid.*: non mi pare sicuro che riferimento sia fatto
qui al personaggio piuttosto che alla commedia); 'Mi piace che
Messer Nicia vi piaccia' (N.M. a Francesco Guicciardini, 17 agosto
1525); 'vi potrebbe far sudare gli orecchi altrimenti che a messer
Nicia' (Filippo de' Nerli a N.M., 6 settembre 1525); 'la semplicità
di Messer Nicia', 'se tutti fossimo come messer Nicia', 'ho
scartabellato, come fra Timoteo, di molti libri', 'ragionamo della
commedia' (N.M. a Francesco Guicciardini, 16–20 ottobre 1525);
'a che porto è la commedia' (N.M. a Francesco Guicciardini, post
21 ottobre 1525); 'comincerò a rispondervi dalla commedia'
(Francesco Guicciardini a N.M., 26 dicembre 1525); 'a proposito
della commedia', 'questo è quanto alla comedia' (N.M. a Francesco
Guicciardini, 3 gennaio 1526); 'el desiderio de V.S. de l'intendere
del recitare de la sua *Comedia de Callimaco*' (Giovanni Manetti a
N.M., 28 febbraio 1526: la ripetizione, in questa lettera, del titolo
esterno delle prime due stampe, può facilmente spiegarsi assu-
mendo che il Manetti, il quale fece da suggeritore nelle rappresentazioni veneziane della commedia, dovette servirsi di un esemplare
delle medesime e che gli spettacoli veneziani fossero in quel modo
annunciati, e non obbliga già a ritenere che Machiavelli stesso, nel

chiedere notizie della rappresentazione, avesse adoperato quel titolo).[5]

Da quanto precede non solo risulta dunque che alla data della terza edizione la commedia aveva già avuto un sensibile lancio editoriale (operante ancora due anni dopo la pubblicazione della terza, e proprio con il reiterato titolo originario a stampa: *Commedia di Callimaco e di Lucrezia*), ma anche è dato arguire che nella cerchia di Machiavelli essa fosse comunemente nota con il titolo non ufficiale di *Messer Nicia*—e tale risulta essere rimasta pur dopo la terza edizione. In tale situazione l'isolato e specioso intervento d'autore sul titolo (e se pure non fosse stato d'autore la sostanza della questione non cambierebbe) può bene apparire oggi a noi legittimo bibliograficamente in quanto determinato dall'esigenza di eliminare una patente discrepanza tra titolo interno (verso 34 del *Prologo*) e titolo sul frontespizio. Con tutto che nella tradizione drammatica una discrepanza del genere non sarebbe neppure eccezionale: basti pensare, per rimanere in un ambito di pertinenza machiavelliana, alla *Casina* plautina: titolo 'esterno' riconosciuto ormai genuino, con tutto che non risulti corroborato dalle parole del prologo

> Comoediai nomen dare vobis volo.
> Clerumenoe vocatur haec comoedia
> Graece, Latine Sortientes... (vv. 30–31),

anche ove *latine Sortientes* sia inteso come spiegazione del titolo greco, e non già come titolo della commedia latina.[6] Quel che importa qui notare è che nella situazione sopra prospettata quel mutamento di titolo non poteva certo risultare vantaggioso dal punto di vista editoriale (direi addirittura commerciale), dopo il successo delle rappresentazioni corroborato a sua volta da un duplice lancio editoriale all'insegna di *Callimaco e Lucrezia*. Quanto al *Prologo*—che costituisce oggi per noi una delle testimonianze più vive e dolorose, con quella rassegnazione solo apparente e con l'insopprimibile e dignitosa coscienza del proprio valore, dello stato d'animo di Machiavelli dopo la delusione del *Principe* e la mancata restituzione all'ufficio—nessuno sembra allora averci fatto gran caso, tanto meno fuori di Firenze, teste la lettera di Francesco Guicciardini del 26 dicembre 1525, a proposito della rappresentazione che si sarebbe dovuta fare a Faenza: 'et perché [gli attori] non si accordano allo argumento [cioè il *Prologo*], quale non intenderebbono, ne hanno fatto un altro, quale non ho visto, ma lo vedrò presto; et perché desidero non sia con l'acqua fredda, non credo possiate errare a ordinarne uno altro conforme al poco ingegno delli auditori, et nel quale siano più presto dipinti loro che voi'.[7] A oltre un anno di distanza dalla terza edizione, il titolo restituito non vi è neppure menzionato, mentre il *Prologo* che quella restituzione sembra aver determinato dovrà essere addirittura soppresso ai fini della recitazione. Con questo non si vuol negare la validità del rilievo del Ridolfi quanto alla causa, per dir così, formale della restituzione; ritengo però che, date le circostanze fin qui indicate—circostanze tutte che avrebbero consigliato ai fini editoriali il mantenimento del titolo esterno di *Callimaco e Lucrezia* con cui la commedia era già nota ai lettori, ovvero la sanzione del titolo più fortunato circolante privatamente, cioè *Messer Nicia* —, la ragione del mutamento, pur poggiando formalmente sulla discrepanza suddetta, vada indicata nel motivo stesso della mandragora, in quanto inerente alla struttura drammatica dell'opera, e in ultima istanza al suo significato: motivo la cui funzione reale trascende, caratterizzando l'intero svolgimento dell'azione, quella pretestuale, o addirittura marginale e accessoria, solitamente attribuitagli dai critici. Al qual proposito sono tipiche le frettolose osservazioni di un critico della levatura di Santorre Debenedetti, che sembrano aver dissuaso editori più recenti dall'indagare l'effettivo rapporto tra il titolo e l'opera: 'La mandragola fu scelta ad arte, per aggiungere un tratto alla semplicità di M. Nicia, perché ancora a questo tempo il popolo aveva in essa una fede superstiziosa, che ci è testimoniata per tutta l'Europa; è dunque evidente che la virtù della mandragola in casi d'amore, ben nota ai Greci, e la commedia del comico Alexis, e la favola di Apollodoro non hanno col nostro soggetto nulla a che fare'.[8] In sostanza il Debenedetti veniva a ridurre quello che, stando al titolo voluto dall'autore, doveva pur essere il motivo fondamentale dalla commedia, a spunto invece secondario, anzi addirittura marginale ed accessorio ('per aggiungere un tratto alla semplicità di M. Nicia'): e come tale, par di poter dedurne, se non addirittura eliminabile, almeno sostituibile con qualche altro spunto superstizioso, ferma restando la trama della commedia. Ove così fosse, né il titolo voluto e ribadito dall'autore risulterebbe giustificato—a preferenza per di più del titolo extra-editoriale desunto dal nome del protagonista comico (della cui semplicità

la credenza nelle virtù della mandragora non sarebbe che un
tratto accessorio), né la trama stessa della commedia troverebbe—
come infatti non sembra aver fin qui trovato—il suo presupposto
basilare.

A meglio intendere la validità, in rapporto all'opera, di quel
titolo che, come tale, doveva allora suonare, in genere e specie,
inaudito—e ricollegandomi al Debenedetti dirò a tal proposito
che il precedente della perduta commedia di Alexis, ἡ Μανδρα-
γοριζομένη, 'la mandragorizzata', cioè 'la donna drogata con la
mandragora' (a quale effetto, in realtà, non risulta dai trentadue
versi superstiti[9]), è improbabile che potesse aver influenzato
la scelta—, giova anzitutto riconsiderare i versi 34–36 del
Prologo:

> La favola *Mandragola* si chiama.
> La cagion voi vedrete
> Nel recitarla, com'io m'indovino.

La dichiarazione risulta notevole per la sua ambigua allusività,
specie se la confrontiamo con la parallela ma esplicita dichiarazione—che è del tutto indipendente da Plauto—nel prologo della
Clizia: 'Questa favola si chiama Clizia, perché così ha nome la
fanciulla che si combatte'. Viva la faccia. Per aggiungere: 'Non vi
aspettate di vederla' ecc. (in realtà anche sul titolo della *Clizia* ci
sarebbe qualcosa da dire: poiché la questione sarebbe però
analoga a quella che concerne il titolo della *Casina*—non dico per
la genuinità, ma per la ragione—rinvio va fatto anzitutto alle
discussioni in proposito dei filologi classici[10]). Quanto alla dichiarazione concernente il titolo della *Mandragola*, pur nella sua
voluta evasività ('La cagion voi vedrete Nel recitarla, com'io
m'indovino'), essa era in realtà tale da poter indurre i critici a
maggiore cautela nella loro sottovalutazione del motivo titolare
della commedia. Intanto che cosa significa 'vedrete nel recitarla'?
Mi pare di poter escludere che sia semplicemente un'allusione
all'unica, se pur iterata, menzione esplicita della 'mandragola'
nell'atto II scena VI, quale pretesto per lo svolgimento della
trama. È un fatto che quel nome non verrà più pronunciato, né
per il rimanente dell'atto II né per tutto il resto della commedia:
atti III, IV e V. Ove esclusivamente quella fosse stata l'allusione,
gli spettatori non avrebbero comunque potuto 'vedere' la
ragione del titolo *nel recitarla*. È vero che forse non la videro

(come mostrato dal titolo delle prime due stampe e dalle allusioni nel carteggio): ma non si può dubitare che una ragione basilare —non solo cioè accidentale (la menzione suddetta) o circostanziale (il pretesto della mandragora per lo sviluppo dell'azione)—, dovesse essere ben presente alla mente dell'autore.

Si può escludere che egli avesse voluto alludere semplicemente alla menzione del presunto ritrovato fecondativo, inteso come pretesto dell'azione, anche perché al ritrovato stesso farà sempre riferimento (ad esclusione, come si è detto, di due occorrenze nell'atto II, scena VI), con il termine generico di *pozione* (a. II, sc. II e sc. VI: quattro volte; a. III, sc. XI, a. IV, sc. II) o di *medicina* (a. IV, sc. III), a non dire del *bicchiere di hypocràs* che Callimaco ha effettivamente preparato per racconciare lo stomaco e rallegrare il cervello alla brava Lucrezia (a. IV, sc. I): *bicchiere/becchiere* ricorre nell'atto IV, scena III e v. La ricorrenza di *pozione* è comunque prevalente, e l'infelice 'riduzione' plurilingue della *Mandragola* ad opera di Andrea Calmo, stampata nel 1552, fu intitolata appunto *La Pozione*:[11] sarà lecito ritenere che neppure al Calmo riuscisse di vedere la 'cagion' effettiva del titolo originale? Nella stessa dichiarazione del *Prologo* pare del resto di poter notare una sfumatura scettica quanto alla reale comprensione del titolo da parte del pubblico: Machiavelli non è scrittore da aggiungere un pleonastico *com'io m'indovino* (normalmente inteso: 'a quanto io posso facilmente prevedere'[12]) tanto per fare la rima con *vino* (v. 37); certo non in un dettato così attentamente scandito quale quello del *Prologo*. È proprio in quella clausola che mi pare di poter notare la sfumatura suddetta: una certezza apparente che invita in realtà a fare bene attenzione alla commedia *nel recitarla*, per tutto il corso cioè della rappresentazione, dal primo all'ultimo atto, per poter cogliere, con la ragione del titolo, il filo conduttore che sottende alla trama. Ai fini dimostrativi di questa nota conviene riportarci direttamente alle tre enunciazioni essenziali dell'atto II, scena VI, in due delle quali occorre appunto la menzione esplicita della madragora:

(*a*) Non è cosa più certa a ingravidare una donna che darli bere una pozione fatta di mandragola.

(*b*) Quello uomo che ha prima a fare seco, presa che l'ha cotesta pozione, muore infra otto giorni, e non lo camperebbe el mondo.

(*c*) E' ci è rimedio [...] Fare dormire sùbito con lei un altro che tiri, standosi seco una notte, a sé, tutta quella infezione della mandragola. Dipoi vi iacerete voi senza periculo.

Chiunque tenga presente lo sviluppo della 'favola', noterà facilmente che, mentre di per sé le enunciazioni *a* e *b* sono destinate a rimanere allo stadio di pretesto per lo sviluppo dell'azione, è in realtà solo con la conseguente enunciazione *c* che viene fornito lo schema effettivo e risolutivo della stessa. Ai fini della giustificazione del titolo, si tratta ora di vedere in che misura ciascuna di queste tre enunciazioni pertenga alle credenze tradizionali relative alla mandragora: in ultima istanza però la giustificazione sarà veramente tale solo se lo schema narrativo e drammatico risultante nella commedia dalla enunciazione *c* si rivelerà tracciato sul paradigma di una precisa pratica superstiziosa relativa alla pianta in questione.

L'enunciazione pretestuale *a*, sebbene di per sé non caratterizzi lo schema dell'azione, rientra senza dubbio nell'ambito delle credenze superstiziose, e su di essa si è soffermata essenzialmente l'attenzione di quegli annotatori che, pur frettolosamente, hanno ritenuto non del tutto ozioso prestare la loro attenzione all'elemento titolare della commedia.[13] Proprio questa attenzione pressoché esclusiva mi sembra possa aver fin qui impedito di cogliere il fondamentale rapporto tra titolo e favola. La ragione di tale esclusivismo si spiega anzitutto in virtù della esplicita testimonianza costituita dalla enunciazione stessa; la quale testimonianza a sua volta trova appoggio in una duplice tradizione: medica e biblica. Già in epoca greco-romana e nella prima era cristiana si nota infatti nelle credenze relative agli effetti della mandragora, accanto alla superstizione che essa induca la pazzia, l'altra secondo cui essa influisce nelle relazioni sessuali, essendo ritenuta efficace come filtro amoroso o come afrodisiaco.[14] Le proprietà erotiche della mandragora potevano risultare da menzioni reperibili in Teofrasto, in Dioscoride, in Giuliano l'Apostata e nel capitolo IV del *Physiologus* sugli elefanti.[15] Ma tali proprietà, con la connessa proprietà fecondativa che qui appunto interessa, dovettero acquistar credito soprattutto con la versione biblica dei Settanta, in cui l'ebraico *dûdâ'îm* (letteralmente 'pomi dell'amore') è reso con μανδραγόραι e con μῆλα μανδραγορῶν, rispettivamente per l'occorrenza nella Cantica VII, 10–13 (dove il contesto suggerisce l'illazione afrodisiaca), e per quella nel Genesi, XXX, 14-16, che sembra essere decisiva invece per l'illazione fecondativa,[16] pur nella varietà delle interpretazioni patristiche (il rinnovato concepimento da parte di Lia e la cessazione della sterilità di Rachele seguono infatti, pur ellitticamente, alla presentazione dei *dûdâ'îm* fatta da Ruben alla madre e al baratto che questa ne fa con la sorella). Il riferimento biblico esime dall'indagare la fortuna della fiducia superstiziosa nella proprietà fecondativa della mandragora: basti qui notare che l'enunciazione *a*, pur risultando formalmente pertinente al titolo, di per sé non si rivela elemento determinante di quest'ultimo: essa è infatti destinata a fungere da spunto pretestuale per lo sviluppo della commedia, e come tale sostituibile sia specificamente (ove occorresse il nome di altro presunto fecondativo)[16a] che genericamente (si rammenti *La Pozione* del Calmo). Dico *di per sé*, e non in quanto la si consideri in rapporto alle enunciazioni che seguono.

L'enunciazione *b* è più complessa, per il confluire in essa di tre motivi superstiziosi, due dei quali pertengono a tradizioni relative alla mandragora, mentre il terzo, che è il più sensazionale, pertiene a tutt'altra tradizione. Giova identificare i tre motivi (sebbene nel suo complesso l'enunciazione stessa sia destinata, come l'antecedente, a fungere di per sé da spunto pretestuale dell'azione, essa è però almeno in parte insostituibile specificamente, come risulterà dall'analisi di *c* di cui costituisce la premessa inevitabile). È soprattutto con riferimento a questa enunciazione che Wilhelm Hertz, nel suo poderoso studio sulla leggenda della fanciulla avvelenata e avvelenatrice (*Giftmädchen* o *pucelle venemeuse*),[17] ha dedicato una pagina alla commedia di Machiavelli, da lui inserita appunto nell'ambito della sua indagine sulla tradizione del *concubitus venenatus*. A meglio identificare le premesse leggendarie dell'enunciazione giova però considerarla anzitutto nei suoi elementi costitutivi: a cominciare dalla premessa (implicita ma necessaria) che la mandragora sia velenosa. Quanto alle possibili fonti classiche per questa credenza, ci troviamo in presenza di autori tutt'altro che estranei agli interessi di Machiavelli, con tutto che la credenza stessa sembri essere stata per lo più formulata in margine a trattazioni mediche in relazione all'uso narcotico e anestetico della mandragora (che è poi l'uso più evidente nelle fonti classiche): ma in tale rapporto la nozione di pericolosità pertiene in maggiore o minore misura alla trattazione di tutti gli anodini (ed è responsabile per il limitato uso di anestetici sia nell'antichità classica che in epoca medievale). Come già si è visto per l'enunciazione *a*, neppure questo motivo implicito nella enunciazione *b* può essere quindi considerato come esclusivo o caratteristico della mandragora (che viene questa volta pronominalmente definita *cotesta pozione*: si ricordi ancora *La Pozione* del Calmo). Gioverà comunque ricordare in breve che Machiavelli poteva trovare in Frontino, là dove narra della cattura di un intero esercito nemico da parte del cartaginese Maharbale—grazie all'esca costituita da vino drogato appunto con la mandragora— la definizione di 'mandragora... cuius inter venenum et soporem vis est' (*Stratag.*, II, 5, 12); a non dire, proprio in un testo a lui familiare, della dichiarazione apuleiana: 'Dedi venenum, sed somniferum, mandragoram, illud gravedinis compertae famosum et morti simillimi soporis efficax' (*Metamorph.*, X, 11), dove però l'effetto venefico risulta negato. Che la mandragora fosse ritenuta mortifera risulta per contro esplicitamente da una nota del Siceliota alle *Ideae* di Ermogene (ἔστι δὲ ἡ μανδραγόρα βοτάνη καρωτική καὶ ἀναιρετική), e la sua pericolosità è rilevata da Teofrasto, Dioscoride e Plinio.[18] Nello schema della commedia questo motivo è comunque destinato a rimanere anch'esso pretestuale, e neppure risulterà di per sé caratterizzante in rapporto al motivo esplicito della stessa enunciazione *b*: risulterà invece, come vedremo, tematicamente pertinente, per via di adattamento, alla fondamentale enunciazione *c* e nell'ambito di quella andrà quindi ricondotto. È del resto chiaro che *b* rappresenta nel suo insieme una premessa a *c*, che ne assorbe i genuini elementi della superstizione tradizionale relativi alla mandragora e a questa soltanto: per tale ragione converrà anche rinviare le considerazioni del secondo motivo mandragoresco che affiora in *b* con la specificazione 'quello uomo che ha *prima* a fare seco', per cui si altera, mediante l'innesto di un particolare esclusivo alla tradizione della mandragora, il secondo nucleo leggendario utilizzato in *b*: la già menzionata tradizione della fanciulla velenosa. A meglio intendere la forzatura operata da Machiavelli nella utilizzazione di questa leggenda mediante l'innesto di particolari pertinenti alla superstizione della mandragora—motivo 1 (velenosità: non esclusivo) e motivo 2 ('chi ha *prima* a far seco': esclusivo o per lo meno caratteristico, come vedremo)—giova qui indicare alcuni momenti essenziali di quella tradizione: in particolare dall'angolo visuale italiano e toscano, rinviando peraltro al citato studio dello Hertz per una esauriente analisi sul piano europeo ed extra-europeo. A cominciare dallo pseudo-aristotelico *De secretis secretorum* o *De regimine principum* (originariamente scritto in arabo e diffusosi nelle lingue occidentali dopo il secolo XII). Il passo che interessa la leggenda è il seguente:

O Alexander, recole facta reginae Indorum, quando tibi mandavit, causa amicitiae, multa enxenia et dona venusta, inter quos [*sic*] missa fuit illa venustissima puella, quae ab infantia nutrita fuit et imbuta veneno serpentum: itaque sua natura versa erat in naturam serpentum. Et nisi illa hora sagaciter inspexissem in ipsam et arte magica judicassem, ideoque audacter, horribiliter et incessanter et inverecunde suum figebat visum in facies hominum, perpendi siquidem quod interficeret solo morsu, quod experimento postea didicisti et probasti, et nisi hoc certissime ostendissem, mors tua fuisset in ardore coitus consequuta.[19]

L'aneddoto passò, come è noto, dal *Secretum* ai *Gesta Romanorum* ed ebbe quindi diffusione su piano europeo. Notevole per l'Italia e la Toscana l'utilizzazione (complicata dall'episodio della regina Candace) da parte dei rifacitori in versi de *Li Tresor* di Brunetto Latini (la riduzione in versi fu fatta, come precisò il D'Ancona, poco tempo dopo l'apparizione del libro, e fu nota a qualche erudito del secolo XVI).[20] Mi limito a riportare qui l'essenziale ai fini del nostro discorso:

[...]
Truovo che Alesandro fu molto lussurioso
E di giaccre con pulcelle fu volenteroso.
La reina del reame di Sizire
Or venne per volerlo far morire:
Li presentò una pulzella,
Non si legge se ne trovasse una più bella,
Ché l'era de la gente angielicha estimata.
Questa pulcella era di veleno nutricata,
Sì che Alesandro quando co' llei coisse
Immantanente morisse.
In questo modo fu la pulzella nutrichata:

qui segue la spiegazione dettagliata (la regina fece mettere una neonata dentro l'uovo di un serpente che la covò e nutrì; poi la prese con sé, allevandola come essere umano),

E una de le più belle creature del mondo diventò.
Quando Alesandro venne nel paese, la reina presentò;
Alesandro, quando la vide, si prese di costei,
Disse [a] Aristotile: Voglio giacere co 'llei.
La sua persona Alesandro governava
Secondo ch' Aristotile il consigliava,
[...]
Aristotile vide la fanciulla sì elegante,
E 'l viso suo sì varicante
Vidde, e l'aspetto e la guardaura,
Disse [a] Alessandro: Io veggo e conosco in questa creatura
Atto et reggimento di serpente,
E pasto velenoso ebbe primamente.
Se alcuno co 'llei carnalmente giacerà
Per lo fermo sappi ch'ella l'avelenerà.
[...]
Disse Alesandro: Non sarebe dottore chrederlo mi facesse,
Se altra esperienza non ne vedesse.
Disse Aristotile: Gran fretta non avere:
S'io posso avere uno serpente, te 'l farò vedere
[...]

Ebbe infatti il serpente e lo fece porre in un vaso dagli orli intrisi di dittamo: il serpente si lasciò morire di inedia al centro del vaso pur di non oltrepassare il dittamo:

Disse Aristotile: Quest'è la sperienzia che vedete:
Se alla pulciella intorno intorno farete
Uno cerchio col succhio della detta erba,
Immantanente vi diventerà acerba,
Et giamai il dittamo non passerà
E anche iv' entro tostamente morrà.
[...][21]

Messo in pratica il consiglio di Aristotele, la previsione si avverò.

Se mi sono indugiato a citare sia dal *Secretum* che dal *Tesoro* versificato, è per mostrare come la leggenda della fanciulla avvelenata e avvelenatrice non risulti in realtà riflessa nell'intrigo della *Mandragola*, né quanto allo schema drammatico né quanto agli elementi caratteristici: ad eccezione, s'intende, del comune motivo 'fisiologico' relativo alla possibilità del congiungimento velenoso, il quale è però destinato anch'esso a rimanere, di per sé, spunto pretestuale nello sviluppo della commedia; a non dire che tanto nel *Secretum* quanto nel rifacimento versificato del *Tesoro*

manca la specificazione avverbiale *prima*—la quale è invece
essenziale per il recupero dello spunto stesso nell'ambito della
tradizione propria alla mandragora—conforme del resto agli
sviluppi cinquecenteschi dalla leggenda (*cf.* ad es.

Johann Lange:
'Nam *quicumque* cum puella ab Alexandro repudiata concubuerat,
eius contagione infecti perierunt');[22] è da notare infine che nelle
discussioni tradizionali sulla specie di veleno di cui fu nutrita la
fanciulla, non v'è accenno alla mandragora, ma piuttosto alla
cicuta o al napello.[23] Era necessaria tale dimostrazione anche
perché i pochi che si sono soffermati sui motivi superstiziosi della
commedia hanno indicato proprio questo della *pucelle venemeuse*,
accanto all'altro della virtù fecondativa della mandragora, come
essenziali alla originaria ideazione di Machiavelli. Così lo Hertz
('Kennern der klassichen Komödie der Italiener wird bei unserer
Besprechung des *concubitus venenatus* in ergötzliche Erinnerung
gekommen sein, mit welch mutwilligem Humor Machiavelli für
die Liebesintrige seiner *Mandragola* von jenem Aberglauben
Gebrauch gemacht hat... Daß der Mandragoras unfruchtbaren
Frauen zum Kindersegen verhelfen solle, ist bekannt genug. Daß
er aber die an die višakanyâ des indischen Dramas erinnernde
Wirkung habe, wird sonst nirgends erwähnt. Das ist die Erfindung
Machiavellis, der mit dem Glauben an die Möglickeit solcher
Vergiftungen sein geniales Spiel treibt'),[24] e così il Sanesi ('la
Mandragola... trasse il proprio titolo e la propria favola, o, per dir
meglio, l'embrione da cui la fantasia del poeta seppe far germo-
gliare la favola, da un doppio ordine di leggende e di pregiudizi
popolari intorno alla virtù di un'erba medicinale... e intorno alla
fanciulla avvelenata e avvelenatrice'); il quale Sanesi, dopo aver
rapidamente accennato a una varietà di superstizioni relative alla
mandragora, si soffermava appunto sull' 'altra più mirabile
potestà, e che a noi principalmente interessa, di fare ingravidare le
donne', rinviando al distico di un' ecloga di Teodolo (sec. X), e
alla *Practica de aegritudinibus a capite usque ad pedes* (Venezia 1486)
di Giovanni Michele Savonarola (già citato dallo Hertz): questo
ultimo 'per il più diretto influsso che poté avere sulla concezione
drammatica del Machiavelli'.[25] In realtà, dopo quanto fin qui
notato, risulta addirittura superfluo osservare che, se influsso
diretto ci fu per la annoverazione che il Savonarola fece della
madragora 'fra i mezzi più atti a produrre o ad agevolare la
fecondazione', questo non affettò certamente la 'concezione

drammatica' di Machiavelli, ma poté se mai fornire lo spunto pretestuale che si è detto discutendo la enunciazione *a*. Spunto che acquista, tematicamente, valore di necessità per l'azione drammatica solo se lo si considera in rapporto alla enunciazione conclusiva (*c*), che andrà a sua volta verificata nell'ambito delle credenze tradizionali relative alla mandragora.

Giova anzitutto ripetere tale enunciazione, che conviene integrare ormai con l'enunciazione *b* (la quale ha perduto la sua autonomia, essendosi rivelata di per sé insostenibile come paradigma dell'azione drammatica, costituita come è di due motivi pretestuali, il secondo dei quali addirittua estraneo alla tradizione mandragoresca, cui viene però riallaciato—come ora vedremo—in virtù della forzatura avverbiale *prima*):

[quello uomo che ha prima a fare seco, presa che l'ha cotesta pozione, muore infra otto giorni...] e'ci è rimedio... Fare dormire sùbito con lei un altro che tiri, standosi seco una notte, a sé, tutta quella infezione della mandragola. Dipoi vi iacerete voi senza periculo.

Anche qui si tratta, ovviamente, di motivo pretestuale: ma tutti sanno come da pretestuale si tradurrà, nella sua essenza, in attuale: nel senso che l'azione tutta del dramma si sviluppa e si esaurisce paradigmaticamente, proprio *nel recitarla*, conforme all'enunciazione stessa. Ne deriva che solo ove l'enunciazione *c* (integrata dalla sua premessa *b*) sia rapportabile, pur parodicamente, a una precisa credenza relativa alla mandragora, potrà risultare appieno giustificata la ragione del titolo. Inutile dire che sarebbe superfluo cercare nelle note alle edizioni correnti della commedia qualsiasi rinvio al preciso motivo superstizioso che è alla base di questa determinante enunciazione. Va subito osservato che esso è da ricercare nelle pratiche tradizionalmente attribuite ai rizotomi per l'estrazione delle radici della mandragora. Il motivo neppure rimase ignorato a chi tentò rapportare la vicenda drammatica alle credenze superstiziose: basti pensare ai già citati Hertz e Sanesi, i quali lo inserirono però senza alcun rilievo correlativo nei rispettivi cenni alla serie di superstizioni relative alla mandragora.[26] Stupisce quindi che in esso non si sia saputo identificare il *pattern* specifico della favola machiavelliana: tanto più che, sia sul piano storico-culturale che su quello ambientale, l'autore poteva risultare non ignaro di questo aspetto magico della superstizione. Storicamente, i primi riferimenti noti a pratiche superstiziose relative all'estrazione della mandragora risalgono a Teofrasto e a Plinio: essi sono tuttavia ancora parziali rispetto alla pratica che si stabilirà in seguito (Plinio, il quale sembra dipendere qui, pur non direttamente, da Teofrasto IX, 8, 8, dichiara: 'Effossuri cavent contrarium ventum et tribus circulis ante gladio circumscribunt, postea fodiunt ad occasum spectantes').[27] È solo con il V secolo che risulta ormai elaborata tale pratica: come appare da alcune miniature del codice Dioscoride di Juliana Anicia.[28] In esse risultano applicate alla mandragora pratiche di estrazione già descritte da Josephus Flavius (*Bell. Iud.*, VII, 6, 3) con riferimento alla *baaras*, e da Aelianus (*Nat. Anim.*, XIV, 27) con riferimento alla *aglaophotis*: l'identificazione della *baaras* e della *aglaophotis* con la mandragora è sostenuta con validi argomenti da studiosi moderni;[29] quanto alla prima, Josephus dichiara:

[...] iis, qui eam attigerint, indubia mors imminet, nisi quis forte illam ipsam radicem ferat de manu suspensam. Capitur etiam et alio modo sine periculo, qui talis est. Undique eam circumfodiunt, ut radicis quam minimum terra tegatur: deinde canem ei alligant, qui cum eum, a quo ligatus est, comitari cupit, illa quidem facile evellitur, canis vero continuo moritur, tanquam vice eius, a quo herba tollenda erat, traditus.[30]

Abbiamo una notazione cinquecentesca che è per noi preziosa in quanto formulata dal medico senese Pietro Andrea Mattioli (1500-1577), non pure conterraneo ma contemporaneo o quasi di Machiavelli. Giova qui citare per esteso alcuni brani del suo commento al cap. LXXVIII ('*Della Mandragora*'), contenuto nei *Discorsi ... nelli sei libri di Pedacio Dioscoride Anazarbeo della materia medicinale*; essi contengono in proposito quelle nozioni essenziali, di carattere popolare come pure erudito, che è lecito ritenere non fossero ignote a Machiavelli stesso; mostrano inoltre come fosse già allora evidente l'analogia *baaras*-mandragora (per comodità di trascrizione adopero l'edizione di Venezia, 1573, p. 688):

È veramente cosa favolosa il credere, che habbiano le Mandragore le radici di forma humana, come si crede il vulgo ignorante, et le semplici donniciuole: et che non si possano cavar di terra, se non con pericolo, attaccandovi un cane, et impeciandosi l'orecchie per non udirne il gridare, per credersi questa gente sciocca, che le radici gridino, et amazzino chi le cava sentendosene grido. Imperoché quelle, che

portano attorno alcuni Ciurmadori, et Ceretani, dando falsamente ad
intendere alle semplici donniciuole sterili, che mangiandone, fanno far
figliuoli, sono radici di canne di brionia, et d'altre piante intagliate in
tal forma, et artificiosamente fatte: et poscia ripiantate con granella
d'orzo attorno a quei luoghi, ove si vuole, che nascano quelle radicette,
che fanno i capelli, la barba, et gli altri peli [...] E però ho voluto qui
avisare il mondo di cotal manifesta truffaria, et far palese a ciascuno,
come tal falsità sia regnata, et regni ancora a i tempi nostri nelle mani
di cotali assassini. I quali, per dar più fede alla cosa, allegano, che
Pithagora chiamò la Mandragora, *Anthropomorphos*, cioè forma d'uomo.
Sopra al che è da sapere che Pithagora non gli pose tal nome senza
causa: perciochè per il più si ritrova la Mandragora havere la radice
biforcata, simile alle gambe dell'uomo, et cavandosi quando ha il suo
frutto, il quale è simile a un pomo attaccato per breve picciuolo tra le
frondi in su la sommità della radice, si rassembra veramente alla forma
d'un uomo senza braccia. Il che pochi hanno saputo dichiarare: anzi
che per il più sento i moderni scrittori biasimare, et Pithagora, et
Columella, non intendendo la cosa, che habbiano favolando scritto, che
habbia la radice della Mandragora forma humana. Ma per finire di dire
la fabula, nella quale recitano essere grandissimo pericolo a cavare la
radice della Mandragora, se non si fa cavare da un cane, dico che ciò
ne pare stato cavato da Josepho historico hebreo, il qual se ben scrive,
che ciò si osservava in Giudea nel cavare d'una altra pianta, si può però
pensare, che tutto questo sia stato transferito nella historia della Mandragora appresso al vulgo da coloro che ingannando la gente vanno
vendendo le Mandragore. Ma accioché meglio sia noto a ciascuno
questa truffaria, recitarò qui quel che scrive Josepho al xxv capo. del
VII libro delle guerre de' Giudei [...]

Non è certo mia intenzione discutere qui i vari aspetti della
superstizione dall'antichità classica (e forse biblica)[31] in poi: si è
fatto rinvio nelle note agli studi fondamentali sulla questione.[32]
La citazione dei *Discorsi* del Mattioli vale del resto a indicare, per
l'epoca che qui interessa, non solo la diffusione in Italia di tali
credenze,[33] ma insieme lo sfruttamento cui esse davano luogo da
parte dei ciarlatani, e per contro il senso critico che esse susci-
tavano negli spiriti colti. Che è quanto basta insomma a farci
apprezzare l'attualità della parodia machiavelliana. La quale
risulta appunto tale ove si badi al nucleo principale della esposizione del Mattioli: la pratica della estrazione, che non senza
ulteriori dettagli sarà precisamente formulata—conforme a quella
che doveva essere la 'prassi' secolare—nella *Dissertatio de Mandragora* di Johann Schmidel (Lipsiae 1671):

§53. Die Veneris ante Solis exortum auribus gossypio oppletis, ceraque aut pice occlusis exire iubent, crucis figuram terno tripodis [l. *tripudii?*] circumductu plantae inscribere, tum circumfodere totam, sic ut terrae non nisi extrema fibra obhaereat; ita solicitatam caudae canis alligere funiculo, statimque aufugere, frusto panis cani obverso; id illum appetentem nitendo radicem evellere, moxque audito eius eiaculatu concidere mortuum.[34]

Ridotta al suo nucleo essenziale, la pratica consiste dunque nel fatto che il rizotomo rischierebbe la vita ad estrarre personalmente la radice della mandragora: egli deve quindi servirsi di un cane che effettui l'operazione per lui (rimanendone ucciso). Non è difficile accorgersi come allo schema elementare

rizotomo—cane—mandragora

corrisponda nella favola machiavelliana il rapporto

Nicia—garzonaccio (Callimaco travestito)—*Lucrezia*.

Dall'angolo visuale del protagonista (non si dimentichi che *Messer Nicia* è il titolo attribuito alla commedia nel carteggio) questo rimarrà un rapporto valido, a cominciare dalla scena VI dell'atto II, sino alla conclusione della commedia. Diversi e più complessi rapporti sono anch'essi evidenti, a seconda che si consideri preminente l'uno o l'altro dei tre ruoli di Callimaco: (i) ruolo genuino di giovane innamorato; (ii) ruolo fittizio di medico venuto da Parigi; (iii) ruolo di garzonaccio. Dell'ultimo si è detto: ma va notato che, mentre il primo è destinato a rimanere ignoto al protagonista, e per questo rispetto non risulta quindi funzionale, il secondo rimarrà bensì anch'esso costante agli occhi di Nicia, ma in effetti non fa che ampliare la relazione suddetta, ferma restando la combinazione derivante dal terzo ruolo (che è poi quello effettivo per la soluzione della favola). Tale ampliamento non altera infatti il paradigma offerto dalla pratica dell'estrazione della mandragora: lo estende ad includere il personaggio del ciarlatano (e per quanto Callimaco non sia tale per natura, vi si adatta per consiglio di Ligurio, che è a sua volta il carattere socialmente responsabile del perdurare e diffondersi di quella superstizione). Si potrebbe insistere sul rapporto basilare: basti aver notato che esso è esemplato parodicamente sulla pratica superstiziosa della estrazione della mandragora. A tal proposito, se veramente il nome di Nicia riflette quello dell'omonimo generale spartano—come ha sostenuto il Parronchi, nel suo saggio sull'allegoria politica della commedia, a sostegno del parallelo Nicia-Soderini[35]—direi che tale riflesso valga piuttosto per la proverbiale superstizione del generale Nicias, rilevata da Plutarco nel cap. VIII περὶ δεισιδαιμονίας.[36] Si potrebbe insistere anche sulla presenza nell'azione drammatica di particolari che sembrano parodiare alcuni aspetti di quella superstizione—a cominciare dal motivo medico del 'segno' (ciò che sembra richiamare una superstizione tramandata da Josephus);[37] mentre Nicia che si finge sordo potrebbe riflettere ancora il rizotomo che deve otturarsi le orecchie; i tre giri, proprio tre, che da Nicia vengono fatti fare al 'garzonaccio' per disorientarlo, potrebbero corrispondere ai tre cerchi che il rizotomo deve tracciare con la spada—o con il tripode?—intorno alla radice (non si dimentichi inoltre lo 'stocco' di Nicia durante l'impresa notturna); la paziente persuasione fatta per indurre Lucrezia ad acconsentire, finché non rimarrà che da compiere l'atto risolutivo del *concubitus*, potrebbe corrispondere alle istruzioni classiche di scavare il terreno intorno alla radice finché questa non rimanga attaccata che per mezzo dei propri filamenti prima dell'estrazione ad opera del cane; il ricorrere anzitutto a Sostrata per ottenerne l'aiuto potrebbe riflettere l'invocazione alla 'madre Terra', che secondo una tradizione doveva precedere il mistero dell'estrazione;[28] mentre Nicia che deve far 'lavare' la donna dopo il congiungimento (e la farà infatti lavare) ricorda il rizotomo che deve lavare la radice dopo l'estrazione per poterne ormai usufruire senza pericolo—: ma essi potrebbero anche essere coincidenziali (se non fossero invero troppi); mentre qui importa soprattutto notare, a riprova di quanto suggerito, la prescrizione *ante Solis exortum*, che si cristallizza, come si è visto, nella compiuta specificazione dello Schmidel, e che costituisce un elemento notevole della tradizione. Qui occorre una breve digressione, che ci riporterà, per terminare, donde siamo partiti: ai contributi preziosi del biografo di Machiavelli.

Ha notato giustamente il Ridolfi che nella *Mandragola* 'sono indicate con una straordinaria cura le ore durante le quali l'azione scenica si svolge' ore computate secondo il coevo uso italiano, cioè da tramonto a tramonto, tanto da poter 'stabilire con assoluta certezza... che la commedia fu scritta tra la metà di gennaio e la metà di febbraio'. Lo studioso fornisce infatti il seguente prospetto cronologico dell'azione essenziale:

2 ore di notte (= 7 p.m.): Callimaco manda la pozione a Nicia (atto IV, scene 2ª, 3ª);

3 ore di notte (= 8 p.m.): atto IV, scena 7ª;

4 ore (di notte) (= 9 p.m.): cattura di Callimaco travestito;

9 ore (= 2 a.m.): Callimaco si fa conoscere da Lucrezia (atto V, scena 2ª);

13 ore (circa 6 a.m.): Nicia fa levare Callimaco (atto V, scena 4ª);

13 ore ¼ circa: 'e' fa appunto l'alba' e Callimaco è liberato (atto V, scena 1);

ore 13 e ½ *c.*: 'è chiaro il giorno', Nicia e compagni vanno a rivestirsi.

L'ultima notazione indica che 'doveva mancare circa una mezz'ora alla levata del sole' e se ne ritrae che 'le 13 ore di notte sonavano in quella stagione circa un'ora prima dell'aurora':[40] ciò che vale a confermare la data di composizione sostenuta dal Ridolfi. Giova tuttavia domandarsi il perché di tanta ricorrente precisione cronologica da parte dell'autore; a giustificare la quale non sembra di per sé sufficiente il motivo prudenziale che la burla si svolga celata, nell'interesse comune degli ingannatori e dell'ingannato (per questo rispetto sarebbe stata sufficiente qualche enunciazione generica, allo stesso modo che nella *Clizia,* sia pure per diverso motivo, è insistentemente detto che le nozze debbono avvenire 'questa sera'). Occorre forse riferirsi pur qui a un aspetto ben noto della superstizione relativa all'estrazione della pianta che dà il titolo alla commedia: che questa si effettui cioè, come si è visto, *ante Solis exortum.* Non a caso le prime essenziali disposizioni date al semplice Nicia nell'atto II, scena VI, includono la specificazione: 'Dipoi, la mattina, ne manderete colui *innanzi dì*'; non a caso le ultime parole del frate a Lucrezia nell'atto III, scena XI, sono: 'preparatevi a questo *misterio, ché si fa sera*'; e non a caso è dato avvertire un certo timor panico nelle parole di Nicia: 'io sentii sonare le tredici ore; e *dubitando che il dì non sopraggiungessi* me n'andai in camera. Che direte voi, che io non poteva far levare quel rubaldone?... Pure e' si levò, io vi chiamai, e l'abbiamo condotto fuora' (cui segue la esplicita ripresa parodica del motivo superstizioso nella commiserazione di 'quel povero giovane,

ch'egli abbi a morire sì presto, e che *questa notte* gli abbi a costare
sì cara': atto V, scena ii).

La digressione non può arrestarsi qui. È ancora il Ridolfi a
rilevare—preceduto però nel rilievo dal Singleton—con le
seguenti parole la straordinaria formulazione della chiusa dell'atto
IV: 'Siamo alla fine del penultimo atto e alla fine della giornata in
cui i primi quattro atti si svolgono. Col quinto atto sarà un altro
giorno, ma frattanto l'azione in vari modi continua, e il Machiavelli, fattosi inaspettatamente aristotelico, quasi direi avanti
lettera, si rivolge agli spettatori per bocca del suo ribaldo frate
filosofante, prevenendo una ipotetica ed impossibile critica, con
queste strabilianti parole: 'E voi, spettatori, non ci appuntate:
perché in questa notte non ci dormirà persona, sì che gli Atti non
sono interrotti dal tempo...'. Lo studioso precisa che 'l'accenno
alla famigerata unità di tempo v'è bene evidente', con tutto che
siamo nel 1518 e l'autore aveva dietro di sé solo l'esempio degli
antichi modelli, mentre 'tutta la precettistica, tutta la polemica dei
retori, anche prima della grande "crisi aristotelica", erano di là da
venire'.[41] Dovendosi intendere in questo modo, la contraddizione
fra il rilievo della 'impossibilità' di una critica del genere da parte
degli spettatori e quello della 'evidenza' della scherzosa preoccupa-
zione regolistica da parte dell'autore, sembra davvero insanabile e
non facilmente riducibile all'ulteriore rilievo che 'questo sfoggiato
scrupolo aristotelico, sotto la penna spregiudicata di un Machiavelli, in una tale commedia, ha una sapidità tutta sua, una grazia
comica a parer mio impareggiabile':[42] a parer nostro, di noi che
possiamo oggi giudicare *post eventum*, senza dubbio; come pure,
è da supporre, a parere già dei lettori di una generazione più tarda
di quella del Machiavelli. Ma ai suoi spettatori dell'anno 1518
è probabile che una tale osservazione 'aristotelica' fosse in
realtà destinata per un motivo di coerenza tematica: in rapporto,
direi, alla superstizione connessa con l'estrazione di quella
mandragora da cui la commedia prende il titolo. Infatti il momento culminante del 'mistero' sarebbe dovuto avvenire durante
la notte, comunque prima del sorgere del sole. Le parole in
apparenza 'strabilianti', 'E voi, spettatori, non ci appuntate:
perché *in questa notte* non ci dormirà persona, sì che gli Atti non
sono interrotti dal tempo', potrebbero quindi essere rapportate,
senza peraltro perdere di grazia comica, alla dichiarazione del
Prologo: 'La cagion voi vedrete Nel recitarla...', e alle enuncia-

zioni degli atti II e III circa il verificarsi notturno del 'mistero'. Si noti del resto la disinvoltura con cui Machiavelli stesso non esita nella *Clizia* ad allontanarsi dalla falsariga della *Casina* interrompendo pur lì, in situazione analoga, l'azione scenica tra sera e mattina nel passaggio dal IV al V atto, e prolungando l'azione fuor di misura rispetto al sintetico epilogo latino. Alla chiusa del IV della *Mandragola* quel che gli premeva soprattutto annunciare al pubblico degli spettatori è che 'el dottore andrà di camera in sala, *perché la cucina vadia netta*' e che 'Callimaco e madonna Lucrezia *non dormiranno*': dove metafora ed eufemismo valgono a prefigurare parodicamente il momento essenziale del 'mistero' notturno, che sarà poi rievocato in dettaglio nelle scene II e IV dell'atto seguente.

Non mi illudo che le mie osservazioni possano risultare senz'altro probanti della giustificazione qui proposta del titolo della commedia (vorrei solo sperare che le obiezioni non poggino sul rilievo scandalizzato della validità artistica dell'opera o del suo valore morale: ciò che non risulterebbe comunque sacrificato dall'impostazione parodica); lo spazio mi vieta di proseguire l'indagine, sia con riferimenti interni alla vicenda che con rinvii esterni, i quali potrebbero a loro volta investire l'intero corpus 'letterario' di Machiavelli.[43] Quanto ai primi, vorrei per lo meno avvertire come lo stesso 'lieto fine'—al di là del beffardo motivo para-boccaccesco, e con tutta la carica etica di stampo machiavelliano—sembra parodiare un preciso sviluppo simbolico-cristiano della stessa superstizione.

Le parole di Lucrezia a Callimaco: 'io ti prendo per signore, padrone, guida, tu mio padre, tu mio defensore, e tu voglio che sia ogni mio bene' (a. V, scena IV)—cui si è voluto attribuire significato allegorico (secondo il parallelo Lucrezia–Firenze, Callimaco–Lorenzo) in virtù soprattutto dell'espressione 'mio padre',[44] la quale ricorre peraltro nell'*Andria* in simile rapporto e senz'ombra di allegoria[45]—introducono, dopo che Callimaco si è fatto 'conoscere', alla soluzione della favola, al di là ormai delle nozioni popolaresche della superstizione. Il motivo parodico non sembra peraltro cessare: esso culminerà con l'invito del frate ad entrare in chiesa. A intendere questa ultima fase della favola occorre forse tener presente il simbolismo elaboratosi intorno alla mandragora con l'esegi biblica.[46] A cominciare dall'esposizione

che della Cantica, VII, 13, diede Aponius,[47] contemporaneo di
Agostino, per il quale la mandragora, di forma umana, ma priva
della testa, emanerà la sua fragranza nel giorno del giudizio
universale. Le mandragore starebbero cioè a indicare simbolica-
mente le genti pagane vissute nell'oscurità della terra: esseri
umani solo in apparenza dotati di ragione, ma in realtà senza la
'testa della fede' cioè senza Cristo (Aponius non trascura peraltro
il motivo superstizioso circa la pratica dell'estrazione, che risale
allo pseudo-Apuleio[48] per l'applicazione esplicita all mandragora:[49]
il punto essenziale è che la radice non viene estratta direttamente
dal rizotomo; ciò avverrà, allegoricamente, alla fine del mondo,
quando gli uomini ancora lontani da Cristo saranno tolti al regno
oscuro della terra). Il motivo è ripreso da Beda, il quale a sua volta
specifica che prima dell'avvento glorioso di Cristo le nazioni
avevano un capo solo apparente, cioè l'Anticristo.[50] Tale simbolismo, presente in Cassiodoro con riferimento al salmo LI,[51] fu
trasmesso al Medio Evo con la *Glossa ordinaria*;[52] esso confluisce
nell'interpretazione simbolica della mandragora priva di testa,
quale risulta anche dal commento alla Cantica erroneamente
attribuito a San Tommaso e dovuto in realtà a Egidio Romano:
per il quale la mandragora è un'erba la cui radice ha membra
simili a quelle di un essere umano acefalo; questo significa il
popolo ebraico che è ancora senza capo; ma alla fine del mondo
gli Ebrei riceveranno la parola e la fragranza della Chiesa e
saranno finalmente riuniti a Cristo, loro capo.[53] Lo stadio finale
di questo simbolismo della mandragora è raggiunto con l'esposizione che della Cantica diede Honorius Augustudunensis,[54] per
il quale l'opera stessa rappresenterebbe una rivelazione della fine
del mondo: la regina Mandragora (intesa come simbolo degli
Ebrei rimasti fino allora sotto il potere dell'Anticristo) è solenne-
mente scortata dalle altre tre regine alla presenza del Cristo: solo
allora la acefala Mandragora sarà coronata con una testa che è
quella stessa del Logo.

Già da questo *excursus*, di necessità saltuario ed ellittico, del
simbolismo cristiano relativo alla mandragora, è dato rilevare
qualche elemento analogico con motivi ricorrenti parodicamente
nella favola machiavelliana e che si esplicitano nel finale della
commedia. Per tale aspetto simbolico della tematica tradizionale
occorre tener presente uno schema di rapporto tra i personaggi
diverso da quello fondamentale per la identificazione parodica al

livello popolare della superstizione. Questa volta a Lucrezia–Mandragora (popolo infedele) si sovrapporrebbe dapprima Nicia (capo solo apparente), quindi Callimaco (capo reale o 'Logo'). Si considerino in proposito queste due dichiarazioni nell'atto finale:

scena IV. [parole di Lucrezia riferite da Callimaco:] [...] io voglio iudicare che e'venga da una celeste disposizione che abbi voluto così, e non sono sufficiente a recusare quello che 'l cielo vuole che io accetti. Però io ti prendo per signore, padrone, guida; tu mio padre, mio defensore, e tu voglio che sia ogni mio bene [...]

scena V. [Messer Nicia a Lucrezia:] Dico che egli è bene che io vadia inanzi a parlare al frate, e dirli che ti si facci incontro in sullo uscio della chiesa, per menarti in santo, perché gli è proprio, stamane, come se tu rinascessi.

(la prima delle quali sembra sviluppare—pur, s'intende, letteralmente a diverso proposito—, l'osservazione di Ligurio su Callimaco finto medico nell'atto II, scena I; 'io credo che Dio ci abbia mandato costui').[55]

E si consideri, nelle scene V e VI, l'atteggiamento sprezzante di Lucrezia verso Nicia (che ben si giustifica, si intende, a livello letterale, per la naturale reazione psicologica della donna), e i rilievi dello stesso marito spodestato: 'Guarda come ella risponde! La pare un gallo!' (un gallo, si badi: la Lucrezia–Mandragora ha ormai alzato la testa o, se si preferisce, la cresta?); 'Tu se' stamani molto ardita! Ella pareva iersera mezza morta'. Non escluderei insomma che Machiavelli avesse inteso, con quest'ultimo atto, investire parodicamente l'interpretazione simbolico-cristiana del motivo biblico della mandragora. Tanto più in quanto dall'indagine che precede risulta evidente, nelle linee essenziali come pure in alcuni particolari, l'aderenza parodica dell'intrigo della commedia al nucleo fondamentale delle superstizioni popolari relative all'estrazione della pianta. Con l'ultimo atto si esaurirebbe quindi coerentemente questa tematica mediante l'ulteriore parodia dei relativi sviluppi simbolici. Del che neppure sarebbe dato stupirsi: 'la favola *Mandragola* si chiama'.[56]

Note

[1] Per i dati bibliografici e cronologici faccio senz'altro rinvio agli studi ben noti di R. Ridolfi; in particolare: 'Composizione, rappresentazione e prima edizione della *Mandragola*', *La Bibliofilia*, a. LXIV (1962), pp. 285–300; 'La

seconda edizione della *Mandragola* e un codicillo sopra la prima', *ibid.*, a. LXVI (1964), pp. 49–62; 'Introduzione' a *La Mandragola di Niccolò Machiavelli per la prima volta restituita alla sua integrità* (Firenze 1965), pp. 7–50 (saggi raccolti in *Studi sulle commedie del Machiavelli*, Pisa 1968, pp. 11–101).

² Le citazioni dalla *Mandragola* sono qui desunte dalla citata edizione critica a cura del Ridolfi.

³ *Ibid.*, 'Introduzione', pp. 17–18 (cf. *Studi* ecc. *cit.*, pp. 71–72).

⁴ *Ibid.*, p. 22 (cf. *Studi* ecc. *cit.*, p. 76).

⁵ Le citazioni dal carteggio sono desunte da N. Machiavelli, *Lettere* a cura di F. Gaeta (Milano 1961), pp. 389, 390, 432, 437, 438, 439, 440, 444, 447, 449, 452. Da notare che il titolo *Nicia... Comoedia* è ripetuto anche dal Giovio (*Elogia clarorum virorum*, Venezia 1546, c. 55).

⁶ Per la questione del titolo *cf.* Plauto, *Casina* a cura di E. Paratore (Firenze 1959), 'Nota introduttiva', pp. 12 sgg. Dalla stessa edizione è tratta la citazione.

⁷ *Cf.* N. Machiavelli, *Lettere, ed. cit.*, p. 447.

⁸ S. Debenedetti, 'Prefazione' a *Opere del Machiavelli, Mandragola* (Strasburgo s.d.), pp. 5–23, a p. 14.

⁹ *Cf.* Ch. B. Randolph, 'The Mandragora of the ancients in folklore and medicine', *Proceedings of the American Academy of Arts and Sciences*, vol. XL (Boston 1905), pp. 487–537, a p. 501. Per la questione della derivazione del titolo da Alexis e relativa bibliografia, rinvio a Di Tommasini, *La vita e gli scritta di N. Machiavelli*, II, 1 (Roma 1911), pp. 387–8, in nota.

¹⁰ *Cf.* Plauto, *Casina, ed. cit.*, 'Nota introduttiva', pp. 40–41.

¹¹ Sulla 'riduzione' del Calmo si vedano le osservazioni di V. Rossi, *Le lettere di Messer Andrea Calmo* (Torino 1888), 'Introduzione', pp. lx-lxii, lxv-lxvi, lxxix. È da notare che il titolo originale fu invece tradotto dal La Fontaine: '*La Mandragore, Nouvelle tirée de Machiavel*' (*cf. Œuvres de J. De La Fontaine*, ed. H. Regnier, tome Vme, Paris 1889: *Contes, Troisième Partie*, II, pp. 22–59).

¹² Così appunto annota M. Bonfantini (N. Machiavelli, *Opere*, Milano– Napoli 1963, p. 986 n. 2).

¹³ Le annotazioni degli editori moderni alla voce *mandragola* (*l.c.*) sono pressoché inesistenti: per quanto mi risulta, non si va al di là di quanto notato da E. Raimondi, in *Opere di Niccolò Machiavelli* (Milano 1966²), p. 1286 n. 37: 'è una erba, alle cui bacche si attribuivano virtù fecondatrici'; o, al più, dal Bonfantini (con riferimento all'occorrenza nel *Prologo*): '*Mandragola* (meglio mandragora) è il nome d'una pianta medicinale usatissima nel medioevo, cui si attribuivano virtù miracolose, anche per la curiosa forma della radice, nella quale si può ritrovare il disegno schematico di un minuscolo corpo umano' (*ed. cit.*, p. 986, n. 2).

¹⁴ *Cf.* Randolph, *op. cit.*, p. 500 (e la documentazione relativa). Non tengo qui conto delle osservazioni fatte in epoca classica circa gli effetti narcotici o anestetici della mandragola (su cui pure è da vedere il contributo citato).

¹⁵ *Cf.* Randolph, *op. cit.*, pp. 502, 532 (citazioni da Teofrasto, IX, 9, 1; Dioscoride, I, 570; Giuliano, *Epist.* XXIII; *Physiologus*, IV; notevole anche la menzione, fatta da Esichio, di Μανδραγορῖτις come epiteto di Afrodite).

¹⁶ *Cf.* Randolph, *op. cit.*, 503–504; 532.

¹⁶ᵃ Proprio per aver badato unicamente alla proprietà fecondativa della

mandragora, il Mastelloni poté dire, a proposito del titolo, che 'se il Machiavelli avesse scelto il nome di un'altra medicina, la sua comedia avrebbe avuta
la stessa catastrofe, e noi non staremmo discutendo della sua originalità'
(*La Mandragora: studi e osservazioni*, Napoli 1896, p. 22).

[17] *Cf.* 'Die Sage vom Giftmädchen', in *Gesammelte Abhandlungen* von W.
Hertz (Stuttgart und Berlin 1905), pp. 156–277 (il saggio era già apparso
nel 1893).

[18] *Cf.* Randolph, *op. cit.*, pp. 509, 511, 512, 533, 534 (per le citazioni da
Frontino, Apuleio, e Siceliota), e p. 525 (dove la nozione di pericolosità è
segnalata in Teofrasto, *Caus. Plant.*, VI.4.5; Dioscoride, I, 571; Plinio,
XXV, 150).

[19] La citazione (tratta dall'edizione bolognese del *Secretum secreti* 'impensis
Benedicti Hectoris', 1518, p. 6) è in A. D'Ancona, 'Il *Tesoro* di Brunetto
Latini versificato', *Atti dell'Accademia dei Lincei*, s. IV, Classe di scienze
morali ecc., vol. IV, *Memorie* (1888), pp. 111 sgg., a p. 141.

[20] *Cf.* D'Ancona, *op. cit.*, p. 111.

[21] *Ibid.* (dal ms. A), pp. 137–140.

[22] Citato da W. Hertz, *op. cit.*, p. 195, n. 8.

[23] *Cf.* W. Hertz, *op. cit.*, pp. 250 sgg.

[24] W. Hertz, *op. cit.*, pp. 259–260. Quanto alla credenza nella virtù fecondativa della mandragora, lo Hertz rinvia all'Anhang' II (pp. 273–277), dove
è contenuta anche una documentazione concernente le altre proprietà
tradizionalmente attribuite all'erba.

[25] I. Sanesi, *La Commedia*, vol. I (Milano, Vallardi, s.d.), p. 204. Il distico
di Teodolo, rimasto ignoto allo Hertz, si trova citato in E. Carrara, *La poesia
pastorale* (Milano, Vallardi, s.d.), p. 62.

[26] *Cf.* W. Hertz, *op. cit.*, 'Anhang' II, p. 276 ('Auch das bekannte Verfahren,
die Wurzel durch einen Hund aus der Erde ziehen zu lassen, erwähnt er und
fügt hinzu, er sei selbst davon Zeuge gewesen, habe jedoch die Behauptung,
daß der Hund dabei sein Leben verliere, falsch gefunden'); Sanesi, *op. cit.*,
p. 204 ('...aveva, infine, radici di forma umana le quali procuravan morte
sicura a chiunque tentasse di sradicarle, cosicché non v'era altro mezzo, per
evitare un effetto così funesto, che quello di legarvi un cane affamato e incitarlo
poco da lungi con un tozzo di pane perché egli, traendo di tutta forza,
svellesse quell'erba a costo della propria vita'); da notare che il Sanesi dipende
dallo studio dello Hertz (o piuttosto dall'esposizione fattane da L. Biadene,
Varietà letterarie e linguistiche, Padova 1896, pp. 1 sgg.) sia per la leggenda della
fanciulla velenosa che per quella della mandragora (*cf.* p. 471, nota alle
pp. 204–205). Al motivo del cane accennò anche il Tommasini (*op. cit.*,
p. 387, n.), accanto ad altre superstizioni e relative fonti, senza peraltro rile-
varne la portata per lo schema della commedia.

[27] Plinii *Naturalis Historiae* lib. XXV, 148 (*cf.* Randolph, *op. cit.*, pp. 490,
531).

[28] *Cf.* Randolph, *op cit.*, p. 491. Si veda anche P. Capparoni, 'Intorno ad una
copia delle scene raffiguranti l'estrazione della Mandragora, che ornavano il
codice così detto: "Dioscoride di Juliana Anicia" da lungo tempo scomparse',
La Bibliofilia, a. XXIX (1937), pp. 152–168 (con 12 facsimili), il quale descrive
le due scene della estrazione della mandragora come si trovano nel codice

98   Giovanni Aquilecchia

3632 della Biblioteca Universitaria di Bologna: 'Codice Bolognese c. 377r, *Dioscoride dà istruzione per l'estrazione della mandragora* [Fig. 10, p. 165]' (pp. 162–163); 'Codice bolognese carta 378r, *La scienza presenta a Dioscoride la mandragora estratta mentre ai piedi di essa giace il cane morto* [Fig. 11, p. 166]' (pp. 164–166). Il luogo di Dioscoride che ha provocato le illustrazioni (e la relativa amplificazione simbolica) è il IV, 75, del *De materia medica*.

²⁹ La identificazione della *baaras* con la mandragora fu sostenuta da P. J. Veth in *Internationales Archiv für Ethnographie* VII (1894): *cf.* Randolph, *op. cit.*, p. 499, nota †; la *baaras* e l'*aglaophotis* sono state identificate entrambe con la mandragora da H. Rahner, *Griechische Mythen in christlicher Deutung* (Zurich 1957); per comodità di citazione rinvio alla edizione inglese di B. Battershaw: *Greek Myths and Christian Mystery*, London 1963, cap. V, 2, '*Mandragora: the everlasting root of man*', pp. 223–277, a pp. 239–245.

³⁰ *Cf.* Flavii Iosephi Hebraei *De bello iudaico*, VII, 6 (*Opera omnia graece et latine*, ed. F. Oberthür, Lipsiae 1787, pp. 1077, 1079). *Cf.* anche, per lo stesso motivo applicato alla mandragora, l'*Herbarius*, 131, dello pseudo-Apuleio (*Corp. Med. Lat.*, IV, p. 222): *cf.* Rahner, *Greek Myths* ecc., p. 238; sempre utile il ricorso alla documentazione fornita da E. von Lippmann, 'Alraun und schwarzen Hund', *Abhandlungen und Vorträge zur Geschichte der Naturwissenschaften*, I (Leipzig 1906), pp. 190 sgg., oltre che dallo Hertz e dal Randolph nelle opere citate.

³¹ *Cf.* J. Frazer, 'Jacob and the Mandrakes', *Proceedings of the British Academy* (London 1917–18), pp. 57–79, il quale ritiene, con riferimento al passo del Genesi, che 'a later Jewish version of the same story, which relates how Reuben obtained the mandrakes' ci tramandi in realtà una sezione originariamente incorporata nel testo biblico; in questa versione un'asino anziché un cane funge, pur accidentalmente, da mediatore tra la mandragora e l'uomo (pp. 75–77).

³² V. anche la bibliografia raccolta da J. Frazer, *op. cit.*, p. 61, n. 2, come pure i riferimenti bibliografici forniti dal Randolph e dal Rahner nei rispettivi contributi. Da notare infine R. Harris, *The Ascent of Olympus*, Manchester, The University Press, 1917, cap. '*The Cult of Aphrodite*' (pp. 107–140), in particolare per la '*Note on the Method of extracting Mandrake Roots*' (p. 135), e per la '*Note on the Mandrake in the Fathers*' (pp. 139–140).

³³ Notevole per la sfera di cultura toscana il *Fons memorabilium universi* di Domenico Bandini d'Arezzo, il quale mostra il proprio scetticismo sia quanto alla presunta virtù fecondative della mandragora che quanto alla superstizione relativa all'estrazione (*cf.* L. Thorndike, *A History of Magic and Experimental Science*, vol. III, New York 1934, p. 566). Per l'epoca moderna la superstizione relativa all'estrazione della radice è documentata in Italia, a non dir altro, da A. Del Nino, *Usi abruzzesi* vol. I (Firenze 1879), cap. XXXIX, '*La festa di San Giovanni*' (pp. 86–88); stando alla dichiarazione di uno zappatore sulmonese, la pratica era allora osservata sulla Majella nella festa di San Giovanni: 'La mandragora, secondo quel tale, è una pianta con radice a forma umana, che produce effetti mirabili, guarisce tutti i mali, ec. ec. Chi la svellesse, morrebbe. Epperò la pianta, bene scalzata, suol legarsi alla coda di un cane. Il cane che è battuto, nel tentare la fuga, sradica la pianta, ma nel tempo stesso muore' (pp. 86–87).

'*La favola* Mandragola *si chiama*' 99

[34] Citato da Randolph, *op. cit.*, p. 531 (*cf.* p. 494, nota || per la lezione *tripodis*).

[35] *Cf.* A. Parronchi, 'La prima rappresentazione della *Mandragola*: Il modello per l'apparato—L'allegoria', *La Bibliofilia*, a. LXIV (1962), pp. 37–86, a p. 59: 'Nicia è il nome del generale ateniese, saggio e prudente, ma anche irresoluto e inutilmente temporeggiatore, che dopo aver concluso la guerra del Peloponneso, tenne invano l'assedio a Siracusa, finché tentò di ritirarsi e, non essendovi riuscito si arrese a patto di aver salva la vita, ma fu ucciso lo stesso (413 a. C.). In modo analogo il Soderini...' ecc., dove la forzatura analogica è evidente.

[36] *Cf.* L. Thorndike, *op. cit.*, vol. I (New York 1923), p. 204.

[37] *Cf.* Flavii Josephi *De bello iudaico*, *l.c.*: 'Accedentibus eamque evellere cupientibus captu haud facilis est; sed refugit, nec prius se sistit, quam quis urinam mulieris... affuderit' (*Opera omnia, cit.*, p. 1079).

[38] *Cf.* Rahner, *Greek Myths* ecc., p. 233.

[39] *Cf.* Rahner, *op. cit.*, p. 265 (con riferimento a *PL*, 197, 1151 A).

[40] *Cf.*, per le citazioni e per il prospetto cronologico, R. Ridolfi, 'Composizione, rappresentazione...' *cit.*, pp. 289–290 (cf. *Studi* ecc. *cit.*, pp. 18–19).

[41] Ridolfi, *op. cit.*, pp. 291–292 (cf. *Studi*, ecc. *cit.*, pp. 21–22). *Cf.* Ch. S. Singleton, 'Machiavelli and the spirit of comedy', *Modern Language Notes*, LVII (1942), pp. 585 sgg., a p. 585: 'Whatever the exact date of composition of the *Mandragola* may have been, it was certainly writtten before one would expect much attention to be given to Aristotle or to any derivative theory of the Unities. Yet one readily notices the strict observance which the play seems to make of them. . . . The comedy is even explicit (with a smile) . . .' e qui segue il riferimento alla chiusa dell'atto IV.

[42] Ridolfi, *op. cit.*, p. 292 (cf. *Studi*, ecc. *cit.* p. 22).

[43] Mi limito ad osservare che non poche delle opere 'letterarie' di Machiavelli sono ispirate a precisi motivi 'magici': es. *Asino d'oro*, *Belfagor*, canti carnascialeschi (in particolare *De' diavoli iscacciati di Cielo* e *De' ciurmadori*: nel quale ultimo è notevole il continuato equivoco erotico della credenza superstiziosa, con impostazione quindi analoga a quella qui prospettata per la *Mandragola*, sebbene con diverso e ben più scoperto procedimento).

[44] *Cf.* Parronchi, *op. cit.*, p. 62: 'Quel "padre", appellativo quanto mai inadatto per un amante, come nota giustamente il Sumberg, richiama l'appellativo di *pater patriae*, e va soggiunto allora che in Firenze tale appellativo, da Cosimo in poi, era legato ai Medici'.

[45] *Cf.* nell' *Andria*, a. I, sc. v, le parole di Panfilo: 'Criside mi disse di Glicerio... io ti do a costei marito, amico, tutore, padre...' (N. Machiavelli, *Tutte le opere*, ed. G. Mazzoni e M. Casella, Firenze 1929, p. 632).

[46] Si veda il fondamentale studio del Rahner, *op. cit.*, pp. 267 sgg.

[47] *Cf. Explanatio in Canticum* XI, ed. H. Bottino–J. Martini (Romae 1843), pp. 210 sg.

[48] L'interpretazione è del Rahner, *op. cit.*, p. 267.

[49] *Cf. Herbarius*, 131 (*Corp. Med. Lat.*, IV, *l.c.*).

[50] *Comment. in Genesim*, XXX (*PL*, 91, 257 C): *cf.* Rahner, *op. cit.*, p. 268.

[51] *Cf. Expositio in Psalterium*, LI, 7 (*PL*, 70, 375 B).

[52] *PL* 113, 921 A; *cf.* Rahner, *op. cit.*, *l.c.*

C.E.I.L. – H

[53] *Cf.* S. Tommaso, *Opera omnia*, XIV (Parma 1863), p. 421 (commento *Sonet vox tua*, 7).

[54] *Expositio in Canticum* (PL, 172, 347–496); *cf.* Rahner, *op. cit.*, pp. 272–274.

[55] Va notato che anche questa osservazione è stata utilizzata a sostegno della tesi allegorico-politica: *cf.* Parronchi, *op. cit.*, p. 67.

[56] Per la stesura di questi appunti non ho potuto tener conto di due importanti studi recenti, nei quali, pur non trovando luogo la questione del titolo o delle superstizioni e del simbolismo relativi alla mandragora, non manca tuttavia il rilievo del carattere, rispettivamente, rituale-parodico e religioso-trascendente nella soluzione del dramma: *cf.* E. Raimondi, 'Il teatro di Machiavelli' in *Studi storici*, a. X, 1969, pp. 749–98; L. Vanossi, 'Situazione e sviluppo del teatro machiavelliano', estratto da *Quaderni del circolo filologico-linguistico padovano*, II, 1970.

J. H. Whitfield

The poetry of Michelangelo[1]

My younger son had occupied himself, as a fledgling art historian, with the birth of landscape painting in late sixteenth-century Italy. At the interview for his first job they offered him the teaching of nineteenth-century art, with impressionism and all that. 'It's a challenge,' he replied, and, hopefully, they gave him the post. By which token it may be felt that I have either some apprehension, or some guilt. And I shall confess that here I have belonged rather to the Italian, than to the English fold. Nor shall I disguise the fact that the English were a century and a half in advance of the Italians in their enthusiasm for the poetry of Michelangelo; so that you, if you have been doing your homework, may well have compared to my disadvantage the half page in the Pelican *Short History of Italian Literature* with John Addington Symonds and his companions in the nineteenth century. I shall attempt no self-defence, but I must warn you sadly (and I hope not sourly) that if you have been reading the *Sonnets* of Michelangelo translated by John Addington Symonds you may not have come near the poetry of Michelangelo. Perhaps I may express what I mean by a true anecdote. One of my colleagues was acting as external examiner in a Scottish university, and tried benevolently to extract from a tongue-tied girl what she had liked. 'Dante,' at last she said. Yes, why? 'Well, at least he did write in English.' Of course, and so did Michelangelo; but there is this little difficulty: that where Michelangelo says 'go', John Addington Symonds says 'wing my way'. He constantly wraps the bare statements of Michelangelo in the full rhetoric of the English nineteenth-century literary tradition of the sonnet. The challenge for me is this also, that you may well expect me to quote Michelangelo to you comfortably, with the words and the face of John Addington Symonds. And whatever expedient I devise, I can not do that; though I shall think it part of my task to give some record of that century's concern with Michelangelo and his poetry.

First, though, let us see how the Italian academic tradition came to lose sight of Michelangelo as poet. Now a madrigal of his was set to music as early as 1518, and might have seemed to show the way to general appreciation. Instead, the collection that Michelangelo himself once planned was never published, and though before his own death in 1535 Francesco Berni had written a line which has re-echoed since

E' dice cose e voi dite parole
(He speaks things, while you speak words),

and though a few other compositions found their way into music
or print, though in the funeral exequies in Florence in 1564 the
crown of poetry too was claimed for him, in effect all his production remained a private matter, buried after that till the late date
of 1623. In this latter year (the year of Marino's *Adone*, the year of
Shakespeare's First Folio) Michelangelo Buonarroti the younger
put out the first edition of the *Rime*. The time was late, the manner
of publication an insult to the memory of Michelangelo, for his
nephew rewrote at will to give what seemed to him a better
flavour; and he of course suppressed the evidence, leaving the
poems addressed to Tommaso Cavalieri altered uniformly to a
'she'. From now on in Italy Michelangelo's poems are condemned
to a neglect only broken in 1863, when Guasti republished them
from the manuscripts. Even so, it has taken another hundred
years before Italian criticism has taken notice of them, and in
between we may take Toffanin's brief chapter in the *Cinquecento*
as typical of academic unresponsiveness. It was headed *Le poetesse
e Michelangelo*, and sweeps him on one side unceremoniously. With
this unawareness there went too a theoretic distrust. For Croce,
the activities of men are mutually incompatible: the more Dante
is a poet, the less he can be a thinker; the more Michelangelo is an
artist, the less he can be a poet. The *Rime*, then, are dilettante toys,
in an alien form, and a good Crocean supplies the answer to his
own question, *Michelangelo fu anche poeta?* with a plaintive *no*. It is
in this way that it takes another century, to the edition of 1960 by
Girardi of Michelangelo's *Rime* in the Scrittori d'Italia, before a
new approach can be made. All useful criticism in Italy itself
comes in this new wave. There is also now a useful paperback
issue by Laterza of Girardi's edition of the *Rime*, and it is here
that you must begin if you wish really to grapple with Michelangelo as poet. But I must warn you of a difficulty: the paperback
has no index of first lines, and you may pity me trying to match
up Symonds and another English nineteenth-century translator
with Michelangelo himself, neither of these having an index
either.

That was, of course, their privilege, living in less systematic
times; but you may well rejoin, Had they no merits, having seen

the importance of Michelangelo as poet a hundred years and more before Italy itself? It was Wordsworth who opened the chorus, with two sonnets 'From the Italian of Michelangelo', and Southey continued it with the sonnets on Dante. Moreover, lives of Michelangelo succeeded each other through the English nineteenth century. I would not have you think that they were all percipient. Here is R. Duppa in 1846, as patronising as Fubini in his answer to the Crocean question:

Of the sonnets, religion and love are the prevailing subjects. In the former Michelangelo is sometimes very successful; in the latter he is either monotonous or quaint; a jargon of Platonism and crude metaphysical divinity, acquired from the prevailing taste of the times, with little mind and no sensibility, supply the place of real feeling. He who only imagines that he loves is sure to be mistaken; and that which is worthless to himself, is still more cold and insipid to others.

After which advertisement, how many readers? Yet there were others, as John Edward Taylor, the printer-scholar, who wrote an essay on Michelangelo considered as a Philosophic Poet in 1840 (reprinted 1852), his essay followed by fifty pages of translations. And here you will find a very different assessment. The centre of Taylor's argument, and of the wide-ranging survey of Italian literature up to Michelangelo, is the importance of Platonism in Italian poetry. And we may take his illustration from a forgotten history of philosophy as helpful for us at a later stage.

Visible things were regarded by Plato as fleeting shades, and Ideas as the only permanent substances. . . . His conceptions on this subject are beautifully expressed in a passage of his *Republic*, in which he compares the state of the human mind, with respect to the material and the intellectual world, to that of a man who, in a cave into which no light can enter but by a single passage, views upon a wall opposite to the entrance the shadows of external objects, and mistakes them for realities.

Now compared with Duppa, J. E. Taylor showed a great percipience and respect. His best phrase (Michelangelo was the Dante of Art, Dante the Michelangelo of Poetry) will show the reverence with which he views his subject; and though his translations are all perforce from the old, corrupt, edition, yet there are one or two which obviously form the basis for John Addington Symonds later on. The defect lies perhaps in that his essay is less on Michelangelo's poetry, than on earlier Italian poetry as all Platonic, and so leading to Michelangelo. But the torch burnt on: in 1857 J. S. Harford published the *Life of Michelangelo* in two volumes, with many translations from the letters and the poems, and here for the first time the Italian text (still of course the bad text) appears alongside the translations— and more, perhaps, of these last than in Taylor. And then, on the other side the watershed, the *Sonnets* by J. A. Symonds in 1878, and his *Life* of Michelangelo, of 1893, followed by that of Sir Charles Holroyd, Keeper of the National Gallery, in 1903. This latter life, as befits the calling of Sir Charles, makes little of the poetry, and we may take it as the close to a century of British concern. Meanwhile, before coming to my subject (which is Michelangelo, and not the English nineteenth century), I must say one or two things about John Addington, though I have spent most of my life avoiding his influence. Coming after Guasti (1863), Symonds knows the authentic text of Michelangelo's poetry (though still chronologically confused). He does not burk the problems which arise from Michelangelo addressing love poetry to Tommaso Cavalieri and Febo del Poggio. But after that we may perhaps pause in our admiration for John Addington, for when he comes to translate his victim, then he deploys all the resources of another century, and of an over-copious sonnet tradition. If you have the patience to compare his sonnets with those of Michelangelo, you will find the translator respects the concepts on which these were based. But he overlays them with a rhetoric which falsifies their tone, and makes their face unrecognisable. If you are going to come to grips at all with the poetry of Michelangelo, you must abandon the English nineteenth century, and spend ten shillings on the Laterza paperback.

But here, as an Englishman, speaking presumably to Englishmen, I may pause for one moment more. For you may well have been struck already by one or two dates. Michelangelo died in 1564. It was the date of Shakespeare's birth. His poems were first printed (garbled) in 1623, the year of the First Folio; and Shakespeare's *Sonnets* had been printed also in 1609. Now these dates exclude the possibility of influence (unlikely also, since Shakespeare had less Italian than either Latin or Greek, presumably). Yet it is not only the consonance of time, and fame, which brings Shakespeare and Michelangelo together. Out of all the lyric tradition, here are the two who verge on homosexual love: Mr

W. H. stands opposite the Dark Lady of the *Sonnets*, as Tommaso de' Cavalieri alongside Vittoria Colonna. Not only that, but for both of them the answer is different from that of the permissive society. For this, see in Shakespeare the sonnet

> A woman's face with Nature's own hand painted,

and in Michelangelo (*inter alia*) 105

> Non vider gli occhi miei cosa mortale
>
> (My eyes have seen no mortal thing),

with its later line

> Voglia sfrenata el senso è, non amore
>
> (Sense is unbridled lust, it is not love),

which may remind us of a celebrated sonnet of Shakespeare,

> The expense of spirit in a waste of shame
> Is lust in action

The consciousness, too, which Shakespeare has, of words (his words) outriding time,

> Not marble, nor the gilded monuments
> Of princes, shall outlive this powerful rhyme . . .
>
> Since brass, nor stone, nor earth, nor boundless sea,
> But sad mortality o'ersways their power . . .,

is matched by Michelangelo's knowledge that his art can outlast Nature and life itself (239 *Com'esser, donna, può quel c'alcun vede*), where man turns to ashes, and his image lasts in stone,

> onde dall'arte è vinta la natura
>
> (Thus Nature's overcome by art.)

Yet both Shakespeare and Michelangelo can come together in an image of Man confronted with the ruthless hand of Time:

> Time doth transfix the flourish set on youth,
> And delves the parallels in beauty's brow,
> Feeds on the rarities of nature's truth,
> And nothing stands but for his scythe to mow.

Against the elaboration of which fascinating rhetoric (recalling T. S. Eliot's awareness of the contrast between Dante's and

Shakespeare's poetry) we may set the bare bones of Michelangelo's lament:

> Muovesi 'l tempo, e compartisce l'ore
> al viver nostr'un pessimo veleno;
> lu' come falce e no' sian come fieno

> (Time moves, a bitter poison marks the hours
> out of our life; Time like a scythe and we like hay).

I must not stay too long among these casual, though interesting, parallels with Shakespeare. Nor must I mislead you into thinking Michelangelo unsophisticated. Certainly, however good your Italian, you will be grateful for the paraphrases which Girardi (as Guasti before him in 1863) has added in elucidation of the poems. And sometimes the elaboration of a conceit may remind us of Donne rather than of Shakespeare. You will remember that little poem called *A Feaver*, in which his mistress's fever becomes, by hyperbole, the fire that is the essence of the world's end:

> O wrangling schooles, that search what fire
> Shall burn this world, had none the wit
> Unto this knowledge to aspire,
> That this her feaver might be it?

Now turn to Michelangelo (241) *Negli anni molti e nelle molte pruove*, in which all achievement is late, the greater the later, and so can least last. What then of Nature, which has reached its utmost in your beauty, and therefore must end soon, so that I can neither think nor say which hurts or helps the most, in seeing you, either my great delight, or the world's end:

> né so pensar né dire
> qual nuoca o giovi più, visto 'l tuo 'spetto,
> o 'l fin dell'universo o 'l gran diletto.

That being said, the nineteenth century swept aside, as an historic curiosity, Donne and Shakespeare being left, as accidental encounters in adjacent time, we are left with Michelangelo. Now there are two simple, though opposite, propositions that must come first. We may not take it that because his *Rime* have been so long neglected, therefore they cannot have poetic worth. But on the other side, we must not say, Michelangelo's genius as an artist is supreme, therefore his poetry has equal rank. For his art is his art, and his poetry, his poetry, and we cannot merely presume a judgment equal on both sides. Next, we must look (as some recent Italian criticism has done) to the areas of catchment, the influences which predetermine the nature of his poetry. And here the date of Michelangelo's birth is a basic and significant factor. 1475: it leaves him mainly open, in spite of his longevity, to the currents of fifteenth-century Florence: the neo-platonism of Marsilio Ficino, the austere Christianity of Savonarola. And behind these, of course, are the great exemplars of Florentine (or Italian) poetry, Dante and Petrarch. Now for the first of these we have some salient connections. There is the presumption of equal stature in differing fields; there are the sonnets specifically addressed to Dante (which Southey and others translated), with the explicit homage of Michelangelo:

> Fuss'io pur lui! c'a tal fortuna nato,
> per l'aspro esilio suo, co' la virtute,
> dare' del mondo il piú felice stato   (248)

> (Would I were he! for born so fortunate,
> for his sharp exile, with his worth,
> I'd give the happiest condition in the world)

—which recalls the proud line of Dante himself (*l'esilio che m'è dato onor mi tegno*). And two sonnets away, a closing line,

> simil uom né maggior non nacque mai   (250)

> (neither a like nor else a greater man was ever born).

In one who feels so strongly the weight of Dante, and who writes in Tuscan verse, there will be obvious places where he echoes Dante. And half a dozen, at least, of these will be discoverable to the reader of Michelangelo's *Rime*. It is not enough to make them seem in any way dantesque.

Indeed, though Michelangelo never expresses for Petrarch the reverence he has for Dante, or ever mentions him by name, yet his *Rime* can be more easily explained in juxtaposition with those of Petrarch. Here again I must issue the caveat which attaches to that birth-date of Michelangelo. For Petrarchism will flower with Bembo after the first quarter of the sixteenth century, but there is no sign that Michelangelo is ever aware of Bembo, nor does he attempt the orthodox imitation of Petrarchan themes which Bembo and his many followers bring back to artificial life.

Perhaps the only influence from the sixteenth-century fashion, quite different, and so far unclaimed,[2] is that of Ariosto. This is in the composition in *ottava rima* (the metre of the *Orlando furioso*), No. 67 *Nuovo piacere e di maggiore stima*, written before 1534 (the definitive edition of the *Furioso*, which took all Italy by storm, is 1532), where echoes of Politian and of the *Nencia* of Lorenzo have been seen for the opening stanzas. But the last two verses are pure Ariosto, written under the strong imprint of those personifications which are the engine-power of the *Orlando furioso*:

> Cogli occhi onesti e bassi in ver 'la terra,
> vestito d'oro e di vari ricami,
> il Falso va, c'a iusti sol fa guerra;
> ipocrito, di fuor par c'ognuno ami;
> perch'è di ghiaccio, al sol si cuopre e serra;
> sempre sta' n corte, e par che l'ombra brami;
> e ha per suo sostegno e compagnia
> la Fraude, la Discordia e la Bugia.

> L'Adulazion v'è poi, ch'è pien d'affanni,
> giovine destra e di bella persona;
> di più color coperta di più panni,
> che 'l cielo a primavera a' fiori non dona:
> ottien ciò che la vuol con dolci inganni,
> e sol di quel che piace altrui ragiona;
> ha 'l pianto e 'l riso in una voglia sola;
> cogli occhi adora, e con le mani invola.

You will forgive me if here I do not pause to translate, since this is a sidetrack in Michelangelo's verse. But I cannot refrain from adding the celebrated stanza from Canto XIV of the *Furioso*, of which this is a palpable echo. In this Canto, to make assurance sure, you will find pictured both Fraud and Discord, but it is Fraud which has always stolen the picture:

> Avea piacevol viso, abito onesto,
> Un umil volger d'occhi, un andar grave;
> Un parlar sí benigno, e sí modesto,
> Che parea Gabriel, che dicesse, Ave.
> Era brutta, e deforme in tutto il resto,
> Ma nascondea queste fattezze prave
> Con lungo abito, e largo; e sotto quello
> Attossicato avea sempre il coltello.

That we may take as Michelangelo's return for the celebrated
lines of praise which Ariosto gave him in the same *Furioso*,

> quel che a par sculpe e colora,
> Michel, piú che mortale, Angel divino.

But from this marginal point, let us go back to the central links
with Petrarch. In the *Secretum* Petrarch wrote of Laura as the
hook of salvation, which saved him from the turpitude of youth.
But in the *Canzoniere* he remains uncertain whether she is this, or
a temptation. Hence the hesitations which make the pattern of the
Canzoniere. Now with Michelangelo the terms are not precisely
the same, since this time there is no Laura. But they are precisely
similar, when we have put for Laura the concept of *beauty* itself.
La bellezza: is this the divine spark which carries Michelangelo
upwards, or is it a temptation which lures him downwards, and
at the last an irrelevancy, to be forgotten? On the one side there
is his conviction, stated in two poems of *c.* 1520:

> Amore è un concetto di bellezza
> immaginata o vista dentro al core,
> amica di virtute e gentilezza.   (38)

> (Love is an idea of beauty, imagined or seen
> within the heart, the friend of virtue and
> of gentleness).

And on these grounds Love can speak to him (in 39):

> I' son colui che ne' prim'anni tuoi
> gli occhi tuo infermi volsi alla beltate
> che dalla terra al ciel vivo conduce.

> (I am he who in your youth turned your
> weak eyes to beauty, beauty which takes
> you though alive from earth to heaven).

And on the strength of those two statements there can follow,
some time after 1528, the line which sums them up:

> l'amor mi prende e la beltà mi lega   (41)

> (Love takes hold of me, and beauty binds).

It is on the fringe of this first attitude that the rare note of sensual
appetite appears. You will find it in a sonnet of 1507, now No. 4,
so on the second page of the Girardi edition (instead, No. XX,
'The Garland and the Girdle', in John Addington): the garland

in which each flower seems to wish to be the first to kiss her head, the dress which clasps her breast, and then pours down, the ribbon on her breast, and the belt which seems to say: here will I always press.

> E la schietta cintura che s'annoda
> mi par dir seco: qui vo' stringer sempre.
> Or che farebbon dunche le mie braccia?

(What would my arms do then?)

Nor is this desire to seize and to enjoy unjustified. In a fragment of *c.* 1511, which starts from an obvious dantesque echo, we can see the answer to the unspoken question:

> Colui che 'l tutto fe', fece ogni parte
> e poi del tutto la più bella scelse,
> per mostrar quivi le suo cose eccelse,
> com'ha fatto or colla sua divin'arte.   (9)

(He who made all, made every part,
and then from all chose out the best,
to show in you his highest things,
as he has done with godlike art).

That is to say, the miracle of feminine beauty is the highest act of creation. And even when Michelangelo, at the age of 50, feels the need to write of himself as 'old', yet he can still claim there is no shame in using divine things:

> E se motteggia o finge,
> chi dice in vecchia etate esser vergogna
> amar cosa divina, è gran menzogna.
> L'anima che non sogna,
> non pecca amar le cose di natura,
> usando peso, termine e misura.   (25, *c.* 1524-5)

(And if men jest or jibe, saying that in old age
it is shameful to love divine-created things,
it is a lie. The soul which does not dream
sins not in loving natural things, if it keeps
weight, bounds and measure).

Nevertheless, it is here that there intrudes the note for which I have recorded already the consonance between Michelangelo and Shakespeare.

And Time that gave doth now his gift confound.
Time doth transfix the flourish set on youth,
And delves the parallels in beauty's brow,
Feeds on the rarities of nature's truth,
And nothing stands but for his scythe to mow.

lu' come falce e no' sian come fieno.   (17)

And following immediately that line (which I quoted before) there comes the lament,

La fede è corta e la beltà non dura.

(Faith is brief, and beauty does not last).

It brings Michelangelo to a short composition (21, before 1524) which seems to me to have one congener in Italian sixteenth-century poetry. This is the final chorus of Tasso's rather unhappy tragedy, *Il re Torrismondo* (though, as you will see when we come to Michelangelo's poem, Hamlet and the gravediggers are not out of sight). Here is Tasso, for once splendidly, and wholly, tragic:

> Ahi lacrime, ahi dolore!
> Passa la vita, e si dilegua, e fugge,
> Come giel che si strugge,
> Ogni altezza s'inchina, e sparge a terra,
> Ogni fermo sostegno,
> Ogni possente Regno
> In pace cadde al fin, se crebbe in guerra;
> E come raggio il verno imbruna, e more
> Gloria d'altrui splendore;
> E come alpestro, e rapido torrente,
> Come acceso baleno
> In notturno sereno,
> Come aura, o fumo, o come stral repente
> Volan le nostre fame, et ogni onore
> Sembra languido fiore.
>   Che piú si spera, o che s'attende omai?
> Dopo trionfo, e palma
> Sol qui restano a l'alma
> Lutto, e lamenti, e lagrimosi lai.
> Che piú giova amicizia, o giova amore?
> Ahi lagrime, ahi dolore!

So Tasso on the universal theme of the brevity of human lot, and barer and less harmonious, but equally insistent, Michelangelo (21):

> Chiunche nasce a morte arriva
> nel fuggir del tempo; e 'l sole
> niuna cosa lascia viva.
> Manca il dolce e quel che dole
> e gl'ingegni e le parole;
> e le nostre antiche prole
> al sole ombre, al vento un fummo.
> Come voi uomini fummo,
> lieti e tristi, come siete;
> e or siàn, come vedete,
> terra al sol, di vita priva.
> > Ogni cosa a morte arriva.
> Già fur gli occhi nostri interi
> Con la luce in ogni speco;
> or son voti, orrendi e neri,
> e ciò porta il tempo seco.

> (All who are born arrive at death,
> with flight of time; the sun leaves
> nothing live. The sweet, the painful
> fails, and wits and words; our ancient
> race are shadows in the sun, mist in the wind.
> We like you were men, happy and sad, like you;
> Now as you see we are, earth in the sunlight,
> lost from life.
> > All things arrive at death.
> Our eyes were whole, with light in every cavity;
> now they are empty, fearsome, black,
> and time brings this about.)

But it is here, of course, that there springs to Michelangelo's mind the superiority of his art. You will be aware of those accounts, first of the opening of his coffin in Florence, when he was three weeks dead, and when he seemed still as one who slept, with no corruption, and no corpse-like smell; then of a similar adventure in the eighteenth century, when his body still appeared intact. We should not have a similar expectation today. But his sculpture? And to Michelangelo also this phenomenon, of the lesser power outbidding the greater one, appealed. You will find in one of the sonnets for Vittoria Colonna (239 *Com'esser, donna, può quel c'alcun vede*), where the image lasts, while its owner dies,

onde dall'arte è vinta la natura			(239, 1545?)

(Thus Nature's overcome by art),

and he adds in the next line,

I 'l so, che 'l pruovo in la bella scultura,

while the close of the sonnet foresees, a thousand years after the death of Vittoria Colonna the proof of her beauty, and the reason of his love, in what he carves. *La bella scultura*: the ideas of Michelangelo, on the primacy of sculpture over painting, are to be found scattered in the *Rime*. Here, close by (237, *c.* 1545), it is *la prim'arte*; and these confirm the conclusion to the most cele-brated *sonetto caudato*, the best-known of what we may call Michelangelo's occasional poetry, the one which grotesquely particularises the consequences for his person of the twenty months labour, as a painter, in the Sistine Chapel (5, 1509-10 *I' ho già fatto un gozzo in questo stento*). It ends:

La mia pittura morta
difendi orma', Giovanni, e 'l mio onore,
non sendo in loco bon, né io pittore.

(Defend my dead painting now, Giovanni,
and my honour, for I am not in a good place,
nor I a painter).

After what you have heard, and seen, you will have views of your own on such a judgment. But the important fact is, that it is Michelangelo's own. And it gives tremendous relief to certain attitudes. One of those is his indignation against the corruption of papal Rome, and the warlike nature of Julius II, his turbulent patron. You will find it first in the sonnet that immediately follows the one on his cramped labours on the Sistine scaffolding, which is addressed to Julius II himself (6, *c.* 1511),

Signor, se vero è alcun proverbio antico,
questo è ben quel, che chi può mai non vuole

(No proverb truer than this ancient one,
That he who can, will never will);

and it takes fire in that nearby sonnet (10, signed Vostro M. in Turchia 1512), which has always been paralleled to the invectives of Dante, or the Babylonian sonnets of Petrarch (against the papal court of Avignon). Its strength, naturally, does not derive from those, respectable, literary connections, but from the convictions of Michelangelo. From his convictions, and his pride: the necessary corollary to those two sonnets on the Rome of Julius II, and the commentary on all Michelangelo's grappling with the temporarily great who were perforce his patrons, you will find in a late fragment (of *c.* 1552, 282):

> Con tanta servitú, con tanto tedio
> e con falsi concetti e gran periglio
> dell'alma, a sculpir qui cose divine.

> (In so much servitude, with so much weariness,
> and with false thoughts, great danger to my soul,
> carving things here that are divine).

A sculpir qui cose divine: it is the one lightning-flash, the sole place where the veil of modesty which Michelangelo interposes between himself and the world lifts for a moment, and he claims consciously what none of us would dare dispute, the splendour of his own genius.

And still in this context, you would not forgive me if I passed over what Michelangelo has to say, within the *Rime*, of the nature of his art. And here, since I did not say it before, I may throw in an experience. In my desire to read the relevant, I sought a famous book which I had read long ago, but of which my memory was blandly (blankly) innocent: Walter Pater, *The Renaissance*. And in a row beneath the copy on the shelf in stack were the works of Stephen Phillips, with the title *Paolo and Francesca* staring me in the face. I had come for Pater, but I had also then to feed my students on *Inferno* V, and so I took both books away. Now Stephen Phillips' poetic drama was played in 1899, printed in 1900, and if you are lucky in your copy you will find what all the critics said about the greatness of his poetic achievement in the advertisement section at the end. They are written over some respectable academic names still not quite out of sight; but the play, that great achievement which was to resurrect poetic drama, is the feeblest wish-wash piffle-wiffle. Oh yes, you will say, but Walter Pater? Well, of course, I shall not speak so slightingly of him, especially as I only re-read the essay specifically entitled *The Poetry of Michelangelo*. But I can tell you now, in case your own homework on Michelangelo is still to do, and will be inspired or directed by what we tell you here, that in twenty-six pages you will find perhaps half a page which speaks directly of the poetry; and in the rest nothing more nutrient than what you might have found in Stephen Phillips. And now you will wonder why I dragged them in at all: it is just because, though you will find nothing whatever in Pater, who professed to speak of Michelangelo's poetry, you will find a good deal in Sir Anthony Blunt, who only volunteered to write on artistic theory. There you will find what, in the *Rime*, is specifically concerned with art. And having said that, it may be enough for our purpose if I look to the one sonnet which you will all feel I must not fail to quote, *Non ha l'ottimo artista alcun concetto* (151, 1538–44). There is somewhere in Vasari the illustration of the waxen image in a bath of water. As the water-level sinks, so do the features emerge. Or, as Michelangelo puts it in the next composition (152), it is by subtraction from the hard stone that the living image within appears. It was Mario Praz who observed that, by a curious coincidence, Donne in *The Crosse* has the same image:

> As perchance, Carvers do not faces make,
> But that away, which hid them there, do take.

And in noting other affinities in the religious lyrics, Praz added that the dates allowed no influence.[3] And here, in this most famous of all Michelangelo's sonnets, the idea both in the mind and in the marble, and if the hand obeys the brain, it can come forth at command. Remember, though, this is not a poem on art theory, but Michelangelo, as artist, can not forget his art when he writes love-poetry. And plainly, this sculpture image is stronger than the other, out of painting, also in a composition for Vittoria Colonna (111, 1536 *S'egli è, donna, che puoi*), where the final appeal is to her to draw on him as he on stone or on blank paper, where there is nothing, but yet there is what I choose to put:

> Disegna in me di fuora,
> com'io fo in pietra od in candido foglio,
> che nulla ha dentro, e èvvi ciò ch'io voglio.   (111)

By now you will be feeling that, like Hamlet, I have mislaid a somewhat blunted purpose: the parallel I proposed with Petrarch. But there is still another, obvious, side to the relationship of

Michelangelo with the beautiful, and you will find it best expressed in the poems for Tommaso de' Cavalieri. Tommaso de' Cavalieri is, as I have hinted, the Mr W. H. of Michelangelo's poetry, and you may feel that we are with him entering the danger zone. That is not true. The lure of the senses, for Michelangelo, is where we saw it first, in that early sonnet on the garland and the belt; and if there is any offence to be given by his poetry it will be found in the attempt to reject the senses at this point. You will find it in 260 (one of the poems written for Tommaso de' Cavalieri, *Non è sempre di colpa aspra e mortale*) in which the first tercet is a rejection of woman, because love for her brings down to sense a lover who would soar up:

> L'amor di quel ch'i' parlo in alto aspira;
> donna è dissimil troppo; e mal conviensi
> arder di quella al cor saggio e virile.

> (The love of which I speak aspires on high;
> woman is too unlike; it ill befits
> a wise and virile heart to burn for her). (260)

The expense of spirit in a waste of shame: it was for Tommaso also that the earlier sonnet was written from which I instanced the parallel with Shakespeare:

> Non vider gli occhi miei cosa mortale
> allor che ne'bei vostri intera pace
> trovai, ma dentro, ov'ogni mal dispiace,
> chi d'amor l'alma a sé simil m'assale;
>   e se creata a Dio non fusse equale,
> altro che' l bel di fuor, c'agli occhi piace,
> piú non vorria; ma perch'è sì fallace,
> trascende nella forma universale.
>   Io dico c'a chi vive quel che muore
> quetar non può disir; né par s'aspetti
> l'eterno al tempo, ove altri cangia il pelo.
>   Voglia sfrenata el senso è, non amore,
> che l'alma uccide; e 'l nostro fa perfetti
> gli amici qui, ma piú per morte in cielo. (105)

(My eyes saw no mortal thing when I found full peace
in your beauteous eyes, but within, where all ill
displeases, Him who assaults my soul with love like
to Himself; and if the soul had not been made akin
to God, it would not seek for more than for

the outward forms which please the eyes; but since
these are deceitful, it transcends them to gaze
on universal form. I say that for those who live,
what dies can not fulfil desire; nor does it seem
eternity belongs to time, where hair turns white.
The senses are unbridled appetite, which kills the soul,
not love; but ours makes perfect friendship here,
and more, with death, in heaven above.)

There is nothing in the whole series of poems for Tommaso
de' Cavalieri which belies the plain statements of that sonnet.
This is not homosexuality in action, but the process by which
beauty is taken upwards to its source; and this impetus gives an
afflatus to the poems for Tommaso which is not equalled in the
colder exchanges with the pious, and middle-ageing, Vittoria
Colonna. Let me just refer you here to two sonnets of the series,
Veggio co' bei vostr'occhi un dolce lume (89) and *I' mi son caro assai più
ch'i' non soglio* (90).

Meanwhile, however, there is riding up an attitude which is
Christian rather than platonic, to remind us that the High
Renascence, in its highest representative, is not the pagan movement dreamed up by nineteenth-century thought. The prelude is
in a sonnet of 1534, *Vorrei voler, Signor, quel ch'io non voglio* (87):

> Vorrei voler, Signor, quel ch'io non voglio:
> tra 'l foco e 'l cor di ghiaccia un vel s'asconde
> che 'l foco ammorza...
>   I' t'amo con la lingua, e poi mi doglio
> c'amor non giunge al cor...
>
> (I would I would, Lord, what I do not will:
> between heart and fire a film of ice is hid
> which damps the fire . . .
> I love Thee with my tongue, and then lament
> love does not reach the heart . . .)

So we pass to the moving, and eloquent, closing sequence of
Michelangelo's *canzoniere*. The apprehension of beauty (and I need
not labour for you the Sappho–Leopardian contrast of his own
graceless form) is the breath of his being.

> Che poss'io altro che così non viva?   (274, 1547)
>
> (What can I do, but live like this?)

To which the answer comes two lines later, in the last line of the same sonnet,

> il cangiar sorte è sol poter divino
>
> (only the power of God can change one's lot).

Thus though there crowd about us at this point in the *Rime* the attestations of his responsiveness to beauty (which is to say, as you will know, to human beauty, for Michelangelo's awareness is all of Man, and little of Nature), we know that we are bound to pass through them, to what for Michelangelo at least must cancel them. On the one side, then, the full confession of his susceptibility:

> Passa per gli occhi al core in un momento
> qualunche obbietto di beltà lor sia,
> e per sí larga e sí capace via
> c'a mille non si chiude, non c'a cento,
> d'ogni età, d'ogni sesso...   (276, 1547–50)

> (Whatever beauteous object meets my eyes
> passes at once into my heart,
> and by so broad commodious a way,
> it is not shut, not to a hundred
> or a thousand such; of every age, of every sex.)

Or alongside that, 279:

> La forza d'un bel viso a che mi sprona?
> C'altro non è c'al mondo mi diletti

> (What may the strength of a fair face spur me to?
> For nought else pleases me in all the world),

with its claim that beauty is the work of God, so that no guilt attaches to the love of it,

> Se ben col fattor l'opra suo consuona,
> che colpa vuol giustizia ch'io n'aspetti,
> s'i' amo, anz'ardo, e per divin concetti
> onoro e stimo ogni gentil persona?   (279 Tardo)

> (For if indeed creation and Creator are akin,
> what fault can justice find in me,
> who love, or rather burn, and for their
> godlike qualities honour and esteem
> all gentle souls?)

And, of course, what I quoted earlier, the flash of resentment against the conditions of Rome under which he works, with the flash of revelation, that his own assessment of himself is the same as ours, comes in this late period:

> Con tanta servitú, con tanto tedio
> e con falsi concetti e gran periglio
> dell'alma, a sculpir qui cose divine.

This is Michelangelo the lightning-conductor, transmitting the beauty that comes from God in the forms of godlike art. Then equally logically he turns away,

> Piú l'alma acquista ove piú 'l mondo perde;
> l'arte e la morte non va bene insieme   (283, 1552)

> (The soul gains most where the world's most lost;
> art and death do not go well together.)

So Petrarch had turned from Laura,

> Che quanto piace al mondo è breve sogno

> (All that pleases in the world as brief as is a dream),

so Michelangelo, in a substantial, not an imitative gesture, for this is life, not literature, renounces art, the idol and the monarch of his life (*Giunto è già 'l corso della vita mia*, 285, 1552–4), with its specific

> Né pinger né scolpir fie piú che quieti

> (To paint or sculpt can bring no comfort now),

and its appeal, instead, to the Christ, who had been the centre of all Michelangelo's late art, and who now replaces it in his own person. All Michelangelo's dazzling career he now enters in the chronicle of wasted time:

> Carico d'anni e di peccati pieno   (293, 1555)

> (Laden with years and full of sin),

he asks only to hate the world, and have the earnest of eternity:

> Mettimi in odio quanto 'l mondo vale
> e quante suo bellezze onoro e colo,
> c'anzi morte caparri eterna vita.   (288, 1555)

For those who still hanker for those old views on the pagan nature of the Renascence world there is no better antidote than the last *Rime*, or the last works, of Michelangelo.

Notes

[1] This is the text, only very slightly modified, of a lecture given at Attingham Park on 8 December 1967, as a contribution to a symposium on Michelangelo, with Professor Niklaus Pevsner on his art, and Professor Nicolai Rubinstein on the historical background.

[2] But *cf.* now the article, 'Postilla per la poesia di Michelangelo' in *Le Parole e le Idee* IX (1967), pp. 206–209.

[3] M. Praz, *Machiavelli in Inghilterra* (Tumminelli, 1943²), pp. 236–237.

Conor Fahy

The two 'Neapolitan' editions
of Ortensio Lando's Forcianae
Quaestiones

Both Richard Copley Christie and Walter Llewellyn Bullock, whose collections of sixteenth-century printed books, now in the Manchester University Library, provide such a rich source of first-hand material for work on the Italian Cinquecento, had a special interest in Ortensio Lando.[1] Christie's interest was probably religious in origin, occasioned by the connection between Lando and Étienne Dolet, who became friends at Lyons in the autumn of 1534, and it was sustained by the faint but unmistakable links which bound Lando to the Protestant cause, then and throughout his life. For Bullock, it was rather Lando the *poligrafo*, contemporary of Aretino and Doni, collaborator of famous printers like Sebastianus Gryphius of Lyons and Gabriele Giolito of Venice, who attracted his attention. Despite, or possibly because of, this diversity of interest, Christie and Bullock assembled between them what is now the richest collection of Lando editions in any library. Since the present writer, under Kathleen Speight, had the pleasure of working for several years literally surrounded by the Bullock books, this seems a peculiarly suitable occasion on which to try to solve one of the many bibliographical problems associated with Lando's works. The occasion is all the more welcome in that it also provides an opportunity of acknowledging the help received from the Librarian of Manchester University, Dr F. W. Ratcliffe, and from his predecessor, the late Dr Moses Tyson, in the work the present writer has undertaken on Lando in recent years.

The two earliest editions of Lando's *Forcianae Quaestiones* are the following:

1. ☙ FORCIA/NAE QVAESTIONES,/ in quibus uaria Italorum inge/nia explicantur, mul=/taq̄3 alia scitu non/ indigna./ Autore Philalethe Polytopiensi Ciue./ MAVRITII SCAEVAE CARMEN./ *Quos hominum mores uarios, quas deniq; mentes/ Diuerso profert Itala terra solo,/ Quiś ue uiris animus, mulierum & strennua uirtus,/ Pulchrè hoc exili codice lector habes.*/ NEAPOLI EXCVDEBAT MAR/TINVS DE RAGVSIA. AN=/NO M. D. XXXV./

Col. [D7*r*]: NEAPOLI EX OFFICINA/ MARTINI DE RA=/GVSIA. ANNO/ 1535./

8ᵛᵒ. A–D⁸. Pp. [2], 3–61, [3].

A1*r*. Title-page.
A1*v*. Blank.

A2r. ⁊⸖ FORCIA/NARVM QVAESTIO=/num libri. II. ad Franciscum Tur=/chium Patricium Lucensem:/ Autore Philalethe Po=/
lytopiensi ciue./ QVANTA ME BENE=/*uolentia prosequatur Vincen=/
tius Bonuisius* ... [C1r] *Sicq̃;/ in tecta discessimus, tanta elati laeticia, ut
ferè desipere/ uideremur./*
C1r. ⁊⸖ FORCIA/NARVM QVAESTIO=/NVM LIBER II./ NON
POSSEM VER=/*bis consequi quanta nos iucun=/ditate illa festiua narratio
affe/cerit* ... [D5v] *Vale & meo no/mine domesti/cos oēs/ salu/ta./* (*)/
D6r. ANTIOCHVS LOVIN=/TVS FRANCISCO/ TVRCHIO/
S.P.D./ AVDIO FRANCISCE/ *te mihi grauiter succensere...*[D7r]
Vale & me/ tui studiosissimum/ ama./
D7v, D8r, D8v. Blank.

29 lines (B8r, C8r = 30 lines), 120 (126) × 67 mm; italic type, 20 lines
= 82.5 mm; three woodcut initials, Q (A2r), N (C1r), A (D6r),
apparently belonging to the same figured alphabet, 28 × 28 mm.

Copies:[2] Bergamo, Biblioteca Civica, Antesala F.4.retro. 13 (2);
Cambridge, Clare College Library, S.8.5; Florence, Biblioteca
Nazionale Centrale, 3.L.6.519; Forlì, Biblioteca 'A. Saffi'; Lucca,
Biblioteca Governativa, H.XXX.A.20; Manchester, John Ry-
lands Library, 4965.2; Manchester, University Library, Christie
9.c.18; Munich, Bayerische Staatsbibliothek, A.Gr.a.666; Naples,
Biblioteca Nazionale, Misc.XXXIII, A.33; Oxford, St John's
College Library, Ss.7.16; Paris, Bibliothèque Nationale, X.20079
(3); Pavia, Biblioteca Universitaria, 5.B.32; Rome, Biblioteca
Angelica, 1.6.57; Rome, Biblioteca Nazionale, Misc.A.256.21;
Rome, Biblioteca Vaticana, Barberini Y.XII.107.

2. ⚜ FORCIA ⚜ /NAE QVAESTIONES, IN/ quibus uaria
Italorum ingenia expli/cantur, multaq; alia scitu/ non indigna./
Autore Philalethe Polytopiensi Ciue./ MAVRITII SCAEVAE
CARMEN./ *Quos hominum mores varios, quas deniq; mentes/ Diuerso
profert Itala terra solo,/ Quis ve viris animus, mulierum & strennua virtus,/
Pulchrè hoc exili codice lector habes./* NEAPOLI EXCVDEBAT MAR/
TINVS DE RAGVSIA. AN=/NO. M. D. XXXVI./
Col. [C8r]: NEAPOLI EX OFFICINA/ MARTINI DE RA/GVSIA.
ANNO/ 1536./

8ᵛᵒ. A–C⁸. Ff. [2], 3–24.

A1r. Title-page.
A1v. Blank.

A2r. ✠ FORCIA ✠ /NARVM QVAESTIONVM LIBRI.II.
AD/*Franciscum Turchium Patricium Lucensem, Auto/re Philalethe Polytopiensi ciue.*/ QVANTA ME BENEVO=/*lentia prosequatur Vincentius Bōui/sius...*[B5*v*] *Sicq̃; in tecta discessi=/mus, tanta elati laeticia, vt ferè desipere videremur.*/
B5*v*. ✠ FORCIA ✠ /NARVM QVAESTIONVM LIBER.II./
NON POSSEM *Verbis consequi quan=/ta nos iucunditate illa festiua narratio affe/ cerit...*[C7*r*] *Vale et meo nomīe domesticos oēs saluta.*/
C7*v*. ANTIOCHVS/LOVINTVS FRANCISCO TVR/CHIO S.P.D./
AVDIO *Francisce te mihi grauiter succense/re...*[C8*r*] *Vale & me tui studio=/sissimum ama.*/

31 lines (C2*r* = 30 lines, C6*r*, C7*r* = 32 lines), 122 (129) × 77 mm; italic type, 20 lines = 79 mm; three woodcut initials, Q (A2*r*), N (B5*v*), A (C7*v*), each apparently belonging to a different alphabet, none of which resembles that of the 1535 edition; Q = 34 × 34 mm; N = 27 × 26 mm; A = 25 × 23 mm.

Copies:[3] Bergamo, Biblioteca Civica, Sala I.logg.H.2.17; Cambridge (Mass.), Harvard University Library; Florence, Biblioteca Nazionale Centrale, 3.L.6.519; London, British Museum, 8405.b.41; Manchester, University Library, Bullock 343424; Manchester, University Library, Christie 9.c.19; Modena, Biblioteca Estense, A.16.B.7; Munich, Bayerische Staatsbibliothek, H.Lit.P.295*m*; New Haven, Connecticut, Yale University Library; New York, Columbia University Library; Paris, Bibliothèque Nationale, K.7399(4); Parma, Biblioteca Palatina, B*.VI.2328; Philadelphia, University of Pennsylvania Library; Pisa, Biblioteca Universitaria, Misc.437.3; Rome, Biblioteca Vaticana, Ferraioli V.7623.int.11; Rome, Biblioteca Vaticana, Rossiana 6190; Treviso, Biblioteca Comunale, 2365/2; Venice, Biblioteca Marciana, Misc. 1387.5; Washington, D.C., Folger Shakespeare Library.

As these lists of copies would suggest, both editions are quite well known. The 1536 edition was mentioned by Tiraboschi and by Cristoforo Poggiali;[4] the 1535 edition was first referred to, as far as I know, in the *Catalogo delle opere di Messer Ortensio Lando* published by Salvatore Bongi in his edition of Lando's *Novelle*.[5]

Recently, in the course of work in progress on an edition of some of Lando's works, I had occasion to consider carefully these two editions, as a result of which it became clear that grounds existed for doubting the authenticity of their Naples imprint. These can be set out as follows.

1. One of the difficulties in accepting the Neapolitan origin of these editions lies in the presence of the following passage in Book I of the work:

Olim splendidissime vestiebant Mediolanenses: sed postquam Carolus Caesar in eam urbem tetram et monstruosam Bestiam immisit, ita consumpti et exhausti sunt, ut vestimentorum splendorem omnium maxime oderint, et quemadmodum ante illa durissima Antoniana tempora nihil aliud fere cogitabant quam de mutandis vestibus, nunc alia cogitant, ac mente versant. Non potuit tamen illa Leviana rabies tantum perdere, neque illa inexhausta depredandi libidine tantum expilare, quin a re familiari adhuc belle parati sient, atque ita vestiant quemadmodum decere existimant. Et certe nisi illa Antonii Levae studia egregios quosdam immitatores invenissent, meo quidem iudicio, nulli cederent.[6]

These outspoken and explicit comments are directed against one of the principal Imperial servants in Italy, Antonio de Leyva, appointed Captain General of the armies of the *lega italica* in 1533, with headquarters in Milan, and created Lieutenant General of Milan on the death of the last Sforza duke, Francesco II, at the beginning of November 1535, when the city of Milan acknowledged Charles V as its lord.[7] It is hard to believe that they were openly published in the same year 1535 in a signed edition in the other major Imperial city of Italy.

2. In the last few pages of the *Forcianae Quaestiones* there is an account of some of the circumstances leading to the publication of the work. The author tells us that shortly after he had completed the text, it became necessary for him to visit Naples. Once there, he found that someone else, an otherwise unidentified *studiosus iuvenis*, had also written down an account of the discussions at Forci which provide the substance of Lando's book. Hearing that the young man was being urged to publish his work, Lando attempted to obtain the manuscript. Failing to achieve this by fair means, he resorted to foul—he stole it. He then sent this young man's text, together with that of his own work, to Francesco Turchi, dedicatee of the *Forcianae Quaestiones*, apparently resident at Lyons. Turchi was opposed to the publication of any work bearing his name, so Lando advised him to be sure to remove all traces of it, if publication occurred at his end. For his part, Lando undertook 'omni mea opera, cura, gratia et diligentia' to see that the *Forcianae Quaestiones* was never

published.[8] How then, one might justifiably ask, did the work with its dedication ever see the light of day? The answer is supplied by the letter from Antiochus Lovintus to Turchi which appears at the end of the text. In this letter Lovintus accepts responsibility for the publication, which he knows is contrary to Turchi's wishes, excusing himself on the grounds of the work's great interest, and of the fact that it was already circulating in manuscript, 'plusquam in trecenta exemplaria', in fact.[9] Whether or not Lovintus was a real person, there is little doubt that the letter was written by the author of the *Forcianae Quaestiones*; similar fictitious letters appear at the end of other pseudonymous works of Lando.[10]

This whole bizarre account of the events surrounding the publication of the *Forcianae Quaestiones* should obviously be taken with a pinch of salt, and since Lando's trip to Naples is an integral part of the story, one's suspicions naturally extend to the Naples imprint. These suspicions are increased by what we know of Lando's biography at this time. If it is true, as the testimony of Johann Albrecht von Widmanstetter affirms, that about 1530 Lando had been an Augustinian hermit in the monastery of S. Giovanni a Carbonara in Naples,[11] then it seems strange that after leaving the order under a cloud he should return to a city where he was known as a renegade monk and there arrange the publication of a book, particularly one describing events occurring in Lucca and dedicated to a Luccan merchant resident in Lyons.

3. Further grounds for doubting the authenticity of the Naples imprint are provided by some aspects of the typography of the two editions. Two separate and distinct italic founts are used, in itself rather surprising for a Neapolitan printer of this period, particularly for one who can hardly be called an important figure in the history of printing, since no other editions of his are recorded. While the italic of the 1536 edition is cramped and inelegant (Fig. 2), that of the 1535 is of high quality (Fig. 1).[12] The three woodcut initials of the 1535 edition clearly belong to a single figured alphabet, and are quite different in style to the three heterogeneous initials found in the 1536 edition. Other italic founts recorded for Naples are those used by Caterina Mayr in 1520 and by Sultzbach in the 1530's, but they are quite distinct from those used in the two *Forcianae Quaestiones* editions.[13] No other Neapolitan printer of the period seems to have had an italic fount. Indeed, Martinus de Ragusia is something of a

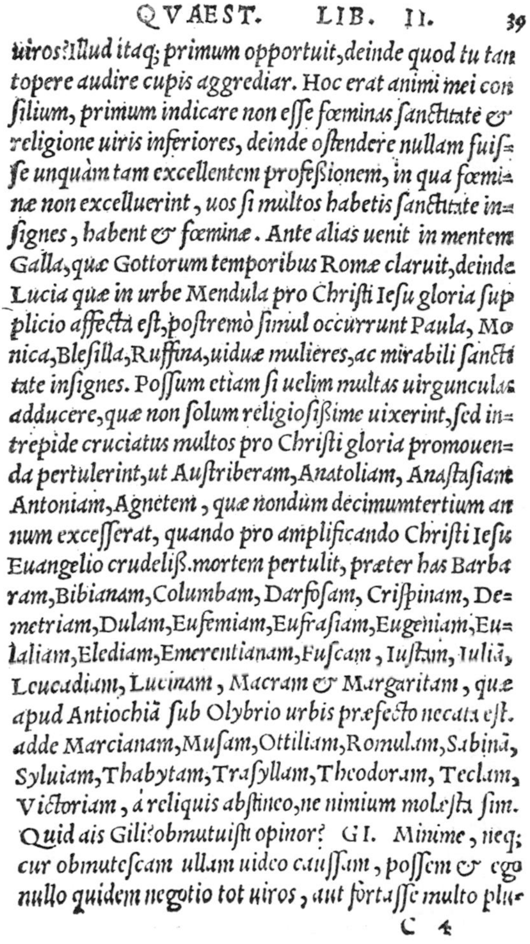

QVAEST. LIB. II. 39

uiros?Illud itaq; primum opportuit,deinde quod tu tan
topere audire cupis aggrediar. Hoc erat animi mei con
silium, primum indicare non esse foeminas sanctitate &
religione uiris inferiores, deinde ostendere nullam suis=
se unquàm tam excellentem professionem, in qua foemi=
næ non excelluerint, uos si multos habetis sanctitate in=
signes, habent & foeminæ. Ante alias uenit in mentem
Galla,quæ Gottorum temporibus Romæ claruit,deinde
Lucia quæ in urbe Mendula pro Christi Iesu gloria sup
plicio affectà est,postremò simul occurrunt Paula, Mo
nica,Blesilla,Ruffina,uiduæ mulieres,ac mirabili sancti
tate insignes. Possum etiam si uelim multas uirgunculas
adducere,quæ non solum religiosissime uixerint,sed in=
trepide cruciatus multos pro Christi gloria promouen=
da pertulerint,ut Austriberam,Anatoliam, Anastasiam
Antoniam,Agnetem , quæ nondùm decimumtertium an
num excesserat, quando pro amplificando Christi Iesu
Euangelio crudeliß.mortem pertulit, præter has Barba
ram,Bibianam,Columbam, Darsosam, Crispinam, De=
metriam,Dulam,Eufemiam,Eufrasiam,Eugeniam,Eu=
laliam,Elediam,Emerentianam,Fuscam , Iustam, Iuliá,
Leucadiam,Lucinam , Macram & Margaritam , quæ
apud Antiochiã sub Olybrio urbis præfecto necata est.
adde Marcianam,Musam,Ottiliam,Romulam,Sabiná,
Syluiam,Thabytam,Trasyllam,Theodoram, Teclam,
Victoriam , à reliquis abstineo,ne nimium molesta sim.
Quid ais Gili?obmutuisti opinor? GI. Minime , neq;
cur obmutescam ullam uideo caussam , possem & ego
nullo quidem negotio tot uiros , aut fortasse multo plu=

C 4

FIG. I. Lando, *Forcianae Quaestiones*, 1535, p. 39,
C4r

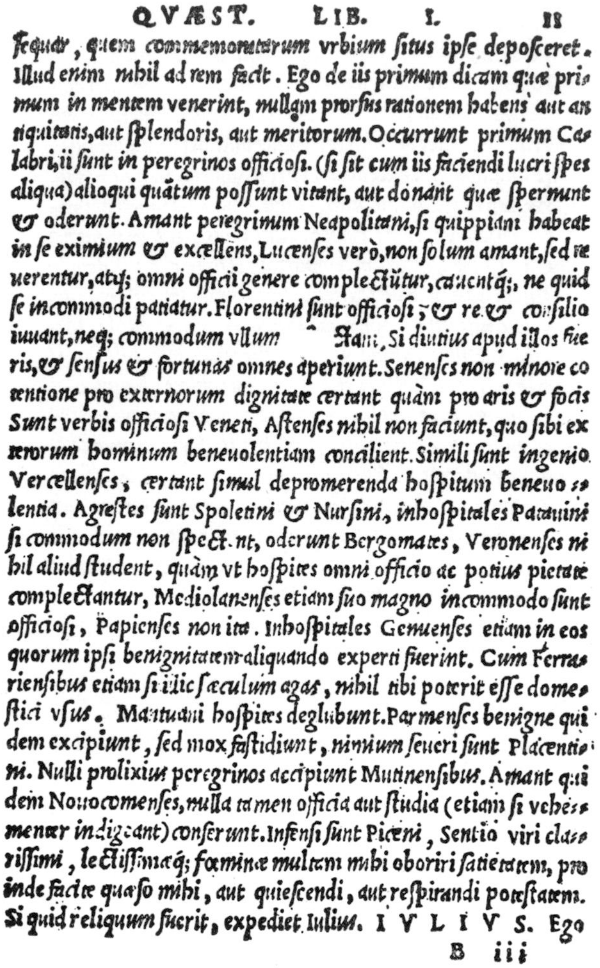

QVÆST. LIB. I. 11

ſequãr, quem commemoratarum vrbium ſitus ipſe depoſceret.
Illud enim nihil ad rem faclt. Ego de iis primum dicam quæ pri
mum in mentem venerint, mullam prorſus rationem habens aut an
tiquitatis,aut ſplendoris, aut meritorum.Occurrunt primum Ca
labri,ii ſunt in peregrinos officioſi. (ſi ſit cum iis faciendi lucri ſpes
aliqua)alioqui quãtum poſſunt vitant, aut donant quæ ſpermunt
ᵺ oderunt.Amant peregrinum Neapolitani,ſi quippiam habeat
in ſe eximium ᵺ excællens,Lucenſes verò,non ſolum amant,ſed ue
uerentur,atᵽ; omni officii genere compleclũtur,cauentᵽ;, ne quid
ſe inconmodi patiatur.Florentini ſunt officioſi ; ᵺ re ᵺ conſilio
iuuant,neᵽ; conmodum vllum ⁀ ſtant, ſi diutius apud illos fue
ris,ᵺ ſenſus ᵺ fortunas omnes aperiunt.Senenſes non minore co
tentione pro externorum dignitate certant quàm pro aris ᵺ focis
Sunt verbis officioſi Veneti, Aſtenſes nihil non faciunt,quo ſibi ex
rerorum hominum beneuolentiam conciliẽt.Simili ſunt ingenio.
Vercellenſes, certant ſimul depromenda hoſpitum beneuo ſe
lentia. Agreſtes ſunt Spoletini ᵺ Nurſini, inhoſpitales Patauini
ſi conmodum non ſpecl.nt, oderunt Bergomates, Veronenſes ni
hil aliud ſtudent, quàm vt hoſpites omni officio ac potius pietate
compleclantur, Mediolanenſes etiam ſuo magno incommodo ſunt
officioſi, Papienſes non ita. Inhoſpitales Genuenſes etiam in eos
quorum ipſi benignitatem aliquando experti fuerint. Cum Ferra
rienſibus etiam ſi idic ſæculum agas, nihil tibi poterit eſſe dome
ſtici vſus. Mantuani hoſpites degluibunt.Parmenſes benigne qui
dem excipiunt, ſed mox faſtidiunt, nimium ſeueri ſunt Placentie
ni. Nulli prolixius peregrinos accipiunt Mutinenſibus.Amant qui
dem Nouocomenſes,nulla tamen officia aut ſtudia (etiam ſi vehes
menter indigeant) conferunt.Inſenſi ſunt Piceni , Sentio viri clas
riſſimi, lectiſſimaᵽ; fœminæ multam mihi oboriri ſatietatem, pro
inde facte quaſo mihi, aut quieſcendi, aut reſpirandi poteſtatem.
Si quid reliquum fuerit, expediet Iulius. I V L I V S. Ego
B iii

FIG. 2. Lando, *Forcianae Quaestiones*, 1536, f. 11r, B3r

mystery in sixteenth-century Neapolitan printing, emerging from nowhere with his two italic founts and obvious typographical skill, and disappearing into oblivion as suddenly as he appeared. While these three considerations did not constitute, either individually or collectively, conclusive proof of the falsity of the Naples imprint, they did seem to be of sufficient weight to justify enquiries into other possible places of origin of the two editions.

To suspect that a book has a false imprint is one thing; to demonstrate that it was printed somewhere else is quite another. In the absence of documentary evidence, which for obvious reasons is rarely available in these cases, one has to work solely on the elements offered by the books themselves. In the case of the two editions of the *Forcianae Quaestiones* the most valuable pieces of evidence seemed likely to be the three woodcut initials, since woodcut alphabets were still at this period individually produced. Identification by type alone, though often necessary in the absence of other information, is a highly technical and often unreliable exercise; in our case, by the mid-1530's italic type was much used in Italy, Switzerland and France, and many founts were virtually identical.

A hint of where it might be fruitful to begin the search came from a collation of the text of the two editions. Among the variants was the following series, involving comments hostile to the Venetians:

1535	1536
Noctu autem [Veneti] dum scortantur, ac potant, Hispanicis palliolis utuntur. *Si non habeant, dant omnem operam ut aliunde, quo iure, quaque iniuria corradant, cogunturque interdum peregrini suos deserere.* Ferrarienses ac Mantuani nihil tam diligenter curant... (p. 16, A8*v*)	Noctu autem dum scortantur, ac potant, Hispanicis palliolis utuntur. Ferrarienses ac Mantuani nihil tam diligenter curant...(f. 7*r*, A7*r*)
Fingunt condonare Veneti, *sed si aliquando nanciscantur ulciscendi locum, nulli crudelius ulciscuntur.* Obliviscuntur iniuriarum Mutinenses, ac Regienses...(p. 20, B2*v*)	Fingunt condonare Veneti, obliviscuntur iniuriarum Mutinenses, ac Regienses...(f. 8*v*, A8*v*)

C. E.I.L.

Sunt Veneti omnium libidinosis-simi, sine delectu amant, sunt etiam in amore nulla constantia... ubi potiti fuerint, statim despici-unt, eandem non saepe adeunt, *si se facilem non praebeat de inferenda vi cogitant.* Cognovi Ferrarienses amoribus deditissimos...(p. 21, B3*r*)

Sunt Veneti omnium libidinosis-simi, sine delectu amant, sunt etiam in amore nulla constantia... ubi potiti fuerint, statim despici-unt, eandem non saepe adeunt. Cognovi Ferrarienses amoribus deditissimos...(f. 9*r*, B1*r*)

Student placere Mediolanenses oppiparis conviviis...coreis Man-tuani, Perusini minis ac blasphemi-is, Veneti illa sua *ridicula* mag-nificentia et *insana* iactantia, Bononienses donis...(p. 24, B4*v*)

Student placere Mediolanenses oppiparis conviviis...coreis Man-tuani, Perusini minis ac blas-phemiis, Veneti illa sua magnifi-centia [et] iactantia, Bononienses donis...(f. 10*r*, B2*r*)

Senenses non minore contentione pro externorum dignitate certant quam pro aris et focis. Sunt verbis *tantum* officiosi Veneti, *re ipsa nihil prorsus.* Astenses nihil non faciunt...(p. 26, B5*v*)

Senenses non minore contentione pro externorum dignitate certant quam pro aris et focis. Sunt verbis officiosi Veneti, Astenses nihil non faciunt...(f. 11*r*, B3*r*)

Even without having established the relationship between the texts of the two editions, these variants suggested that it would be worth while looking for the 1536 woodcuts in Venetian editions, since one obvious explanation of the situation was that passages considered offensive to Venetians or to their govern-ment had been removed from the 1536 edition by a Venetian publisher. Thanks to the invaluable 'Index of Printers and Publishers' at the end of the British Museum's *Italian Short-title Catalogue*, a search that would otherwise have been too laborious to undertake soon ended in success. Among the publications of one of the first printers examined, Melchior Sessa, who printed and published an edition of Lando's *Cicero relegatus et Cicero revocatus* in 1534, the woodcut initial A used in the 1536 *Forcianae Quaestiones* was found in a 1533 edition of Brunetto Latini's *Tesoro* and in a 1539 folio edition of Pietro Aron's *Toscanello in musica* (Fig. 3). There is no doubt that it is the same block: it is characterised by a small crack just above the top of the letter, by another break in the cross-piece of the A, and by a third fracture in the top left-hand border. Also in the 1539 *Toscanello* was the distinctive and ugly Q which appears in the 1536 *Forcianae Quaestiones* (Fig. 4). This evidence leaves little doubt as to the Venetian origin of the 1536 *Forcianae Quaestiones*. The selling or

(a)   (b)   (c)

FIG. 3. Woodcut initial A in: (a) B. Latini, *Tesoro* (Venice, Sessa, 1533), Q5v; (b) Lando, *Forcianae Quaestiones*, 1536, C7v; (c) P. Aron, *Toscanello in musica* (Venice, Sessa, 1539), A4v. [(a) and (c) are reproduced by courtesy of the Trustees of the British Museum]

handing down of blocks and type from one printer to another, or their lending around among printers of the same town, particularly among those linked by business dealings, is far from uncommon. But here, if the 1536 *Forcianae Quaestiones* really is by

(a)   (b)

FIG. 4. Woodcut initial Q in: (a) Lando, *Forcianae Quaestiones*, 1536, A2r; (b) P. Aron, *Toscanello in musica* (Venice, Sessa, 1539), I4v. [(b) is reproduced by courtesy of the Trustees of the British Museum]

Martinus de Ragusia, we would have a case in which a printer lent or sold a couple of blocks to a colleague, who took them off to the other side of Italy, printed a book, and then returned and gave or sold them back to their original owner. Of course, this is not impossible, but, as a distinguished contributor to this volume reminded us some years ago, 'Il possibile è per definizione materia di romanzo, non di storia. Compito dello storico è di sceverare dal possibile il probabile e dimostrarlo tale.'[14] The most probable explanation of the evidence is that the book was printed at Venice. Sessa was head of one of the biggest printing and publishing concerns of the period. His own press was unable to handle the volume of business, and he made considerable use of other printers, such as Giovanni Antonio Nicolini da Sabbio and Bernardino Bindoni. However, both the 1533 Brunetto Latini and the 1539 *Toscanello* were printed as well as published by Sessa. The inference is that the 1536 *Forcianae Quaestiones* was actually printed on his press. This is supported by the evidence of the type used (Fig. 2). Though it is hard to achieve certainty in such matters, there is no doubt that the italic of the 1536 *Forcianae Quaestiones* answers the description of Sessa's italic given by Luigi Balsamo:

...il corsivo usato in edizioni di Marchio Sessa...degli anni 1531–36...è scadente e irregolare nel disegno, ha lettere non ben allineate o caduche ...Vi è usata come iniziale la v; la z corta ha il tratto superiore legger- mente mosso; la x presenta ingrossate le estremità delle aste. Si notano ancora la d e l'a zoppicanti, ed inoltre l'h con l'ansa che si restringe in basso più sensibilmente che nei disegni precedenti. I particolari più caratteristici risultano: le numerose legature (compresi in e un, la doppia l), e soprattutto i gruppi ra e re, frequenti, in cui la vocale rientra sotto il braccio della r.[15]

Thus type and woodcut initials both come from the same source, the printing press of Melchior Sessa.

The happy conclusion of these enquiries into the printing of the 1536 *Forcianae Quaestiones* naturally acted as a spur to tackle the problem of the 1535 edition. If success here was rather longer in coming, the writer has only his own obtuseness to blame, since clues were available both in the account of publication given by Lando in the text and in the true story of the 1536 edition, described above. The observations of friends on the typography and iconography of the 1535 edition[16] suggested that its place of origin was probably to be found outside Italy, and it was in this sense that enquiries were begun. Lando was known to have had links with Lyons in the 1530's, where another 1534 edition of his *Cicero relegatus et Cicero revocatus* had been published, but assuming that it would have been stretching coincidence too far to suppose that the two 'Neapolitan' editions of the *Forcianae Quaestiones* had been printed in towns already associated with the printing of Lando's *Cicero*, work was first directed towards Basle, another important printing centre with which Lando had some connections. The choice of Basle was also partly motivated by the existence of an 'Index of Printers and Publishers' in the British Museum's *German Short-title Catalogue*, without which valuable tool, as has been said, this sort of research is so demanding of time as to be uneconomical. But Basle proved not to be the home of the figured alphabet used in the 1535 *Forcianae Quaestiones*. It became clear that if the research was to continue the task of looking through the Lyons printers had to be faced. In the absence of an 'Index of Printers and Publishers' from the British Museum's *French Short-title Catalogue*, this seemed a mammoth undertaking, until Mr J. Jolliffe, of the Department of Printed Books of the British Museum, kindly made available the relevant parts of his own index to the printers and publishers of the British Museum's collection of early French books. With this invaluable aid, success was soon achieved. The woodcut initials of the 1535 *Forcianae Quaestiones* were found, not in the editions of Lando's friend, Sebastianus Gryphius, the printer and publisher of the 1534 Lyons *Cicero*, but in those of the brothers Melchior and Gaspard Trechsel, of a family of German origin, whose father, Jean, and stepfather, Jean Klein, had been printers in Lyons since 1488. The initials occur in several of the editions printed by the brothers between 1530 and 1539. In particular, they are found numerous times in a handsome Ptolemy printed in 1535 (Fig. 5).[17] This volume also contains most of the other letters of the same woodcut alphabet.

The finding of the woodcut initials of the 1535 *Forcianae Quaestiones* in the books of a Lyons printer obviously puts an end to the existence of Martinus de Ragusia. In the case of the 1535 edition, it hardly even seems within the bounds of possibility that a printer should have borrowed so frequently used a series as Trechsel's figured alphabet of woodcut initials, gone off to Naples to print the 1535 *Forcianae Quaestiones*, and then come back to Lyons to return it to the Trechsels; but even suppose this to be possible, if the existence of Martinus is to be maintained one has then to believe that he hurried off to Venice, borrowed Sessa's blocks and type, and set off again to Naples, to

FIG. 5. Woodcut initials Q, N and A in: (*a*), (*b*), (*c*) Ptolemy, *Geographicae enarrationis libri* (Lyons, Melchior et Gaspard Trechsel, 1535); (*d*), (*e*), (*f*) Lando, *Forcianae Quaestiones* (1535). [(*a*), (*b*) and (*c*) are reproduced by courtesy of the Trustees of the British Museum]

print the 1536 edition! Clearly, Martinus de Ragusia is a fictitious person. Both of the 'Neapolitan' editions of the *Forcianae Quaestiones* have false imprints; the 1535 edition was printed at Lyons, the 1536 at Venice.

Short of a detailed study of italic founts in Lyons, it is not possible to identify with certainty the owner of the italic used in the 1535 edition; the matter is made more delicate by the fact that the founts used in the 1530's by Gryphius and the Trechsels are almost identical. At present, all that can be said is that the type of the 1535 *Forcianae Quaestiones* is closely related to both the Gryphius and the Trechsel italics, but that one of its characteristic features, the go ligature, with the lower part of the g sharply inclined to the right, has not yet been found in either.

The fact that neither of the two earliest editions of the *Forcianae Quaestiones* was printed at Naples has some implications for Lando's tortured and uncertain biography. In the first place, it eliminates a visit to Naples in 1535 which some critics have postulated as necessary in order to account for the two editions. Secondly, it makes it likely that Lando's first association with Lyons lasted longer than the present writer suggested in an earlier contribution.[18] In reconstructing Lando's biography one is often reduced by the dearth of facts to piling hypothesis upon hypothesis. Let us see what new hypotheses can be extracted from our new evidence. While the passage on Antonio de Leyva quoted earlier may refer to the period before the death of Francesco II, it certainly seems more apposite if written after that event, when Antonio, from being Captain General of the *lega italica*, had become the acting head of state. This situation would seem to justify better such phrases as 'postquam Carolus Caesar in eam urbem tetram et monstruosam Bestiam immisit', and the references to 'illa durissima Antoniana tempora' and 'illa Leviana rabies'. If this hypothesis is correct, it places the date of publication after 2 November 1535. One must bear in mind that the Lyons practice of dating 'ab incarnatione' would allow the work to be published up to 24 March 1536 (our style) and still carry the date 1535. We can perhaps connect the probable publication of the 1535 *Forcianae Quaestiones* late in that year or early in 1536 with the letter of Sebastianus Gryphius to Giovanni Angelo Oddone, dated 2 February 1535-6, from which we learn that

Lando had been in Switzerland and possibly Germany from before the middle of November 1535 until some time not long before the letter was written. This would suggest that publication occurred early in 1536 after Lando's return from this trip—that is, of course, if the 'Hortensius' referred to by Gryphius really *is* Ortensio Lando.[19]

The unravelling of part of the mystery of the *Forcianae Quaestiones* presents us with some further problems. Why was a false imprint necessary for the 1535 *Forcianae Quaestiones?* This is not an easy question to answer. After all, Lando's *Cicero relegatus et Cicero revocatus* had been openly published by Gryphius the previous year, and the main subjects discussed in the *Forcianae Quaestiones* (the manners and customs of Italy; the equality or superiority of women to men) were no more controversial than Lando's unorthodox contribution to the debate on Ciceronianism. All in all, the most likely explanation of the false imprint seems to be that it was connected with the air of Evangelism which hangs over Lando's account of the state of religion in Lucca. Even this explanation is not wholly convincing, however, since the most explicitly Evangelical statements occur in the last few pages of the book, in a passage also containing the account of the author's trip to Naples, and there are grounds for believing the whole passage to have been added to the text after the false imprint had been decided upon.[20] If the false imprint of the *Forcianae Quaestiones* was indeed due to the contents of the work, it is more likely to have been insisted upon by the printer than by Lando, a bird of passage in Lyons, satisfied with the anonymity or pseudonymity under which he continued to hide his identity until the very last years of his life. But that Lando was at least an accessory to the decision is shown by his bizarre story of the work's publication. Indeed, one is tempted to believe that whoever took the decision to publish under a false imprint, the choice of Naples was Lando's. The very improbability of Lando's book being published at Naples at that time would have made the choice appeal to his paradoxical sense of humour.

Equally puzzling is the case of the 1536 edition. Why was the false imprint repeated? One possible explanation would be to regard the 1536 edition as a piracy.[21] But the type of piracy involved—reprinting a popular work, and continuing the original imprint to help pass the reprint off as authorised—was not at all common in sixteenth-century Italy. Since no copyright laws existed, a publisher, if he came across a work he thought would sell, simply printed an edition under his own name, careful only to avoid offending the susceptibilities of his own government, or abusing a local *privilegio*. If Sessa, or whoever, really thought the 1535 *Forcianae Quaestiones* had been printed at Naples, it is hard to see why, in publishing an edition in Venice, he did not affix thereto his own imprint (as he had done in 1534 for Lando's *Cicero relegatus*). On the whole, it seems more likely that the publisher of the 1536 *Forcianae Quaestiones* continued the false Naples imprint because he knew or thought it to be false. This knowledge or suspicion could have come to him in more than one way, and on the evidence at present available it is difficult to say where the probabilities lie. It could have been, for example, that a copy or copies of the 1535 edition came to his attention in a consignment of books from outside Italy, and/or that he recognised the style of the Lyons printers, and/or that he knew enough about the state of printing in Naples to realise the un-likelihood of the publication there of a similar book. In these cases, the decision to continue the false imprint would have been solely his, occasioned perhaps by the prudent consideration that if the 1535 edition justified a false imprint, it might be as well to play safe with the 1536. On the other hand, the 1536 publisher could have repeated the false imprint because he had been asked to. Such a request could have come only from one or other of the parties involved in the 1535 edition, either the publisher, that is, or Lando. A possible reason might exist in the desire to bolster up the fiction of the Naples imprint and of the existence of Martinus de Ragusia. Unfortunately, we do not know very much about relations between Venetian and Lyons printers at this time. As for Lando, there are no known links between him and Sessa beyond those created by the 1534 *Cicero* and the 1536 *Forcianae Quaestiones*: later, when Lando made Venice his base for a few years (*c.* 1545–*c.* 1554), he seems to have worked for and used other printers and publishers—Andrea Arrivabene, Bernardino Bindoni, Giolito, Bartolomeo Cesano.

For the moment, then, it seems as if the false imprint in these editions of the *Forcianae Quaestiones* must remain something of a mystery.[22]

140 Conor Fahy

Notes

[1] See *Catalogue of the Christie Collection*, etc. (Manchester 1915). There is no published catalogue of the Bullock Collection.

[2] This list does not claim to be exhaustive. Press marks are given where known.

[3] See n. 2. I am indebted to Professor Paul F. Grendler for supplying me with references to copies in North American libraries.

[4] G. Tiraboschi, *Storia della letteratura italiana* (Milano 1822–6), Tomo VII, p. 1185; C. Poggiali, *Memorie per la storia letteraria di Piacenza* (Piacenza 1789), I, p. 188.

[5] *Novelle di M. Ortensio Lando* (Lucca 1851), p. xxxiii.

[6] *Forcianae Quaestiones*, 1535, pp. 15–16, A8r-v. The passage is repeated in the 1536 edition (f. 7r. A7r).

[7] *Storia di Milano. IX. L'epoca di Carlo V* (1535–1559), (Milano 1961), pp. 3–9.

[8] 'Vix libellum complicaram cum subito nuntiatum est Neapolim excurrendum esse quo cum pervenissem, repperi descriptos fuisse hosce nostros sermones a studioso iuvene, cumque intellexissem urgeri a multis ut excudendos daret, data est a me diligenter opera, ne in lucem venirent; hos cum non possem neque pecunia, neque precario elicere, curavi ut furtim surriperentur. Eos etiam cum iis quos mea manu scripsi mitto. Sed tamen vereor ne (ut est in proverbio) e patella elapsi in prunas decidamus, siquidem Neapoli non est ea impressorum copia quam intelligo Lugduni esse. Vide modo tu, postquam tam iniquo fers animo tuum nomen scriptis commendari, ne quispiam ex impressione referat; ego tua caussa diligenter omni mea opera, cura, gratia et diligentia neque usquam imprimantur curabo' (*Forcianae Quaestiones*, 1535, pp. 57–58, D5r-v).

[9] *Ibid.*, pp. 59–60, D6r-v.

[10] Lando's *Paradossi* (1543) and *Commentario delle cose d'Italia* (1548) terminate with letters from Paulo Mascranico and Niccolò Morra respectively, both clearly written by the author. The *Catalogo delli inventori delle cose*, also by Lando, and published in the same volume as the *Commentario*, ends with a *Brieve apologia di M. Ortensio Lando per l'autore del presente catalogo*, which fulfils the same function as these letters.

[11] Von Widmanstetter's testimony is discussed in my article 'Per la vita di Ortensio Lando', *Giornale storico della letteratura italiana*, 142 (1965), pp. 243–58. Recently, Professor Paul F. Grendler (*Critics of the Italian World (1530–1560): Anton Francesco Doni, Nicolò Franco and Ortensio Lando*, Madison, Milwaukee–London, 1969, pp. 24–25) has drawn attention to a letter by Lando to the Swiss reformer Joachim von Watt (Vadianus), which calls in question the accuracy of the date 1530 for Lando's residence in the monastery of S. Giovanni a Carbonara, since it appears to have been written in 1529, and describes its writer as having taken refuge in Switzerland for religious reasons 'una cum uxorcula' (*Die Vadianische Briefsammlung der Stadtbibliothek St. Gallen, hgn. von Emil Arbenz*, iv, St Gallen, 1902 (Mitteilungen zur Vaterländischen Geschichte, hgn. vom Historischen Verein in St. Gallen), pp. 188–189). Further investigation is required to see if this apparent chronological clash can be resolved.

[12] The illustrations have been reproduced as closely to actual size as possible.

[13] For the Mayr and Sultzbach italics, see L. Balsamo–A. Tinto, *Origini del corsivo nella tipografia italiana del Cinquecento* (Milano 1967), pp. 119–120, 149. The Sultzbach italic is an early example of those inspired by the designs of Ludovico degli Arrighi, and is rather widely spaced (20 lines = 107 mm). The Mayr italic, also used by Marcello Silber at Rome, is closer in size (20 lines = 85 mm) and style to the *Forcianae Quaestiones* founts, particularly to that of the 1535 edition, but has a characteristic tail on the bar of the e, absent from the latter.

[14] C. Dionisotti, 'Appunti su antichi testi', *Italia medioevale e umanistica*, 7 (1964), p. 95.

[15] Balsamo–Tinto, *op. cit.*, p. 111. The measurement of twenty lines given by Balsamo (81 mm) is slightly larger than that of the 1536 *Forcianae Quaestiones* (79 mm). However, as Balsamo rightly remarks (*op. cit.*, p. 41, n. 31), the varying atmospheric conditions endured, in their hundreds of years of life, by the books on whose paper such measurements are carried out justifies us in ignoring small discrepancies of this sort.

[16] The writer is greatly indebted to Dennis E. Rhodes and to the late Roberto Weiss for their help in this matter.

[17] For the Trechsels and Jean Klein, see H. Baudrier, *Bibliographie lyonnaise* série XII (Lyon–Paris 1921), pp. 230–306. Other Trechsel volumes in the British Museum containing the woodcut initials in question are J. Rainerius, *Oratio*, 1532 (N: A2r), S. Champier, *Campus Elysius Galliae*, 1533 (Q: H2r), and *Periarchon*, 1533 (A: Aa3r), C. Hegendorff, *Dialecticae legalis libri*, 1534 (Q: I7r), Xenophon, *De Cyri minoris expeditione*, 1536 (A: A2r; Q: D1v, F1r, H1v, O8r), S. Champier, *De monarchia ac triplici imperio*, 1537 (A: A3r), *Les simulachres et historiees faces de la mort*, 1538 (Q: H1r). In the 1535 Ptolemy, the N appears four times, the Q thirteen times, and the A twenty-five times.

[18] 'Per la vita di Ortensio Lando', *cit.*, pp. 251–255.

[19] For the text of the letter see Baudrier, *op. cit.*, série VIII (Lyon–Paris 1910), pp. 32–33; Grendler, *op. cit.*, p. 27, n. 25. The possibility that the style of dating used in this letter might be 'ab incarnatione' was overlooked by the present writer in his discussion of Lando's Lyons visit in the contribution cited in n. 11.

[20] This statement is based on the presence in the volume of two conflicting references to the composition of the work. The first of these occurs at the conclusion of the discussions reported in Book II, which, like those of the first book, had taken place at Forci. Addressing the dedicatee of the work, Lando writes: 'Dum haec ad te scribebam, torquebar inclementius,'—a reference to an attack of fever which he suffered at Forci after the discussions —'alioqui fuissem fortasse paulo diligentior... Perscripsimus autem istaec, ut tu quoque gaudium hoc nostrum gauderes, atque me tui amantissimum, qui nullum locum praetermitto tui exhilarandi, intelligeres...' (*Forcianae Quaestiones*, 1535, p. 53, D3r). The text then goes on to recount how Lando and some others went back to Lucca and then, after receiving hospitality and discussing religion, made their way to Milan, via Florence and Bologna. It is at this point that the second reference occurs: 'Ego vero, cum primum

in urbem' (i.e. Milan) 'veni, atque domi meae omnia ut vellem esse cognovi, coepi literis quantum memoria suppeteret Forciana gesta consignare' (*ibid.*, p. 57, D5r). We then have Lando's account of his visit to Naples and the events surrounding publication (see n. 8). The discrepancy between the two references suggests that Lando first intended to bring the work to an end shortly after the conclusion of the account of the Forci discussions, where the first reference occurs, but later added all that comes after that point.

[21] That the text of the 1536 edition depends on that of the 1535 edition can readily be shown. In the latter, Antiochus Lovintus' letter to Francesco Turchi begins thus: 'Audio Francisce te mihi graviter succensere atque infortunium minari, propterea quod Forcianas *quaestio* tuo nomini dedicatas excudendas dederim' (p. 59, D6r). The reading 'quaestio', for 'quaestiones', occurs at the end of a line, and is clearly a compositorial error. This error is repeated in the middle of a line in the 1536 edition (f. 23*v*, C7*v*).

[22] While correcting the proofs of this article I have been informed by Mrs Natalie Z. Davis, of the University of Toronto, that she has discovered a link, in the nature of a large loan, between the Trechsel brothers and the Protestant Étienne de La Forge. The loan, paid by La Forge to Melchior in 1533, was still unredeemed in 1542. Whether the loan was a simple business transaction, or concealed an interest in Protestant literature on the part of the Trechsels, the burning at the stake of La Forge in 1535, as a result of the 'Affaire des Placards', is likely to have made the Trechsels wary for a while of open links with writers of unorthodox opinions—all of which may have some relevance to the false imprint of the 1535 *Forcianae Quaestiones.* Mrs Davis will be giving full details of her discovery in her forthcoming book on Protestant printers in Lyons, *Strikes and Salvation.*

Peter Armour

*Galileo and the crisis in Italian
literature of the early Seicento*

Galileo is one of those men whose life, works and personality have presented so many different facets to people of different ages that it is almost legitimate to talk of the accumulation of a myth, universally meaningful through time and capable of constant examination and reinterpretation. Even in his own age he was both idolised and victimised, and it has always been possible to approach the subject of this remarkable man from a variety of points of view, to reinterpret both the man and the dramatic role which he played in a conflict itself capable of reinterpretation apparently *ad infinitum*. From the vast amount of evidence available in the twenty volumes of the Edizione Nazionale,[1] Galileo has been studied under the aspects of astronomer and Copernican propagandist, victim of the Holy Office, unflagging observer of nature's laws, founder of that mixture of hypothesis and experimentation known as the scientific method, precursor of Newton. He has also been accused of betraying science and his conscience by his abjuration, of tactlessly closing the door upon the development of science in Italy, of beginning the dissolution of the Pythagorean and medieval unity of science and religion, a unity from which Kepler took his cue, and which Bruno and Campanella both tried to reformulate in Galileo's own time. Recently, and perhaps significantly, increasing prominence has been given to an aspect of Galileo once considered marginal—his consciousness of literature, his literary tastes and his own prose style, and his respect for the expression and the logic of the word. That the master of science was also a master of Italian prose has been a commonplace since the times of Parini and Leopardi,[2] but now Galileo, the man or the myth—it no longer matters which—can be made to show us a unique blend of science and the humanities. Since the fundamental study by Vaccalluzzo,[3] Galileo's function as a literary critic, friend and adviser of poets, and master of prose has been integrated more and more fully into the picture of the great man who did so much in fields now considered the antithesis of imaginative literature. The particular usefulness of this approach to Galileo lies in the fact that Galileo's influence on literary criticism and on scientific writing in general was very small[4] and thus one can more easily concentrate upon the man himself, on his cultural education and environment, on his personality and mental processes, and on the troubled and critical age in which, through these qualities in Galileo and others, science took a definitive turning in its history.

That the early seventeenth century was a troubled and critical age is the thesis of two fine essays: a study by G. Getto of the history of criticism of the Baroque age and of its twentieth-century re-evaluation, and a perceptive account by C. Calcaterra of the contradictory elements inherent both in the word 'baroque' and in the age to which the adjective has been assigned.[5] Both see Baroque as a religion and a philosophy in crisis, although neither gives full prominence to the fact that this definition applies specifically to the Catholic Church and the Aristotelian philosophy in crisis, so that their analysis of the age in general is less valid for countries other than Italy and possibly Spain. The restlessness which they detect in the Baroque age in Italy is that of man uncertain of the stability of reality and striving for possession of the world and of God again. Hence, the return to medieval certainties of the post-Tridentine Church and of the neo-Scholastics and other Peripatetics is as much a part of this definition of Baroque as the search of the Marinist poets for new and unconventional styles, the visions of Bruno and Campanella, and the rational approach of Galileo and his followers which, by way of Descartes in particular, led to a resolution of the crisis in the rationalism of the Enlightenment. Calcaterra discusses the ambiguity contained in the word 'baroque', which can be applied both to those tied to the specious arguments of the old syllogism *in baroco* and to those who attempted to replace the old schemes with a new view of God and man, with a sense of reality as marvellous but deceptive and specious, and with a wilful rejection of the old precepts and conventions which led to the association with the word 'baroque' of the ideas of flamboyance and eccentricity, virtuosity and even delirium. This highlighting of the two chief contradictory trends of the age leads to the paradoxical interchangeability of the words 'baroque' and 'anti-baroque', so that they must be considered not as opposites but as poles between which many minds oscillated. A study of Galileo's literary interests in the years 1590–1610 illustrates not only the emergence of these two poles and the oscillation even of Galileo between them, but also the originality of Galileo's approach to the solution of the crisis. Galileo fought all his life against the arguments *in baroco* of the Peripatetics, but his implied principles of literary

criticism are Aristotelian in origin,[6] and he himself later claimed
to be a more faithful follower of Aristotle than the Peripatetics
themselves (letter to Liceti, 25 August 1640; XVIII, 234). He
used language and words with an exuberance and originality of
thought, style, and metaphor worthy of a more sober Marino,
and yet he openly expressed his dislike of mannered conceits, and
in this respect the years 1590–1610 are important in that both
Calcaterra and Panofsky[7] detect a reaction against Mannerism
during this period and see this as an important prelude to the
Baroque. Galileo's taste for the classics, the Tuscans, and Ariosto
has caused some people to see him as a man who reacted against
the Seicento in favour of an older Renaissance world,[8] and yet
Galileo himself received a classical education very different from
that of the men of the Renaissance, and his own works and
prose-style have no true antecedents in the age of Ariosto and
Machiavelli.[9] It seems, therefore, that the two 'poles' of the
Seicento—rigid preceptism and extravagant innovation—are
both equally absent from Galileo, and in fact, because unlike
many of his contemporaries he believed in the stability and comprehensibility of reality and in the oneness of truth, of both
science and faith, he offers a singularly balanced middle way
between the two extremes. His is the third way, the way of
rationalism and of sanity, the way of the future, leading to the
Enlightenment. Arguments concerning his 'gusto primo-rinascimentale' and 'antisecentismo',[10] or his 'secentismo' and Baroque
taste, seem to neglect the fact that Galileo's originality lies in the
way he succeeded in showing something of both, because he
lived through this period of crisis, was influenced by both trends,
and succeeded in finding a sane and rational solution between
them. An examination of Galileo's literary interests throughout
his life but especially up to 1610 not only casts a valuable light
upon this crisis in Italian literature and upon the contradictory
elements at work but is also a necessary path towards defining
Galileo's own solution to the crisis and the genesis of the forms
and style of his own prose works of 1610 and after.

Galileo's education began with the usual Latin and Greek.
According to Viviani (XIX, 601), he first devoted himself to
proficiency in Latin literature because of the poverty of his family,
and, as a member of the merchant class and son of a well-known
musician and musical theorist, he may well have considered

following the career of letters. With his exceptional memory, say his son and Viviani (XIX, 596, 627), he soon had by heart much of Virgil, Ovid, Horace, and Seneca. All three of his earliest biographers (Vincenzio Galilei, Viviani, and Gherardini) testify to his memorisation of much of the *Orlando Furioso*; Viviani says that he knew 'almost the whole of Petrarch, all the poems of Berni, and little short of the whole poem of Lodovico Ariosto', and Gherardini records his ability to recite and adapt to his own purpose passages from Berni and Ariosto and also reports his familiarity with and liking for Ruzzante (XIX, 596, 627, 644–5). To this list we can, of course, add Galileo's knowledge of Dante. According to the same sources, his conversation was greatly enriched and enlivened by his deep knowledge of these authors. Fragments of translations from Greek and Latin have come down to us (IX, 283–90), and as late as 1604 Galileo was still interested enough in literature to embark upon a translation of the 'Homeric' *Batracomiomachia* into Italian (XX, 585). Favaro's reconstruction of Galileo's library[11] gives further evidence of his interest in the humanities: besides the works of music, philosophy, medicine, and astronomy, which one would expect, we find a very wide range of Latin and Italian classics and a large number of contemporary poems, fables, dramas, and romances, including Franciosini's translation of *Don Quixote*, about which, however, we have unfortunately no record of the reactions of the admirer of Ariosto.

Galileo himself turned his hand to literary composition, and Favaro includes in the Edizione Nazionale six sonnets, the *Capitolo contro il portar la toga*, and two drafts of a comedy. Favaro ascribes five of the sonnets to Galileo's youth, but the last one, a riddle, to the very end of his life (IX, 26). Together with the *capitolo*, these works confirm Galileo's acquaintance with Petrarch, Petrarchism, and Berni. Of the comedy, the second draft is considerably more complex than the first, and since it appears to be set in Padua, it may well have been drawn up after 1592 (IX, 21). The complicated system of love affairs, the contrived *inganno*, the transvestite hero, and the general salacity all claim relationship with Cinquecento comedy of the later variety, in which the intrigues of Ariosto and Machiavelli have become a rather bewildering mass of *peripezie* and the amusing amorality of the former a hectic and ultimately monotonous hedonism.

Before leaving Tuscany, and probably in about 1588, Galileo had entered the field of literary controversy with two lectures read to the Accademia Fiorentina *Circa la figura, sito e grandezza dell'Inferno di Dante* (IX, 31–57). In these he supports the dimensions of Dante's Hell as calculated by the Florentine Manetti and denied by Vellutello. It is said that Galileo delivered these lectures in a bid to secure a chair of mathematics at Pisa, and this theory would certainly account for their mathematical rather than critical emphasis.[12] However, they could also indicate that Galileo was still in the position of a dilettante, with general interests in literature and the arts as well as in mathematics. This quality never completely left him, even after his commitment to mathematics on his appointment to Pisa in 1589 and to Padua in 1592. Presumably at about the same time as he gave the lectures on Dante, Galileo became a member of the Accademia Fiorentina, and undoubtedly throughout his life he preserved that strong sense of *fiorentinità* which was later to ally him rather with the Accademia della Crusca than with the linguistic experimenters of Padua and Venice. Galileo's association with various academies is evidence of his participation in the general cultural trends of the time. In 1599, he became a founder member of the Accademia dei Ricovrati in Padua, and three years later he was one of its *censori sopra le stampe* (XIX, 207–208). In 1605, he was inscribed in the Accademia della Crusca (XIX, 221), and of course in 1611 he was given membership of the newly formed and rather exclusive Accademia dei Lincei (XIX, 265), which, although devoted primarily to philosophy and mathematics, instructed its members not to neglect 'the ornaments of elegant literature and philology, which, like graceful garments, adorn the whole body of science'.[13] Finally, in 1622, Galileo took office as Consul of the Accademia Fiorentina, choosing as his counsellors Mario Guiducci and Tommaso Rinuccini. According to Salvini, when Galileo handed over the consulate in the following year, Michelangelo Buonarroti made a speech and presented Galileo with the traditional silver cup on which was engraved a representation of the Arno, symbolising 'il pregio della fiorentina eloquenza' (XIX, 444–445).

Galileo's reputation in literary matters is not, however, confined to his membership of various academies. It is clearly an aspect of his personality of which his contemporaries were aware but of which only scattered evidence survives for us. We do, however, possess certain annotations made by Galileo to Ariosto, Petrarch, and Tasso. These are usually dated from about the same period as the lectures on Dante, namely 1588–90. None of them can be considered typical of the literary controversies of the time, since they avoid any formulation of aesthetic theory or polemic on the basis of abstract theory and citation of authorities. They are all annotations or marginal notes, evidence of a habit to which Galileo was always addicted. Indeed, from the annotations to Ariosto (IX, 151–194) and to Petrarch,[14] it is hard to draw any other conclusion than that Galileo was registering his own ideas on a careful reading of the works, although a touch of what we might call sixteenth-century pedantry emerges from the fact that he suggests corrections even to Ariosto.

The annotations to Tasso, however, (IX, 61–148) have a more complicated history and cast considerable light on the involvement of Galileo in the literary crisis of the period 1590–1610. Although these also are generally dated from about 1590, there is no certainty about the origin of the *Considerazioni al Tasso* as they have come down to us. Viviani mentions a commentary by Galileo on the parallel passages of Ariosto and Tasso, dates this from Galileo's time in Pisa, and believes that Galileo gave it to Jacopo Mazzoni and was, to his regret, unable to regain it (XIX, 627). Even if most of the *Considerazioni* which we possess date from the same period, it seems possible that some date from after Tasso's death in 1595.[15] We also know that for many months and even for some years, Galileo made notes comparing Ariosto and Tasso on blank pages inserted into a copy of the *Gerusalemme* and that he lost this copy some time around 1620 or later (XVIII, 120, 192). In short, the only likely *terminus ad quem* for the composition of the *Considerazioni* is 1609, when Cigoli asked for Galileo's notes to the first stanza on behalf of Jacopo Giraldi (X, 244).[16] Galileo could thus conceivably have been working spasmodically on a commentary upon Tasso for as much as twenty years, from his time at Pisa (Viviani) to his last years in Padua. It would seem safest to assume that the *Considerazioni* which we possess derive substantially from the annotations in the interleaved copy of the *Gerusalemme*. The manuscript (a copy with some pages missing) was seen by Serassi about 1780 but was not published until 1793. The editor of this edition claims that Serassi had not published the manuscript because he was jealous of Tasso's honour and that the missing pages had been removed by a Tassist zealot; however, even he takes the precaution of including in the edition a discourse by G. Iseo in favour of Tasso.[17] C. Ricci, who believes that the *Considerazioni* were transcribed from the interleaved book, surmises that Galileo himself kept this work of his youth from circulation because growing esteem for Tasso made his own virulence out of place, and that after he had lost the book it fell into the hands of a Tasso enthusiast who made a copy and then destroyed the original.[18]

Whatever the origin of the *Considerazioni* as we know them, three facts are certain: that Galileo was interested in the controversy over the comparative excellence of Ariosto and Tasso; that he made fuller and more elaborate notes on Tasso, and over a longer period of time, than he did for Ariosto and Petrarch; and that his friends and others knew of these notes as possibly even destined for publication. Both Viviani and Gherardini testify that Galileo refused to compromise on the question of Ariosto's immense superiority to Tasso (XIX, 627, 645), but the length and detail of the *Considerazioni* and the device of interposing blank pages for notes indicate that Galileo took his critique of Tasso fairly seriously and was eager to be as methodical as possible. He may even have intended to draw on them later to compose a continuous commentary, as he was afterwards to write up *Il Saggiatore* from marginal notes made to Grassi's *Libra*. Indeed, the similarities between the *Considerazioni* and *Il Saggiatore* are interesting in this respect. Spongano's definition of the latter as 'una continua disamina di fallacie e di errori di logica'[19] could certainly be applied in part to the former, and Galileo applies to Grassi's style some of the adjectives (*spezzate, intarsiate, riportate in iscorcio*; VI, 261) which he had used of Tasso (IX, 63, 129–130). In *Il Saggiatore*, Galileo also mentions or quotes Ariosto more frequently than in any other of his works (VI, 232, 270, 310, 317, 330, 338). However, whilst the notes to Grassi were extended and published as a continuous critique, those to Tasso remain for the most part fragmentary and certainly linguistically crude, and it seems unlikely that Galileo ever seriously considered revising and collating them for publication. Nevertheless, his friends knew of their existence and indeed showed some interest in and respect for Galileo's views. Cigoli, as we have seen, wrote to Galileo in 1609 asking for his notes to stanza one for Jacopo Giraldi, a member, like Galileo, of both the Accademia Fiorentina and the Accademia della Crusca (X, 244). In 1614, Gualdo, reporting the news from Padua, told Galileo that Paolo Beni, the great theorist and champion of Tasso, was in a hurry to print his commentary on the first ten *canti* of the *Gerusalemme*, because he was afraid lest Galileo should publish his own commentary first (XII, 81–82), and this, as we shall see, occurred during the most critical period of Beni's polemic with the Crusca. If Galileo ever intended to complete his work on Tasso, he had obviously shelved the project by this time, and his interests were turned to the repercussions of his astronomical discoveries. Eventually he mislaid his annotations, but knowledge of them lived on in Venice, and between the years 1637–9 Francesco Rinuccini, the Tuscan Resident there, made several requests to Galileo for his notes on Ariosto and Tasso (XVII, 242, 260–261; XVIII, 116, 122–123). In his replies, Galileo confessed that he had lost his annotated copy some twelve or fifteen years previously, but he presents Rinuccini with a few of his ideas on a comparison of the two poets and reasserts his belief in the superiority of Ariosto (XVIII, 120–121, 192–193). Although Galileo's views remained basically the same up to these last years of his life, the strength of his antipathy to Tasso and his earlier interest in the controversy have gone and it is not difficult to guess the reasons.

The *Considerazioni al Tasso* have often been used to prove that Galileo was at heart a man of the High Renaissance, with no stomach for the literary tastes of the Seicento.[20] Such a view, however, ignores the whole state of Italian letters in the years 1590–1610 in which the *Considerazioni* were composed. It is in this period that we find the initial conflict of ideas and styles, and an indication of the way in which Galileo was to resolve the conflict in his own prose works.

In the first place, we must remember that Galileo's contribution to the controversy over Ariosto and Tasso differs from the general pattern in that he makes no use of abstract theory in his arguments and that the chief criterion of his judgment on Tasso is a personal one—his worship of Ariosto. Part of his study of Tasso involved him in comparing parallel scenes and episodes from Ariosto, and he openly admits to preferring Ariosto in the majority of cases and accuses Tasso of being ill-advised to invite such comparisons. Even when he praises Tasso, it may be because of qualities akin to those of the 'divinity of Ariosto' (IX, 136). Thus, the fact that the *Considerazioni* invoke no theory derives largely from the fact that they are a justification of a personal taste. Having said this, however, we can nevertheless define three basic qualities which Galileo found in abundance in Ariosto and largely lacking in Tasso: attention to the *verosimile*, realistic *osservazione del costume*, and clarity of style. Thus we can reconstruct Galileo's implicit theoretical assumptions: he believes that narrative poetry should enrich but not openly transgress the laws of verisimilitude; he asks that the characters should have an objective psychological coherence and appreciates heroism and nobility in love and in ideals; and he reacts against verbal affectations and contortions which mark the degeneration of Renaissance limpidity into Mannerism, obscurity, and linguistic impurity. Of these assumptions, the first two associate Galileo with the Aristotelian poetics of the Cinquecento, and the third connects him with the linguistic standardisation undertaken by the Accademia della Crusca on the basis of Tuscan models of the past. So, although Galileo in attacking Tasso invokes neither Aristotelian precepts nor the rules of the Crusca for winnowing, milling, and baking the Tuscan of the past, he has nevertheless been accused of being in this respect a traditionalist, to be ranked alongside the Aristotelian critics and the Crusca in the refusal to accept Tasso's revolutionary brand of poetry.

Two basic misunderstandings have here succeeded in clouding the issue. The first is the assumption that the revolution initiated by Tasso was the introduction of the poetry of the subjective into the description of love and of knightly ideals. However, this surely is a discovery of a later age; in the period 1590–1610, Tasso's innovations were not seen as 'romantic' in this sense but as a strange and solemn mixture of classical rhetoric and vernacular mannerism. That Galileo is impervious to Tasso's subjectivism is not merely true, it is patently obvious. Galileo refused to accept Tasso's introspection and disturbed relationship with reality (Geymonat and Brunetti); he rejected the subtly sick and complex element in Tasso's art (Jannaco); he and Tasso were simply incompatible (Chiari).[21] All this is true, but it is in a sense beside the point, because Galileo was far from being alone in this. This incomprehension of the 'romantic' Tasso was not merely typical of Florentines such as Galileo, but of many others including Tasso's own early champions. Thus, although the failure to detect Tasso's subjectivism may underlie much of the polemic of the years 1590–1610, the crisis in itself concerns not Tasso's interior torment but his means of expression in general, and his language and style in particular.

The second misunderstanding is that Galileo's implacable rejection of Tasso is a rejection also of *secentismo*. This view, however, begs two questions: that Tasso was the sole begetter of Seicento literature, and that aversion to Tasso was untypical of the Seicento. Neither of these is true, least of all in the period 1590–1610 when *secentismo* itself was still in the process of being defined. Tasso's major contribution to *secentismo* was the introduction of a rhetoric of *concettismo*, of word-transposition, and of musical rhythm, the liberation of the epic from rigid peripatetic rules, the dissolution of the sense of absolute objectivity and stability in the world and in man. Neurotic, in many ways contradictory, and fodder for both peripatetics and antiperipatetics alike, he was in many ways the original *anima in baroco*. In these twenty years of crisis, this prelude to the Baroque, there was a widespread reaction against Tasso's actual epic from many quarters, and yet his stylistic influence was working, at times openly, at times secretly, to emerge somewhat changed and adapted to the needs of the Baroque age. Tasso's influence on *secentismo* is thus twofold: his epic precipitated a conflict between Renaissance and Mannerist ideals and between Tuscan and non-Tuscan standards, a conflict from which the Baroque was born; and his stylistic innovations, either as direct influences or because they anticipated the aesthetic demands of the Seicento, worked through this period to survive in fields very distant from the serious, classicising epic. Thus it is that major writers of the Seicento, such as Galileo, Tassoni, and Boccalini, could show aversion to, or doubts concerning, Tasso's epic whilst still belonging to a trend in which Tasso's stylistic influence can be traced.

There is, however, a way in which *secentismo* rejects Tasso, and that is in rejecting the *genre* which he himself chose for his major work. Although there were many attempts to write serious epics in the Seicento, the *genres* in which the spirit of *secentismo* is most evident show little open acknowledgment of Tasso. Indeed, the Baroque age opened with the controversy over Tasso and Ariosto, and only extremists such as Beni resolved it unequivocally in Tasso's favour; for the most part, the early Baroque age acknowledged either the superiority of Ariosto or an approximate equality of these two very different epic poets. Thus, if Baroque literature assimilates Tasso, it also looks back to Ariosto. The negative aspects of Seicento literature are the moralising poems of a Cesarini or epics such as Margherita Sarrocchi's *Scanderbeide* on the fifteenth-century Albanian hero, Scander-beg, enemy of the Turks. *Secentismo*, defined in its positive sense, is surely bound up with the schools of Marino and of Tassoni, with the world of the senses encoded in the cipher of *concetti* and with the emergence of the heroicomic epic. Neither of these will take us back to the *Gerusalemme Liberata*, except in the general ways described above. Indeed, both, reacting in different ways against the solemn epic and epic solemnity, have their roots in an earlier age, in the sensuality, the spirit of discovery, the pastoral ideal, and the satirical approach to heroism of the late Quattrocento and early Cinquecento. The *Gerusalemme* sought to change these elements radically, or even deny them; the Baroque age, ushered in with a controversy over Ariosto and Tasso, includes as an integral part a reappraisal of humanistic classicism and its liberation from certain conventions and precepts which had been imposed upon it. Thus only in a sense is Tasso the father of *secentismo*; his greatest immediate heir is not Marino but Milton. So we return to those crucial years 1590–1610, when the stylistic controversy precipitated by the *Gerusalemme* was still to be resolved, and when, to return to our earlier paradox, the phrase *in baroco* can be applied both to the sophistries of the Peripatetics and preceptists and to the restless search for a solution outside the rules laid down.

In this period, a very typical feature is precisely a reaction against Mannerism and a reappraisal of Renaissance classicism. D. Della Terza has recently pointed out that Tasso himself belonged to the reaction against the *Gerusalemme Liberata* when he agreed to rewrite it as the *Conquistata*, and it is true that in some ways Tasso's own corrections attempt to deal with some of the points criticised independently by Galileo.[22] In this respect, both Tasso and Galileo show the influence of the aesthetic preceptists and the Tuscan purists, but Tasso's solution, to achieve the unities by amplification, is an attempt to regress to earlier principles which Galileo, in his antiperipatetic role, would

certainly have condemned. The solution Tasso proposed in the
Conquistata is vastly different from the solution Galileo himself
was later to find between Cinquecento and Seicento. However,
Tasso's enforced withdrawal from his own innovations was a
prelude to a fairly general artistic reaction against Mannerism in
favour of a return to Renaissance classicism. Calcaterra defines
this as a reaction against the *anima in baroco* which continues
through the Seicento and most of the Settecento, and which in
itself is to be integrated into any positive definition of the word
'baroque'.[23] It is, however, the art critic Panofsky who argues
most convincingly for the return to High Renaissance ideals of
artists of the period 1590–1615.[24] The Carracci brothers and
Domenichino in Rome and Cigoli in Florence were all part of
this trend. Indeed, Panofsky quotes the story that, during an
argument about the comparative merits of Ariosto and Tasso,
Annibale Carracci replied that he believed Raphael to be the
greatest of all painters. Seen against this background, some of
Galileo's celebrated remarks about Tasso appear not antiquated
but very much part of the trend: whilst Tasso's poem is uneven
marquetry (*tarsia*), Ariosto's is a harmonious oil-painting showing
mastery of *sfumatura* (IX, 63); whilst Tasso's poem is like an
eccentric's study with curiosities such as a petrified crab, a dried
chameleon, insects in amber, clay figurines, and a few sketches
by Bandinelli or Parmigianino, Ariosto's is a rich gallery of rare
and excellent ancient sculptures, paintings, and *objets d'art* (IX,
69); whilst Ariosto is clear and natural, Tasso forces his allegory
into the literary equivalent of the anamorphosis (IX, 129–130), of
which Panofsky gives a superb example from Holbein's *Am-
bassadors* and an apposite quotation from Shakespeare:

> Like perspectives, which rightly gaz'd upon
> Show nothing but confusion; ey'd awry
> Distinguish form . . .
>   (*Richard II*, II, ii)

In this way, eyeing not awry but through Galileo's own literary
criticism, some form begins to emerge concerning this period of
crisis between Mannerism and Baroque. Galileo is not, in Chiari's
words, 'antisecentista e antiperipatetico in letteratura come nella
scienza'[25] but is at this stage reacting against Mannerism on the
basis of a spontaneous and non-dogmatic acceptance of Aristo-

telian aesthetic criteria. Galileo himself reflects the general crisis, and his criticism of Tasso shows his own solution. One point, however, remains to be observed: that Galileo's adherence to the movement of reappraisal of Renaissance classicism in the years 1590–1610 may have bequeathed to him a prejudice of considerable interest to the historian of science. Panofsky, referring to the emphatic rejection of the ellipse by High Renaissance artists and to the reduction of heavenly and bodily movements to the circle in Renaissance science, suggests that in this period Galileo too became subject to the obsession with circularity, Koyré's *hantise de la circularité*, and it may be that Galileo's antipathy to Mannerism, which used the ellipse in art and obliquity in literature, made him incapable both of penetrating Kepler's 'peripatetic and enigmatic' style (the words are Sagredo's—XI, 398) and of accepting Kepler's discovery of the elliptical orbits of the planets.[26]

Galileo's solution to this crisis between Mannerism and the return to the Renaissance is original: despite his use of peripatetic principles, he invokes no precepts; despite his association with Tuscanising academies, he lays down no linguistic rules; despite his love for Ariosto, he notes Tasso's occasional good points. In short, Galileo's reactions as recorded in his notes are those of a man inspired by a love of sane literature.[27] As in his reactions to the other crises of his day, he is a follower of Aristotle but not a Peripatetic, an imaginative writer but not a flamboyant rhetorician. His way is, as we have already seen, the way of sanity and reason, the way of the future. He accuses Tasso of longwindedness and pedantry; he notes Tasso's grammatical errors and *parole stravolte* and his use of empty words like *grande* and *cose*; he accuses him of stylistic affectation, of hiding his poverty of imagery under *scherzetti* and 'arzigogoli simili a quelli del *Sator Arepo*' (IX, 74); he notes particularly the logical errors, the orotund orations put in the mouths of ignorant persons (IX, 83, 90, 93, 120), the placing of an enormous garden in the middle of a palace (IX, 138), and even the inability of the wind to disperse echoes, dreams, and shadows (IX, 132–133); and he dismisses Tasso's characters, especially the insipid love of Tancredi (IX, 69-70, 111–112) and the lack of character of the soldiers (IX, 100, 102). It was said that he called the Christian hero 'Goffo freddo'.[28] These are censures which, within limitations perhaps, the unprepared reader of Tasso might move against him even today after the Romantics have

discovered something else in the *Gerusalemme* and when poetry
has acquired a long tradition of subjectivism, illogicality, and lack
of verisimilitude. One may disapprove of Galileo's rationalistic
solution, but it would seem to be with us still.

This is Galileo's middle way between the attacks launched upon
Tasso by the Peripatetics and the Crusca and the excessive support
given to him by such theorists and polemists as Paolo Beni. In
literary affairs, during Galileo's years in Padua, it was Beni who
was ahead in proposing the more extravagant solution to the
crisis, and it was his aesthetic theory which to a large extent the
Seicento was to echo. Galileo and Beni were fellow-professors in
Padua for some eleven years, and one cannot resist speculating
upon the discussions the professor of mathematics and the
professor of classics might have had. Beni carried the banner of
a *volgare illustre* ennobled by Greek and Latin rhetoric and is
considered the heir to the attempt by Trissino and Speroni to
hellenise Italian.[29] This linguistic controversy had for long been
centred on the academies and schools of Florence and Padua in
conflict, and the emergence of Tasso as the bone of contention
may be seen as a polarisation of this older disagreement and also
as evidence of the crisis in the new Aristotelianism of which Padua
was the centre or, from another point of view, the fortress.
During Beni's time in Padua (1599–1625), he evolved an aesthetic
theory based on the new Aristotelianism which dismissed Dante,
shrugged aside Ariosto, and upheld Tasso as the fountainhead of
a new and more perfect poetry, by which Beni meant the epic,
pre-eminent for its 'amplitude' and 'more durable and richer
voluptas'.[30] Against clarity and precision, Beni advocated the
necessity for magnificence and ornament in poetry; to paraphrase
his own words, poetry, richly ornamented, must ride in triumph
over pedestrian speech; like a bride she must be adorned with
pearls and gold, jewels and purple.[31] This theory achieved full
elaboration in the Commentary to Aristotle's *Poetics* (Padua,
1613), which Toffanin describes as the theoretical basis of *secentismo*, and Jannaco (quoting Spingarn) as the last of the great
Italian commentaries to exert an influence over the whole of
Europe.[32] Certainly, Beni passed on to the Seicento the stylistic
theories distilled from his enthusiastic study of Tasso, although
secentismo, as we have seen, did not derive exclusively from him
but explored many areas remote from the serious epic.

In the meantime, however, Beni had come into conflict with the Accademia della Crusca, and the references to this conflict in the correspondence of Galileo and his friends cast light upon the crisis which produced both Beni's extravagant neo-Aristotelian theories and Galileo's practical and rational approach. Beni's *Comparazioni d'Omero, Virgilio e Torquato* appeared in 1607, and Galileo's own views on Tasso were known about this time, as Cigoli's letter of 1609 indicates (X, 244). No direct connection between Beni's works and Galileo's critique of Tasso can be established, but Galileo's friends seem to have been aware of the disagreement of the two men on the subject. Galileo certainly knew Beni, since the latter both knew of and confirmed Galileo's astronomical discoveries of 1610. It was Beni who almost immediately communicated the news to G. B. Manso, friend and biographer of Tasso, in Naples. Manso replied that both the contents and the descriptive style of Beni's letter had aroused great wonder in Naples and a twinge of jealousy in G. B. Della Porta, and he enclosed a letter for Beni to give to Galileo (X, 291–296). After Galileo's departure from Padua, Gualdo continued to keep him informed of the turbulent career of the professor of classics in that university. Beni's attack on Livy in 1611 seemed to Gualdo somewhat tendentious (letter to Galileo, 25 February 1611; XI, 56), but it was the appearance of the *Anticrusca* which caused the greatest stir.[33] Published in Padua almost immediately after the appearance in Venice of the *Vocabolario della Crusca* (1612), Gualdo saw it mainly as an attack on Boccaccio and the Tuscan tongue (letter to Galileo, 23 November 1612; XI, 435), and Pignoria awaited news from Galileo of its reception in Florence (letter to Galileo, 23 November 1612; XI, 436). A reply to the *Anticrusca* was published in Verona in 1613 by Orlando Pescetti, and in the following year Beni defended himself in *Il Cavalcanti*, using the pseudonym Michelangelo Fonte and artfully dedicating his book to Cosimo de' Medici.[34] With this work, however, Beni appears to have gone too far. The Venetian authorities, who had allowed the publication of the *Vocabolario della Crusca*, were displeased that Padua was producing works which so severely criticised the Accademia. On the appearance of *Il Cavalcanti* they sacked the Paduan censor, Livelli, and introduced a rule banning the publication of any book in the Venetian territory without its prior revision in Venice. Gualdo from Rome relayed this news to Galileo and reported that Beni was preparing to print his commentary on the first ten *canti* of the *Gerusalemme* and was in a hurry lest Galileo should anticipate him by publishing his own commentary. Gualdo sarcastically calls this work a bid by Beni for a recognition of his supremacy but regrets that the Venetian restrictions are hindering its publication, because its appearance would give Galileo a good opportunity to publish his own 'most acute and learned notes' (Gualdo's letters to Galileo of 5 July and 13 December 1614; XII, 81–82, 118–119). Gualdo is perhaps not entirely serious here; by 1614, Galileo was a celebrity in astronomy and hardly likely to publish some rough and unpolished literary notes, and by 1616, when Beni's commentary eventually appeared under the title of *Il Goffredo*, Galileo was already in the forefront of the Copernican campaign, which was to occupy him for the next seventeen years. There is, however, a further possible reason why Galileo should never have published these virulent notes on Tasso, and that is that, although he retained his healthy opposition to affectation and Mannerism as developed in him during those earlier years, and although he continued most emphatically to prefer Ariosto to Tasso (letters to F. Rinuccini of 5 November 1639 and 19 May 1640; XVIII, 120–121, 192–193), he had come to accept, at least in part, the importance and influence of Tasso. Already in the *Considerazioni*, Galileo had noted one or two good points in the *Gerusalemme*, among them the council of the devils (IX, 95), Alete's oration and Goffredo's reply (IX, 79–80), the death of Dudone (IX, 89), Armida's story (IX, 100–101), and Tasso's rhetorical and broken lines, with *enjambement,*

> Amor, ch'or cieco, or Argo, ora ne veli
> Di benda gli occhi, ora ce gli apri, e giri,

which he preferred to Ariosto's

> Quel che l'uom vede, Amor gli fa invisibile,
> E l'invisibile fa vedere Amore   (IX, 75).

Nor was Galileo averse to decorating his own prose with metaphor, allegory, the terse *concettino*, the sense of the wonder of the universe, the touches of colour and sarcasm and even of horror.[35] These elements, considered as undeniable evidence of *secentismo* in Galileo, are indications of the general stylistic liberation which the controversies over Tasso initiated, and, as we have seen, this liberating effect was felt by many who, like Galileo, continued to dislike the actual *Gerusalemme*. That Galileo sensed the new direction of contemporary literature is not at all surprising, as he was not only a man who found pleasure in reading widely, but he was also closely associated with many writers of the time. He was asked to advise and criticise poets such as Strozzi (X, 82–83) and Ciampoli (XIII, 254), and Margherita Sarrocchi sent him her epic *Scanderbeide* for correction (XI, 262, 324); he was interested in the prodigious peasant poet G. D. Peri (X, 405–406); innumerable people sent him plays and poems; many of his friends and supporters were poets, the most notable being, of course, Michelangelo Buonarroti; and his own discoveries inspired a considerable amount of poetry, including verses from both Marino and Chiabrera.[36] Thus Galileo, opponent of the *Gerusalemme*, was constantly aware of the development of a new style in literature in the wake of the controversy over Tasso, and Colapietra even notes an echo in the *Dialogo dei Massimi Sistemi* of one of Tasso's most famous lines.[37] Hence, some recognition by Galileo of Tasso's importance and a desire to be more conciliatory may have inspired his solitary tribute to Tasso in the *Dialogo*: 'come leggiadramente cantò il Poeta sacro: *Qual l'alto Egeo...*' (VII, 463).[38]

   Galileo's awareness of literary questions and involvement in the world of literature thus gives us a valuable insight into the apparently contradictory elements at work in this critical period in Italian literature, when, in the controversy over Ariosto and Tasso, both peripatetics and antiperipatetics, classicists and *secentisti* could be found on either side. Galileo eventually found the answer in a rational and practical approach which avoided both rigid philosophical and linguistic rules and extravagant unconventionality. As a Tuscan, he relied on his native sense of language, and as an enthusiast for Ariosto and an opponent of Mannerism he inherited a sense of literary form and balance which he was to put to good use. Yet his deep conviction of the comprehensibility of the book of nature and the oneness of truth is based on discoveries, laws, and reasoning unknown in Ariosto's time, whilst his exuberance in revealing these new wonders avoids the affectation, the contortions, and the riddles of some of his own contemporaries. As in science, so in his own prose style, Galileo is, in Spongano's words, 'a thousand miles away' from the writers of the early Cinquecento,[39] but he is at least as far from Bartoli also. From the controversies of 1590–1610 he emerged with a mixed style, in which clarity and logic were paramount, but not at the expense of the explanatory digression, the telling metaphor, the life of the imagination.

Galileo's appreciation of clear and rational imaginative literature contributes greatly to an understanding of his mental processes as a scientist and as a propagandist for Copernicus. Without it, he would have written either rambling and elegant disquisitions, rich in citation and irrelevant fancy, or the bald statements of theory and fact which later became the pattern for scientific prose. That Galileo himself achieved a balance between these two extremes not only gives an important insight into the mental processes of this early rationalist and man of humanity and culture, but it is very much a part of the story of his life and of the advancement of Copernicanism. Without the literary awareness which he possessed and the sense of form which this gave him, Galileo would not have been such a danger to his opponents or such an influential campaigner for the heliocentric world-system. Galileo's style played almost as great a part as his message in bringing him into conflict with the Holy Office and in spreading the new cosmology about Europe. If Galileo differs from many other *secentisti* in having something indisputably important to say, nevertheless it was to a large extent his way of saying it which beguiled or enraged his readers, and indeed Galileo remains extremely persuasive even when his theories are wrong, as in the well known cases of the comets and the tides. Thus one can say that the setback to Copernicanism in Italy but its triumph elsewhere result to a large extent from the fact that Galileo was in mind and in style superior to his opponents and that the Copernican message was put into words by the 'greatest prose-writer of the Italian Seicento'.[40] Thus our study of the crisis in literature of 1590–1610, with the conclusion that Galileo was an advocate of rationality, sanity, and clarity in a blend of baroque and anti-baroque, comes to have important effects on the history of ideas. Even in Latin Galileo is a powerful writer, and the crucial *Nuncius Sidereus*, which is plain to the point of baldness, carries an enormous sense of excitement in the revelation of the new heavens.

It is, however, in the Italian works that Galileo's apparently innate feeling for words and style had its greatest influence. That he should have written in Italian at all was a product of his reaction against the preceptists and pedants and of his humanistic desire to reach as wide a literate public as possible, for the glory of Italian science and to help solve the additional crises which his own discoveries had provoked. In general, Galileo's works have the clarity, moderation, and naturalness which he had found lacking in Tasso, but they carry also an exuberant use of language and metaphor, a delight in discovering, revealing, reasoning, and arguing, and a discursive, indeed digressive, style which belong very much to the spirit of the age. The style is mixed, but with a unifying and dynamic factor: the progressive communication of the truth about nature. In his work, therefore, pages of mathematical disquisition, powerful descriptions of the glories of nature, and the construction and demolition of real or dummy opponents all play a vital part, and it is the creator of this prose, Galileo with his sense of the human scale, who brings these elements together in a unique blend, with the power to influence the mathematician, the philosopher, the *honnête homme*. Galileo does not discover or reveal nature's laws from the angle of fact alone, but he approaches them with the two faculties of logic and imagination. He himself calls his hypotheses *fantasie*, and it was this ability to follow up his *fantasie* with demonstration and logic which was his weapon in establishing the scientific method and in waging his cultural campaign. The anti-Aristotelian idea of 'philosophising with the fantasy' is an apparent paradox, and it has been used to explain how Galileo and Marino were contemporaries, in other words as a criterion of Galileo's *secentismo*, but in fact it should be seen as the basis for distinguishing between the solutions proposed by the two men. In Marino's case, the phrase means to allow the imagination to break Aristotle's rules by creating a style which follows the sinuous and conflicting lines of an unstable and inaccessible reality;[41] for Galileo it means to use the imagination to reach a stable and accessible reality, and then to demonstrate the fantasy with experiment, and finally to persuade others of its truth. It is thus incorrect to conclude, as does Marzot, that Galileo's works, built upon *fantasie*, remained even for him 'una solennissima chimera'.[42] Galileo and Marino do have one thing in common, that the world perceived by the senses is illusory, and from this Galileo deduced his important theory of secondary qualities, but Galileo believed the evidence of the telescope and of his own eyes as an experimenter and so ascertained the one ultimate reality: that the book of nature is written in the language of mathematics (VI, 232), and so he formulated the primary qualities upon which science came to be founded.

An examination of the form of Galileo's major works on Copernicanism will bring us to a final definition of his '*secentismo*' along the lines already laid down. His set-piece letters, *Il Saggiatore*, and the *Dialogo dei Massimi Sistemi* show us a Galileo who is aware of a long literary tradition and who produces his own solution from the crisis of this tradition at the beginning of a new century and, for science, a new age.

The letter was a form of writing particularly favoured by Galileo for the advancement of his views. The Cinquecento had provided the tradition of the public private letter,[43] and it was particularly suited to Galileo's discursive and natural style, in which the pen follows the logic of the thought but is allowed a moderate amount of freedom. Besides this, of course, the letter had the political advantage of making its recipient its protector. The *Letters on Sunspots* were addressed to Welser, a minor German potentate indeed but a fluent Italian speaker, a friend of Clavius, and the patron of Apelles, the first announcer of the sunspots. They were destined for publication from the first, even though this meant changing a tendentious quotation from the Bible in Welser's first invitation to Galileo (XI, 437–438). Similarly, the controversy brewing over the interpretation of Scriptures induced Galileo to write, not a Scholastic treatise, but a series of letters to churchmen (Castelli and Dini) and finally to the Dowager Grand Duchess of Tuscany, Christine of Lorraine. This latter, prepared carefully by Galileo and Castelli, must surely have been intended for publication, but events overtook it with the decree of 1616. The set-piece letter was thus the first literary form chosen by Galileo for his propagation and defence of the new world-system. There are many other examples of this form as used by Galileo throughout his life, though they were destined for circulation rather than publication. The last of these is the letter *Sopra il candore della luna*, to Prince Leopold of Tuscany, of March 1640.

Il Saggiatore can be seen as marking the transition in Galileo's choice of form from the letter to the dialogue. It is in the form of a letter, addressed, after long and careful deliberation, to Virginio Cesarini, the Pope's newly appointed Maestro di Camera. Yet this device is little more than a political safeguard. The work itself springs from annotations made by Galileo to a copy of Sarsi's *Libra astronomica et philosophica*. It is in fact a series of extended annotations and is the least consciously literary of Galileo's works. He imposes no form upon it; he merely takes Sarsi paragraph by paragraph and systematically destroys the arguments of the transparently masked Jesuit. It is, as we have seen, a similar procedure to the method he had applied to Tasso. Galileo must undoubtedly have spent some considerable time in detecting and demolishing Sarsi's logical and scientific errors and in polishing his own blade of sarcasm, but he allows no evidence of the throes of literary composition to intrude. He chose a simple, practical, and original method, brilliantly reflected in the metaphor of the title, of subjecting to minute weighing the arguments of Grassi–Sarsi and his own replies and barbed comments. At most, it is a parody of the peripatetic commentary. There is no question of classicism or of Seicento fantasies: the problem was to reply, and Galileo found the most rational of solutions. It now has a place in the history of literature.

The *Dialogo dei Massimi Sistemi*, however, was from the beginning consciously literary. Galileo worked on it for several years, and there are many references in his letters to his problems in giving words and shape to his ideas. That he should have embarked upon this *magnum opus* at all is due to his awareness of literature and of its power to persuade and sway. The apparent dawning of a new freedom with the accession of Urban VIII induced Galileo to compose a work which would not have the mere simplicity of quotation and refutation of *Il Saggiatore* but would deal with a whole host of arguments and angles and embody the position of the *honnête homme*, his reader, in the face of the conflict of the time. The fundamental conflict of the *Dialogo*, says Fiorentino, is not an invention of the fantasy but a historical fact.[44] This fact, perhaps the underlying motive for Galileo's choice of the dialogue, confirms our view that in the crisis of the Seicento Galileo reacted in literary affairs with a spontaneous and practical mixture of originality and awareness of a long humanistic tradition. There were, of course, other reasons which made the dialogue a suitable form: it allowed Galileo to pretend to be presenting both sides of the argument, a political safeguard which may well have occurred to Galileo after his interview with the new Pope Urban VIII and which certainly became an increasingly necessary fiction to get the book through the hands of the censor, but ultimately this reason does not explain the device of a dialogue in the presence of an *honnête homme*. Such a device is better understood if we see the *Massimi Sistemi* as the culmination of Galileo's cultural campaign, its manifesto, in Geymonat's words,[45] that is, not just as a work of science and philosophy but as a work of propaganda for a world-system and for a rational and experimental approach to the wonders of nature. This propaganda was directed precisely to the *honnête homme*, and so the dialogue responds to a practical need to introduce an intelligent layman to represent Galileo's own audience. The dialogue had a long tradition as a method of conveying ideas in an attractive way and in a realistic and human situation; it also serves to reflect Galileo's own personality, with his liking for company and witty conversation. Thus once again we find Galileo choosing a rational and practical solution on the basis of an apparently innate sense of the human scale and of a literary tradition stretching from Plato's supper-party to that of Bruno, and it may be that Galileo's use of the dialogue was suggested to him above all by the more proximate example of the unfortunate and unmentionable prophet of the new universe who had also tried to find a solution to the crisis of post-Renaissance religion and philosophy and had died for it in the Campo de' Fiori.[46]

Thus Galileo's literary awareness and sense of reality and of the power of the word led him to adopt the dialogue as his form, and in it all those influences from the years 1590–1610 seem to converge. The form, the balance, the humanisation may seem to derive from Renaissance models, but the content is a mixture of mathematical explanation, philosophical argument, the poetry of the extended metaphor, and touches of humour, mixed in a free and discursive style, something new and partially Baroque but not extravagantly so. The interlocutors of the *Massimi Sistemi* may seem outwardly to reflect the civilised society of the *Decameron* or the *Courtier*, but beneath this there is the irreducible opposition of revolution and a dogmatism treated with deliberate cruelty. The characters themselves are principally intended to convey attitudes, but many of Galileo's friends complimented him on his skill at characterisation: Campanella defined Simplicio as the laughing-stock, Salviati as the Socrates, and Sagredo as the sceptical man of sense and compared Galileo's work favourably to Plato's (letter to Galileo, 5 August 1632; XIV, 366), and Micanzio claimed that he could almost hear Sagredo himself speaking (XIV, 350). However, it is above all Simplicio who shows Galileo's skill in depicting character. A composite figure, or exemplar, drawn from Galileo's peripatetic adversaries, he is both a dummy enemy built for demolition and a precursor of Manzoni's comic pedant, Don Ferrante; by any standards he is a fine product of literary imagination, an entrenched and old-fashioned philosopher such as all ages can recognise.[47] Unfortunately, in creating this character at this time, Galileo allowed his exuberant wit to go too far, and by enraging his adversaries he brought down upon his head the power of inquisitorial authority, that product of the baroque age to which Galileo's rationalism and trust in truth made him ultimately vulnerable. Although it is not proved that the Pope saw Simplicio as a caricature of himself,[48] nevertheless the whole conception of Simplicio was tactless, and so Galileo was ultimately betrayed by his own solution to the crisis of the age, by his own rational belief that the truth would prevail by the double persuasiveness of logic and imagination.

Notes

[1] Galileo Galilei, *Opere*, Edizione Nazionale, ed. A. Favaro, etc. (Florence, Barbèra, 1890–1909, reprinted 1929–39 and 1964–6), 20 vols. Subsequent references to this work will be made in parentheses with the volume number in Roman numerals and the page number in Arabic numerals.

[2] *Cf.* G. Parini, *Dei principi particolari delle belle lettere*, chapter V; G. Leopardi, *Zibaldone*, ed. F. Flora (Milan, Mondadori, sixth edition, 1961), vol. I, pp. 45, 886; vol. II, pp. 1070–1071. Foscolo, although reproaching Galileo for attacking Tasso, anticipated modern opinion in his *Poemi narrativi*, Edizione Nazionale (Florence, Le Monnier), vol. xi, pt. 2, p. 181: 'Galileo owed the richness, the purity, and the luminous evidence of his prose to his constant study of poetry.'

[3] N. Vaccalluzzo, *Galileo letterato e poeta* (Catania, Giannotta, 1896).

[4] R. Spongano, *La prosa di Galileo e altri scritti* (Messina–Florence, D'Anna, 1949), pp. 114–115, mentions the negative aspect of Galileo's influence in the

insistence of many later scientific writers on *piacevolezze* rather than on direct scientific reasoning. However, Galileo's contribution to the vocabulary of physical science in the vernacular was decisive; *cf.* B. Migliorini, *Storia della lingua italiana* (Florence, Sansoni, third edition, 1961), chapter 9, especially pp. 477–478; M. V. Giovine, *Galilei scrittore* (Genoa, Albrighi & Segati, 1943), pp. 49–101; and M. L. Altieri Biagi, *Galileo e la terminologia tecnico-scientifica* (Florence, Olschki, 1965).

⁵ G. Getto, 'La polemica sul Barocco', in *Orientamenti Culturali: Letteratura Italiana: Le Correnti* (Milan, Marzorati, 1956), pp. 417–504; C. Calcaterra, 'Il problema del barocco', in *Questioni e correnti di storia letteraria* (Milan, Marzorati, 1963), pp. 405–501.

⁶ R. Colapietra, 'Il pensiero estetico galileiano', *Belfagor*, xi (1956), pp. 557–69, argues from this that Galileo is an Aristotelian critic attacking the antiperipatetic elements in Tasso; M. V. Giovine, *op. cit.*, pp. 21–32, from the same premise draws the opposite conclusion: that Galileo was an anti-peripatetic attacking a poet who was still in part the slave of Aristotle.

⁷ Calcaterra, *op. cit.*, pp. 459 ff.; E. Panofsky, *Galileo as a Critic of the Arts* (The Hague, Nijhoff, 1954), pp. 15–20.

⁸ Among many who have supported this view to some extent, I note: A. Chiari, 'Galilei e le lettere italiane', in *Nel terzo centenario della morte di Galileo Galilei* (Milan, Vita e Pensiero, 1942), pp. 351–381; F. Foti, 'Galilei critico', *Nuova Antologia*, 502 (1968), pp. 361–369; F. Maggini, 'Galileo studioso di letteratura', *Convivium*, xvii (1949), pp. 847–861; C. Jannaco, *Il Seicento* (Milan, Vallardi, second edition, 1966), pp. 548–551; N. Sapegno, 'Galileo scrittore', in *Galileo Galilei: Celebrazioni del IV Centenario della Nascita* (Rome, Accad. Naz. dei Lincei, 1965), pp. 101–115. G. Varanini, *Galileo critico e prosatore* (Verona, Fiorini & Ghidini, 1967), pp. 9–77, after an exhaustive survey of the *Considerazioni*, sees Galileo as a conservative in the period of crisis, adhering to the ideals of 'una tradizione saldamente instaurata ma già minacciata e scossa' (p. 76).

⁹ R. Spongano, *op. cit.*

¹⁰ U. Bosco, 'Gusto letterario primo-rinascimentale di Galileo', to be republished in *Saggi sul Rinascimento Italiano*, Florence, Le Monnier; A. Chiari (ed.), *Galileo Galilei: Scritti letterari* (Florence, Le Monnier, 1943), p. xiii, uses the phrase 'un Galileo antisecentista'.

¹¹ A. Favaro, 'La libreria di Galileo Galilei', *Bullettino di bibliografia e di storia delle scienze matematiche e fisiche*, xix (1886), pp. 219–293.

¹² A. Chiari (ed.), *G. G.: Scritti letterari* (1943), pp. xi–xii; F. Foti, *op. cit.*, pp. 361–362; F. Maggini, *op. cit.*, pp. 850–852.

¹³ S. Drake, *Discoveries and Opinions of Galileo* (New York 1957), p. 77.

¹⁴ First published by N. Vianello, 'Le postille al Petrarca di Galileo Galilei' *Studi di filologia italiana*, xiv (1956), pp. 211–433.

¹⁵ F. Maggini, *op. cit.*, p. 853.

¹⁶ F. Maggini, *loc. cit.* A. Belloni, *Galileo Galilei* (Turin, Paravia, n.d.), pp. 104–105, sees the *Considerazioni* as Galileo's reaction to Beni's fanatical support of Tasso and thus by implication dates them from after 1599, when Beni arrived in Padua.

¹⁷ *Considerazioni al Tasso di Galileo Galilei e Discorso di Giuseppe Iseo sopra il*

Poema di M. Torquato Tasso per dimostrazioni di alcuni luoghi in diversi Autori da lui felicemente emulati (Rome, Pagliarini, and Venice, Valle, 1793).

[18] C. Ricci, *Le Considerazioni al poema del Tasso di Galileo Galilei* (Ariano, Soc. per Costruzioni ed Industrie, 1889).

[19] R. Spongano, 'Galileo scrittore', in *Libera Cattedra di Storia della Civiltà Fiorentina: Il Sei-Settecento* (Florence 1956), p. 120.

[20] See note 8.

[21] L. Geymonat and F. Brunetti, 'Galileo Galilei', in E. Cecchi and N. Sapegno (eds.), *Storia della Letteratura Italiana: Il Seicento* (Milan, Garzanti, 1967), p. 183; C. Jannaco, *op. cit.*, p. 542; A. Chiari (ed.). *G. G.: Scritti letterari* (1943), p. xvi.

[22] D. Della Terza, 'Galileo letterato: Considerazioni al Tasso', *La Rassegna della Letteratura Italiana*, lxix (1965), pp. 77–91, and 'Galileo, Man of Letters', in C. L. Golino (ed.), *Galileo Reappraised* (Berkeley and Los Angeles, Univ. of California, 1966), pp. 1–22.

[23] C. Calcaterra, *op. cit.*, pp. 459 ff.

[24] E. Panofsky, *op. cit.*, pp. 15–20.

[25] A. Chiari (ed.), *G. G.: Scritti letterari* (1943), p. xiii. However, in the augmented edition of the same work (Florence, Le Monnier, 1970) Chiari gives a good example of the general confusion and ambiguity surrounding the whole critical problem by using also the significantly different (if not contradictory) phrase 'secentista antibarocchista' (p. xv).

[26] E. Panofsky, *op. cit.*, pp. 20–28; D. Della Terza, *op. cit.* (1965), pp. 87–88.

[27] C. Ricci, *op. cit.*, p. 43, refers in this respect to Galileo's love of "sana letteratura". An interesting fragment by Galileo against literary pedants has come down to us (IX, 228–229). On this general character of healthiness and vigour in Galileo's critique of Tasso, *cf.* M. V. Giovine, *op. cit.*, pp. 33 ff., and F. T. Prince, *The Italian Influence in Milton's Verse* (Oxford, Clarendon Press, 1954), pp. 43–46.

[28] Quoted by C. Jannaco, *op. cit.*, p. 81.

[29] G. Toffanin, *Il Cinquecento* (Milan, Vallardi, seventh edition, 1965), pp. 481, 645.

[30] C. Jannaco, *op. cit.*, p. 323.

[31] G. Toffanin, *op. cit.*, p. 632.

[32] G. Toffanin, *op. cit.*, pp. 564–565; C. Jannaco, *op. cit.*, pp. 27–28.

[33] On the history of this controversy, *cf.* C. Jannaco, *op. cit.*, p. 94, and B. Migliorini, *op. cit.*, pp. 453–455.

[34] B. Migliorini, *op. cit.*, p. 454, sees this dedication as a cunning move by Beni.

[35] R. Colapietra, 'Caratteri del secentismo galileiano', *Belfagor*, viii (1953), pp. 570–578.

[36] A full description of Galileo's relations with contemporary poets can be found in N. Vacculluzzo, *Galileo Galilei nella poesia del suo secolo* (Milan–Palermo–Naples 1910), with publication of contemporary verses inspired by Galileo.

[37] R. Colapietra, 'Il pensiero estetico galileiano', *Belfagor*, xi (1956), p. 564.

[38] *Cf.* note by F. Flora in *Galileo Galilei: Opere* (Milan–Naples, Ricciardi, 1953), p. 801.

[39] R. Spongano, *La prosa di Galileo e altri scritti*, pp. 103 ff.; M. V. Giovine, *op. cit.*, analyses in detail Galileo's vocabulary, grammar, and syntax and also concludes that Galileo's style is mixed and original.

[40] R. Spongano, *La prosa di Galileo e altri scritti*, p. 96.

[41] C. Calcaterra, *op. cit.*, pp. 414–415.

[42] G. Marzot, 'Variazioni barocche nella prosa di Galileo', *Convivium*, xxii (1954), pp. 678–689, and xxiii (1955), pp. 43–67. The ambiguity of certain critics with regard to Galileo's *fantasie* is simply but perceptively resolved by W. Mays, 'Scientific method in Galileo and Bacon', in *Galileo nella storia e nella filosofia della scienza: Atti del Symposium Internazionale di Storia, Metodologia, Logica e Filosofia della Scienza* (Vinci–Florence, Gruppo Italiano di Storia delle Scienze, 1967), pp. 309–316: '... in Galileo's method, intuition and imagination play a key role in the formulation of the law under which the empirically determined series of measurements are subsumed. One of the implications of such an approach is that scientific discovery is akin to artistic creation ...' (p. 313).

[43] R. Spongano, *La prosa di Galileo e altri scritti*, pp. 93–96.

[44] F. Fiorentino, *Bernardino Telesio, ossia studi storici su l'idea della natura nel Risorgimento italiano*, vol. II (Florence, Le Monnier, 1874), pp. 280–2. A. Banfi, *Galileo Galilei* (Milan, Il Saggiatore, 1961), p. 267, also detects in the *Massimi Sistemi* Galileo's 'senso del conflitto di cultura'.

[45] L. Geymonat, *Galileo Galilei* (Turin, Einaudi, 1957), discusses Galileo as a propagandist with a politico-cultural programme and calls the *Massimi Sistemi* 'il manifesto copernicano' (chapter VII). A. Banfi, *op. cit.*, talks in a similar way of Galileo's 'missione illuministica' (pt. II, chapter IV).

[46] G. Gentile (ed.) *Galileo Galilei: Lettera a Cristina di Lorena* (Florence 1943), p. 83, points out the similarity of ideas between Bruno and Galileo in the controversy between science and scriptural interpretation and suggests that Galileo had read Bruno but dared not publicise the fact. S. Timpanaro, *Scritti di storia e critica della scienza* (Florence 1952), pp. 104–105, suggests the possible influence of the *Cena delle ceneri* on Galileo's thought, and F. A. Yates, *Giordano Bruno and the Hermetic Tradition* (London, Routledge & Kegan Paul, 1964), pp. 358–359, suggests briefly, and not entirely accurately, a formal parallel between the *Cena* and the *Massimi Sistemi*.

[47] F. Fiorentino, *op. cit.*, pp. 280–282.

[48] G. Abetti, *Amici e nemici di Galileo* (Milan, Bompiani, 1945), p. 232; F. Soccorsi, *Il processo di Galileo* (Rome 1947), pp. 40–41.

Felicity M. Firth

Goldoni: a view from the pit

'Siamo tutti mercanti,' says Colombina in *La famiglia del-l'antiquario*, an accurate statement in its context which riles Doralice, the noblewoman of one week's standing. 'Fu mercante,' says the anxious Rosaura in *Le femmine puntigliose*, explaining her husband's position, and she is emphatic in her use of the past tense.

Contempt for the honourable exchange of goods and money is an attitude which is ridiculed in Goldoni's theatre, and as we shall see, by the nature of that theatre itself. It is the one form of human foolishness which meets in his plays with the hard edge of censure, most of our failings being recorded merely with amusement, tolerance, and a little added colour.

Colombina's 'siamo tutti mercanti' coming from Goldoni's pen has an aphoristic ring which lifts it out of its context. Here we feel we have a key which will open up for us a new view of Goldoni's theatre and a better understanding of his bourgeois ethic. The World and the Theatre, he claimed in his preface to the 1750 edition of his plays, were his education, and so they continued to be. They were also, in another dimension, his market and his market-place.

Menego Cainello, the gondolier who lounges outside the theatre in *La putta onorata* giving his views on the contemporary drama, is no figure of fun. He and his fellows provide a kind of consumers' advisory service to the Venetian theatre-going public. Here he asks about the play currently running, and about the audiences it is attracting. 'Ghe xe assae barcarioi drento?' he asks. 'Pi de cento,' someone answers. In that case, 'co la piase ai barcarioi, la sarà bona.' There is no patronage or irony in his being given this to say; if the taxi-drivers like it, then it is good. This is the measure of the reality to Goldoni of his notion of a popular theatre. Though he relinquished the techniques of the *commedia dell'arte* he was not willing to let go of its audience. His aim was to wean it, 'zente bassa' and all, on to a more substantial diet. Anselmo, the Brighella of the theatrical company depicted in *Il teatro comico*, explains the way that public taste is moving. Comedy based on character has gained in popular favour, and now every man is his own drama critic: 'L'Italia adesso corre drio unicamente a sta sorte di commedia... in poco tempo ha tanto profittà el bon gusto nell'animo delle persone, che adesso anca la zente bassa decide francamente sui caratteri e sui difetti delle commedie.'

What the public wants, as Menego Cainello puts it, are 'de quele comedie che gh'ha del sugo', and Goldoni, true trading son of Pantalone, makes it his business to know his market. The customer's pleasure is law. 'Io stimo,' he writes in his preface of 1750, 'che più scrupolosamente che ad alcuni precetti di Aristotele o di Orazio, convenga servire alle Leggi del Popolo.' The trading parallel itself is drawn in his exquisite *Una delle ultime sere di carnovale*, in which he presents himself 'allegorically' as a designer of cloth, and his relationship with the public as that of dealer and consumer:

Gh'ho tanto respetto e tante obbligazion coi aventori de sta bottega, che sarave un ingrato se trascurasse de corrisponder alle finezze che i m'ha praticà.

My aim in this essay is to illustrate the workings of this 'dealer–consumer' relationship between Goldoni and his public, to point out some of the ways in which, often instinctively it seems, he knew how to appeal to the most fundamental drives and instincts in his audience, to give them subtle pleasures, from the sheer joy of spontaneous laughter, the 'dilettevole solletico all'uman cuore' of which he writes in the preface already quoted, to the satisfaction of various baser tendencies to be specified later.

He had a strong sense of the essentially social nature of the drama. His plays are distinguished for the warmth of the welcome they afford the audience. The playwright plays host, makes a study of his audience's comfort, pleasure and taste. All this Goldoni achieves with a rare degree of realism. Critics are probably right in attributing to him a psychological unevenness in his presentation of character on the stage, but there is no doubt that in his consideration of his audience he gives evidence of a very profound knowledge indeed of what Momigliano calls 'i più interni retroscena dell'anima'.

His first lesson in the mechanics of audience reaction he must have derived from the *commedia dell'arte*, the fundamental message that while a popular audience can take a fair dose of artistic or psychological discrepancy in its stride, it will be outraged if for a moment it is asked to tolerate boredom. So while the improvised comedy, languishing on the diminishing returns of crudity, was fighting off the bugaboo with increasingly frantic brandishings of Arlecchino's slapstick, Goldoni started to rebuild the popular theatre on the foundation of an almost subliminal engagement of emotion.

He gives us what he knows we like; not what we think we like; this in his day would have meant an adaptation if not a continuation of the old tradition. Nor does he give us what he thinks we ought to like; there is no forcing of public taste.

The most fundamental trick of all is the magic of the domestic scene itself. To be admitted to the inside of someone else's house in the theatre as in life is a warming and refreshing experience. The brightly lit interior, the firelight on the wall; no doubt the psychologists have a word for it; in surroundings at once familiar and unfamiliar we let go our tensions and responsibilities, and knowing that no excessive demands will be made on imagination or intellect, we wait to be entertained. We are suddenly alive to someone else's set-up, to the strains and stresses of another household and to the colour of its coffee-cups. Goldoni makes use of this receptive state of mind and welcomes us with pleasantly associated objects. Teapot, samovar and goblet have a substantial stage history, and it is not for nothing that the 'chicchere' and 'biscottini' or their equivalent, are brought on in almost every Goldonian play. Perhaps the most daring instance of this kind of welcome is the play *Una delle ultime sere di carnovale* where a card-game and a supper party form the main action, the pairing off of three sets of lovers in the last scene being in the nature of a formal appendix for the sake of appearances.

A little finite world where we know the postman and the baker and the district nurse—the secret of Coronation Street and Tannochbrae; the secret too of *Il campiello, Le massere, Le baruffe chiozzotte*, plays set in a small domestic ambience where we quickly find our bearings. The horizon widens slightly, the cross-section of the community is minimally enlarged and the same sense of familiarity, of knowing where we are, pervades our pleasure in *La bottega del caffè, Il ventaglio, La locandiera*. If this sense of security and recognition can reach a foreign reader across two centuries and half a continent, what must its original impact have been? All the Venetian plays are infused with this delightful and in no way contemptible spirit of what we now might call *campanilismo*. But perhaps the word acquires a rather special connotation anyway when applied to Venice.

We are lured towards the warmth and brightness of Goldoni's

scenes as fish towards a brilliantly coloured fly. The hook on
which we dangle for the duration of each play is the principle of
identification, explicitly described by Anselmo in *Il teatro comico*:
'Adesso che se torna a pescar le commedie nel mare magnum della
natura, i omeni se senta a bisegar in tel cor, e investindose della
passion o del carattere che se rappresenta, i sa discerner se la
passion sia ben sostegnuda, se el carattere sia ben condotto e
osservà.'

Goldoni manipulates us so that we invest ourselves with the
passions of his characters, and some of the means he uses to do
this are basic indeed. Our sympathy with certain characters is
engineered on a basis of defensive solidarity in the face of a loath-
some third party; we side with Lucietta against Lunardo; with
Meneghina against Cecilia, with poor Bettina against Beatrice,
with Marcolina and good little Zanetta against feckless Pellegrino
and the unbearable Sior Todero Brontolon. Another device he
uses is almost the old pantomime trick of kindling the spirit of
sexual antagonism in the audience by playing one sex off against
the other—'Come along, the ladies, all together now, please!'
One element is provoked while the other chuckles. Pantalone in
Le femmine puntigliose provokes this response with his remedy for
wilfulness in a wife:

Pantalone: L'averia bastonada.

Florindo: Bastonare una donna civile?

Pantalone: Bastonarla in una camera serrada, che nessun savesse gnente,
per salvar el decoro; ma bastonarla.

Paron Fortunato's 'Donne danno, donna malanno, malanno,
danno, malanno' in *Le baruffe chiozzotte* has the same effect. The
same purpose is served by the scene in *I rusteghi* in which Lunardo
and Simone hug each other in their delight in their common
hatred of women. 'Donne, donne, e po donne' sighs Simone, to
which Lunardo replies, 'Chi dise donna, vegnimo a dir el merito,
dise danno.' The hackles of at least half the audience can safely be
considered raised. In *La locandiera* the women look to Mirandolina
as to an avenging champion, while the men, whether they hope
the misogynous Cavaliere will resist or fall, cannot fail to regard
him as their representative.

The defeat of the over-dominant male is a frequently recurring
motif; the overbearing female too, has to be taught her lesson.

The sex war is carried on in pitched battle or light skirmish varying in intensity from play to play; hostilities are never quite total, though there is a cruel moment in *La locandiera* when we wonder whether perhaps Mirandolina has not gone too far. More often the sallies take the form of light banter: 'A sti omeni no gh'è da creder,' says Polonia in *Una delle ultime sere di carnovale*, 'no gh'è da fidarse: i xe tutti compagni'; gentle manoeuvres merely aimed at promoting allegiances in the auditorium.

The plays of Goldoni are also geared, whether by instinct or by art, to engage a whole host of petty emotions, trivial drives and urges we may not care to own to, such as curiosity, acquisitiveness, the desire for approval, the passion for conformity, the need to look up to people, the need to look down on people, and supremely, our delight in recognising our neighbours' foibles if not our own. Why do we love to see Checca and Rosina in *La casa nova*, eyeing through their metaphorical lace curtains their neighbours' furniture as it is moved into the flat below?

Checca: Aveu visto quel specchio co la soaza negra?

Rosina: Antigaggie.

Checca: E quei caregoni de bulgaro?

Rosina: I mobili de so bisnono.

Checca: I butterà via un mondo de bezzi in pittori, in favri, in marangoni, e po no i gh'averà una camera de bon gusto.

Rosina: Possibile che no l'abbiémo da véder?

Checca: De dia! la voî véder se credesse d'andarghe una festa, co no le ghe xe.

Goldoni cajoles the merchant soul of Venice. The social and material rat-race—could one call it perhaps the mania for keeping up with the Pantaloons?—is a theme which lights a spark in every affluent breast. Checca and Rosina are afraid that their neighbours will have better furniture than themselves. When they see stuff being moved in which is no better than their own their reaction is of intense relief, which they have to disguise as scorn. 'Fancy them with all that money having rotten old rubbish like that!' We seem to have heard it before.

Goldoni is writing comedies for an audience drawn from a commercial urban community built on centuries of mercantile tradition. He has an instinctive understanding of the whole complex of human values and reactions which is part of this inheritance. Where life is based on trade, if a man is any 'good' he will have something to show for it; the extent of his possessions will be the measure of his worth. It cannot be stressed too much that there is no evaluation of the bourgeois ideal in Goldoni. Extreme attitudes towards it or within it may be seen to be ridiculous, but the ethic itself is neither praised nor questioned. Its exponents are his subjects and there is warmth and zest in his treatment of them, but the ethic is simply accepted as part of the picture to be painted. Aspects of it are shown to be good; in the Pantalone–Anselmo figure we have the patriarchal merchant at his best, wise, kind and authoritative; in *La buona famiglia* we have a recipe, a very pattern of merchant virtue in the life of a whole household. At the same time abuse and excess in lives lived by this creed as in those lived by any other is shown to lead to uncomfortable or intolerable situations. In *I rusteghi* we see the middle-class values of thrift and privacy blown up by one man's monomania and turned to monsters. Goldoni documents people as he sees them, materialistic beings in a material world. He is factually aware that a large part of their emotional stability is rooted in hard cash. Love and despair are treated lightly. His characters may blush, tremble and swoon with these emotions, but their hearts' true treasure is in 'bezzi contai.'

The spuriously superior attitude to possessions we have come to know in the post-romantic era, in literature if not in life, would have been incomprehensible in eighteenth-century Venice. Only in a very rare lyrical moment in Goldoni's plays is the idea entertained that the world might ever be well lost for love. The sentiment is barely breathed by Bettina, the irrationally faithful heroine of *La putta onorata* and *La buona moglie*, who could live, she says, 'si ben, soto una scala, ma col mio caro Pasqualin.' Goldoni flatters his audience by reflecting their own inevitable attitude favourably. Bettina's wistful dream of love under the stairs has no chance against the solid weight of Pantalone's 'Co no gh'è da magnar l'amor va zoso per i calcagni', and he is supported by the voice of common sense in many persons, from the motherly Checca in *La casa nova*—'L'amor no fa boggier la pignatta' to Angiola, the old battle-axe of *Le donne de casa soa*:

> I amori delle putte i xe pettegolezzi;
> Passa presto l'amor, co no che xe più bezzi

Love, as prudent parents tell their children to this day, will not pay the coal bill.

Indeed the ways are many in which the merchant soul and its by-products are the same today as they always were, and those of us who have known life in industrial and commercial places are able to respond to Goldoni with an extra degree of warmth and recognition. The mania, for instance, for doing one's housework well and then telling people about it in detail, is a common characteristic of the Goldonian housewife, epitomised perhaps by the infuriating Betta of *Le donne de casa soa*, who fills a whole scene at the beginning of Act III with a minute account of her cleaning routine, which she punctuates with assurances that if you want anything done properly you should do it yourself. Familiar too is the way that the characters in the *Villeggiatura* trilogy take their best clothes with them on holiday. In the country their one idea is to recreate on a spectacular scale the pleasures of the town, the parties, the concerts, the *conversazioni*. This *smania* is surely behind the modern bourgeois holiday ideal, a place where one can enjoy the ultimate in urban luxury, but in superficially rural surroundings. Goldoni would have understood those package tours to Majorca and the Costa Brava; he would have appreciated the Blackpool tower, vision of Paris made concrete on the coast of Lancashire.

An essential feature of Goldoni's sympathetic hold over his audience is his ability to draw his social climbers, bullies, spoil-sports, spendthrifts, misers, silly women and giddy girls, without appearing to judge them and so demand of us the exertion of moral indignation. His characters carry their defects innocently; Mirandolina just happens to be a man-eater; Rosaura (in *Le femmine puntigliose*) a snob; Lunardo was born a miserable old devil, and Sior Todero a miser and a bully. We like or we dislike, and are thankful not to have to judge. The processes are pleasant; identification with some and a hearty horror of the others.

The same absence of censure marks Goldoni's attitude to materialistic competitiveness. The rat-race is effectively a feature of society and by refusing to condemn it Goldoni allows us to dabble in participation, to share a little, for our own entertainment, in the hopes of the contenders. Certainly, the advantages of moderation are set forth, especially through the person of Pantalone, wherever he appears. In *Le femmine puntigliose* he deplores the rage for keeping up with one's neighbours and sees it as the commonest cause of ruin:

Questa xe la più forte rason de tutte. Per far quel che fa i altri, andar in malora per complimento, farse burlar per usanza. Questa xe la rovina dei omeni, questo xe el desordine delle famegie. Per far quel che fa i altri, se se precipita, se se descredita.

Yet we are allowed to be partly sympathetic. We still hope that poor silly Rosaura will get her invitation to rub shoulders with the nobs of Palermo. The climbing instinct is latent in us all, and Goldoni encourages our identification to increase the urgency of his story.

In the *Villeggiatura* trilogy he brings the audience's gambling instinct into play. Leonardo is eaten up with the desire to 'comparire'. On the brink of ruin he knows that he is mad to spend so much on cutting a fine figure:

Lo veggo anch'io, che faccio più di quello che posso fare; ma lo fanno gli altri, e non voglio esser di meno,

but he hopes to win the hand and dowry of Giacinta, daughter of his lavish and hospitable neighbour Filippo, and the plot hangs on the question of whether his resources will last while he spends ostentatiously in the pursuit of his object. Further suspense and uncertainty are provided by the fact that Giacinta loves and is loved by Guglielmo. With Leonardo's marriage to Giacinta in the last act of the play *Il ritorno dalla villeggiatura*, hearts are left in splinters but finances and face have been saved. We find we have the feeling that this is a happy ending.

On our perpetually burning interest in the financial fortunes of Goldoni's characters depend many of his plots, and sometimes at a very basic level, to the extent that Florindo in *La serva amorosa*, Eleonora in *Il cavaliere e la dama* and Bettina in *La buona moglie*, actually keep us guessing as to where their next meal is coming from. Goldoni accompanies his engagement of our materialistic curiosity with that of allied emotions. In a society where a man's possessions are the measure of his worth, appearances assume a more than normal importance. Pride in appearance covers the widest possible field, from trivial externals to weighty matters of honour and reputation. Again our adherence to the ethic is taken for granted, flattered, and used in the manipulation of our sympathies. We are shocked with Gnese in *Le Massere* at

the prospect of Anzoletto the merchant's son being seen in the
street with a bucket, as we feel resentment against Angiola in
Le donne de casa soa for asking her husband's business partner to
walk publicly home from the market carrying a basket of fish.
Occasionally the code is gently mocked. Sabina's horror in
Le avventure della villeggiatura at the sight of Ferdinando without a
watch, 'specialmente in campagna', is surely meant to be funny.
To twentieth century ears it is reminiscent of Wilde.

Goldoni's bourgeois characters are more acutely conscious of
the dignity of their origins than are his nobles, and are quick to
protest if they fear that they are being undervalued. 'Ben arlevada'
and 'civil' are labels claimed by almost every woman in his
dialect plays. Sometimes most colourfully they insist on the
respectability of their beginnings, as does Marcolina in *Sior
Todero Brontolon*:

M'hai trovà in t'un gattolo? M'hai tolto senza camisa? Gh'ho dà
siemile ducati e son civil più de lori: che i so vecchi xe vegnui co le
sgalmare, e casa mia xe più de cent'anni che la gh'ha negozio impiantà,

or epigrammatically, like Checca in *Le donne di casa soa*:

So una putta civil, e son vostra sorella
E no m'avè trovà in t'una sportella.

When the nobility boasts of its origins the words are made to
sound foolish; the bourgeois sounds foolish when he rejects his.
We are encouraged to rejoice in our middle status. Anzoletto in
La casa nova and Doralice in *La famiglia dell'antiquario* make the
mistake of trying to kick back the ladder up which they have
climbed. Both are faced with ruin as a result and we feel profound
satisfaction that it is only through appeal to their merchant
families that they are able to re-establish themselves.

The wish to be thought well of, the desire for respect rather
than for the qualities which inspire it, is presented as a straight
and serious motive. To the eighteenth century Venetian indeed
to lose the good opinion of others was to lose everything, was
even a sufficient reason for leaving one's town or country.
Goldoni himself left Venice to avoid public mockery in 1743
after the scandal in which he was duped by his brother Gianpaolo.
By extension the code demanded a good appearance on all fronts.
One must be seen to be astute and successful in business, honourable, conventional, respected, domestically well organised, well

dressed, well fed, well served, and even happy. The worst fear expressed by Goldoni's characters is that of criticism. Rosaura in *La moglie saggia* is prepared to undergo every sort of domestic unhappiness in order to avoid this worst of failures:

è assai meglio soffrire le domestiche dispiacenze, di quello sia esporsi alle dicerie, alle critiche, alle derisioni del mondo.

This is really the predicament of the 'rusteghi' in the final scenes of their play. Lunardo has planned the marriage between Filipetto and Lucietta; their marriage but not their meeting. He forbids them to marry in order to re-establish his public image, in case it should get about that the lovers have met without his consent, so flouting his authority. He admits that the only obstacle to their marriage is this 'affronto' to his own honour.

Fabrizio, the ordinary honest family man in *La buona famiglia* states the code in these terms: 'La compassione, la carità, tutto quel che volete, ha da cedere il luogo al rispetto e alla convenienza.'

Giacinta's is possibly the extreme case. Her conflict in the *Villeggiatura* trilogy is not as she thinks the Cornelian tussle between love and honour, but the worldly one between passion and reputation. Why has she not broken her understanding with Leonardo long before and given her hand with her heart to Guglielmo?

Che cosa mi ha trattenuto finora dal recedere da un impegno che non è indissolubile, e preferire ad uno sposo, sì poco amato, un oggetto amabile agli occhi miei? Non altro che il mio decoro, il giusto timore di essere criticata.

She justifies herself in a long impassioned speech to the man she loves, which includes the words: 'Qual nome ci acquisteremo noi fra le genti? Qual figura dovremo fare nel mondo?'

'Scomparire', 'fare cattiva figura', these are the crimes to be avoided at whatever cost. 'L'onore', she concludes, giving her motive the grand name that Goldoni's public would have readily accorded it, 'si dee preferire alla vita'.

In only apparent contrast to the middle-class desire to be thought well of is the fetish for unobtrusiveness. One wishes to 'comparire' but one does not wish to 'farsi scorgere'. If one may borrow an expression from John Osborne's Archie Rice, another entertainer who aimed to enthral a popular audience, Goldoni is here playing upon what one might call the 'thank God we're normal' syndrome of the man in the piazza. Excess and eccentricity make us vulnerable; we draw confidence from the uniformity of our behaviour. This common attitude can be made use of by the playwright; it sharpens our amusement at his eccentrics, and he can use it to kindle in us the glow of self-congratulation at our own normality and good sense. The elderly Sabina in *Le avventure delle villeggiatura*, running after the scrounger Ferdinando, is reprimanded by Giacinta:

Eh! via, signora zia, non vi fate scorgere, non vi rendete ridicola in questo modo.

'Non vi fate scorgere' becomes a catch-phrase, used even by kindly Anselmo in *La buona famiglia* to dry the tears, surely justified, of Costanza his daughter-in-law when she fears she has lost her husband's love.

Pantalone in *Le femmine puntigliose* draws the audience round him in a comfortable spirit of complacency as he describes the effete and foppish ways of some of the aristocracy; here the spark of male pride is fanned in the audience at the same time as the spirit of conformity:

Gran cossa xe questa! I omeni i xe arrivai a un segno, che debotto no i gh'ha de omo altro che il nome. Le donne le ghe comanda a bacchetta... Le xe cosse che fa morir da rider, andar in conversazion dove ghe xe donne coi cavalieri serventi.

He goes on to describe the absurdities of 'serventismo', and it is furthermore a comfort to those who cannot afford to indulge in certain forms of pretentiousness, or who have not the time, to be reassured of their folly and fatuity.

The bourgeois ideal is to live and work quietly after the manner of one's forebears. Privacy and one's own business are the household gods. Fabrizio, another embodiment of bourgeois rectitude from *La buona famiglia* insists:

Basta, pensiamo a noi, e lasciamo che il cielo provveda agli altri. Se possiamo far del bene, facciamolo, ma senza intrinsecarsi troppo negli affari altrui.

'Go home,' says Pantalone, to the socially aspiring Florindo in *Le femmine puntigliose*, 'tender ai so negozi, e seguitar le pratiche e le usanze e le corrispondenze de so sior barba.'

In the end, a quiet modest demeanour even pays. When

Pantalone in *La famiglia dell'antiquario* finds his own daughter Doralice already equipped with a 'cavaliere servente' after only four days of marriage to a nobleman, he tells her that her first 'fumo della nobiltà' has gone to her head:

Sè muggier de un conte, sè deventada contessa, ma el titolo no basta per farve portar respetto, quando no ve acquistà l'amore della zente colla dolcezza e colla umiltà... Portè respetto ai vostri maggiori; siè umile, siè paziente, siè bona, e allora sarè nobile, sarè ricca, sarè respettada.

Sobriety of life is not only its own reward but is a practical means of ensuring for oneself both financial security and public regard.

Goldoni is uninhibited in encouraging us to a whole-hearted enjoyment of the peculiarities of foreigners. By conveying to us an absurd sense of their 'otherness' he draws us together in a glow of insular—or rather peninsular—warmth. The three suitors of *La vedova scaltra* have about them the timeless air of the popular funny joke—'Once upon a time there was an Englishman, a Frenchman and a Spaniard.' Madame Gatteau in *Una delle ultime sere di carnovale* with her extraordinary speech patterns; Isidoro the Levantine merchant in *Le donne de casa soa*; Arlecchino's impersonation of an Armenian in *La famiglia dell'antiquario*; from nearer home even the superb and archetypal but well-nigh incomprehensible Paron Fortunato of *Le baruffe chiozzotte*; all these excite the 'dilettevole solletico nell'uman cuore' by their freakishness. Most delightfully ridiculous of all is Alì, the Impresario from Smyrna. His verbs are all in the infinitive but the naïveté of his speech belies his iron determination not to be made a fool of. Reclining on his sofa smoking his hookah he interviews Carluccio, 'musico soprano'. 'Smirne,' he exclaims, 'non aver bisogno di tua persona. Se voler andar Turchia, io ti mandar Costantinopoli, serraglio de Gran Signore.' Nibio the theatrical agent explains the phenomenon of the male soprano voice, commending its beauties. Carluccio exhibits his theatrical temperament as terms are discussed. He demands an apartment, a carriage, a wardrobe, his own choice of libretto. The barely articulate impresario concludes the interview summarily: 'Se più voler,' he threatens, brandishing his pipe in Carluccio's face, 'se più seccar, romper pipa.'

The characters in Goldoni's plays are divided into those who work and those who do not, and our sympathy is secured for those who do. The trading and artisan element in the audience is in this way again flattered with a sense of its own worth. A defence of commerce is made by Anselmo, the Pantalone figure of *Il cavaliere e la dama*. He has been called 'un vil mercante, un uomo plebeo' by the noble Don Flaminio. The merchant's reply is a statement of faith: 'La mercatura è utile al mondo, necessaria al commercio delle nazioni, e a chi l'esercita onoratamente come fo io, non si dice uomo plebeo.' Small trade, crafts and manual work are seen in the same light. The artisan figures going about their business in the opening scene of *Il Ventaglio* are possessed of a sure dignity and sense of purpose. They are quick-witted and capable of reactions superior to those of the gentry living on income with the time to chase baubles. The servants in all the plays bear out this contrast, perhaps nowhere more gracefully than in the opening scene of *Le avventura della villeggiatura*. Drinking chocolate in their quarters in the early morning, the servants have just put their masters and mistresses to bed. Brigida conveys the sheer physical joy of being up early after a good night's sleep:

> Oh! io ho dormito benissimo. Quando ha principiato la conversazione, io sono andata a dormire. Hanno giuocato, hanno cenato, hanno ritornato a giuocare, ed io me la godeva dormendo. A giorno la padrona mi ha fatto chiamare; mi sono alzata, l'ho spogliata, l'ho messa a letto, ho serrato la camera, e mi sono bravamente vestita. Ho fatto una buona passeggiata in giardino, ho raccolto i miei gelsomini, e ho goduto il maggior piacere di questo mondo.

The servants here and *passim*, the cooks in *Le massere*, the fishermen and lace-makers in *Le baruffe chiozzotte*, the actors in *Il teatro comico*; the weavers in *Una delle ultime sere di carnovale*, the gondoliers in *La putta onorata* and *La buona moglie*, the shopkeepers in *La bottega del caffè* are examples of scores of Goldonian characters all seen in the act of working. Work is the norm, and the normal attitude is that of Menego Cainello the gondolier: 'Servimo, xe vero, ma el nostro xe un servir nobile, senza isporcarse le man.'

I have tried to show some of the ways in which Goldoni captivates his audience, especially when he does so through what I have called its bourgeois sensibilities. In reading his plays and some of the views of his critics I have been impressed by the contrast between Goldoni's genial pragmatism, his zestful study of public tastes, capacities and susceptibilities, and the non-materialistic approach of his literary critics; perhaps no merchant soul has studied him. I have felt that there was perhaps a need for some baser spirit to acknowledge a debt, to point out some of the humbler undercurrents of his drama, the fundamental mechanics of his magic, by which those to whom he appeals are drawn in to participate in the true dramatic experience, defined in its essence by one modern critic, J. L. Styan, as 'the exercise of that unique faculty of sharing the experience of others'.

Uberto Limentani

La traduzione foscoliana dei
Discorsi nel Parlamento in
morte di Francesco Horner

L a prima opera[1] che, a quanto consta, il Foscolo abbia pubblicato dopo il suo arrivo in Inghilterra è l'opuscolo contenente la traduzione in italiano dei discorsi pronunciati alla Camera dei Comuni in morte di Francesco Horner: simbolo e comprova dell'ingresso trionfale del poeta nella cerchia più alta ed autorevole del partito Whig, quella, cioè, che aveva per suo centro Holland House.

Francis Horner[2] era stato la grande speranza del partito Whig. Venuto a Londra dalla nativa Scozia non ancora venticinquenne per esercitarvi la professione forense, dopo soli tre anni, ad onta della sua estrazione piccolo borghese, era già entrato in Parlamento all'indomani della morte di Charles James Fox, in un'epoca in cui la Camera dei Comuni era riserva esclusiva del ceto patrizio e, in minor misura, dei giuristi più insigni: la grandezza dell'uomo, per carattere e per intelletto, non aveva tardato ad essere riconosciuta; ma, oltre alla stima generale, egli si era conquistato anche l'affetto di quanti lo avvicinavano: l'equilibrio e la saggezza, la vastità degli interessi e l'acutezza della mente, la bontà del tratto, la probità e la salda fede nei suoi principî trasparivano, a detta di tutti, dal suo aspetto: 'the commandments were written on his face', disse di lui Sydney Smith.[3] Era stato uno dei fondatori e dei collaboratori della *Edinburgh Review*, si era distinto per i suoi brillanti saggi di economia politica, si era fatto rapidamente un nome fra i maggiori giureconsulti della capitale, ed era emerso in un Parlamento ricco di uomini di altissima levatura, sì da apparire chiaramente avviato verso le vette più alte della carriera politica; era naturale che questo geniale Whig, cui arrideva l'avvenire, si vedesse aperte le porte dei palazzi dell'aristocrazia, e che, introdotto a Holland House dal suo amico John Allen, il factotum e confidente di Lord Holland, vi trovasse così cordiale accoglienza da diventare intimo dei padroni di casa, ospite abituale e, con le sue lettere, regolare informatore di Lady Holland su quanto accadeva in Parlamento.[4]

Fu al principio dell'estate del 1816 che cominciò a manifestarsi la grave malattia polmonare che doveva in pochi mesi condurlo alla tomba e che alla fine di settembre indusse i suoi medici a consigliargli di lasciare le isole britanniche e di svernare in Italia. L'interessamento di Lord e Lady Holland per la salute dell'infermo appare costante attraverso la frequente corrispondenza scambiata con lui; nella quale comincia a figurare, tra la folla di begli ingegni che si davano convegno nelle sale di Holland House, Ugo Foscolo, giunto in Inghilterra il 12 settembre, e introdotto dopo pochissimi giorni, e cioè il 21 settembre,[5] da Giuseppe Binda nell'ospitale palazzo. L'impressione prodotta dall'esule italiano in questo ambiente può essere giudicata da quanto Lord Holland scriveva a Francis Horner il 28 settembre,[6] annunciandogli l'arrivo del famoso scrittore:

Here is John Russell [...], not a little delighted with one of our guests, Foscolo—a native of the Greek Islands; who, while completing his education in Italy, was overtaken by the great events of 1796 and 1797, joined the Cisalpine Republic, and forfeited Bonaparte's favour, by the uncourtly mixture of admonition which he infused into a speech of congratulation on his election to the Presidency of the Italian republic in 1802. He has since that time served in the army, been imprisoned, persecuted, and suspected, till, on the battle of Leipsig, he espoused the falling fortunes of Bonaparte[7] with zeal, and has now refused to take oaths to the Austrian government, and come to settle here for twelve years, during which he hopes to be able to compose something that may give him an existence with posterity. His learning and vivacity are wonderful, and he seems to have great elevation of mind, and to be totally exempt from affectation, though not perhaps equally so from enthusiasm, violence, and resentment.

Frattanto lo Horner aveva annunciato la decisione di partire dalla Scozia per l'Italia insieme col fratello Leonard, ed era stato invitato da Lady Holland a soggiornare in un appartamento messo a sua disposizione, e fornito di ogni comodo, durante la sosta a Londra. Il 1mo ottobre Lord Holland, nel reiterare l'invito della consorte, aggiungeva[8]:

Has she [i.e. Lady Holland] told you about Foscolo, our late inmate here? He is without exception the liveliest and cleverest man I know, and I should think full of good qualities as well as talent. In genius and vivacity like Erskine;[9] but Erskine with fixed opinions, great and various knowledge, and affections as warm as his imagination. We are all here *engoués* with him.

E lo Horner, di rimando, nell'accettare l'offerta d'ospitalità: 'Your accounts of Foscolo are so interesting, that I am quite impatient to see him.'[10]

Il soggiorno dello Horner a Holland House durò più dei tre giorni originariamente previsti e deve essersi protratto dall' 11 al 19 o al 20 ottobre;[11] il Foscolo, reduce da Mudeford, lo incontrò

forse più d'una volta: certo egli lo conobbe il 14 ottobre;[12] ed
è chiaro, come si vedrà fra un momento, che essi concepirono
un'alta stima l'uno dell'altro. È rimasta notizia di due delle lettere
di presentazione ad amici italiani che il Foscolo diede allo Horner.
Di quella alla Donna gentile sopravvive solo la menzione che il
Foscolo ne fece in una lettera a lei diretta ('Ho dato per te una
lettera al signor Horner, l'oratore più insigne del Parlamento, e
che viene in Toscana a rifarsi in salute. Dio voglia che ci arrivi,
perch'è partito quasi morente! Aiutalo come e quando potrai'[13]);
di un'altra, del 19 ottobre, indirizzata al letterato torinese Giuseppe
Grassi, col quale il Foscolo era in rapporti d'amicizia da molti anni,
è stato conservato il testo:[14]

Il signor *Horner*, distinto fra gli oratori del Parlamento, s'avvia a Pisa
a rifarsi in salute; e passerà per Torino, dove, facendovi capitar questo
foglio, voi potrete far conoscenza seco, e udire novelle di me. E ve lo
raccomando anche—e *in visceribus*,—perché potrà darsi che la sua
infermità lo stringa a sostare in Torino; e voi gli sarete, ne sono certis-
simo, liberale di consigli e di conforti, e mi sdebiterete non foss'altro in
parte delle affettuose accoglienze ch'io ricevo tutto dì dagl'Inglesi,
segnatamente dagli amici di quest'uomo celebre.

Giunto a Torino il 12 novembre, lo Horner consegnò questa
lettera al destinatario il giorno seguente, e ricevette da lui informa-
zioni che lo confermarono nel proposito di scegliere a residenza
Pisa, come narrato in una lettera della stessa data a Lady Holland:
'I have heard something today, which is in favour of Pisa again;
from M. Grassi, a gentleman to whom Foscolo gave us a letter.
Pray tell him that we are pleased with his friend, and that we are
obliged to him for taking much trouble to give us information.'[15]
Lo stesso Grassi accusava poi ricevuta della lettera, scrivendo al
Foscolo l'8 gennaio 1817:

Horner mi ha parlato di voi con tanta sincerità di lode, che nulla
più. Egli mi disse la stima in che il vostro immenso ingegno è presso i
grandi di cotesta capitale dell'impero britannico; ed io ne presi quella
parte che si conviene alla vera e salda amicizia che da tanti anni vi
professo.[16]

Arrivato a Pisa il 28 novembre, parve dapprima che lo Horner
riacquistasse le sue energie; ma l'8 febbraio, quasi inaspettatamente, decedeva all'età di trentott'anni. La notizia fu resa pubblica
in Inghilterra alla fine del mese e destò immensa impressione ed

universale cordoglio; il 28 febbraio apparve nel *Morning Chronicle* un commosso necrologio, redatto dal vecchio amico dell'estinto, John Allen.[17] La scomparsa di un uomo che non solo era ritenuto il più atto a guidare il partito Whig a più alti destini, ma aveva già così bene meritato della patria, come economista e come statista, da suscitare le maggiori speranze, fu vista come una disgrazia nazionale dai suoi compagni di fede politica e in pari misura dai suoi avversari: sì che, quasi spontaneamente, gli uni e gli altri si unirono nel proposito di tributargli un solenne omaggio in Parlamento 'by a general understanding throughout the House', come scriveva già il 1° marzo John Whishaw.[18] Un simile tributo d'affetto per la scomparsa di un parlamentare che non aveva ancora attinto le vette più elevate della carriera politica, né aveva rivestito alcuna carica importante era cosa fuori del normale, e lo notava John Allen nella lettera di condoglianza al padre dello Horner:

So strong and general is this feeling, that, on the strength of it, his friends have thoughts of venturing on a measure, which, though not quite unprecedented, is nevertheless unusual, and somewhat irregular. In moving the customary writ for the borough which he represented, it is intended to say a few words on his merit and character. Lord Morpeth has most kindly undertaken this office, and it is some consolation to think, that if poor Horner could have looked forward to the possibility of such a measure, there is no man in the House of Commons he would have selected in preference to Lord Morpeth, for the discharge of this tribute to his memory. Some others may possibly follow Lord Morpeth, and even from the opposite side of the House: my only fear is that too many will come forward.[19]

Lo stesso giorno in cui fu scritta questa lettera, il 3 marzo 1817, ebbe luogo la commemorazione alla Camera dei Comuni: otto deputati, quasi tutti fra i più in vista, come un Canning, un Romilly, un Manners Sutton si alzarono a ricordare lo Horner; e cinque di essi erano Tories, ossia del partito avverso a quello del defunto; alcuni, sia Whig che Tory, erano stati suoi intimi amici, come Lord Morpeth e Sir Samuel Romilly; altri ammiravano e amavano in lui solo il grande parlamentare che avevano tante volte ascoltato. La seduta del 3 marzo parve ai contemporanei un eccezionale momento di tregua, in cui tacque per breve tempo l'acerba battaglia della Camera dei Comuni e gli accaniti rivali parlarono con voce concorde: avvenimento davvero memorando.

Non mancano le testimonianze: il direttore dell'*Edinburgh Review*, Francis Jeffrey, scriveva a John Allen il 14 marzo:

What took place in Parliament seems to me extremely honourable to the body; nor do I believe that there is or ever was, a great divided political assembly where so generous and just a testimony would have been borne unanimously to personal merit, joined especially as it was in that individual, with a stern and unaccommodating disdain of all sorts of baseness or falsehood. It is also a national trait, not less honourable, I think, to all parties, that so great a part of the eulogium of a public man, and in public assembly, should have been made to rest on his domestic virtues and private affections.[20]

E Sir James Mackintosh, che assistette a 'this affecting, improving and most memorable scene', come egli la definì nel suo diario, aggiunse:

I may say without exaggeration, that never were so many words uttered without the least suspicion of exaggeration; and that never was so much honour paid in any age or nation to intrinsic claims alone. A Howard[21] introduced, and an English House of Commons adopted, the proposition of thus honouring the memory of a man of thirty-eight, the son of a shopkeeper, who never filled an office, or had the power of obliging a living creature, and whose grand title to this distinction was the belief of his virtue.[22]

Altrove, lo stesso scrittore sottolineò l'insolita commozione che pervase quel giorno

a divided assembly, unused to manifestations of sensibility, abhorrent from theatrical display, and whose tribute on such an occasion derived its peculiar value from their general coldness and sluggishness.[23]

Naturalmente fu a Holland House che la morte dello Horner destò il maggior compianto. Lord Holland fece stampare privatamente in un opuscolo il testo dei discorsi, come era apparso nel resoconto ufficiale dei dibattiti parlamentari,[24] e cioè riveduto dalla maggior parte degli oratori.[25] E il Foscolo tradusse in italiano appunto questo opuscolo, e ne affidò la stampa, in un numero assai limitato di esemplari, ai tipografi Schulze e Dean, ai quali era stato indirizzato nel precedente mese di febbraio dallo Zotti per la riproduzione di due incisioni per l'*Ortis*.[26] L'iniziativa del Foscolo fu soprattutto un delicato atto di cortesia e d'amicizia verso Lord e Lady Holland, cui era legato da un debito di riconoscenza per averlo introdotto nel bel mondo della capitale, e

ai quali un gesto simile non poteva non riuscire gradito; si noti
poi che egli era in termini d'amicizia con almeno un paio di
coloro che avevano preso la parola; ma il Foscolo volle anche
rendere omaggio alla memoria d'una persona che aveva sia pure
brevemente conosciuta e apprezzata.[27] Egli aveva visto in lui uno
spirito affine, un uomo 'destituito di prosapia e di ricchezza' (come
scrisse traducendo il discorso di Lord Morpeth), che aveva saputo
'con la prospera coltura del proprio ingegno, e col solo esercizio
degli onorati suoi studj [...] meritare invidia ed ammirazione dagli
uomini più facoltosi e più alteri.' E poi l'anima del poeta dei
Sepolcri era particolarmente aperta al sentimento d'una nazione
che celebrava un suo morto illustre e che si proponeva di custo-
dirne l'esempio e la memoria come sprone ai posteri per nobili
imprese: 'Ma quanto è più lunga e più generosa, tanto è più utile
a noi l'afflizione per gli uomini egregj i quali dopo d'averci amati
e istruiti, sanno beneficarci anche dalla lor sepoltura,' si legge
nella dedica del libretto.

Il raro opuscolo[28] consta di ventitré pagine, e reca la nota
dedica, firmata, 'Al nobile giovinetto Enrico Fox figlio di Lord
Holland,'[29] il quindicenne erede dell'illustre nome, col quale il
Foscolo si era legato di tenera amicizia, e di cui conosceva
l'attaccamento per lo Horner; la versione del necrologio 'estratto
dal *Morning Chronicle*'[30] precede quella dei discorsi,[31] che riproduce
fedelmente il testo dell'opuscolo fatto stampare in inglese da Lord
Holland. Letta oggi, quando è difficile far rivivere le emozioni e
le passioni del momento, questa serie di discorsi non sembra
conservare che un limitato interesse, legato all'occasione in cui
furono pronunciati, ed ingenera una certa monotonia, per la
ripetizione degli stessi concetti e degli stessi sentimenti; essa,
tuttavia, non riesce inutile per la migliore conoscenza del Foscolo
traduttore.

'E meccanico sono stato io pure—né traducendo si può far
altro', aveva scritto il Foscolo in altra occasione;[32] ma certo
l'epiteto, che mal s'adatta alle traduzioni foscoliane, non s'addice
nemmeno a questa, ove il testo inglese è rifoggiato e ripensato sì
da diventare prosa italiana; consapevolmente o inconsapevol-
mente, egli mirò soprattutto a dar nerbo e concisione al suo stile
senza che ne scapitasse la fedeltà (anche se non aveva imparato a
scriverlo in maniera corretta, appare chiaro da questo lavoro che
conosceva già molto bene l'inglese anche nelle sue sfumature); la

pacata e rotonda facondia delle grandi occasioni parlamentari usata quel giorno dai vari oratori con una certa ampollosità si trasforma in una specie diversa d'eloquenza: quella di una stringata e vigorosa orazione foscoliana. Basteranno alcuni esempi, tratti a caso dal testo, per vedere come il traduttore abbia saputo cercare e trovare l'espressione lapidaria: '[a person] whose inflexible virtue and integrity rendered him one of the most distinguished members of this House, one of the brightest ornaments of the profession to which he belonged, and held him forth as a finished model for the imitation of the rising generation'[33] diventa: '[lui che] per l'inflessibile integrità era additato come insigne nel Parlamento, come decoro de' giure-consulti, e come specchio alla sorgente generazione.' E ancora: 'whenever he was found in public life, he was respected and admired—whenever he was known in private life, he was most affectionately beloved':[34] 'in pubblico, era l'ammirazione del mondo; e in privato, l'amore de' suoi.' Altrove la versione è un po' libera senza per questo riuscire meno felice: 'the hope was vain and the attempt fruitless,'[35] 'e la speranza che lo confortò ad espatriarsi non valse se non a far ch'ei morisse in terra straniera,' in cui il Foscolo aggiunge qualcosa del suo, come fa quando traduce, con efficace adattamento, 'I can confidently appeal [...] to this House, where his exertions will be long remembered with mingled feelings of regret and admiration'[36] con: 'e n'attesto [...] questa Camera, che un dì lo ascoltava ammirandolo, che oggi lo brama; e lo bramerà'; oppure: 'but his career was prematurely closed'[37] con un assai più conturbante 'ma gli si fé incontro la morte'. Solo assai raramente l'amor di concisione lo porta a semplificare troppo, sì che il significato del testo originale risulta alterato: 'It was the mind that appeared in speeches that gave them character'[38]—'e il carattere de' suoi discorsi sgorgava dall'anima sua.'

La traduzione deve essere stata eseguita alla fine d'aprile o al principio di maggio del 1817, a giudicare dalla data della dedica (12 maggio 1817), e, sebbene stampata in un numero esiguo di esemplari, deve essere stata conosciuta abbastanza largamente, almeno nell'ambiente Whig, poiché di essa viene data notizia da tutti gli scrittori del tempo che accennano all'opuscolo fatto apprestare da Lord Holland. Non è noto a quali dei suoi cono-scenti il Foscolo l'abbia inviata, ad eccezione di Lady Holland, la

La traduzione foscoliana dei 'Discorsi nel Parlamento'   195

cui copia esiste tuttora;[39] e del bibliofilo Thomas Grenville, che aveva ricevuto dal Foscolo nello stesso torno di tempo un Omero[40] e un *Ortis*,[41] e quattro anni più tardi sarà il destinatario di una delle preziose copie dell'edizione privatamente stampata degli *Essays on Petrarch*; esiste infatti il biglietto di ringraziamento,[42] con la data del 27 giugno 1817, in cui il Grenville loda 'the taste and feeling' della dedica, e preconizza che 'the memory of poor Horner will live in Italian as well as in English literature.'

Il testo dei *Discorsi nel Parlamento*, che vengono qui dati alle stampe per la prima volta dal 1817, riproduce esattamente quello della copia conservata al British Museum.

Note

[1] V. sui *Discorsi nel Parlamento in morte di Francesco Horner*: E. R. Vincent, *U.F.: An Italian in Regency England* (Cambridge University Press, 1953), pp. 43–45 (e trad. italiana: *U.F. esule fra gli Inglesi*, Firenze, Le Monnier, 1954, pp. 34–35). Poco utile è l'articolo di L. Rava, 'U.F. in memoria di Francesco Horner: con la lettera al figlio di Lord Holland', nella *Rivista d'Italia*, anno XXV, vol. I (1922), pp. 65–70.

[2] V. su F.H.: *Memoirs and Correspondence*, a cura del fratello Leonard Horner (Londra, J. Murray, 1843), 2 voll.; e l'ed. accresciuta del 1853 (Boston, Little, Brown and Co.); Lady Holland, *A Memoir of the Reverend Sydney Smith* (Londra, Longman, Brown, Green Longmans, 1855), 2 voll.; *The Economic Writings of F. H. in the Edinburgh Review, 1802–1806*, a cura di F. W. Fetter (London School of Economics, 1957).

[3] Lettera a Leonard Horner, nella cit. ed. di Boston delle *Memoirs and Correspondence*, vol. II, p. 464.

[4] V., su Holland House in questo periodo: Princess Marie Liechtenstein, *Holland House* (Londra, Macmillan, 1874), 2 voll.; L. Sanders, *The Holland House Circle* (Londra, Methuen, 1908); C. Segrè, 'Lady Holland e i suoi ospiti italiani', in *Relazioni letterarie fra Italia e Inghilterra* (Firenze, Le Monnier, 1911), pp. 317–420; Lord Ilchester, *The Home of the Hollands, 1605–1820* (J. Murray, 1937); E. R. Vincent, *op. cit.*

[5] V. lettera 17 settembre a Giuseppe Binda (*Epistolario*, Firenze, Le Monnier, 1853, vol. II, p. 274) in cui Foscolo dice che sarà presentato 'sabato mattina' agli Holland. Il 21 settembre era appunto un sabato.

[6] Lettera CCLXXIV nelle cit. *Memoirs and Correspondence* (1ª ed.), vol. II, pp. 341–342.

[7] Il duplice atteggiamento del Foscolo nei riguardi di Napoleone a cui qui si allude (v. anche E. R. Vincent, *op. cit.*, p. 26) non era dissimile da quello degli stessi Whigs e in particolare di Lord e Lady Holland, che avversarono Bonaparte quando era un oppressore, all'apice della potenza, e si adoperarono energicamente a suo favore quando era oppresso durante la prigionia a Sant'Elena.

C.E.I.L. – O

[8] Lettera CCLXXVII, *Memoirs and Correspondence cit.*, vol. II, p. 346.

[9] Lord Thomas Erskine (1750–1823), il famoso giurista e Lord Chancellor, Whig ed intimo amico di Fox.

[10] Poscritto aggiunto il 6 ottobre alla lettera 4 ottobre 1816 a Lady Holland (*Memoirs and Correspondence cit.*, lett. CCLXXVIII, vol. II, p. 349).

[11] *Memoirs and Correspondence cit.*, p. 43.

[12] E. R. Vincent, *op. cit.*, p. 43.

[13] Lettera del 25 ottobre 1816, in *Epistolario cit.*, vol. II, p. 285.

[14] *Epistolario cit.*, vol. II, p. 282.

[15] *Memoirs and Correspondence cit.*, vol. II, pp. 364–365.

[16] *Epistolario cit.*, vol. III, p. 374.

[17] *Memoirs and Correspondence cit.*, vol. II, p. 411. Prima di entrare al servizio di Lord Holland nel 1801 lo Allen (1771–1843) aveva insegnato medicina a Edimburgo, e lo Horner aveva ascoltato un suo corso di lezioni. Anche lo Allen aveva appartenuto al gruppo di scozzesi che aveva fondato la *Edinburgh Review*.

[18] Lettera a Thomas Smith, nelle *Memoirs and Correspondence cit.*, vol. II, p. 415.

[19] *Ibid.*, pp. 413–414.

[20] *Memoirs and Correspondence cit.* (ed. di Boston 1853), vol. II, pp. 456–457.

[21] Lord Morpeth.

[22] *Memoirs of the life of Sir James Mackintosh* (Londra, E. Moxon, 1835), vol. II, p. 339. L'intero passo del diario del Mackintosh in cui è descritta la seduta è citato da E. R. Vincent, *op. cit.*, p. 44.

[23] Nota a pp. 314–315 della *Dissertation on the progress of Ethical Philosophy chiefly during the seventeenth and eighteenth centuries* di Sir James Mackintosh (Edimburgo, Adam and Charles Black, 2ª ed., 1837).

[24] Che sia stato Lord Holland a far stampare l'opuscolo è attestato da Lord Ilchester (*The Home of the Hollands cit.*, p. 318) e da Sir Samuel Romilly, che pronunciò uno dei discorsi commemorativi (*Memoirs of the life of Sir Samuel Romilly written by himself*, Londra, J. Murray, 1840, vol. III, n. a p. 282). Il titolo del raro opuscolo, che consta di 23 pp., è: *Motion for a new writ for the Borough of St. Mawes, in the room of Francis Horner, Esq. deceased; on Monday, March 3, 1817* (London, Printed for Ridgways, Piccadilly. 1817). Esso riproduce fedelmente il testo ufficiale (*The Parliamentary Debates*, Londra, T. C. Hansard, vol. XXXV, 1817, col. 841–850). Il necrologio tratto dal *Morning Chronicle*, riprodotto nelle pp. 21–23 dell'opuscolo, appare in una nota in calce alla col. 841 dei *Parliamentary Debates*. Questi recano, dopo il discorso di Lord Lascelles, la formula: 'The motion was then agreed to', che fu omessa nell'opuscolo.

[25] Della revisione del testo dei discorsi dà notizia Sir S. Romilly, *op. cit., ibid.*

[26] mss. Lab. XLII, 166. La lettera è stata pubblicata da G. Gambarin nel vol. IV dell'Ed. Naz., p. LXXIII.

[27] Esiste fra i mss. Lab. (XLII, 249) un foglio manoscritto in latino, non di mano del Foscolo, contenente quattro distici 'In obitum Francisci Horner' e firmato da 'the Hon. W. Spencer'.

[28] *Discorsi nel Parlamento in morte di Francesco Horner tradotti dall'inglese*

(Londra, dai torchi di Schulze e Dean, 13, Poland Street, 1817). Sotto il titolo si legge un distico catulliano ('Multas per gentes et multa per aequora vectus, Advenio has miseras hospes ad inferias'), adattato dal Carmen CI, vv. 1-2. (Il Foscolo sostituì 'hospes' a 'frater').

[29] Pp. III–IV. La dedica fu riprodotta per la prima volta dal Carrer, e poi nell'*Epistolario* (Firenze, Le Monnier, 1853), vol. II, p. 298, con l'omissione delle parole '[perchè] vivete in libera patria', per motivi di censura.

[30] Pp. V–VI. Nell'opuscolo in inglese fatto stampare da Lord Holland il necrologio fa da appendice ai discorsi.

[31] Pp. 9–23.

[32] Lettera del 28 ottobre 1813 a Camillo Ugoni a proposito della traduzione del *Viaggio sentimentale* (*cit.* da M. Fubini, vol. v dell'Ed. Naz., p. XLII; ora nell' *Epistolario*, Ed. Naz., vol. IV, p. 411).

[33] Discorso di W. Elliot.

[34] Discorso di C. Manners Sutton.

[35] Discorso di Lord Morpeth.

[36] *Ibid.*

[37] *Ibid.*

[38] Discorso di C. Grant.

[39] Essa è conservata nella Brotherton Library (Università di Leeds), e reca la dedica di mano del Foscolo: 'A Milady/Holland/Enrico Fox/ e Ugo Foscolo rispettosamente/offerivano/. Hollandhouse 28 giugno MDCCCXVII.'

[40] E. R. Vincent, *op. cit.*, p. 52.

[41] Il Granville scrisse al Foscolo il 17 maggio, ringraziando per il dono dell'*Ortis* (MSS. Lab. XLII, 196).

[42] MSS. Lab. XLII, 250.

DISCORSI

NEL PARLAMENTO

𝔍𝔫 𝔐𝔬𝔯𝔱𝔢

DI

FRANCESCO HORNER

TRADOTTI DALL' INGLESE.

Multas per gentes et multa per aequora vectus,
Advenio has miseras hospes ad inferias.
CATUL.

LONDRA

DAI TORCHI DI SCHULZE E DEAN,

13, Poland Street.

1817.

[p. 2 *occhietto*]

[3]

AL NOBILE GIOVINETTO

ENRICO FOX

FIGLIO DI LORD HOLLAND.

So di mandarvi un dono che vi rinnoverà amaro nell'anima il desiderio di
Francesco Horner. Ma quanto è più lunga e più generosa, tanto è più
utile a noi l'afflizione per gli uomini egregj i quali dopo d'averci amati e
istruiti, sanno beneficarci anche dalla lor sepoltura. La morte non fu al
tutto immatura per esso: non gli lasciò meritare la invidia, la ingratitudine
e la sazietà de' mortali; e nol ritolse alla terra, se non quando ei s'era già
fatto degno che i suoi concittadini ponessero molte speranze in lui solo. Or
da che non v'è conceduto d'essere spettatore delle sue azioni, contemplatele
nelle sue lodi. Potrete emularle, perchè vivete in libera patria e vedete le [4]
pubbliche virtù venerate nella memoria del vostro zio, ed amate nel padre
vostro: e la Natura vi ha dotato d'indole sì gentile, da non sentirvi felice

se non quando procuccierete fama a voi, ed utile agli altri. Ricordivi dell'amico rapito nel vigor dell'età, ed affrettatevi. E mentre voi, giovinetto, ricalcando i vestigj di quel cittadino salirete animoso per le vie della vita, io stanco e privo di patria, andrò ripensando al sicuro riposo e all'anima divina di quel mortale, e non mi rincrescerà di discenderle.—Addio.

UGO FOSCOLO.

Soho Square,
12 Maggio, 1817.

[5]

ESTRATTO

DAI.

MORNING CHRONICLE,

Venerdì, 28 *Febbraro*, 1817.

DOBBIAMO, e non senza amaro cordoglio, annunziare che FRANCESCO HORNER, membro del Parlamento per *San Mawes*, morì in Pisa addì 8 del mese. A noi è raramente toccato a dolerci di perdita più grave, o a sostenere più irreparabile calamità. All'inflessibile integrità, ed all'ardente sua religione per la libertà, egli univa la moderazione e la discretezza; doti che non sempre accompagnano quelle virtù. La riverenza ch'egli otteneva, e la deferenza ond'era ascoltato nella Camera de' Comuni, sono convincentissime prove del predominio delle virtù morali in una popolare assemblea. Rari fra quanti s'attennero all'Opposizione conseguirono preponderanza ed autorità in Parlamento pari a quella ch'ei senza i casuali sussidj della opulenza e del grado, aveva acquistato; e non tanto per la facondia e l'ingegno, benchè fossero eminentissimi in lui, quanto per l'universale opinione della sua pubblica e domestica rettitudine. Aveva potente intelletto, [6] mente comprensiva, dottrina vasta e accurata, giudizio profondo e luminoso; condotta piana e diritta. La sua eloquenza conformavasi al suo carattere; grave, energica, senz'ombra di vanità o presunzione, e schietta di personalità e di rancore; ma piena di profondo sdegno e magnanimo contro la fraude, l'ipocrisia, e l'ingiustizia. Era caldo, zelante, affettuoso nell'amicizia; disinteressato e signorile nelle azioni; deliberato e costante nelle opinioni; era modesto e verecondo ne' modi. Gli amici suoi non cesseranno mai di piangere la sua morte e la loro disavventura. La repubblica non si ristorerà agevolmente di tanta perdita; e in tempi simili a' nostri, se ne accorgerà amaramente. Esso nasceva nel 1778:[1] fu ascritto nella Facoltà degli avvocati nel 1800; e nel 1807 chiamato al Foro Inglese. Dal 1806 sedeva nella Camera de' Comuni membro di tre Parlamenti successivi. L'ufficio laborioso di commissario per la Liquidazione de' Crediti del Carnatico,[2] fu l'unico impiego ch'egli esercitò; e solo per breve tempo: da che vedendolo incompatibile con gli studj e gli obblighi della sua professione, lo aveva, da più anni in qua, rassegnato.

[7]

DISCORSI

NEL PARLAMENTO,

&c. &c. &c.

[*p. 8 occhietto*]

[9]

DISCORSI

NELLA CAMERA DE' COMUNI

In Morte

DI FRANCESCO HORNER

LORD MORPETH[3]

PROPONGO che l'Oratore[4] emmetta il suo rescritto per l'elezione d'un membro pel comune di San Mawes, da sostituire nel Parlamento a FRANCESCO HORNER defunto.

E se alla proposta aggiungerò alcune parole intorno ad avvenimento sì luttuoso, confido che non avrò taccia di inopportunità o d'arroganza.[5] So che non è solito ufficio, se non in rade occasioni; nè io paragonerò questa con le anteriori; basti che non mancano esempj.

L'amico mio, che oggi io deploro, nè lo rammenterò mai senz'amarissimo desiderio, era già da alcun tempo di sì afflitta salute da non potersi applicare alla sua professione nè a' doveri del Parlamento; e sperò di riaversi sotto cielo più [10] propizio e più ameno. Ma nè la salubrità del clima, nè i sussidj della medicina giovarono contro alla consunzione, che lo struggeva lenta, ostinata; finchè subitamente lo estinse: e la speranza che lo confortò ad espatriarsi non valse se non a far ch'ei morisse in terra straniera. Le angoscie del morbo che s'esacerbava ogni dì, non turbarono mai la serenità del gentile animo suo; e nell'esaurimento delle forze vitali quell'egregio intelletto serbò la sua calma, il suo vigore, e la sua dignità. Forse non mi sarebbe disdetto, se (senza troppo innoltrarmi nel sacrario delle famiglie) accennassi quelle domestiche carità, quelle soavi virtù, che abbellivano insieme e nobilitavano la sua vita privata. Direi come caldamente ei sentiva la pietà figliale e fraterna, e ne adempieva generosamente i doveri; benchè questi pregj, per quanto siano da onorarsi e da amarsi, non pare che possano con rigorosa convenienza raccomandarsi alla contemplazione del Parlamento. Pur quando sono adunati inviscerati immedesimati nel carattere d'un pubblico personaggio, ridiventano di pubblica proprietà; e per l'influenza del loro esempio il capitale della pubblica virtù si arricchisce.

[11] E che uomo pubblico egli si fosse, io mi richiamo a più numerose testimonianze; e n'attesto il Foro del quale egli era ornamento; e questa Camera, che un dì lo ascoltava ammirandolo, che oggi lo brama; e lo bramerà. Nè importa ch'io noveri con quali discipline severe, con quante fatiche ei meritò la sua fama; affermerò solamente ch'ei la piantò sovra le fondamenta inconcusse d'una mente conscia di sè e della sua rettitudine. Era ardente a rintracciare la verità,[6] e irrepugnabilmente tenace negli alti principj del giusto e del retto. Allorch'ei diffondeva fra noi le idee della sua mente limpida e doviziosa, la sua facondia era ad un tempo semplice e casta e virile ed efficacissima ad agitare e dilucidare le gravi faccende. Avresti detto che alla dialettica precisione del giureconsulto s'accoppiasse il corredo di cognizioni ed il senno dell'uomo di stato.

Le sue opinioni politiche furono sì patenti, ed ei le professò sì altamente che sarebbe superfluo s'io le esponessi e illustrassi. Citerò bensì con fiducia i suoi contradditori politici, e affermo; ch'ei non mercò popolarità per modi obbliqui o a prezzo non degno di lui. Saranno ingenui e confermeranno, che quantunque le [12] sue sentenze scoppiassero sempre maschie, deliberate e costanti, non però gli sfuggiva parola che fosse tinta mai d'acrimonia o amareggiata di personalità o di rancore. E appunto da' suoi costumi e dalle doti, che ingentilivano di tanta amabilità la sua conversazione, appariva che quel cuore infatti era libero d'ogni acerba passione.

Or chi considera quanto ei progredí nel foro e fra noi, e in quanto breve spazio di vita, s'accorge che non erano se non preludi di cose maggiori, e i primi passi co' quali ei correva a più nobile fama; ma gli si fe' incontro la morte. Al lutto senza consolazione per la famiglia che lo ha irreparabilmente perduto, e per chiunque il conobbe e lo amava, s'aggiunge (e il dirò pure) che il Parlamento e la Patria presentono in tanta perdita il gran pubblico danno; e in questi tempi ne faremo rigida prova. Nondimeno in questi tempi, mentre tutti si stanno intenti a scrutinio severo della Costituzione,[7] chi per investigarne i difetti e trovarvi riparo, chi per esaltarne i pregj e la perfezione, noi possiamo pur confortarci considerando come un cittadino destituto di prosapia e di ricchezze, ha potuto con la prospera coltura del proprio ingegno, e [13] col solo esercizio degli onorati suoi studj aggiudicarsi tal grado nel mondo da meritare invidia ed ammirazione dagli uomini più facoltosi e più alteri.

Scusimi la Camera, non per avere promosso questo soggetto; ch'anzi confido d'esserne assolto: bensì pel tributo scarso ed innadequato offerto da me alla memoria di tanto amico.

MR CANNING[8]

Fra quante volte fu qui prestato ai defunti l'ufficio, adempiuto ora con sì affettuosa e delicata facondia dal nobile amico mio,[9] non ho memoria che mai potesse cospirare come oggi il consenso di tutti gli animi.

Sarebbe stata mia somma ventura, ed oggi la sconterei con pari cordoglio, se avessi coltivato amicizia con l'egregio ed amabile personaggio, della cui perdita oggi dobbiam condolerci. Nol conobbi che nel recinto di questa Camera; e nelle due ultime diete m'accadde d'allontanarmi: nè ho potuto ammirare i frutti che (a quanto intesi poscia, e non dubito) rispondevano a' primi presagi ed alle felici speranze che non potevano essere deluse che dalla morte. Pur tanto vidi di lui da desumere quale [14] oratore manchi alla Camera, e quale cittadino alla Patria.

E davvero; stavano riposte in esso con meraviglioso concerto tutte quante le doti atte a degna riuscita. Profondità di principj, ampie mire, moltiplicità ed esattezza di cognizioni, e fin'anche il

tenore della sua vigorosa e temperata eloquenza; il candor del suo
foco, se mai lasciavasi allettar dal suo foco; e più che altro, la
modestia singolare la quale velando le sue facoltà le faceva
trasparire con più grazioso splendore, erano doti, che avvalorate
da costumi illibati, gli conciliavano non solo il cuore degli amici,
ma imponevano a un tempo rispetto a' suoi avversarj politici;
quindi l'attenzione e il favore di chi lo ascoltava; quindi la certezza
d'un nome illustre da non potergli essere conteso mai nè invidiato.

Nè finirò senza alludere alla conclusione del mio nobile amico,
alla quale io al tutto consento. Parebbe non doversi frapporre al
nostro lutto nessuna parola, che senta di controversia. Ma da che
pur questa in pochi anni è la seconda volta che qui s'ode citar il
nome d'un oscuro comune per vacanza di rappresentanti insigni
di costumi e d'ingegno,[10] non mi si neghi ch'io [15] con le mie
dichiarate opinioni intorno alla nostra Costituzione parlamentaria,
e rispettando le altrui, asserisca, che dobbiamo in parte rassicurarci
su le imputazioni teoriche contro una Costituzione la quale
praticamente riesce sì bene. Non può essere al tutto vizioso e in-
conveniente al suo scopo un sistema di rappresentazione, per cui
gli uomini simili a quelli che or noi ricordiamo, si succedono in
questa Camera per mettere a prova i doni che hanno sortito dal
Cielo, e farne spettatrice la Patria, dalla quale possono essere un
dì chiamati ad assisterla de' loro consigli, e sostenerne la grandezza
e la gloria.[11]

MR MANNERS SUTTON[12]

Dubito s'io debba inframmettermi, quand'io non sono atto ad
aggiungere nulla a' sensi caldi e veraci egregiamente espressi; ma
spero di non parere presontuoso e impetrare ch'io dal profondo
dell'anima mia possa confermar gli altrui detti.

Tempi addietro la sorte mi consentiva di vivere in domesti-
chezza amichevole con Francesco Horner; il cangiarsi delle circostanze, e il mio dipartirmi dal foro ci hanno disgiunti: [16] pur
(s'io troppo non mi lusingo) ho certezza che il rincrescimento fu
poi sempre scambievole. Quanto a me, posso dire con lealtà che
nè le circostanze mutate, nè i dispareri politici, nè la interrotta
famigliarità hanno mai potuto minimamente intepidire gli affetti
riverenti, devoti, amorosi, che gli ho pur sempre serbato.

La perdita di tante e imponenti doti d'ingegno, d'attività

infaticabile, di severissima integrità riunite con accordo così perfetto in un uomo pubblico, è in questi, anzi in tutti i tempi, sì grave, da poter essere giudicata dal Parlamento. Ma chi non era consolato dalla felicità, e direi dalla beatitudine, d'averlo amico; chi non poteva essere testimonio e godere delle amabili doti che lo rendevano caro a' suoi conoscenti, non può concepire quanti piaceri ed esempi di virtù private oggi manchino alla vita sociale. Ed io stimo con sincerità di coscienza non essere mai vissuto mortale, di cui si possa più veracemente dire: che in pubblico, era l'ammirazione del mondo; e in privato, l'amore de' suoi.

Non abuserò della indulgenza del Parlamento; ben io bramava d'ottenerla per brevi momenti, tanto da sdebitarmi, a mio potere, [17] d'un obbligo di gratitudine, e soddisfare [il] mio cuore; e unire la mia all'universale venerazione, in cui la memoria di tal cittadino deve essere e sarà indubitabilmente tenuta.

MR WYNN[13]

Le virtù[14] che onoravano l'ottimo collega che abbiamo perduto sono state fino ad ora descritte dagli amici miei[15] con amore e con fede; perch'essi ebbero opportunità di osservarle da presso. Per altro non erano virtù sì adombrate dalle pareti domestiche da non apparire luminose anche al mondo; stavano ingenite nell'individuo; ogni sua azione derivava sempre da esse; e però si svelavano a tutti. La gentilezza dell'indole e la mansuetudine ch'egli esercitava fra tutti i suoi conoscenti, lo accompagnavano a' Tribunali ed al Parlamento. Fra l'ardor delle dispute, la veemenza de' dibattimenti politici, e i pertinaci conflitti di dispareri, di contradizioni, e di giudizj, la serenità, e fin anche l'amenità dell'indole sua rimanevansi inalterabili. Nè bollore di controversia, nè impeto d'anima, nè entusiasmo per le proprie idee, nè convinzione degli errori altrui il seducevano a malignare le intenzioni degli av-[18] versarj, o ad inveire contro il loro carattere. La ricordanza di tali virtù sarà amara e lunghissima.

SIR S. ROMILLY[16]

La calda amicizia che per più anni mi strinse all'uomo desiderato oggi dal Parlamento, mi assegna, spero, il doloroso diritto di spassionare con pochi detti l'anima mia; ed è sì piena delle private virtù di lui, che sebbene non fossero conosciute nè pregiate mai

da veruno più che da me, le parole mancherebbero a quanto io
ne sento: onde tacendo dell'amico, non dirò che dell'uomo
pubblico.

Fra le qualità che lo segnalavano, la indipendenza d'animo
risaltava generosissima: ed ei ne sentiva la dignità; e discerneva
quanto importasse; e la pregiava sopra ogni cosa; e la voleva a
ogni patto. Però mentr'ei corredavasi l'intelletto di sì varia
supellettile di dottrine spettanti alla pubblica economia, ed alla
esterna politica dello Stato; mentre assumeva con felice facondia le
questioni gravi che ultimamente si trattavano nella Camera, egli
non che ristarsi pur mai dagli obblighi laboriosi della sua professione, vi perseverava. E benchè il Foro non avesse an- [19] cor cor-
risposto a' suoi meriti, ei vi attendeva indefesso; quasi sdegnasse
di fidare per la propria indipendenza se non se nelle proprie
fatiche, o di aspirare se non per esse agli emolumenti e agli onori
a' quali il suo alto ingegno ascrivevagli di grandi e giusti diritti.

Da dodici anni in qua il Parlamento è andato perdendo alcuni
di que' mortali che l'hanno più illuminato e illustrato; ma la
perdita d'oggi ha una sua propria fatalità. Perchè quegli altri
egregj avevano già tocco il sommo del loro vigore, e sperimentate
tutte le loro forze; e la Camera nel vederseli rapire, ha non foss'altro goduto della trista soddisfazione di saper misurare tutto
quant'era il suo danno. Ma chi si ricorda che da quando Francesco
Horner si fece udire fra noi, il suo ingegno d'anno in anno
s'invigoriva, e che le sue facoltà s'ampliavano; e che la sua
eloquenza risaliva più sempre all'altezza de' soggetti, e li padro-
neggiava—chi si ricorda come ad ogni nuova dieta le sue parole
erano d'ora in ora più pregne di sostanza, d'autorità, e di persuasione, e come il suo intelletto illuminava, e abbracciava le idee,
e si agguerriva di nuove forze—quei può solo accertarsi che per
quanta eccellenza avesse l'a-[20] mico mio fino allor conseguita, ei
di certo, se al Cielo non fosse piaciuto altrimenti, avrebbe palesato
delle facoltà ignote fin allora alla camera, nè forse note a lui stesso.

Or se considerando le qualità straordinarie di Francesco Horner,
prescindessi dallo scopo al quale miravano, tradirei l'animo mio.
La grande eloquenza non è per sè stessa che oggetto di passeggiera
ammirazione, e vanissima: ben è nobilitata dall'uso: e quando
tende virtuosamente a fini magnanimi, alla tutela dell'oppresso,
alla redenzione dello schiavo, alla diffusione del sapere, alla
dispersione delle tenebre dell'ignoranza e della superstizione, alla

verace utilità della patria, e a dilatare la sfera della prosperità del genere umano, allora l'oratore è creato per beneficio de'popoli. E perchè appunto abbiamo perduto un così fatto oratore, io reputo questa come gravissima fra le disavventure che nell'odierna condizione de' tempi potesse e possa affliggere mai la nazione.

[21]   MR W. ELLIOT[17]

Nè io mi negherò il conforto di porgere fra gli altri amici il mio modesto tributo d'affezione e di stima, ed anche di gratitudine, alla memoria di lui che mi fu spesso liberale de' lumi del suo felice intelletto; e che per l'amore religioso alla verità, pel raro criterio, per la dignità e l'efficacia del dire, e per l'inflessibile integrità era additato come insigne nel Parlamento, come decoro de' giure-consulti, e come specchio alla sorgente generazione.

Sono tante le circostanze, e sì diverse le considerazioni che rendono più funesta la sua morte, ed avvenne in tal congiuntura, ch'io non ardirei calcolare tutto il pubblico danno. Ben disse il mio dotto amico,[18] essere perdita grande per oggi, e grandissima per l'avvenire. Poichè (per consigli inaccessibili alla indagine de' mortali) ei fu ritolto alla terra, mentre avviavasi verso gli alti gradi nella repubblica ne' quali, a quanto occhio umano può antivedere, i suoi meriti dovevano collocarlo; e la patria avrebbe goduto de' pieni e maturi beneficj di tante ammirabili doti.

[22]   MR C. GRANT[19]

Io lo conobbi innanzi ch'ei conseguisse il nome di cui fu poscia rimeritato nel mondo; nè posso in questa luttuosa occasione udire onorare la sua memoria, e tacermi. Per dispareri ch'io avessi seco nelle pubbliche controversie,[20] io non cessava dall'ammirar quella mente e quell'anima. Perchè nella sua eloquenza non palesavasi unicamente l'ingegno, ma si spiegava in essa anche un cuore ridondante di probità generosa, di benevolenza, d'umanità e delle virtù tutte che provocando l'applauso persuadono insieme ad amarle; e il carattere de' suoi discorsi sgorgava dall'anima sua. Non descriverò le sue private virtù, le quali, a dir poco, veniano del pari co' suoi pubblici meriti. Gl'interessi e le cure della pubblica vita non intepidivano in lui gli affetti domestici, o la pietà per la sua famiglia. L'ultima volta ch'io conversava seco, ei godeva della speranza delle ferie e del piacere di potersi raccogliere nel grembo de' suoi parenti, e fra le carezze degli amici. Quanto io più ripenso alla mente, alle virtù, ed alla vita di lui, tanto più io mi raffermo ch'esso è degno di lodi meritate da pochi.

[23]   LORD LASCELLES[21]

Non ho mai conosciuto Francesco Horner, se non se in questa Camera; e dove in ogni seria questione abbiamo quasi perpetuamente votato con opposte sentenze.[22] Ho nondimeno asserito assai volte in privato ch'egli era uno de' maggiori ornamenti della sua patria; onde spero perdono se unisco la mia all'altrui voce per pronunziare oggi in pubblico, che la patria non poteva essere afflitta di maggiore disavventura. Gl'istituti del Parlamento non concedono via a decretare a suffragi l'onore dovuto alla memoria di lui; ma sia di conforto agli amici suoi la certezza, che ove fosse stato possibile a raccorli, i pareri sarebbero stati unanimi.

        Londra,
Dai Torchi di Schulze e Dean,
    13, Poland Street

Note

[1] L'opuscolo in cui è publicato il testo inglese reca erroneamente '1779', che il Foscolo corresse nella sua traduzione.

[2] 'Commissioner for the Liquidation of the Carnatic Claims': fu questa la sola carica pubblica dello Horner, onerosa ma non retribuita. Dal marzo 1806 al maggio 1809 egli fece parte della commissione arbitrale incaricata di liquidare i debiti del Nababbo di Arcot e di soddisfare le pretese dei suoi creditori; tali debiti erano sorti in seguito a prestiti concessi dalla Compagnia delle Indie Orientali per spese militari. Il Carnatic è una regione dell'India meridionale, equivalente a un dipresso allo stato di Mysore, che era stata conquistata dalla Gran Bretagna nel XVIII secolo.

[3] George Howard, poi sesto Conte di Carlisle (1773–1848). Lord Morpeth conosceva il Foscolo ed ascoltò le sue conferenze. Apparteneva al partito Whig, aveva avuto vari incarichi ministeriali, e si era messo in vista in Parlamento. Il suo discorso, che diede il tono alla commemorazione, riscosse il plauso universale e fu definito 'feeling and judicious' da Lord Holland (*Further Memoirs of the Whig party, 1807–1821*, Londra, J. Murray, 1905, p. 256); e Sir James Mackintosh (*diario cit.* da E. R. Vincent, *U.F.: An Italian in Regency England*, Cambridge University Press, 1953, p. 44) scrisse: 'Lord Morpeth opened it in a speech so perfect, that it might have been well placed as a passage in the most elegant English writer; it was full of feeling; every topic was skilfully presented, and contained, by a sort of prudence which is a part of taste, within safe limits; he slid over the thinnest ice without cracking it.' Egli era stato prescelto a proporre la mozione a motivo della sua amicizia con lo Horner.

⁴ Lo 'Speaker'.

⁵ Era cosa insolita commemorare un deputato che non aveva occupato le cariche più alte.

⁶ Sydney Smith scrisse in una lettera al fratello dello Horner (Lady Holland, *A memoir of the Reverend Sydney Smith*, Londra, Longman, Brown, Green and Longmans, 1855, vol. I, p. 18): 'Horner loved truth so much that he never could bear any jesting upon important subjects.'

⁷ La riforma della costituzione era uno degli argomenti più dibattuti, ed aveva dato luogo a disordini in varie città; la questione era stata di particolare attualità anche in Parlamento nelle settimane precedenti. I propugnatori della riforma avevano un programma assai vasto, che minacciava perfino l'esistenza della monarchia, e mirava soprattutto a modificare la Camera dei Comuni ed a cambiare un sistema elettorale anomalo sotto molti aspetti, specialmente nelle circoscrizioni in cui l'elezione del rappresentante in Parlamento era praticamente alla mercé di una sola persona, solitamente dell'aristocrazia. Gli antiriformisti consideravano i loro avversari come pericolosi rivoluzionari.

⁸ George Canning (1770–1827), il noto statista e futuro Primo Ministro; fra i più influenti del partito Tory. Nel 1817 era President of the Board of Control, era già stato Ministro degli Esteri, e quando era morto Guglielmo Pitt, ne aveva pronunciato l'elogio alla Camera dei Comuni. Sir James Mackintosh (diario cit., *ibid.*) osserva intorno al suo discorso: 'Canning filled well what would have been the vacant place of a calm observer of Horner's public life and talents.'

⁹ Allude, secondo la consueta formula parlamentare, a Lord Morpeth.

¹⁰ A questo punto il resoconto ufficiale e l'opuscolo fatto stampare da Lord Holland recano una nota a piè di pagina omessa dal Foscolo: 'Mr Windham, who represented St. Mawes in 1806, died member for Higham Ferrers in 1810.' William Windham (1750–1810) in realtà aveva rappresentato dal 1802 al 1806 la circoscrizione elettorale di St. Mawes, di cui lo Horner fu deputato dall'aprile 1813.

¹¹ Il Canning riuscì destramente a inserire, in un discorso che non avrebbe dovuto essere controverso, il tema da lui più volte ripreso nei suoi interventi in Parlamento, della difesa del sistema elettorale esistente. Egli era infatti avverso alla riforma della costituzione; e la felice riuscita in Parlamento dello Horner, che era diventato deputato grazie all'offerta del seggio da parte di chi in pratica ne disponeva, gli forniva un nuovo, efficace argomento a sostegno della tesi da lui propugnata.

¹² Charles Manners Sutton, poi primo Visconte Canterbury (1780–1845), lo statista del partito Tory, che tre mesi più tardi fu eletto Speaker della Camera dei Comuni. 'Manners Sutton's most affecting speech,' scrisse Sir James Mackintosh (*ibid.*), 'was a tribute of affection from a private friend become a political enemy.'

¹³ Charles Watkin William Wynn (1775–1830), anch'egli del partito Tory; ebbe alcuni incarichi ministeriali.

¹⁴ Nel resoconto ufficiale e nell'opuscolo contenente il testo inglese, i discorsi del Wynn, di Sir S. Romilly, del Grant e di Lord Lascelles sono riferiti in forma indiretta, mentre il Foscolo li ha volti in forma diretta.

[15] Anche qui l'espressione 'amici miei' è la solita formula parlamentare; nel testo inglese: 'his Noble Friend (Lord Morpeth), and his Right Hon. Friend who had last spoken (Mr. M. Sutton)'.

[16] Sir Samuel Romilly (1757–1818), uomo politico Whig, giurista e criminologo di fama europea; promosse una riforma del diritto penale che s'ispirava anche alle idee del Beccaria. Era fin dal 1802 intimo amico dello Horner, e conosceva il Foscolo (E. R. Vincent, *op. cit.*, p. 51). Nel suo diario, dove il Romilly riassume il discorso da lui pronunciato, egli ricorda la lunga e stretta amicizia che lo legava allo Horner, e aggiunge: 'I thought myself called upon to mention those merits for which I most highly valued him; and to say that, which, if he could witness what is now passing amongst us, I thought he would most wish should be said' (*Memoirs of the life of Sir S.R.*, Londra, John Murray, 1840, vol. III, p. 281).

[17] William Elliot, uomo politico del partito Whig, appartenente alla cerchia di Lord Holland. Morì nel 1818.

[18] Cioè Sir S. Romilly (secondo l'usanza parlamentare si definisce 'dotto' chi esercita l'avvocatura).

[19] Charles Grant, poi Lord Glenelg (1778–1866), statista Tory che ebbe vari incarichi ministeriali. Il resoconto ufficiale, ma non il testo da cui il Foscolo tradusse, specifica: 'Mr C. Grant, junr.' Sedeva infatti a qual tempo in Parlamento anche il padre del Grant, pure chiamato Charles.

[20] Allude al fatto che apparteneva a un partito diverso da quello dello Horner.

[21] Henry Lascelles, secondo Conte di Harewood (1767–1841). Sir James Mackintosh (*ibid.*) lo definisce in quest'occasione 'head of the country gentlemen of England.'

[22] Lord Lascelles apparteneva al partito Tory.

Beatrice Corrigan

Foscolo's articles on Dante in the
Edinburgh Review: a study
in collaboration

C.E.I.L. – P

The *Wellesley Index to Victorian Periodicals* is not only a major research tool but a stimulus to scholarly investigation. Among the discoveries of its editors in the records of the last century was that an article on Dante in the *Edinburgh Review* for February 1819 (pp. 453-474), was only partly by the hand of Ugo Foscolo, to whom it had always been attributed. The first sixteen pages were his, but the last five were by another writer, identified apparently, in an unpublished letter from Francis Jeffrey to William Allen, as P. M. Roget.[1] This attribution seemed to Mrs Esther Rhoads Houghton of sufficient interest to merit further investigation, and as her own time was limited she invited my collaboration. A second reading of the letter, and of others in the correspondence, showed that Jeffrey had written not 'Roget's' but 'Roger's,' with a misplaced apostrophe; and Mrs Houghton immediately made the correct identification: Samuel Rogers. It is consequently now possible to piece together, at least in part, the story of a strange literary mystification.

Two weeks after his arrival in England, in September 1816, Foscolo had been introduced to the hospitality of Holland House,[2] and had so assured for himself the protection and assistance of a powerful Whig circle, delighted to aid a distinguished soldier, poet, and patriot, who had refused to take an oath of loyalty to the Austrians and to put his pen at their service. Lord Holland's private physician and librarian, John Allen, was a correspondent of Francis Jeffrey, who was constantly urging him to secure distinguished contributors to the *Edinburgh Review*, and Allen evidently seized the opportunity to serve both Jeffrey and Foscolo at the same time. A benevolent conspiracy must have been formed, with Lord Holland's encouragement, among Allen, Sir James Mackintosh (already a regular contributor to the *Review*) and Samuel Rogers, who disapproved of the current fashion of anonymous reviewing and had held aloof from both the *Edinburgh* and the *Quarterly Review*.[3] Rogers first met Foscolo at Holland House on 14 October 1816,[4] and from then on showed him great kindness. In 1817 Foscolo expressed his admiration for *The Pleasures of Memory* and his gratitude to its author by dedicating to Rogers the London edition of *Le ultime lettere di Jacopo Ortis*.

Probably at Allen's suggestion, Jeffrey commissioned an article from Foscolo on the subject of Italian literature, beginning with Dante whose fame was rising again after a long eclipse. Mackintosh promised to translate the article from French—for though Foscolo read English he did not write it with facility, and all his articles were written in what he called *francioso*, to distinguish it from *francese*, a language which he had never learned formally.[5] Rogers agreed to write a review of Cary's three-year-old translation of the *Divine Comedy*, which so far had not received the attention it deserved; this, attached at the end of Foscol'os remarks, would lend them timeliness and an English interest. Mackintosh had long been a friend of Rogers, had written a flattering review of his *Columbus* in the *Edinburgh Review* in 1813, and had spent much time in his company in Paris the same year.[6] In 1816 he had written asking him to use his influence with Byron to induce him to accept payment from Murray for a volume of poems which the publisher was anxious to secure, and divert part of the money to Godwin, then in great distress.[7] Roger's acts of kindness to less fortunate men of letters, Moore and Sheridan among them, had been continuous ever since he came into his fortune, but the manner in which he attempted to aid Foscolo was novel and, probably because of its unfortunate outcome, seems to have remained unique.

Rogers, according to his own account, had been introduced to Cary's Dante by Moore, and 'mentioned it to Wordsworth; and he to Coleridge, who had never heard of it till then, and who forthwith read it'.[8] In a letter of 1817 Wordsworth asked Rogers whether he and Dante 'continued as intimate as heretofore'.[9] On 24 June of that year Crabbe records that while visiting Rogers he met Foscolo, and the conversation turned on Dante.[10] It was at that very period that Jeffrey was carrying on negotiations with Foscolo through Allen, to whom he wrote on 15 June 1817:[11]

My dear Allen,
              I am afraid I have not enabled you to make as precise and as courteous an answer to Foscolo as I ought to have done but I have really been so busy that I could not even get out the present No. of the review in decent time. I am now however most anxious to prepare for the next and I hope Mr. Foscolo will be able to give us an article before the end of July. I forget whether I told you that I perfectly approved of his plan in so far as I understand it—though in reviewing the literature of Italy it would certainly be desirable that he showed so

much acquaintance with that of other countries as to give his judgement authority with their natives. He should recollect in that as he is writing to foreigners whose habitual prejudices must be attended to even when he undertakes to convict them of error the more he mixes of philosophy and general speculation the better—the more he can connect peculiarities of taste with peculiarities in the history and government of different nations—and trace back the operation of those great causes that are the common source of whatever distinguishes one people from another—I conceive in short that such a discourse on Italian literature as might do for an Academy in that country would not be fit for the Edinb. R.—and that Mr F. will do most justice to his own talents and principles in going as often as he can beyond the narrow boundaries of mere literature.

It was probably this letter that gave Foscolo the idea of restricting his article to Dante, treating him within the framework of the Middle Ages. Jeffrey's hope that such an article could be finished in a month was unreasonable, but late in August Foscolo sent an 'articoletto' to Miss Pigou, a young friend of Rogers, promising that he would send other fragments as he composed them, and asking her to transcribe them so that when they were all put together the result would be a paper for the *Edinburgh Review*.[12] Early in November she wrote to him anxiously inquiring where the article was.[13] On 3 March 1818, he wrote to Quirina Mocenni Magiotti that the copyist was at his lodgings, working hard to finish the article which was to be sent that very day to London to the translator.[14] Part of it, however, went astray, and it was not until 3 April that Foscolo wrote to Allen saying that he had that day sent to Mackintosh for translation the recovered paper, revised and partly rewritten.[15]

Meanwhile on 25 March Jeffrey, justly uneasy, had written to Allen: 'I am growing very impatient about Dante—and still more for the primitiae of the Poet—and as you have been kind enough to negotiate these supplies for me you must submit to the discomfort of being dunned for them.'[16] The Poet can only be Rogers, who was to make his debut as a reviewer, and whose contribution was also too long delayed. The following letter from him,[17] though undated, was almost certainly an answer to Allen's reminder:

Dear Allen,
          Many thanks! My stuff is already off—I hope Jeffrey will understand that it is meant to close the article.

But there was still no word from Mackintosh, and sometime in April the long-delayed February number of the *Edinburgh Review* appeared, and the disaster was immediately apparent. On 29 April Jeffrey wrote to Allen from Glasgow in great distress:[18]

My dear Allen,

There seems some fatality about this paper of Foscolo's. You will probably by this time have seen from the review that the thing has been bungled after all. I must now explain to you how it has happened. After waiting four or five days for the sequel of Dante I was compelled to go to Aberdeen for some important trials for which I had been previously retained. I left instructions with my brother to wait 3 days longer for the sequel and if it did not come then to cancell what was printed and finish with another article. On the 2nd day Roger's part arrived under McIntosh's cover and without one line of explanation and it has been printed accordingly as the sequel of the original critique leaving out the second part of Foscolo's and without any notice of a *hiatus*. This disaster has arisen partly from my absence—and my unwillingness to disclose any part of the secret to my deputy—and partly I think I may say chiefly from McIntosh's apparently unaccountable delay and his neglecting to give any notice when he sent Roger's paper that there was any other to come. They wrote to me that the sequel had come and was printing, and it was only on my arrival here yesterday when I saw the review for I have not yet been able to get home that I discovered what had happened. The sequel of Foscolo's part had not arrived in Edinburgh by yesterday's post. What most disturbs me in this matter is the vexation it may probably occasion to Foscolo and the difficulty of knowing how to dispose of the portion of his work which has been thus unluckily omitted. I cannot consent to lose it and wish you would consider what is best to be done for it. As you mention that he has been kind enough to promise another article on Petrarch for next No. perhaps the sequel of Dante might be dovetailed to the beginning of it so as to make a continuous history of the progress of Italian poetry. If this will not do we must first allude to the accident in a note and print the sequel in its true character.

MacIntosh has never written a word to me and altogether I am rather out of humour with him. . . . Shall I remit for Foscolo to you or him—I shall be in Edinburgh tomorrow evening but I can't delay writing you.

Remarkably enough, the secret that Jeffrey had hidden so closely from his deputy has escaped the notice of all scholars. Yet close examination of the article reveals several inconsistencies and peculiarities that might have excited speculation and which are susceptible of explanation only now that the truth is known. Jeffrey's recommendation that Foscolo should attempt to relate Italian literature to a wide general background was probably communicated by Allen to Mackintosh, who offered to supply some allusions to English literature and so make the subject seem less remote to the *Edinburgh*'s readers. The reference to Dibdin's *Bibliographical Decameron* at the end of the first paragraph is probably Mackintosh's, though Foscolo may have been introduced to the work by his English friends. This is followed in the second paragraph by the statement that from the influence of Dante's genius may be dated 'the commencement of the literary history of Europe'. On page 456 Monsignor Dionisi's edition of Dante is said to have done the poet as much harm as Bentley did Milton. The suggestion in a note on page 461 that the legend of Dante's having visited Oxford is probably due to two English prelates at the Council of Constance may also be Mackintosh's, as well as the added comment that the Latin manuscript in which this story is preserved 'has much the air of a literal translation from an English original'.

Undoubtedly by Mackintosh is a long note (p. 465) concerning 'a foreigner of great literary distinction', who was much moved by his perusal of Shakespeare, despite his preference for the Greeks, but was repelled when he saw the plays performed.[19] This can only refer to Foscolo himself, and had it been written by him would seem an awkward reference to his own experience, but it probably struck Mackintosh as a good illustration of Foscolo's theory, expressed in the text, that 'it is the examination of particular beauties ... which lead the reader on from page to page'. A final contribution by Mackintosh is probably the apt quotation from Johnson on page 466.

More important than all these brief interpolations is the quotation from William Warburton's preface to his edition of Shakespeare (1747), also more likely to have been known to Mackintosh than to Foscolo. 'The whole a critic can do for an author who deserves his services,' Warburton had written, 'is to correct the faulty text, to remark the peculiarities of language, to illustrate the obscure allusions, and to explain the beauties and defects of sentiment or composition.' This fourfold definition of the critic's function forms a framework for Foscolo's share of the article and serves to delimit it most usefully, for one of the reasons why the existence of two separate reviews passed unremarked was that they seem so logically fused. Warburton's fourth head leads Foscolo to explain why such discrimination had never been exercised on Dante, and why Gravina found it impossible to prove that the *Italia Liberata* of Trissino was finer than Tasso's *Gerusalemme Liberata*. He then passes on to a tribute to the beauties of Ariosto; the inability of anyone but a poet to judge a poet; the degree of taste and genius in Pope; his habit of analysis, evident even in his translation of Homer; Homer's objective representation of the passions; Shakespeare's genius obscured in Delille's translation. This long series of digressions from Dante concludes: 'Yet the readers of most of the capitals of Europe, at this day, would probably prefer [to the original words of Shakespeare] the couplet of Delille.'

It is certainly Rogers who begins the next paragraph on page 469: 'Of all the translators of Dante with whom we are acquainted, Mr Cary is the most successful.' Yet because there seems a natural transition from the condemnation of one translation to the praise of another the hiatus, as Jeffrey called it, went unobserved, and all the more easily because of the additional references to Pope's Homer on the next page.[20] The mention of 'our own Milton' might, however, have aroused suspicion, as well as an unmistakable change in style from the stiff succession of simple affirmative sentences into which Mackintosh rendered Foscolo's French to the graceful flowing structures, with frequent semi-colons and dependent clauses, which characterised Rogers' prose even in his letters.

There are differences in editorial style as well. Foscolo quotes Dante in Italian, giving canto and line, with Cary's translation in a footnote and a reference to the volume and page of the tiny three-volume edition. Rogers quotes, with one exception, only the translation; with references to canto but not to line and with striking inconsistency in his use of arabic numerals mixed with upper and lower case Latin numerals. Finally, Foscolo would never have contended, as Rogers does (p. 470), that sometimes Cary transcends his model.[21]

The tribute to Mrs Barbauld which concludes the article is particularly characteristic of Rogers. He had met her when he was still young, and formed an enduring respect for her talents. In 1812 he wrote to his sister: 'I expect a very just encomium on

Mrs Barbauld in *The Edinburgh Review*, from a conversation I had in Scotland.'[22] Probably he had tried to persuade Jeffrey to obtain a favourable review of Mrs Barbauld's *Eighteen Hundred and Eleven*, which had been savagely attacked by Southey in the *Quarterly*;[23] and though this kindly attempt failed he remembered six years later his desire to see justice done her.

As well as revealing signs of multiple authorship, the first article on Dante betrays the lack of a competent editor. Both Foscolo and later Foscolo scholars complained of typographical errors; indeed, it is startling to find 'Jordello' three times instead of 'Sordello' (p. 457). But the half-dozen misspellings of Italian are less unfortunate than the substitution of Urban VIII for Boniface VIII (p. 458), the date of 1818 given for Cary's Dante instead of 1814 (p. 453), and the misplaced comma (p. 465) that converts Petrarch into a sixteenth-century poet.

Foscolo's reaction to the mutilated article can be deduced from the flurry of letters that followed its appearance. It is evident that in an interview with Allen he flew into a passion, blamed Mackintosh bitterly both as intermediary and translator, and vowed never again to write for any review but the rival *Quarterly*. But this mood was short-lived and, blaming his outburst on the 'douleur du moment', he consented to give Jeffrey the remainder of his article, revised, expanded, and enriched with extracts from Dante's prose which his friend Roger Wilbraham had translated for him into good English—probably a parting shot at Mackintosh, though he had now forgiven him.[24]

Jeffrey on his side was anxious to make amends and secure the sequel to the article. On 8 May he wrote to Allen:[25]

I enclose a billet for Foscolo and a draught for £85 which will fetch about 80 guineas if instantly cashed. I even thought of making it £100 but this is rather more than we could well afford to go on with if he should write many and long articles—however if you think it right as for our honour and interest and more likely to secure him pray add the additional £15 and I shall send the sum to you immediately.

I think I shall be able to arrange for a translator well enough and should be glad to have the MS as soon as possible in my hands.

The billet enclosed[26] contained an apology to the offended author couched in such flattering terms that Foscolo quoted them to Quirina Mocenni Magiotti as the general opinion of his work, and described to her the airy castles to be erected upon his prospective wealth, though Allen had discreetly modified Jeffrey's generosity.[27] In the same letter Jeffrey urged Foscolo to send for the next number of the *Edinburgh Review* the rest of the Dante article, promising to play better his part as editor, and reminding him that it would be difficult to find a translator superior to Mackintosh. Allen also wrote, begging Foscolo to give Jeffrey his article, and pleading Mackintosh's cause.[28] Mackintosh himself in a brief note apologised for his involuntary error, and requested the honour of being allowed to translate the second part of Dante.[29] No more delicate and considerate amends could have been made.

Even the second instalment of the unfortunate article, however, was destined to cause trouble to both author and editor. On 22 June Foscolo wrote to Allen,[30] apologising for his delay in sending the paper and again blaming his translator, this time William Wallace. On 27 June Jeffrey wrote to Allen:[31]

I hope no new disaster has come between Foscolo and me. I have been expecting his MS for a fortnight and begin now to be rather uneasy especially as he had reason to think that the No. must have been more forward than it is. Pray contrive to let me hear about it—or rather to see it—for nothing else will be very satisfactory.

On 5 July Allen communicated Jeffrey's anxiety to Foscolo,[32] and on 12 July the article reached Jeffrey. But even when it was safely in his hands it presented problems which forced the editor to defer it until the September issue (pp. 317–351). In a letter to Foscolo, written from the Highlands on 5 August,[33] he explained that the delay was caused by other obligations, but commented with his unfailing courtesy and tact on what he termed faults of the translator that he had been forced to rectify. Yet it was not the translator's fault that abbreviations and retrenchments had to be made: the second instalment probably manifested, as had the first in the long digression already mentioned, the extravagances of composition which Foscolo had described so complacently to Samuel Rogers a year before.[34] 'When I think and write of a subject,' he said, 'at first I can bridle neither my ideas, my memory, or my pen. I have recently chanced to write 15 hours on end, and 27 pages in one day. But I need 15 or sometimes 27 days to arrange the disorder inseparable from such abundance, to

220 *Beatrice Corrigan*

give the substance of my ideas without any superfluity, to state facts correctly and display erudition without pedantry.' It is evident from Jeffrey's letter that in the second part of the Dante article Foscolo had left the latter process for his editor to perform.

Despite Foscolo's excursions and Jeffrey's excisions, it is possible to trace in the concluding part the structure of the article as it was originally planned. No reference was made to the accident, but in a succinct opening paragraph the author deplored that 'the limits of a late Number precluded us from entering, as fully as we would have wished, into the subject of Dante'; and expressed his pleasure that he had recently received F. Cancellieri's book, which he proceeded to review. Then he continued the brilliant survey of Italian history in Dante's age which had been interrupted in the first instalment, and which is one of Foscolo's great contributions to Dante studies. Finally he passed on to a consideration of the *Divine Comedy*, quoting liberally from the original and adding Cary's translation for the benefit of his English-speaking readers. This is unmistakably part of the original essay as he had planned it with Rogers, and would have formed a logical prelude to the review of Cary's Dante, as Rogers had hoped Jeffrey would understand.

In Foscolo's famous study, then, many hands may be detected —Mackintosh's, Wallace's, Wilbraham's,[35] Rogers', and, finally, Jeffrey's. The latter may well not only have exercised his editor's discretion in abridgments, but have added the allusions to Shakespeare's use of the word 'worm' for 'serpent' (p. 320), and to Robertson's *History of Scotland* (pp. 321–322). Particularly likely to be his is the reference to the See of Canterbury and the concessions made by 'our England' to Pope Gregory VII. The mention of Leigh Hunt's *The Story of Rimini* (published in 1816) which introduces the account of Francesca da Rimini may also have been suggested by Foscolo's English friends.

The benevolent collaborators kept their secret well, and it was only in his old age that Rogers deplored, not any lack of literary fame, but Cary's ingratitude for the part he had played in winning popularity for the great translation.[36] It was Coleridge alone whom Cary thanked in the preface to the handsome second edition of the *Divine Comedy* in 1819; and Coleridge alone was subsequently credited as the founder of Cary's fame. Yet, as Rogers said, only 120 persons heard Coleridge's lecture in

February 1818, whereas in April the *Edinburgh Review* article reached a wide circle of readers. Rogers' regrets were regarded as senile complaining, and when Foscolo's letter to Quirina Mocenni Magiotti was published by Giuseppe Caleffi in 1835 his complaints about the mutilation of his article seemed meaningless.

Foscolo had some reason to be dissatisfied with the treatment accorded to the entire article. Though his methods of composition were volcanic, his anxiety to be thorough in scholarship shows his classical training. In his footnotes he refers to the principal authorities on Italian literature and bibliography—Crescimbeni, Quadrio, Mazzuchelli, Tiraboschi, Haym—as well as to writers on medieval history and theology. That he was able to find these works in London is proof both of his diligence and of the wide range of the collections available to him, yet the difficulty and delay which he suffered in his research is evident from his letters. To Samuel Rogers on 19 February 1818, while still engaged both on the Dante article and on an ambitious project for a parallel between English and Italian literature, he complained that he had hardly any books but his memory, and that Murray (who was interested in his Parallel) had advised him to use the libraries of his friends.[37] He disliked this procedure, both for the time it cost him and because he shrank from asking favours, yet the only semi-public library available to him was that of the Royal Institution at 21 Albemarle Street, not far from the lodgings in Bleinhem Street which Foscolo occupied in 1818.[38] He seems to have been singularly fortunate in finding the works he needed, and it is evident that there was already considerable English interest in Italian studies. In the first part of the article on Dante he cites four Italian writers, and also refers to Bayle. He mentions as well Gravina's opinion of Tasso, but without a definite reference, as though he were quoting from memory. In the second part he cites twelve Italian authorities and at least five others, including Schlegel and the Abbé de Sade's *Life of Petrarch*, a work which he tried to borrow from Roger Wilbraham in 1819.[39]

This conscientious erudition combined with one of the most sensitive and original critical faculties of his day made Foscolo rebel against the fate inflicted by the *Edinburgh Review* on his Dante article. In 1820, even though he had still not decided to give his essay on Petrarch to the *Quarterly Review*, he had forebodings about its possible treatment at Jeffrey's hands. 'Probably,' he wrote to Gino Capponi, 'it will come out cut in half, and half encrusted with their own wretched scraps of allusion and erudition.'[40]

Yet the fortunes in Italy of the maltreated Dante article were even stranger.[41] In 1819 Foscolo's friend Davide Bertolotti published in *Il Raccoglitore* of Milan a portion of the second paper in the *Edinburgh Review* (pp. 340–346), identifying it as Foscolo's and entitling it, 'Illustrazione dell'episodio di Francesca da Rimini, nella *Divina Commedia*.'[42] The passage opens abruptly, omitting the reference to Leigh Hunt which serves as an introduction in the original, and of course omits as well all references to Cary. The following year another extract was published, this time from the first article (pp. 454–464), as an 'Esame critico dei Commentatori di Dante'.[43] Bertolotti's translation of both passages is very faithful; he has added many notes, amplified and in one case corrected Foscolo's references, corrected the Jordello misprint and others. He omits the allusion to English bishops (p. 461), as well as the long note about 'a distinguished foreigner' (p. 465). Also omitted is a phrase about 'the savage bigotry of the priests', better suited to Protestant than to Catholic readers.

In 1829, two years after Foscolo's death, an article appeared in the *Revue Britannique* in Paris entitled 'Dante Alighieri et son époque'.[44] The translator's notes identify it as Foscolo's and as extracted from the *Edinburgh Review*, but actually it is a curious mixture of free composition and quotations or paraphrases. It begins with remarks (not Foscolo's) on the function of criticism, passes on to Giuseppe Baretti's tribute to Dante as a prophet of scientific discoveries,[45] and then weaves together the translator's own reflections with fragments from the two Dante articles to form a hybrid essay which to the uninitiated reader would seem to have form and unity.[46] The author of this monstrous compilation was almost certainly Philarète Chasles, who had met Foscolo in London in 1819 and listened to his complaints about the British Cyclops who protected him and kept him prisoner.[47] Still bitter over his *Edinburgh Review* misadventures, Foscolo may well have confided them to Chasles, pouring out his heart, as his unsympathetic French auditor remarked, like a true Venetian. Chasles was co-editor of the *Revue Britannique* from 1825 on, and, as he said himself, for a time wrote over a third of the articles. It was this slovenly farrago (even the Jordello misprint was not corrected) that was accepted in Italy as Foscolo's *Edinburgh Review* article on Dante. It was twice translated into Italian in the year of its publication, and one of these versions was reprinted by Giuseppe Caleffi in his edition of selected works by Foscolo in 1836. It also appeared in a Foscolo anthology in 1852, and the mystification was not cleared up until 1880 when Dr Bianchini's article appeared in *Il Propugnatore*. It has taken another ninety years for the quite innocent confusion in the original English version to come to light.

Notes

[1] In the Holland House papers (now in the British Museum), Letter 54. Mrs Kay Marie Baird of Queen's University, Kingston, kindly secured photocopies for me of the relevant letters. I have not altered Jeffrey's spelling.

[2] E. R. Vincent, *Ugo Foscolo* (Cambridge University Press, 1953), p. 32.

[3] P. W. Clayden says in *Rogers and His Contemporaries* (London 1889) that 'Rogers declined to write for the *Quarterly Review* or to be associated with the men who founded it. He was opposed, moreover, to anonymous writing, and regarded anonymous criticism as a kind of fighting in a mask. His only contribution to this kind of literature was a part of a review of Cary's Dante in the *Edinburgh Review*'. I, 58.

[4] Vincent, p. 43.

[5] *Epistolario*, ed. F. S. Orlandini and E. Meyer (Firenze 1954), 3 volumes (vols. 6, 7, 8 of *Opere edite e postume di U.F.*), II, 340.

[6] Clayden, I, 203.

[7] *Ibid.*, I, 210–214. In his *Early Life of Samuel Rogers* (London, 1887) Clayden says: 'It is, indeed, a striking feature in the correspondence between Rogers and his political and literary friends of three generations, that his readiness to do them all kinds of service is constantly assumed and acted upon. Criticism of manuscripts, negotiations with publishers, advice on business or travel, advances of money, are forms of help constantly asked and constantly given.' Pp. 282–283.

[8] Alexander Dice, *Recollections of the Table-talk of Samuel Rogers* (New Southgate 1887), pp. 285–286.

[9] Clayden, *Rogers*, I, 241.

[10] *Ibid.*, I, 246.

[11] Holland House Papers, Letter 49.

[12] *Epist.*, II, 327.

[13] Francesco Viglione, *Ugo Foscolo in Inghilterra* (Pisa 1910), p. 212.

[14] *Epist.*, II, 340–341.

[15] E. R. Vincent, 'Foscolo and John Allen', *Italian Studies*, IV (1949), 7.

[16] Holland House Papers, Letter 53.

[17] BM, Add. MSS, 52, 195; f. 90. The BM has dated this letter only 'Before April 23, 1824', but it is almost certainly 1818.

[18] Holland House Papers, Letter 54.

[19] A few days after his arrival in England Foscolo was taken to Lord Holland's box at Drury Lane to see Edmund Kean in *Othello*. Vincent, *Ugo Foscolo*, p. 34.

[20] Foscolo had been engaged for some years on a translation of the *Iliad*, had published part of his version in 1807, and was still at work on it in 1820 (*Epist.* III, 1). He may have discussed with Rogers Pope's rendering, the only work by Pope that Rogers disliked. Clayden, *Early Life*, p. 59.

[21] Indeed, according to Cyrus Redding, Foscolo considered the best translation of Dante to be that of Nathaniel Howard published in 1807. *Fifty Years' Recollections Literary and Personal* (London 1858), I, 111.

[22] Clayden, *Rogers*, I, 118.

[23] *QR*, VII (June 1812), 309–313. See Betsy Rogers, *Georgian Chronicle* (London 1958), 139–142.

[24] He retracts these outbursts in a letter dated by Vincent (*Italian Studies*, p. 8) as April 1819, but which was possibly written early in May.

[25] Holland House Papers, Letter 53.

[26] Unmistakably the letter of the same date, first published in Italian translation in the *Epistolario* (III, 429–430), and later, still in Italian, by John Purves, 'The Letters of Francis Jeffrey to Ugo Foscolo', *University of Edinburgh Journal*, VI (1933–4), 26–27.

[27] *Epist.*, II, 344–347. Allen paid Foscolo thirty-two guineas for sixteen pages, more than double the remuneration that had been promised. This reference to sixteen pages when the article apparently contains twenty-one has puzzled scholars.

[28] *Epist.*, III, 434–5.

[29] *Ibid.*, p. 434, n. 2.

[30] Vincent, *Italian Studies*, p. 9.

[31] Holland House Papers, Letter 57.

[32] Purves, 114.

[33] *Ibid.*, 114–115.

[34] Clayden, *Rogers*, I, 256–257.

[35] Wilbraham's translation must have been from Latin, a passage from one of Dante's letters (pp. 350–351). A quotation from the *Convivio* is given in the original Italian only, as the translator knew French but not Italian. In 1819 Foscolo asked Wilbraham to translate a passage of Petrarch's Latin, 'con quella dignità e schiettezza di stile che è tutto vostro.' Cesare Foligno, 'Quindici lettere inedite di Ugo Foscolo', *Aretusa* (Naples), I (September–October 1949), 11.

[36] Dice, pp. 285–286.

[37] Clayden, *Rogers*, p. 256. Foscolo describes to QMM in March 1818 his difficulties in finding such works as Tiraboschi and Muratori (*Epist.*, II, 341). He adds that the English dislike lending books. He made use of the library at Holland House, and wrote to the secretary-librarian, Giuseppe Binda, asking him to check references (*Epist.*, II, 333–334).

[38] Vincent, *Italian Studies*, p. 7. The Royal Institution had been founded in 1799 for the promotion of science, and its library was chiefly scientific and historical. See K. D. C. Vernon, 'The Library of the Royal Institution, 1799–1954', *Proceedings of the Royal Institution*, XXXV (1954), 887–889.

39 Wilbraham had been lending Foscolo books since 1817 (Foligno, 1–15), and Foscolo acknowledged his debt to Wilbraham's library in the dedication of his edition of the *Decameron* in 1825.

40 'Probabilmente uscirà mezzo tronco, mezzo intarsiato di cosacce non mie e mezzo addottorato.' He also complains about the errors introduced into his article on Parga in 1819 (*Epist.*, III, 16–17). In a letter to Lady Dacre in 1821 he describes Murray's similar editorial malpractices in the *Quarterly* (*Epist.*, III, 31).

41 They were first disclosed by Domenico Bianchini in 'Lo scritto "Dante e il suo secolo" è proprio di Ugo Foscolo?' *Il Propugnatore*, XIII (1880), 3–11. Dr Bianchini does not analyse Bertolotti's editorial work, suggest Chasles as the author of the *RB* article, or describe his methods as a compiler.

42 *Il Raccoglitore*, I (1819), 53–62.

43 *Ibid.*, VIII (1820), 41–58, 76–79.

44 *Revue Britannique, ou choix d'articles traduits des meilleurs écrits périodiques de la Grande-Bretagne, sur la littérature, les beaux-arts, les arts industriels, l'agriculture, la géographie, le commerce, l'économie politique, les finances, la législation, etc., etc.*, XXV (juillet 1829), 5–33.

45 Baretti's name is not mentioned, but the passage is paraphrased from his *Dissertation upon the Italian Poetry* (1753), reprinted in *Prefazioni e polemiche* (Bari 1911), pp. 106–8.

46 These fragments follow no consistent pattern and are taken indiscriminately from the two articles. The order in which they occur is as follows (the original articles are distinguished as I and II): I, 477; II, 329, 313–319, 330–332, 320–321, 326, 321, 323, 322, 323–29; I, 457, 459, 437–8; II, 333, 345, 349; I, 350.

47 Philarète Chasles, *Mémoires* (Paris 1876), I, 158–159. Much later he published an article (without mention of Foscolo), 'Francis Jeffrey. Fondation, développement et influence de la *Revue d'Edinbourg*', *Revue contemporaine* (15 juin 1853). This was reprinted in his *L'Angleterre littéraire* (Paris 1876).

Stephen N. Cristea

The fortunes of Goethe's Die
Leiden des Jungen Werthers
in Italy

Initial reaction to the subject of '*Werther* in Italy' is almost certain to be conditioned by a reflex which assumes that the topic must already have been studied—must, because this is true of other countries, and because the work is so well known in Italy in the context of Ugo Foscolo's *Ultime Lettere di Jacopo Ortis*. This assumption is a natural one, for not only do there exist comprehensive studies devoted to one country, such as F. Baldensperger's *Bibliographie critique de Goethe en France*,[1] but there are also works dealing with *Werther* within the framework of the whole of Europe, such as K. Hillebrand's *Die Werther-Krankheit in Europa*,[2] J. W. Appell's *Werther und seine Zeit*,[3] and in particular the more detailed and scholarly work by S. P. Atkins *The Testament of Werther in Poetry and Drama*.[4] There are even studies which concentrate on the influence of Goethe in Italy, such as G. Fasola's *Goethes Werke in italienischen Über-setzungen*.[5] However, although references are made to the fortunes of *Werther* in the peninsula in these and other critical works— Atkins spends several pages analysing Sografi's play *Verter*, and then devotes a short section of his bibliography of poems and plays based on *Werther* to Italy, Fasola enumerates the Italian translations of the novel, and Hillebrand discusses the link between *Werther* and the *Ultime Lettere*—there is nothing specifically concerned with this subject.

Goethe's novel is best known in Italy because of its connection with the *Ortis*, and the part it played in the genesis of the Italian work has been argued over at length. For this reason I do not propose to do more than touch superficially on this problem. Rather I intend to look at the work in its own right, both as regards the translations, and the compositions it inspired, to consider its special relationship with the poems of Ossian (an aspect which has never been considered, because hitherto no study had been made of the poems in Italy), and to attempt to bring together in the appendices all the available details relevant to the compositions connected with *Werther* in which Italians are involved.[6]

To an Italian reader *Werther* must have seemed in many respects just another melancholy northern work. It did not appear in Italian until 1782 (it was published in Germany in 1774), almost twenty years after the first edition of *Le Poesie di Ossian*,[7] and over ten years after that of Edward Young's *Le Notti*.[8] The atmosphere of hopeless sorrow that permeates the novel, the feeling that life is a torment, that all action is futile, and that death is the only solution to the human lot cannot have come as anything new. The predominant concern of the writers of the time was to arouse the sentiments of the reader, and the full title of Grassi's translation, *Werther, opera di sentimento*, makes it clear that this novel was a further manifestation of this intention. The reviewer who forced himself to comment on the work in the periodical *Memorie Enciclopediche di Bologna*[9] in 1783 saw it in this light, and disdained to discuss the book for this very reason. I quote the review in full because it is revelatory of the kind of reception which awaited *Werther* in Italy by those who mistrusted the continual exploitation of the feelings of the reader, and saw no justification for it:

> Young, ed Arnaud ànno introdotta la passione per le cose di sentimento. Ma il patetico se non è accompagnato dai tratti sublimi, e pittorici, e da tutte le grazie della poesia, a lungo stanca, ed annoja. E che pretendono tanti romanzieri italiani, francesi, tedeschi, inglesi con presentarci tutto giorno interminabili storie di disgrazie, di sventure, di guai? In questo globo di miserie non vi è niente di più facile, che idearsi degli accidenti degni di commiserazione, e descriverli in prosa.

The reviewer's ideal novel is somewhat different:

> I romanzi per piacere dovrebbero essere brevi, pieni di sali arguti, sparsi di un ingegnoso ridicolo, e di una satira fina, e delicata sopra i cattivi costumi.

and although he recognises that this is not possible for all writers, *Werther* falls short of even his lowest standards:

> Sappiamo bene, che non è per tutti lo scrivere con brio, e l'intrecciarvi la difficile facezia: ma almeno, che essi non ci secchino con i lunghi piagnistei di un amante addolorato, che vede l'oggetto dei suoi ardenti voti fra le braccia di un uomo brutale, e che disperato di poterla conseguire, si ammazza.

It is not the most sympathetic synopsis of *Werther*, and was not calculated to inspire the periodical's readers to obtain a copy.

Turning back for a moment to the years preceding the first Italian translation it seems that *Werther* had made little impression in Italy. This is borne out by Grassi, who wrote in his Dedication to Hess at the beginning of his 1782 translation:

la brama che dimostraste, che quest'Opera fosse da noi meglio conosciuta, spinto avendomi a dare alle stampe questa versione.

In the Venetian periodicals where, since they were the best informed and most up to date, one would expect to find a reasonably detailed account of the work, all I have discovered is the following, in the *Giornale Enciclopedico*, in the section of bibliographical details from abroad:[10]

> Les souffrances & *Le pene del giovane Werther*, in due parti: traduzione dal tedesco: del B.S. di S. Mastricht 1776: in 8. Quest'Opera è celebre nell'Alemagna: ell'è una spezie di Romanzo, ripieno di una sensibilità la più commovente, e scritto in forma di Lettere.

Considering the furore *Werther* had caused in the European countries north of the Alps, this is very meagre information, even allowing for the fact that it was written in 1777, and the brevity of the comment indicates that the editors had not actually read the novel, and that this was a second hand report from a correspondent living abroad.[11] In other journals published in these years the work seems to have been passed over in complete silence, and indeed one wonders if it was known of at all. That *Werther* was read in Italy before Grassi's translation is postulated by M. Kerbaker in his *Shakespeare e Goethe nei versi di V. Monti*,[12] in which he analyses the influence of a French translation of the novel on Monti's early verse. He can offer no proof to substantiate this theory, however, and as Monti only wrote the *Pensieri* in the latter half of 1782 this means that he would have had ample time to see a copy of Grassi. As for Monti's attitude to *Werther*, we know nothing, because there is no mention of the novel in his extant correspondence. It would be dangerous to pay too much attention to this because many of his letters may have been lost, but I cannot help feeling that it would be too much of a coincidence, if all the letters in which he speaks of the novel had been destroyed, especially as so many of them dating from 1782–3 to Fortunata Fantastici still exist. How then can one account for his silence on a work which so obviously influenced him? I suggest that firstly, he did not want to advertise his indebtedness to *Werther*, secondly, that he disapproved of the amount of imitation of foreign literatures then going on in Italy, and thirdly, he did not feel the desire to discuss the novel with friends, because his interest in it was as short-lived as the love affair he was engaged in during this period.[13] As the impassioned and unsuccessful lover Monti could identify with Werther, but when this was no longer the case, the novel ceased to serve as a source of inspiration.

Even after the publication of Grassi's translation there appears to be singularly little comment on the novel, due no doubt, at least in part, to the fact that this genre was despised by the main source of literary information, the periodicals. It is this which makes it so difficult to assess the reaction to *Werther*, for whereas the reviewer of the *Memorie Enciclopediche* had bothered to make a few remarks—admittedly very disparaging ones—in other journals the work was ignored. *Werther* enjoyed such notoriety in Germany and France, provoked so much discussion, and so many imitations of one type or another, that echoes of its fame must, I feel, have reached Italy by the middle of the 1780's, and it is virtually impossible to interpret the lack of comment on it as anything other than wilful omission. Occasionally, it is true, a novel was accorded some grudging praise:[14]

Una casta semplicità si fa sentire in essa, e la distingue dalla quantità de' Romanzi de' quali siamo innondati... sembraci che Madama Smith abbia osservato la natura col fino gusto d'un Pittore, e con l'entusiasmo d'un Poeta.

but usually they are seen as pernicious creations:[15]

nei turpi loro Romanzi [Voltaire, Crebillon, Diderot] ove le bellezze dello stile e della immaginazione ad altro non tendono, che a corrompere i cuori, e non eccitano, che dell'indignazione negli animi onesti e virtuosi.

A reviewer in the *Memorie per servire alla storia letteraria e civile*, as late as 1798, makes a statement about the attitude to novels in general which must have been shared by many Italians:[16]

Quest'è un Romanzo. Finchè non ne avremo di buoni, e originali in Italiano, non disapproveremo, che chi ha la smania di scarabocchiare della carta, s'occupi a tradurre i Romanzi Inglesi, Francesi e Tedeschi, solo faremo istanza perchè siano scelti quei soli libri di tal genere che sono atti ad ispirare l'amor della virtù, e sia rispettata la lingua Italiana...

It is at this point that I come to the second main objection to *Werther*, which is that it ends in suicide. Those who mistrusted the genre altogether were confirmed in their suspicions that novels were dangerous by this apparent glorification of suicide. Even to those who were less extreme in their opinions it constituted a real barrier, which could not be passed over in silence. This explains why the whole of Grassi's long Preface is an attempt to exonerate the action of the hero and justify the ending of the novel. It is obvious from the conclusion to his *apologia in favore dell'opera medesima* that the main objection to *Werther* in Italy was that it was 'dannosa alla Società'. Suicide was contrary to traditional values, it undermined the structure of society, and above all, was condemned as a sin by the Church. This must be kept in mind when reading the *apologia*, since it accounts for the various justifications of the work, not exempt from tautology, that he thinks it necessary to advance. At no point does he say that suicide is automatically excusable—indeed, his final stress is on the necessity of remaining in control of oneself—but he argues that Werther was not guilty, because the balance of his mind was disturbed. It is not simply a case of diminished responsibility and mitigating circumstances, for he suggests that the propensity to suicide is born in the person. As substantiation of this, he says that the desire for survival is the strongest of man's instincts and leads him to accomplish incredible feats, and that therefore anyone who denies this instinct must be 'strascinato da un'intima segreta forza superiore'. He ends by asserting that *Werther* could in fact be beneficial to society since the hero's death was caused by an excess of passion, and the reader would thus be put on guard against the tyranny of the senses, and would learn to defer to the powers of reason and reflection:

chi leggerà i casi di Werther non potrà che conoscere a temere il pericolo, cui porta una inclinazione, che si lasci dal tempo troppo invigorire,... ne paventerà l'esempio e si premunirà contro delle proprie tendenze per non perdere... quel dominio che il savio può e deve su delle stesse conservare.

It is notable that in his preoccupation with the reception of the work on a moral plane Grassi says nothing about the artistic merits of the novel. Apart from the suggestion that a reading of *Werther* was 'utile', the public might well have wondered why they should trouble to read it. Grassi himself had undertaken the translation 'per solo sollievo dell'angustiato mio spirito', not because he was impressed by the distinctive qualities of the work.

In the Dedication to his translation, published in 1788, Salom leaves the reader in no doubt about the finer points of the novel:

> il maggior pregio del *Verter*... dipende dalla delicatezza degli affetti, dalla nobiltà dei sensi, dalla robustezza de' pensieri, e dalla squisita sensibilità ond'esso è tutto pieno... Romanzo sublime nel suo genere.

He is more concerned with the literary presentation of *Werther* and provides a section entitled *Notizie critiche sulla presente operetta*, in which he puts the work into its context, talks a little about the author, and mentions by name Jerusalem and Vezlar (*sic*).[17] His stay in Germany had provided him with this background information, and he informs the reader that he had spoken with someone acquainted with Jerusalem's son, said to be the model for Werther. Even he, however, cannot ignore the contemporary desire for a literature which is useful as well as entertaining, and justifies the novel on the same grounds as Grassi had done:

> Egli mena il nostro Verter dal principio alla fine della sua passione per una serie di paradossi, che dalla sua alterata fantasia vengono abbracciati come veri e giusti raziocinj, e con ciò si propose l'utilità del Lettore, mostrandogli sin dove possa condurre un falso ragionare.

This matter of the suicide continued to be the dominant factor in conditioning the response to the novel, and Grassi's arguments were not convincing enough for Ippolito Pindemonte, who speaks here through the mouth of Abaritte, in the novel of the same name:[18]

> Mi furono raccomandati alcuni romanzi. Senonchè abbattutomi su le prime ad uno, ove mi parea che il principale scopo dello scrittore fosse di render bello ed amabile il suicidio, non volli più leggere i romanzi vostri.

He was not the only one who interpreted *Werther* in this way, and in consequence scorned the work. With Pindemonte it is a case of personal antipathy, but G. B. Giovio voices the concern of society as a whole. He judges *Werther* (along with similar creations such as the *Ultime Lettere, Atala* and *René*) to be responsible for tormenting individuals and families with the spectre of suicide:[19]

> Ma chi poi negare oserebbe, chi non compiangerebbe insieme il danno gravissimo che da tai volumetti qualche sconsigliato sparse nelle

famiglie e nel mondo? Quelle paginette divennero qualche fiata il codice d'alcuni suicidi, e più sovente per quelle il suicidio riuscì la questione favorita e laceratrice fra le mura domestiche.

and is convinced of the appeal and potency of these works:

Pertanto un cuore ben fatto palpita per quelle pagine, per quelle una mente osservatrice i pensieri scopre stillare tutti di vivo sangue dalla prima fino all'ultima linea.

Against this way of thinking we have the example of Leopardi, who, with characteristic lucidity, wrote:[20]

A ogni modo mi sono avveduto che la lettura de' libri non ha veramente prodotto in me nè affetti o sentimenti che non avessi... ma pure gli ha accelerati, e fatti sviluppare più presto.

That the example of *Werther* brought him more rapidly to the idea of killing himself, he admits, but adds that he too would have thought of suicide sooner or later, because it is a desire which comes from the heart. Foscolo takes up the question of suicide in his long letter to Bartholdy,[21] in which he compares and contrasts *Werther* and the *Ultime Lettere*. Grassi had drawn a distinction between impulsive and meditated suicide, and had concluded that only the latter kind should be condemned.[22] Foscolo bears out Grassi's idea that Werther's death was like a fatal illness, not a voluntary act, lucidly decided upon, and he emphasises that in the *Ortis* he was concerned with presenting the hero's act as the assertion of the liberty of the individual. It is the classical conception of suicide, and for Grassi at least the example of Jacopo would have been deemed more pernicious, because his death involved the cooperation of his faculty of reason, not the repudiation of it, as in Werther's case. If we are to believe Ceroni, it was still impossible to appreciate the qualities of *Werther* in the second half of the nineteenth century, because of potential danger lurking in the example of the suicide:[23]

Non si osa lodare tutti questi pregi d'una verità sì viva e toccante senza fare delle riserve sull'ispirazione generale dell'opera e sui risultati da essa prodotti.

Despite the extraordinary success of the work in Germany and France, *Werther* appears then to have aroused little interest before 1782 (certainly there are no compositions before Monti's *Pensieri* which reveal the influence of the novel). That it was known of in Italy is apparent from the bibliographical details that I have been able to locate, and there must surely be others. When it was translated into Italian, and thus became available to a much wider public, it was opposed on two main counts, namely that it was a novel, and that it exonerated (and even appeared to glorify) the act of suicide. However, although this opposition must have mitigated against the popularity of *Werther*, the fact that it was a novel troubled only those men of letters who were preoccupied with the social role of literature which was to disseminate knowledge, to educate through entertainment—a role in which the novels were not thought to participate[24]—and the majority of the readers would have considered this aspect superfluous. As for the suicide, this heightened the pathos, and stimulated further the compassion of the reader. If novels were judged by the amount of *sentiment* they aroused, then *Werther* came high on the list—a 'Storia, che più d'un bel ciglio di molle pianto carco vidde', as Ludger wrote in his Introduction. Grassi found solace while reading the work, rather than an instigation to put an end to his suffering by killing himself, and so too did Salom:[25]

Il mio cuore stretto ed angustiato vi benedì cento volte d'avergli fatto versare dolcissime lagrime, che in larga copia mi grondano dagli occhi, ogni volta ch'io leggo, per esempio, l'ultima lettera della Prima Parte.

To those who argued as Giovio, it could be objected that a reading of *Werther* was cathartic, and that the vicarious experience of Werther's suicide prevented others from attempting a similar solution to their problems.

That the novel did in time become popular and famous in Italy is obvious not only from the reprints of Salom and of Grassi, but also from the works it inspired, both poetical and theatrical. Besides Monti's *Pensieri*, there are the *sciolti*, by the conte Pietro di Maniago, written probably in 1796, which appear to be a poetic transposition of Werther's last two letters:[26]

Fosca è la notte: tenebrosa e fosca.
Sempre è l'ultima notte: oh! di natura
Soave, placidissimo riposo,
Nò, non t'invidio più: ferreo trà poco
il mio sonno sarà: Dolce mia Fiamma,
Dall'esistenza mia sublime prezzo,
Gli estremi accenti miei degna di un guardo:

the sonnets by Vettor Benzone, published in 1798–9:[27]

Alla tomba di Werter

Astro del duolo che la notte bruna
D'una pallida tingi e dubbia aurora:
Tu pingi quel che tua trista fortuna
A morte trasse anzi il suonar de l'ora.

A la soglia di sua bassa dimora
Veggo il tuo raggio avvicinarsi, o Luna,
Egli la sepolcral quiete onora
Del cener freddo che colà s'aduna.

Qualunque volta tu riguardi al basso
Pietoso raggio illuminar ti piaccia
Quello ch'io scrivo sul funereo sasso:

'Qui posato ha la sua pallida faccia
'Werter: Pensosi o voi fermate il passo
'Ch'ite sequendo la medesima traccia.

as well as Sografi's play and various aspects of Foscolo's *Ultime
Lettere*. Maniago was a friend of Foscolo in Venice in 1796, and
tells us of hours spent with the poet, who was deeply moved by
Werther and by his *sciolti*:[28]

> Mi diceva spesso egli stesso, che non aveva mai letto cosa più
> commovente di queste due epistole, ch'egli sapeva a memoria e che
> recitava spesso piangendo.

Others of their circle no doubt joined in these conversations
about the novel, and Maniago's poetic version of the ending.
The name of Carlotta enjoyed great popularity, and to a lesser
extent so did that of Werther (which for instance the Principessa
di Carignano, Giuseppina di Lorena gave to her dog—a sure sign
of the fashionableness of the name![29]). Goethe was known
throughout Italy as the author of *Werther*,[30] and as late as 1809
the translation of *Wilhelm Meister* was offered to the reading public
as *del signor Goethe, autore di Werter*.[31] In 1789 the work was
described as an 'inimitabile quadro delle vicende prodotte da una
passione dolce e gentile in un'anima sensibile',[32] by 1802 the
periodicals refer to it freely,[33] 'ben si vede come il celebre romanzo
del Werther del dott. Goethe è stato il modello...' and after this
the fame of the novel received fresh impetus from its popularity

with Napoleon, and from the praise it was accorded in the works of Mme de Stael, which were so widely read and discussed in the peninsula.[34]

Whereas the influence of *Werther* is immediately recognisable in the works of Benzone and Maniago, and in those of the young Monti and Foscolo, this is not the case with those compositions for the stage which took the novel as their source of inspiration. The whole character of *Werther* was altered and the transposition necessary to enable it to be performed changed it into a *commedia* in the version by Sografi, to a *farsa per musica* in that by Camagna, and to a *melodramma giocoso* in Gasbarri's adaptation.[35] All the seriousness of the German original has been dissipated, with the exception of a few lines in Sografi, and in accordance with the demands of comedy, the tragic ending has been dropped and the suicide replaced with reconciliation. *Werther* is singularly ill suited for the stage: the lack of action and of characters, the amount of interior monologue—these had to be compensated for in some way, and thus new characters are brought in, and a plot is fabricated which retains only the most tenuous links with the novel. If it were not for the title of the play the reader would be excused for failing to identify the source as Goethe's novel. The skeleton of the original remains, insomuch as there is a young man hopelessly in love with another man's wife, but this is a situation which is common to hundreds of eighteenth century tear-jerkers. If Sografi's play is but a pale shadow of Goethe's work, it is nevertheless incomparably better than the other versions which are based on it. It is well written, the characters are drawn with skill, the plot handled with ability, it is lively, witty, and at the end Werther takes on the character of the eternal melancholic, unable to find rest or peace. This final note shows that Sografi realised the implications of the character he was dealing with, even if his nature had led him to write a play which does not end in suicide:

Werther: Ella [la mia passione] mi trasporta l'anima, rende ottuse le mie sensazioni, mi lacera il cuore. Non è per questo, che in mezzo a questa burrascosa agitazione d'affetti, io non senta qualche volta una voce che s'alza imperiosa dal profondo del cuore, che mi ricorda i doveri d'uomo, e che mi rinfaccia la mia debolezza. E solo per questa voce medesima, ch'io ancora potrò vedere la luce del sole, errare sventuratamente di luogo in luogo, cercando invano sollievo ne' mie, affanni, piangendo amaramente sul mio destino.

I do not propose to give a complete résumé of the plot since Atkins has already done so, and it is sufficient to say that a sub-plot has been introduced in which the tutor of Carlotta's children is also in love with her, has his declaration rejected, and then, jealous of Werther, poisons Alberto's mind against his wife and friend on his return from abroad. Alberto is convinced of his wife's infidelity and his friend's betrayal, when in fact the only thing that has happened is that Werther has revealed his love to Carlotta. One of her children overheard the tutor's proposal to her, and it is when this is disclosed to Alberto that he is persuaded that Werther and Carlotta are innocent. Werther is determined to commit suicide as no satisfactory solution to his situation is possible, but decides, before doing so, to force the tutor Giorgio to write a full confession. Werther's servant Federigo has in the meantime swapped the poisoned wine without his master know-ing. During the confession Giorgio, under duress, drinks some of the wine to keep up his courage, and then, when Werther tells him what was in it, immediately goes into psychosomatic agonies. He recovers, only to be dismissed, when the truth is revealed by Federigo before the assembled cast.

Atkins recognised that the libretto of Gasbarri's *Carlotta e Werther*, with music by Coccia, was influenced by Sografi's play, but was not aware that the latter was also the inspiration for Camagna's libretto *Verter*, with music by Pucitta, which had first been performed some twelve years before Gasbarri. Furthermore it would seem that the play about Werther performed in Naples in 1797 which Croce talks of,[36] was either a performance of Sografi, or, failing this, was based on his version, and was not, as he suggests, a parody of an English drama. Croce sounds very sure of his information, but the exact parallel of the plot which he describes and the events in Sografi is more than even the greatest coincidence could account for. It is all the more puzzling since Croce, having told us that the play was a translation from the English, then adds that the translator has not kept to the text, but has invented, 'con un colpo da uomo di genio', new characters and events—which are precisely those that characterise Sografi's play. Did Stegmann,[37] from whom Croce takes his information, see a copy of the English play, or did he misunderstand the situation? Did the producers of the play say that it was based on an English drama to attract a larger audience? Whatever the explanation, this production must have been inspired directly by Sografi's drama, which had been performed three years before in Venice. At the same time as this play was being performed at the Fiorentini theatre a parody was staged at the S. Carlino with Pulcinella taking the leading part. Croce says that it was worth more than the 'dramma parodiato', and gives the following description of the finale:

Il finale era che, dopo che Pulcinella ha tentato, veleno, pugnale e pistole, e li ha messi poi di nuovo da parte, finalmente si decide, anche morendo, di punire la sua amata. S'impiccherà di fronte al suo letto! Tutto l'apparato è pronto, già egli sta per appiccarsi, quando ad un tratto cambia pensiero, afferra il suo rivale e lo impicca, ed egli per fare più strepitosa la vendetta, si corica nel letto di Carlotta!

It sounds stirring stuff, but has nothing to do with *Werther*!

We have travelled almost as far from the original in the libretti of Camagna and Gasbarri. The full title of Camagna's work reveals that it was based on a commedia of the same name (Sografi's play was known as *Verter* at first and then later as *Carlotta e Werther*) but does not say who wrote the latter. The anonymous author is easily identifiable as Sografi, since the same twists occur in the plot, complete with the enamoured tutor, a false poisoning, and a confession under duress. The role of the child who reveals the truth has been altered, and instead, Alberto is informed by one of the servants that Werther and Carlotta did not wish to flee together as Giorgio had asserted. The farce is no more than a series of stock situations acted out by one-dimensional figures, a fact which is emphasised by the introductory list of characters. This defines Ambrogio as the *servo sciocco di Verter*, and calls the tutor *Giorgio Ipocrita*. Giorgio's hypocrisy is accordingly more pronounced than in Sografi, Ambrogio is the stereotyped grumbling and gullible servant, and overall the comic elements in the play are more stressed. Werther and Carlotta become conventional Metastasian lovers, and the genuine emotion of the original is reduced to stylised gestures:

Verter: A qual passo io son ridotto
         Giusto Ciel mi porgi aita...
         Ah si perda pria la vita
         Non si lasci il caro ben.

Ma qual speme se io qui resto,
qual conforto all'amor mio!
Lacerar mi sento oh Dio!
Dalla smania il cor nel sen.

Gasbarri's libretto changes the name of the servants, but little
else, and the location is given as a small village in Germany,
which is identical with Sografi's setting. It is much livelier than
Camagna's version, wittier, and less superficial, and the action is
handled better in the scenes where Alberto is induced to drop
his suspicions and accept the truth. A chorus of servants, cooks
and footmen is included, which allows the poet to introduce such
humorous passages as:

Servi: S'io lo trovo in stanza solo,
            Dal balcon farà un bel volo.

Cuochi: Se mai viene giù in cucina,
            Gli darò una polpettina.

Staffieri: Se in carrozza averlo io posso,
            Lo precipito in un fosso.

and it is the chorus which makes the only reference in any of the
theatrical compositions to the world of nature, so prominent a
feature of the novel:

Nembo fremente s'ode d'intorno,
Muggisce il vento: si oscura il giorno:
Manca la speme di amica stella,
E la procella—crescendo va.

It is on this note of foreboding that the first act comes to a close.
Although this gloomy 'landscape' was appropriate to the novel,
it is out of place in this libretto, and has obviously been put in
because it belongs to the world of Werther, with little concern
for the actual context. There is a return to Sografi in the role of
the child, and the conclusion is made more dramatic by Werther
himself drinking some of the wine which he believes to be
poisoned. This gives rise to a speech in which Werther, bidding
farewell to the world, exclaims

O mia diletta madre!
Chi ti darà conforto,
Quando saprai, che Verter tuo è morto?

It is an interesting point that whereas in the German novel Werther does not appear to have any emotional relationship with his mother (even at the end he only writes: 'Liebe Mutter, verzeiht mir! Tröste sie, Wilhelm!'), by the time we reach Sografi, Werther's love for her, although not stressed, is clearly evident, and then it plays a more prominent role here after the publication of the *Ortis*, where it is an important element of Jacopo's character. It is unlikely that Foscolo was influenced by Sografi,[38] but it is very possible that Gasbarri was thinking of Jacopo Ortis when he wrote his *Carlotta e Werter*. The characters of the two young men must have fused in the minds of many people.[39] This libretto is superior in all respects to that by Camagna, but is no more than a travesty of the novel. That it could have been written and performed as late as 1818 shows the extraordinary popularity of this type of operetta in Italy.

Foscolo in a letter to Vordoni about his dramatic version of the *Ortis* wrote:[40]

Ella—e l'autore della commedia tratta dal Werther prima di lui—ella ha sentito questo bisogno d'azione e di varietà di caratteri—quindi in questi due drammi non resta del protagonista che il solo nome.

He does not mention Sografi by name, but the reference is unmistakable, and we have seen how justified his criticism was. However, Sografi does occasionally recapture a little of the essence of the German hero, particularly in Werther's final speech, which is more than can be said for either of the libretti. His play was highly praised by the critic who wrote the *notizie storico-critiche* to the first edition in 1800:

Giusta condotta, scene affettuose e patetiche, stil naturale, intreccio di accidenti senza confusione, sali faceti, morale onesta, caretteri aperti, *nissun matrimonio*, fanno il Verter, a nostra opinione, una delle migliori commedie moderne.

the first performance was a success:

Ma tale fu l'interesse che prese il pubblico a favor del poeta, e contro l'ingiustizia che si minacciava alla rappresentazione che la stessa non si terminò a cagion degli applausi. Si replicò per molte sere.

and it was performed in towns throughout Italy, with the audiences responding eagerly to the passions of Werther and Carlotta:[41]

> Carlotta piange! ruft Werther
> Im süssesten Schmerze melodischen Lauts,
> Und alle Hände, Fächer, Tücher, Beine, Stöcke
> Erregen das lauteste Getümmel freudigen Beifalls,
> Und tausend Tränen fliessen.

Many people have first come across the name of Ossian in *Werther*, and although it must have been rare for the Italian eighteenth-century reader to come to the novel without a prior acquaintance with the Caledonian bard, the fact that Ossian figures so prominently in the novel must have contributed further to the already widespread interest in the poems in Italy. Melchior Cesarotti's translation of the poems was famous by the 1780's, and so it is interesting to see what the Italian translator did, when he came to that passage where the hero reads to Charlotte his translation of the *Canti di Selma* and a piece from the poem *Berrathon*. The Celtic original had been in verse, Macpherson's version had been in poetic prose, Cesarotti had chosen unrhymed hendecasyllables interspersed with sections of rhymed lines of five and seven syllables, Goethe had used prose—there was no firm precedent, and the translator had to decide for himself. If he chose verse, then inevitably a comparison with Cesarotti awaited him, if prose, then a comparison with Goethe. It was not an invidious decision, especially as this episode is central to the development of the novel, but there existed a simple way of resolving the difficulty. Grassi saw this, and the parts of the ossianic poems which he retains (he omits the first 336 lines of the *Canti di Selma*, which have 360 lines, and which are all translated in the German) are taken straight from Cesarotti, apart from one or two alterations in punctuation. When Ludger came to this passage, he translated it, unlike Grassi, in its entirety, and put it, as Goethe had done, into prose. His translation is closer to the German[42] than Cesarotti's, but less satisfactory stylistically. Salom for his part adds a note to his version of Ossian, saying that amidst all the difficulties of the translation, this section of the work was not the least of his worries. He realised the danger of a comparison with Cesarotti:

mi sono trovato nella dura necessità di tradurre un poemetto, tradotto già dalla sua celebre penna, e per conseguenza non atto che a concitarmi le beffe, ed io ben le meriterei, se avessi con ciò inteso di gareggiare con lui per l'onore del canto.

and to avoid any suggestion of vying with him, he sent him his translation to have it corrected and approved.

Whatever the merits of the various versions, it is impossible to deny the efficacity of the portrait of Ossian which appears in another celebrated letter in *Werther*:[43]

Ossiano ha preso nel mio cuore il luogo, che occupava Omero. Cotesto illustre Bardo mi apre la strada ad un mondo affatto nuovo: erro per delle brughiere in mezzo a degli impetuosi turbini, che involvono, e svegliano le larve de' nostri maggiori dal debole chiaror della luna rese ai nostri occhi visibili... incontro il Bardo stesso, cotesto venerabil vecchio, cui il canuto crine accresce un nuovo decoro: lo veggo errante per le valli investigar le tracce de' suoi padri, oimè! ei non ritrova che i vuoti lor sepolcri! allora cotesto Eroe, rivolte al cielo le umide ciglia, siegue con un occhio rispettoso l'astro della sera, che va a nascondersi dietro i flutti del burrascoso mare...

The young Werther found in Ossian a kindred spirit,[44] suffering all the grief of loneliness and separation from those he loved, finding momentary consolation in his memories and the contemplation of nature, longing for the release of death, and yet wondering if he would be missed on earth, if his tomb would awaken in the passer-by thoughts of the son of Fingal. This feeling of spiritual affinity Werther passed on to his readers, and so it is that *Ossian* and *Werther* become inseparably linked.

It is obvious that Sassoli, employed to complete the *Ultime Lettere* in 1799, and aware of the Ossian–Werther connection, carried this over into the world of Jacopo, and has the hero read aloud from the ossianic poems as he stares out from his room, and discerns the shapes of warriors in the clouds and mist rushing past his window:[45]

Vedeva perfino, o Lorenzo, fra que' nugoloni addensati, le pallide taciturne ombre de' guerrieri Bardi errar lentamente, e inabissarsi poi, e disperdersi colle loro lancie di nebbia. Non mi contenni dal pronunziar con tutta energia alcuni versi divini del celtico Omero.

In Monti's *Sciolti a don Sigismondo Chigi*, and in his *Pensieri*, are to be found echoes of *Ossian* as well as *Werther*, and it is notable that in the *Raccolta di scelte prose alemanne*, the editor, after praising *Werther*, gave his readers Goethe's translation of the *Canti di Selma* as a sample of the work.[46] Inevitably the name of Cesarotti reappears, and the editor quotes from his version in footnotes to facilitate a comparison.

Before the publication of the *Ortis*, the fame and popularity of *Werther* was limited in Italy by the following factors: (1) it only became available in 1782, by which time not only were other works from the north widely known of in the peninsula, but also a reaction against the importation of yet more foreign compositions was gathering momentum; (2) it could only be read in translations that left much to be desired; (3) it ended in suicide, and (4) it was a novel. That it was popular, despite all this, is due to the fact that not only did the hero speak directly to those of his age, giving utterance to all the hopes and fears of a young man passionately in love, but it was the first work to deal sympathetically with a person led to kill himself (the reader is told at the very beginning that he cannot refuse Werther his 'Liebe' and 'Bewunderung'). Many others besides Monti, Foscolo, and Giuseppe Poerio,[47] must have felt that they could identify with Werther in a way which was not possible with any other character in contemporary literature. There was no comparable figure, not even among the inhabitants of Ossian's world, or in the pages of Young. In the last decade of the century the novel became increasingly well known, inspired a number of works, and its popularity is reflected in the enthusiastic reception of Sografi's play. The influence it had was, however, in no way comparable to that which it exerted in Germany and France.

After the publication of the *Ortis* its success was overshadowed by the presence of a native-born *Werther* which did not require translation, and as Foscolo wrote in his *Notizia Bibliografica* to the 1816 Zurich edition of the *Ultime Lettere*:[48]

> Le grida de' giornalisti che l'Ortis fosse imitazione del *Werther* indussero molti in Italia a raffrontare un libro originale con un libro traddotto, e il *Werther*, per un giudizio popolare provocato da un'accusa mal fondata, fu ingiustamente condannato e quasi caduto in disprezzo.

Of all the works inspired by *Werther*, the *Ortis* is probably the only one which goes beyond being a mere imitation and becomes a creative work in its own right. Despite Foscolo's protestations to the contrary, it is clear that the *Ortis* owes much to the German novel, but there is one difference between the two heroes which is of overriding importance—their political feelings. Werther is apolitical, and his interior life is so intense that he is oblivious to much that goes on around him, whereas Jacopo is appalled and outraged at the exploitation of his homeland. He is an Italian citizen at a time when Italy existed only as a geographical entity, he stands for freedom, and his cry of nationalism made him the hero of all those who loved their country, and felt inspired by its former glory. Why then should the Italian reader turn to *Werther* when he had to hand not a comparable, but a superior volume, which was more relevant to his situation than the German novel could ever be? Jacopo was more congenial than Werther because he possessed this added dimension of a social conscience (Werther automatically sides with the underdog, and gives generously to the poor, but their suffering does not lead him to deplore the state of society) and because his suicide could be interpreted as an assertion of personal liberty in the face of foreign oppression, rather than the result of temporary derangement:

No, cara giovine: non sei tu cagione della mia morte. Tutte le mie passioni disperate: le disavventure delle persone più necessarie alla vita mia: gli umani delitti: la sicurezza della mia perpetua schiavitù e dell'obbrobrio perpetuo della mia patria venduta...

> (Letter headed *Mercoledì, ore 5*, written
> shortly before his death.)

Werther continued to stimulate the young reader even after the appearance of the *Ortis*, as we learn from Leopardi's *Zibaldone*:

'Io so che letto Werther mi sono trovato caldissimo nella mia disperazione.'[49]

It was performed repeatedly on the stage in various guises, and Grassi's translation was republished several times. It failed though to engage the hearts and minds of the Italian reader to the same extent as the *Ultime Lettere*, and overall it was far less influential —both as regards the interest it aroused and the works it inspired—than the poems of Ossian.

If I may be permitted to end on a personal note, a Venetian

friend of mine of melancholic disposition was known at school
(some fifteen years ago) as *il giovane Werther*. The acquaintance
with *Werther* in Italy by successive generations of young people
which this indicates, and which is so striking to an English
person, is probably due not to some particular attraction of the
novel for the Italians, but to its connection with Foscolo's novel.[50]
Maturer students of literature in Italy have never ceased to be
interested in the novel, as is apparent from the successive translations and editions of *Werther* after 1850, and in this century, but
most of them must have had this work brought to their attention
in the context of the *Ultime Lettere*.

Appendix A

Italian translations of Werther *before 1850*

Works referred to in the appendices not already mentioned in the text
or the notes are as follows:

F. Blangini, *Souvenirs* (Paris 1835).
G. B. Marchesi, *Romanzieri e romanzi italiani del Settecento* (Bergamo
    1903).
F. Clément et P. Larousse, *Dictionnaire des Opéras* (Paris 1881).

1781	Anon.	*Werther*[51]	[Not published?]
1782	Gaetano Grassi	*Werther*, opera di sentimento coll'aggiunta di un'apologia in favore dell'opera mede-sima.[52]	Poschiavo

[There appear to have been two editions published in this
year, identical except for an enlarged list of printer's errors in
the second edition.]

1788	Corrado Ludger	*Gli affanni del giovane Verther*, tradotti da C.L. in Lingua Toscana dall'originale tedesco.[53]	Londra
1788	D.M.S. [=D. M. Salom]	*Verter*, opera originale tedesca tradotta in italiana.[54]	Venezia
1796	D.M.S.	*Verter* [Identical edition.]	Venezia

1800	G. Grassi	*Werther*	Milano
1801–2	A. F. Arese	*Werther*[55]	Not published
1803	L. C. de Salse	*Werther*, traduit de l'Allemand de Goethe en Français et en Italien.	Paris

[The name of the translator is taken from Fasola.]

1807	G. Grassi	*Werther*	Basilea
1808	G. Grassi	*Werther*	Basilea
1808	G. Grassi	*Werther*	Livorno
1808	G. Grassi	*Werther*	Firenze

[Both Fasola and Marchesi—who probably took the information from Fasola—mention this edition, but I have been unable to locate it.]

| 1809 | Michelangelo Arcontini | *Werther*, opera di sentimento del Dott. Goethe. | Padova |
| 1811 | D. M. Salom | *Werther* | Venezia |

[Identical to 1788 edition, except that it only has frontispiece to vol. 1, which, with minor pictorial alterations, is the same as frontispiece to vol. 2 of earlier edition. The caption underneath the picture has been altered. In 1788 it read:

Sensibil alma, a cui pregiata, e cara
Fia sua memoria nell'obbrobrio involta,
Ei ti sogguarda dalla tomba, ascolta:
Mortal, fa cui, e a non seguirmi impara.

and has been altered to:

Ove sia chi per prova intenda amore,
Spero trovar pietà non che perdono.
                              (Petr., Sonet. 1)

| 1811 | Anon. | *Werther* | Bologna |
| 1823 | Anon. | *Werther*, nuova traduzione in favore dell'opera medesima. | Firenze |

[This is Grassi's translation despite the publisher's claims that it is a *nuova traduzione*.]

| 1827 | G. Grassi | *Werther* | Basilea |

248 Stephen N. Cristea

Appendix B

Theatrical compositions based on Werther performed in Italy

(a) Plays without music[56]

1794   Antonio Simeone Sografi   Verter[57]   Venezia
                                  commedia

[This *commedia* was performed on various occasions: in Naples in 1797, in Milan in 1797–8, in Rome in 1804, in Verona in 1805.]

1797   Anon.   Werther   Naples

[This was a parody of Sografi's play with Pulcinella playing the leading role.]

Also in Naples in about 1795 Werther was the subject of a puppet show: this is mentioned by Atkins, and the information is taken from Stegmann.

(b) Plays with music

1802   Giulio Domenico Camagna   Verter   Venezia
       music by   farsa per musica
       Vincenzo Pucitta   tratta da una com-
                                  media dello stesso
                                  titolo, da rappresen-
                                  tarsi nel nobile
                                  teatro Giustiani in
                                  San Moisè.

[This was also performed in Milano in 1804, and in 1805.]

1811   Anon.   Il Werther   Pisa
       music by   farsa
       Nicolo Benvenuti

[Atkins describes this as an *opera seria*, but Clément and Larousse say it was a *farce*: I have not been able to locate it, but suspect that it was a farce, and that it too derived from Sografi.]

1814   Gaetano Gasbarri   Carlotta e Werther   Favenza
       music by   melodramma giocoso:
       Carlo Coccia   rapp. al Teatro
                           degli Infuocati
                           l'aut. 1814.

[Atkins gives the place of performance as Firenze not Favenza. It was also staged in Rome in 1816, and in Venice, Teatro di S. Benedetto in 1818.]

| 1849 | Almerindo Spadetta music by Mario Aspa | *Carlotta e Werter* melodramma rapp. Teatro Nuovo. | Napoli |
| 1862 | Leopoldo Farnese music by Raffaele Gentili | *Werther* melodramma tragico in 3 atti | Roma |

[Atkins says this was based on Sografi, but the plot bears no resemblance to the latter's *Verter*, nor indeed to Goethe's *Werther*. Suffice it to say that when the play opens a ball is in progress at the castle of Sesenheim, and Werther is engaged to be married to the Baron's daughter Sofia. The fact that he finally shoots himself with guns handed to him by Carlotta represents the only link with the original.
Also performed in Milan in 1864, and in Modena in 1865.]

| 1897 | Anon. | *Werther* dramma lirico | Milano |
| 1899 | Arturo Franchi | *L'ombra di Werther* | Trieste and Roma |

[This play was translated into German and into English]

Appendix C

Poetical and musical compositions based on Werther *and written by Italians published or performed outside Italy.*

(a) *Poetical compositions*

| 1802 | Luigi Balochi | *Werther*, cantata per musica | Paris |

see pp. 139–142 of *Il Merto delle Donne, le Rimembranze, la Malinconia e le pompe funebri: poemetti di G. Legouvé membro dell'Istituto nazionale recati in versi italiani.*
Following Balochi's translation of Legouvé's poems is a short section of his own poems.

The cantata is composed of a mixture of unrhymed hendecasyllables and rhymed settenari, both devoid of any originality. The poem opens with the lines:

> Alla metà del tenebroso giro
> S'appressa omai la notte... Ora funesta
> Prefissa al mio morir!... E come, oh Dio!
> Tregua trovar, vivendo, al dolor mio?

and closes in a paroxysm of emotion, expressed in rows of dots and exclamation marks. The rhymed sections of the poem might have been written by any competent member of Arcadia: 'Come vivere potrei / Lontan dal caro bene? / Mille volte morirei / Di smania e di dolor.'

| 1811–12c. | Giuseppe Marco Maria Felice Blangini | *Werther* cantate à grand orchestre | Kassel |

(b) *Musical compositions*

| 1796 | Gaetano Pugnani | *Werther*: ein Roman in Musik gesetzt. tone-poem. | Vienna Burgtheater |

[Quoted by Atkins—mentioned Josef Richter: *Breife eines Eipeldauers*, 26. Heft vom Jahre 1796.]

Pugnani's composition was also performed in his home town of Turin in about 1795, and there is a description of the performance in Blangini: 'L'intention de Pugnani était de faire une musique tellement imitative, qu'à l'aide de l'orchestre seul il reproduirait les principales situations du roman de Goethe, sans le secours d'aucun texte... L'exécution de ce morceau produisait beaucoup d'effet, mais Pugnani voulut aller trop loin. Au moment où Werther va se tuer, il saisit un pistolet chargé et le tira dans sa chambre: cela effraya quelques auditeurs, d'autres crurent que Pugnani était devenu fou.'

Appendix D

Miscellaneous compositions based on Werther *with which Italians are connected*

| 1791 | Luigi Muzzi | *Verteriade* | Paris |

[Imitation of Goethe's *Werther*, entitled *Werthérie* done by Pierre Perrin and translated by Muzzi. This was read by Foscolo see *Opere*, ed. naz., vol. 14, Lettera 655.]

| 1792 | J. E. Dejaure music by Kreutzer | *Werther et Charlotte*, comédie en un acte en prose, mêlée d'ariettes performed at Théâtre des Italiens 1 February 1792. | Paris |

[Clément/Larousse: 'on remarqua particulièrement l'invocation à la nature chantée sur des paroles imitées d'*Ossian*.' For a description of the piece see Appell, *op. cit.*, p. 34.]

1830 [Gasparri/Coccia?]   *Carlotta e Werther*   Paris
Théâtre des Italiens

[Atkins says a play of this name was performed there, and suggests it might be the Gasparri (*sic*) libretto.]

Atkins gives the following two works which were based on Coccia:

—*Mentre Francesco faceva il brodo*, Duetto, in the opera of *Carlotta and Werter*. Composed by Signor Coccia. London, Birchall and Co., about 1825. 15 pp. Duet of Ambrogio and Giorgio.

—...*brodo*. Duo buffo, sung by Signori De Begnis and Placci. Composed by Signor Coccia and arranged for Piano Forte by Gaetano Pinchiori Cittadini. London, T. Boosey and Co., about 1830. 16 pp

Note. As far as *Werther* in Italian art is concerned, apart from the two engravings to be found in Salom's 1788 translation, I have come across the following compositions:

Werter contemplating on Charlotte's Wedding Ring   Angelica Kauffman pinx. P. Benato sculp[r]. (undated).

[*Dolori del giovane Werther*] *Werther seduto a tavolino in atto di scrivere*   Dionigi Faconti pinx. Alberto Gilli incisore (Torino 1869).

Notes

[1] (Paris 1907).
[2] *Culturgeschichtliches aus dem Nachlasse von K. H.*, article 4, pp. 102–142 (Berlin 1885), siebenter Band von *Zeiten, Völker und Menschen*.
[3] *Dritte, gänzlich umgearbeitete und vermehrte Auflage* (Oldenburg 1882).
[4] Harvard Studies in Comparative Literature, vol. 19 (Harvard 1949).
[5] *Jahrbuch der Goethe Gesellschaft*, 16 (Weimar 1895), pp. 220–240.
[6] I do not claim that this study is exhaustive, and there may well be other works which have escaped my notice.
[7] First published Padova 1763.
[8] First published Marseilles 1770. By 1782 the Italians had met this northern melancholy in Thomson, Gray and Arnaud as well as in Ossian and Young.
[9] Num. 36 (novembre 1783), p. 288.
[10] Vol. 1 (gennaio 1777), p. 126.
[11] This supposition is substantiated by the fact that the bibliographical details given here are incorrect. A *Werther* was published in Maestricht in 1776, but the translator's name was not given (it was G. Deyverdun). B. S. di S. (Baron S. de Seckendorf) also published a translation of *Werther* in 1776, but the place of printing was Erlang.
[12] (Firenze 1897). Kerbaker admits that he has been unable to trace the French translation which supposedly influenced Monti, and I would suggest

that, since no proof is forthcoming about this French work, it is very possible that Monti's source was Grassi's translation (the *Pensieri* and the *Sciolti
a Chigi* are known to have been completed by March 1783). If the *Werther*
he read was not Grassi's translation, then it may have been G. Deyverdun's
version to which, at a superficial glance, his *Pensieri* seem closer than to that
by Baron Seckendorf. Grassi's *Werther* is based on Deyverdun's text, not on
the German original, and thus the French text which Kerbaker sees behind
the *Pensieri* may well be Grassi's translation—a French text in Italian clothing.
There are several other studies which deal with the sources of these poems
by Monti, the most recent being: C. Colicchia, *Il 'Saggio di Poesie' del 1779
e la prima poetica montiana* (Firenze 1961).

¹³ Monti met and fell in love with a girl called Carlotta in the autumn of
1782, and by the same time the following year all was over, see: *Epistolario
di V. Monti*, ed. A. Bertoldi (Firenze 1928), vol. 1, pp. 192–193.

¹⁴ *Nuovo Giornale Enciclopedico d'Italia* (Venezia 1790), p. 117.

¹⁵ *Giornale de' Letterati* (Pisa 1794), vol. 96, p. 288.

¹⁶ Semestre primo, parte 111, p. 130 (Venezia, maggio-giugno, 1798).
The reviewer said this à propos of a work entitled, *Il Duca di Guise, o le
funeste conseguenze della Gelosia*, which had been translated from the French.

¹⁷ It may well be that if there are any late eighteenth century or early
nineteenth century Italian guidebooks to Germany, special mention will be
made of Wetzlar because of its connection with Werther.

¹⁸ *Abaritte, storia verissima* (Londra 1792), cap. XVI, p. 87. (first published 1790).

¹⁹ *Idee sulla tristezza* (Como 1812), p. 258: is in *Raccolta di operette filosofiche
e filologiche scritte nel sec. XVIII* (Milano 1832), vol. 2, pp. 246–281.

²⁰ *Zibaldone*, 64.

²¹ *Opere*, ediz. naz., vol. 15, lettera 667, Milano, 29 sett. 1808.

²² The preoccupation with suicide explains, I think, the popularity of
another figure who killed herself because of unrequited love: Sappho (once
referred to as a 'Werther in gonnella'). The amount of literature dealing with
this figure at this time is striking, and she continues to be a source of inspiration well into the second half of the nineteenth century. I have come
across the following works:

Saffo, tragedia di Maria Fortuna, fra gli Arcadi Isidea Egirena (Livorno 1776).

Le avventure di Saffo poetessa di Mitilene, Alessandro Verri (Padova 1780,
    1782: Vercelli 1783 etc.) Eighteen editions are known.

Saffo, ossia i Riti d'Apollo Leucadio, dramma per musica di A. S. Sografi
    (Venezia 1794).

Saffo, tragedia di Franz Grillparrer (Firenze 1816).

Saffo, tragedia di Stanislao Marchisio (Milano 1821).

Saffo, tragedia lirica di Salvadore Cammarano (Verona 1831) Sixteen
    editions known.

Saffo, tragedia di Leopoldo Marenco (Milano 1868).

Sappho also appears at the close of Foscolo's ode *All'amica risanata* (1802),
is the subject of Leopardi's *Ultimo Canto di Saffo* (1822) and A. F. von
Kotzebue saw a sculpture of Sappho, done at that time in Rome in 1804, see:
Erinnerungen von einer Reise aus Liefland nach Rom und Neapel (Berlin 1805).

[23] See preface to his translation of *Werther* (Firenze 1858).
[24] Grassi had stressed the 'utility' of the novel to placate the opposition of such people.
[25] See *Lettera del traduttore all'Autore* printed in the Introduction to his translation.
[26] MS. Cod. Magliabechiano, 11, VII, 80, Bib. Naz. Firenze.
[27] *Anno poetico ossia Raccolta annuale di poesie inedite di autori viventi* (Venezia 1798), p. 24. There is another sonnet with the same title in volume for 1799, p. 12.
[28] Quoted by E. Marinoni, *Prose e Poesie di Ugo Foscolo* (Milano 1913), p. 29.
[29] *Aneddoti di Storia Civile e Letteraria*, no. 2, 'Werther in Italia', p. 136, *La Critica, Rivista di Letteratura, Storia e Filosofia*, anno XXXVII, fasc. 1 (Bari, 20 gennaio 1939). The Principessa erected a little monument to Werther in the grounds of her house (while the dog was still alive) and the verses which adorned the edifice were written by Tommaso Valperga di Caluso.
[30] See Goethe's *Italienische Reise*, undertaken in 1786-7.
[31] *Raccolta di Romanzi* (Milano 1809), num. IV, tom. 1, *Gli anni del noviziato di Alfredo Meister*.
[32] *Raccolta di scelte prose alemanne, con gli elementi grammaticali ad uso degli italiani* (Pavia 1789). Author not given.
[33] See: Marinoni, *op. cit.*, p. 24, taken from *Giornale dell'Italiana Letteratura*, (Padova 1802).
[34] See: *L'Alemagna*, traduzione ital. fatta sulla seconda edizione francese (Milano 1814), vol. 2, p. 256.
[35] See Appendix B. Sografi's play is a mixture of comedy and tragedy, and the best description would be a bourgeois drama with comic overtones.
[36] *I Teatri di Napoli* (Napoli 1891), pp. 650-652.
[37] C. J. Stegmann, *Fragmente über Italien aus dem Tagebuch eines jungen Deutschen* (1798). The only English drama based on *Werther* written before 1797 was that by F. Reynolds (pub. 1786) which had an entirely different plot.
[38] Since his love for his mother was a biographical fact.
[39] A French translation of the *Ultime Lettere* was entitled, *Amour et Suicide, ou le Werther de Venise* (Paris 1820).
[40] Foscolo, *op. cit.*, vol. 15, p. 225, lettera 462, Brescia, 5 giugno 1807.
[41] *Kleines Theater in der Arena* in *Gedichte von L. Tieck* (Dresden 1823), pp. 120-123. This is a lively description of a performance he saw in the amphitheatre in Verona in 1805.
[42] The full title of the translation tells the reader that it is done from the German. Of the three Italian translators Ludger is the only one who does not connect Ossian with Cesarotti, due presumably to his living outside Italy.
[43] Quoted from Grassi's translation, letter of 12 ott., p. 146.
[44] The innumerable unhappy lovers who inhabited the misty landscapes were an added attraction of the Ossian poems. They figure prominently in the *Canti di Selma*, and Werther identifies with them while reading to Carlotta.
[45] Foscolo, *op. cit.*, vol. 4, p. 93. This edition of the *Ortis* was published in 1799, but is dated 1798 because printing had begun with the title page in

that year. At the end of the novel Sassoli lists *Werther* among the books lying about in Jacopo's room, and it is one of the four books Jacopo leaves to Teresa at the conclusion of Foscolo's section.

[46] See note 32.

[47] See: B. Croce, *Una famiglia di patrioti, ed altri saggi critici e storici* (Bari 1919). From prison on the island of Favignana Poerio wrote to his fiancée in 1800: 'Sarebbe impossibile di avere *Werther?* Questo libro diminuirebbe la metà de' miei mali. Io mi sforzo invano di ricordarmi de' squarci più sublimi e analoghi alla mia situazione', and in the following year: 'Se avessi un *Werther* sarei meno afflitto'. This young prisoner, separated from the girl he loved because of his political beliefs, would have found a much closer parallel to his situation in the *Ultime Lettere!*

[48] Foscolo, *op. cit.*, vol. 4, p. 526, note c. This was the edition which purported to be printed in London, 1814.

[49] *Zibaldone* 261–262, written sometime during the years 1815–19. For the influence of *Werther* on Leopardi's verse, see: G. A. Borgese, *Leopardi wertheriano e l'Omero di Ugo Foscolo*, in *Mélanges Baldensperger* (Paris 1930), vol. 1, pp. 63–69.

[50] It is possible that interest in *Werther* in Italy is also stimulated by the popularity there of Massenet's opera *Werther*, performed repeatedly since 1894.

[51] This unknown translation has hitherto been ascribed to Grassi—by Fasola, Appell, Marchesi, etc. That it is not by Grassi is evident from Goethe's letter to Frau von Stein, which contains the only information available about this translation. This letter is dated 12 December 1781, and in it Goethe says he has received an Italian translation of *Werther*, and that the translator has 'Auch meinen vielgeliebten Namen in Annetta verwandelt'. That 'vielgeliebten' name he is referring to must be Lotte—and Grassi faithfully translates this as Carlotta. There is no mention of the name Annetta in Grassi's Italian version. Furthermore, the dedication to Hess at the beginning of Grassi's translation is dated very precisely as '2 Febbraio 1782', which rules out any possibility of the work having been published in the previous year.

[52] Grassi did not base his translation on the German original, but on the anonymous French translation published in 1776 (see note 11). His source is unmistakable because the French translator omits various letters, numbers the ones left in, and excludes most of the *Canti di Selma*, and Grassi's version is identical in all these respects. Baron Seckendorf on the other hand is much closer to Goethe: he does not number the letters and he keeps in the whole of the extracts from Ossian. He is more faithful to the text, whereas Deyverdun frequently alters the phrasing and imagery of the German.

[53] This edition appears to have passed unnoticed in Italy. The stress on the fact that it was translated into the Tuscan language suggests that the translator thought that this would recommend it to English people, who had learnt Italian, and who knew that Tuscan was the purest form of the language.

[54] Salom also saw the Deyverdun translation (he mentions it in his Preface), but because his translation was undertaken, on arrival in Germany, as part of an attempt to learn the language, he used the German text. He admits

that by himself, with the sole aid of the dictionary, he would never have understood Goethe properly, and that he was assisted in the task of translation by an Italian-speaking German. He completed his translation some time in the years 1782-3, but refrained from publishing it then because of the appearance of Grassi's edition. Salom was a doctor by profession.

⁵⁵ Countess Antonietta Fagnani Arese was a friend of Ugo Foscolo, and did this translation at his behest while he was in Florence. He intended to 'polish' her version and then send it to Goethe, but never did so, see: *Carteggio Foscolo-Arese* in Foscolo, *op. cit.*, vol. 14 pp. 207-414, and in particular Foscolo's letter to Goethe, *ibid.*, pp. 129-132. Not surprisingly Foscolo despised the two Italian translations which he knew of—those by Grassi and Salom—and wrote to Goethe that Arese's work would be far superior.

⁵⁶ There are theatrical compositions which appear to have derived their title from *Werther*, but not their subject matter, e.g. *Carlotta ed Alberto ossia le conseguenze di una falsa notizia* (Venezia 1808). There are others in which echoes of *Werther* are to be heard, e.g. *L'amicizia tradita*, tentativo tragico urbano (Venezia 1808), and there are several which attest to the popularity of the name Carlotta at this time, but which lack any other connection with *Werther*, e.g. a trilogy of plays by Francesco Avelloni entitled, *Carlotta calunniata*, *Carlotta oppressa* and *Carlotta vendicata* (Roma 1802-3).

⁵⁷ Published in 1800 in Venice in *Il Teatro Moderno applaudito ossia Raccolta di Tragedie, Commedie, Drammi e Farse*: also in Vienna 1817, in Milan 1830, and in Venice 1832.

C. P. Brand

The Italian exiles in Britain
in the early nineteenth century:
a survey of their writings

The political upheavals of the Napoleonic wars, the Restoration and the revolutions in Italy in the early nineteenth century clearly had a profound effect on the literature of the period. The lives of many writers were seriously disturbed. For a significant group of intellectuals their participation in the wars or revolutions led to exile in other parts of Europe or even America, and their opportunities for writing and communicating with their countrymen at home were severely limited. The actual period of exile varied considerably in length, some Italians spending the rest of their lives abroad, others seizing the opportunity afforded by the fairly frequent amnesties to return home after a few years. But a considerable number of Italians who cared about the fate of their country found themselves at some stage in their lives suddenly plunged into a strange environment, trying to understand and speak a strange language, trying to communicate with a strange people.[1]

Those who came to England, often after an initial period in Switzerland, France or Spain, reacted very positively and sometimes energetically to their new experiences. They found many Englishmen disposed to be sympathetic to both their personal and their political misfortunes and yet often very ignorant about conditions in Italy. In spite of the fashionableness of travel in Italy and a fairly widespread interest in Italian language and the literature and arts of the glorious past the English very generally did not know or care about their Italian contemporaries, their institutions or their way of life.[2] They had just emerged from a long and trying European war, as a result of which Italy had been restored to her old reactionary governments, and most Englishmen did not understand or care what this really meant to the Italians. The exiles set to work to try to tell them, partly through direct contact with British families, but also through the written word—books, pamphlets, articles in the journals, letters to the newspapers. A considerable number of these exile-publications survive in libraries and private collections up and down the country, and they make an interesting and illuminating contribution to the literature and history of the period. Leaving aside the much studied writers such as Foscolo, Mazzini and Panizzi, this article surveys some of the lesser known work written in exile and published in Britain in the early nineteenth century and attempts to show something of the circumstances in which it arose, the motives for its composition, and the reception and influence it had in this country.[3]

As suggested above, one of the prime concerns of the Italian exile was to convince his host nation of the injustice of the Restoration; but often he was also especially interested to see the working of constitutional government and free institutions such as he and liberals all over Europe desired to establish in their own countries, and some of the books published in England were aimed as much at Italians in Italy as they were at the English. In fact a considerable number of these works, though published in England, were in Italian, or French, and a substantial number of books, published later in Italy by exiles who had returned home, taught the lessons learned by them from their experiences in England and France. The latter are not considered here, nor is the range of work published by the exiles in England related to the teaching of the Italian language or Italian literature. There is an extensive corpus of such works and some of these made important contributions to British education and to the history of Italian literature (Foscolo's literary criticism, for example, and Panizzi's editorial work); it is worth noting, however, that some of even the innocent-looking grammars and readers written by the Italians were loaded with political propaganda: 'È mia mente d' intertenirvi, Signore mie, Signori miei, de' pregi della mia lingua, della storia della mia patria, della biografia dei miei concittadini...'[4]

Of the Italians resident in England at the beginning of the century a high proportion were music teachers, singers, instrumentalists or language teachers who came to this country voluntarily in order to earn a living, and these had little interest in politics or did not obtrude their opinions on the political scene. An exception was A. Bozzi Granville, who left Italy in 1807, enrolled in the Royal Navy and subsequently settled in England, where he gained a considerable reputation as a doctor.[5] On one occasion he treated Palmerston and, he tells us, didn't miss 'this opportunity of revealing my opinions on the Italo-Austrian question'. Granville held strong liberal and patriotic views, which he expressed in an Italian periodical published in London in 1813, *L'Italico ossia giornale politico, letterario e miscellaneo da una Società d'Italiani*. He wrote later that this journal was 'founded ostensibly as a means of encouraging Italian literature in this country', but that it was used as a vehicle for patriotic propaganda;

it contained frequent appeals to the English to support the
cause of Italian independence, and articles in defence of the
Italian national character. It combined emotional verse ('Alla
bramata libertà d'Italia') with informative reports ('Il metodo col
quale si mette in esecuzione la legge della conscrizione negli Stati
Italiani'). In the list of subscribers were the Prince Regent, the
Duchess of York, the Duke of Cambridge, Lady Burghersh, and
many other influential people. Three volumes of *L'Italico* were
published, and Granville also brought out another journal, *Il
Patriota Italiano*, at about the same time, but the life of both
periodicals was limited to the years 1813–14.

Of his other works the most interesting was his *Appello ad
Alessandro, Imperatore di tutte le Russie sul destino dell'Italia*,
published in London in 1814 in Italian, English and French, an
impassioned plea for Italian unity: 'È giustizia, è legge a tutte le
nazioni comune, che dopo tanti secoli di divisione finalmente
addivenghino gl'Italiani un popolo solo, una sola famiglia... È
tempo ormai che l'Italia cessi d'essere il teatro sanguinoso su cui
si decidano le dissenzioni delle Potenze continentali occupate in
dividerne le spoglie'. Granville claimed that he sent a copy of
this appeal to Castlereagh and that the latter accepted it, indicated
his approval and said 'he was happy to assure me that it would
have his support'. Granville's list of subsequent publications is
extensive but they are mostly on medical subjects (the quarantine
laws, for example). He did, however, publish two letters to Lord
Palmerston on the Austrian crisis in 1848.

Francesco Macerone was another of the Italian liberals whose
early life was seriously affected by the Napoleonic wars.[6] He was
born in England of Italian parents who had settled abroad for
business reasons. His parents sent him to Naples in 1803, when
he was 15, and the French occupation caught him there and kept
him in Italy for nearly seven years. When Murat joined the allies
Macerone became his adjutant and undertook several missions
on his behalf, two of them to London. When the British government broke off its relations with Murat, Macerone found himself
in a difficult situation: he claims that he pleaded Murat's cause
with Napoleon himself in Paris on several occasions; and the
British government used him for various missions in this connection. He was later imprisoned by the French, freed, and fled to
England, bursting with indignation at the perfidious British.

His *Appeal to the British nation on the treatment experienced by the Emperor Napoleon on the island of St Helena* was published in London in 1817 under the pseudonym of 'M. Santini, custode del gabinetto dell'Imperatore'. Macerone describes in his *Memoirs* the circumstance in which the *Appeal* was printed. He met Santini, a poor, ignorant man, in London and got from him an account of the conditions in which Napoleon was being held on St Helena. Macerone wrote up Santini's story and published it in French and English under Santini's name 'because I had merely transcribed in the two languages the details of the petty and mean vexations and privations to which Governor Lowe exposed his illustrious prisoner. This little work was printed by Ridgway and aroused so much interest that 7 editions were sold in 2 weeks.'[7]

However Macerone was a man of vivid imagination. His *Memoirs* are full of unlikely romantic tales, and the *Appeal* was similarly so exaggerated that it soon fell into disrepute. B. E. O'Meara, one of Napoleon's medical attendants, later made this comment: 'Gave Napoleon a copy of Santini's leaflet, in French, which he read observing as he went through it 'true', 'partly true', 'false', 'stuff'. He ended up by saying that Santini would have done better to confine himself to the strict truth which would have had a much stronger effect on the public mind than all the exaggerations he had promulgated, which seemed to have been invented by someone in England because Santini wasn't capable of writing a pamphlet by himself.'[8] The *Quarterly Review* also considered the *Appeal* must have been written for Santini by someone else, and Lord Holland in the Commons declared frankly that it was not to be taken seriously. The extent of the polemic it aroused in the press and Parliament is, however, an indication of what the exiles could do.[9]

In the same year Macerone published in English a book entitled *Interesting facts concerning the fall and death of J. Murat, King of Naples*, a detailed account of the author's part in the events of 1814 and of his missions on behalf of the allies, the French and Murat. His descriptions of his interview with Napoleon, the Duke of Wellington, Lord Bentinck and others, though not very reliable, are very lively. He describes Blücher's jealousy for example: 'Always the Duke of Wellington! Have they forgotten that there is a Prince Blücher? That there is a Prussian army?' The book is very hostile to Britain, and strongly favourable to Murat, whose downfall was accelerated by 'his complete trust in the good faith and honour of Great Britain'; he praises Murat's 'nobility and generosity'. Macerone's book was heavily attacked and ridiculed—by the *Critical Review*, for example, which asserted that Murat had permitted 'the most inhuman atrocities' to be perpetrated in Madrid, and Macerone published a second edition of his book in order to refute these charges. A heated controversy followed in which the Liberals attacked the government record and the Tories heaped abuse on Murat and Macerone. Sir Robert Wilson in the *Quarterly Review* accused Macerone of abusing the powers entrusted him by the allies; Macerone had admitted that he had been authorised by the Austrian Emperor to offer asylum to Murat if he would agree to take up residence on Austrian territory as a private individual; Murat and Macerone had been provided with passports for this purpose but Murat on arriving in Corsica drew Macerone into his plan for an attack on Naples, whereupon Macerone offered Murat 'that same passport to be nsed against the allies'.[10] Elsewhere the critics complained that Macerone's actions had positively encouraged Murat in his treacherous scheme. Macerone took out a libel action against the *Quarterly*, failed, and then printed an angry protest against British justice, *A few specimens of the Ars Logica Copleiana or Solicitor General's logic as exhibited in the case Macerone v. Murray* (1820).

Macerone also flattered himself that a series of his letters to the *Morning Chronicle* frustrated a Holy Alliance plan to intervene in South America, and quoted a despatch to Bolivar in which it was said that the pamphlet in which he issued his letters 'killed Murillo'. Macerone's flamboyant and exaggerated writings probably helped to discredit more than his own case. He got embroiled in another controversy in 1832, when he proposed a sort of Home Guard to meet the fear of violence that arose at the time of the reform Bill. He published a set of *Defensive instructions for the people with a new system of army called 'Foot Lancers'* asserting 'the right (if not the duty) of all Englishmen to be equipped with arms'.[11] His pamphlet attracted a good deal of attention, most of it adverse: the *Literary Gazette* declared that he had preached 'the old Italian method of stabbing in the back our political rivals'.

The most frequent theme in the political treatises published by the Italian exiles in the years after 1815 was, as one would expect, the protest against the injustice of the Restoration in Italy. Many of the exiles found themselves in Britain as a direct result of their revolt against the conditions imposed by Britain and her allies on Italy in 1815, and they repeatedly pressed home on the British the effects of the settlement. An anonymous book, printed in Edinburgh in 1819, pointed out the advantages of the Napoleonic regime in Italy, the impetus towards unification, 'le leggi fondamentali di cui il nuovo dominatore avea dovuto giurare l'osservazione'.[12] All this was destroyed by the allies: 'Voi, o Principi, cangiaste si fatta Italia e ve ne chiamaste Liberatori'. The restoration of feudalism, of industrial monopolies, of restrictions on freedom of the press, commerce and movement had made Italy 'non più il giardino ma il deserto del mondo'. And the anonymous author calls passionately for a reunification of the scattered and mutilated limbs of his country.

It was probably the same anonymous author who in 1824 published a protest against Lady Sidney Morgan's famous travel book on Italy, in which she had attacked the Regno Italico.[13] The author, who says he was Milanese and a witness on the Milanese scene for thirty years, asserts that, republican as he is, he must admit that 'il nome splendido di Regno d'Italia, che ci dava un posto importante e consono ed il pegno di un futuro fortunato ad esso corrispondente, era per noi un acquisto prezioso', and he refutes Lady Morgan's criticism of Napoleonic influence in Italy: 'in quanto agli Italiani, sì morti com'erano da tanti secoli, egli li suscitò alla vita'.

The largest influx of Italian exiles came in the third decade of the century and consisted substantially of men who had taken part in the Carbonaro risings in 1820 and 1821. One of the leaders of the revolution in Naples, General Guglielmo Pepe, fled to England, via Sardinia and Spain, in 1821.[14] He had served under Murat in Naples and narrowly escaped imprisonment in 1814 for his liberal opinions, but he was given command of a division in 1818 and used his authority to help impose a constitution on Ferdinand in 1820. On his arrival in England he published *A narrative of the political and military events which took place at Naples in 1820–21 with observations explanatory of the national conduct in general and of his own in particular during that period*, with a dedication to Ferdinand appealing to him to restore constitutional government. Pepe was concerned to justify first the revolution itself, then the military defence of the city by the Neapolitan forces. Many English liberals, Shelley among them, had welcomed the uprising enthusiastically as proof of the seriousness of the Italian liberals' desire to win free institutions. The ignominious collapse of the constitutional forces in Naples was a bitter disappointment to them and was pointed to by the Tories as proof of Neapolitan weakness and treachery. Pepe insisted that the rising was not merely military in character; that 'not only was the nation unanimous in its wish for the abolition of absolute power but that to preserve its liberties it displayed the greatest energy and was disposed to make every sacrifice'.[15] The failure of the revolution was to be attributed to bad administration, particularly in military matters, to the ill-health, inexperience and inability of the regent and his loss of heart at the first military reverses.

In the course of his narrative Pepe referred briefly to General Carascosa, formerly commander of the first corps of the Neapolitan army: 'This Corps, not having passed the river Liri, never had occasion to see the enemy. The Austrians having obtained possession of the Abruzzi, it made a movement to retreat behind the Volturno (a large river about five leagues from Naples); and there it suddenly disbanded'. This statement was probably the origin of the duel to which the angry Carascosa challenged Pepe when the former arrived in London in 1823.[16] Santarosa seems to have been present at the duel, as a rather inexpert second. There was a reconciliation but, soon after, their quarrel was renewed when Carascosa published his account of the Neapolitan revolution, in which, according to Pepe, 'not only the liberal party but the whole Neapolitan people was unfairly discredited'. Carascosa had held important offices under Murat, had been confirmed in his rank on the restoration of the Bourbons, and promoted War Minister by the constitutional government in 1820. His conduct at this time was severely criticised by various other Italian exiles, and his own account was published in French in London in 1823 under the title *Mémoires historiques, politiques et militaires sur la révolution du Royaume de Naples en 1820–21*. Apart from his attempts to explain his own ambiguous floating from one side to the other, he attacked popular risings in general and Carbonarism in particular as being corrupted by ambitious intrigues: the Neapolitan forces were badly organised, untrained and generally indifferent to the constitution: 'la masse des citoyens désirait une constitution mais elle était loin de vouloir l'obtenir par la révolte'. In all this he had attempted to do his duty as a soldier, and when the resistance collapsed in Naples he fled to Malta and thence to England, 'n'ayant plus d'autre sol en Europe où je puisse reposer ma tête'.[17]

Pepe was certainly justified in his complaint that Carascosa's book discredited the Neapolitans. The *Ecclesiastical Review* drew the obvious conclusion that intrigue, insubordination and cowardice characterised the whole episode. Pepe broke off relations with Carascosa and published a reply in Paris.[18] The latter emigrated to France in 1831 and continued to write pamphlets on political and military subjects; he must have kept in touch with the state of public opinion in England because he published a *Réponse à un baronet anglais à l'égard de l'Autriche en Italie*, and his autobiography was printed in England in 1846.

Another refugee from Naples was the lawyer Guglielmo Paladini who took part in the revolutions of 1799 and 1820. He fled to England after the Carbonaro rising and met Santarosa there. He became an enthusiastic admirer of Britain and the British constitution and in 1827 published his *Progetto di un nuovo patto sociale per lo regno delle Due Sicilie*,[19] dedicating it to the British nation: 'O terra felice! O invitta generosa nazione paragonabile solo a te stessa... Chi se non tu, d'ogni timore incapace, accolse le perseguitate vittime delle più ingiuste proscrizioni?' His book, he tells us, was 'un tentativo di portare i principi della costituzione inglese in aiuto agli abitanti delle Sicilie'. He attributes the failure of the revolution in Naples to the hostility of the aristocrats, and tries to convince his readers of the need to establish a new popular regime: 'Egli è l'interesse e dev'essere il desiderio del popolo inglese di vedere i principi d'un liberal governo estesi al più che sia possibile. L'Inghilterra non può aver alcun comun interesse coi principi su cui è fondata la Santa Alleanza'.

A strange figure who aroused some heated controversy among the Italian exiles at this time was Count Ferdinando dal Pozzo, who arrived in England in 1823 and stayed until 1831, when he went to Paris.[20] He was a Piedmontese and an ardent local patriot; he had held various offices in Piedmont under the

Napoleonic regime and compromised himself in 1821 when he became minister for domestic affairs in the revolutionary government. He fled to Switzerland and then to London, where he published, in 1823, his protest against the suppression of the revolution, *Observations sur la nouvelle organisation judiciaire établie dans les états de S. M. le Roi de Sardaigne par l'édit du 27 septembre 1822*. Like so many of his compatriots, he was grateful for the asylum granted him and the privileges inherent in a constitutional government: 'Devenu maintenant citoyen temporaire de l'Angleterre je me trouve d'une double manière rassuré et encouragé même dans mon entreprise. Non seulement les lois restrictives du Piémont, en fait de presse, ne m'atteignent plus... mais je jouis ici de tous les droits dont l'Angleterre laisse participer les étrangers'. Dal Pozzo took a special interest in the current controversy over Catholic emancipation; while professing himself a Catholic he had a strong dislike of priests and admired the system of control exerted by the Austrians on the Church in their territory. He explained this system in a book published in London in 1827 entitled *Catholicism in Austria or an Epitome of the Austrian Ecclesiastical Law, with a dissertation upon the rights and duties of the English government with respect to the Catholics of Ireland*. He advocated civil and political rights for the Catholics in England and a similar control over the practice of the Catholic religion to that which he had outlined in his book about Austria:

The legislature of this country . . . should lay protecting hands upon [the Catholic Church], place it, without any concordat, and only by the indisputable right of sovereignty, under the control of the State government; regulate the exercise of its worship; disentangle it from superstitions . . . and from the exaggerated pretensions of the Court of Rome.

He hoped that his book would reveal to Englishmen 'the interior structure of this vast, ancient and very complicated machine'.[21] His book attracted considerable interest in England; the *Morning Chronicle* quoted from it in a leading article and it was discussed in the Lords by the Duke of Wellington and the Earl of Winchelsea—who read a long extract aloud.[22]

Dal Pozzo repeated these views in a further book published in London in French two years later, *De la nécessité très urgente de soumettre le catholicisme romain en Irlande à des règlements civils spéciaux*. He advocated that the Catholics should have 'l'égalisation de droits... avec les autres sujets de la Grande Bretagne'. He devotes a whole chapter to explaining 'Pourquoi le catholicisme exige de plus grandes restrictions, un plus grand nombre de dispositions de la part de l'autorité civile... que tout autre culte'. His proposal that the possessions of the Catholic Church in Ireland should be confiscated by the Crown, which would use the proceeds to pay the salaries of both Catholic and Protestant priests, met the obvious response in the *Foreign Quarterly Review*, the *Morning Chronicle*, etc.: without belittling the Austrian system, it was obvious that 'many things can be done in Austria which cannot be done in this country'.[23] A few years later, after the passing of the Catholic emancipation laws in England, he turned his attention to advocating *The complete emancipation of the Protestant Vaudois of Piedmont* in a work presented to the Duke of Wellington, quoting the King of Sardinia's words to a British Minister: 'Do you emancipate the Irish Roman Catholics and I will emancipate the Vaudois.' He planned also to write a novel in Italian for the English young ladies studying the language, but I don't think this ever materialised. His most important work, published in 1833 in Paris with the title *Della felicità che gl'Italiani possono e debbono dal governo austriaco procacciarsi*, proposing a reconciliation between the Italian liberals and the Austrians, provoked clamorous opposition from the exiles in England, who were extremely resentful of Austrian domination—and the Tories at once pointed to Dal Pozzo's book as proof that not all Italians were groaning under the Austrian yoke and that there were alternatives to the violent revolution preached by the *Giovane Italia* movement.[24]

Among the Italians most hostile to Dal Pozzo's book was Pietro Anichini, who had left Italy in 1809 and was then established in business in London. He replied to Dal Pozzo in 1835 in a book published in London in Italian, *Considerazioni sull'opuscolo del Conte dal Pozzo... e cenni intorno ad un articolo della rivista trimestrale straniera* (the *Foreign Quarterly Review*). Anichini attacked the Austrian police State, 'la più inquisitoriale, la più sanguinosa, la più crudele polizia', and bewailed the lot of his compatriots in Austrian prisons. He termed himself an 'Ausonian', and he objected to Dal Pozzo's local, Piedmontese patriotism, his lofty conviction that the states of Italy must always be divided.

Dal Pozzo had lived long enough in England, Anichini insisted, to know that divisions and differences characterised almost every English county: 'Ma ad onta di queste sofistiche scipitezze presenta forse il mondo intero più maestoso esempio d'unione di nazionali interessi' than Great Britain?[25]

Anichini apparently wrote his various political and religious tracts in his leisure time after business hours: 'As a former grenadier, a tradesman and now a business-man, literature has always been and remains my trusty friend; I devote my whole day from nine in the morning to seven in the evening to the labours of my humble profession, but my evenings often until 3 in the morning to the religion of knowledge.' His works are mostly favourable to the British, and he expresses gratitude for the many acts of generosity he has benefited by, but he also found much to criticise. He wrote a letter to *The Times* in 1820 to protest against the insults heaped on Italy as a result of the unscrupulous conduct of the Italian witnesses at the trial of Queen Caroline, and when *The Times* refused it he printed it privately as *A letter to the most noble the Marquis of Lansdowne*, 'by an Ausonian.' He used the same pseudonym a few years later for his *Analytical and historical view of the Catholic religion with reference to political institutions* (1826), where he insisted on 'the pernicious effects which the Catholic Church has had on the liberty and well-being of humanity'. He declares he is a devout Christian but rejects 'the triple foundation of ignorance, intolerance and despotism' on which the Catholic Church was based. Catholics should recognise the spiritual but not the temporal authority of the Pope. After Catholic emancipation he directed his attention to the rights of the Jews, and subsequently to *The present laws of marriage, adultery and seduction in England* (1836), which he thought representative of 'all the inflexible tyranny of the most ignorant periods of papism'. Anichini's works were reviewed in several British journals, but they did not create much impression in this country.

Rather better known than Anichini was Foscolo's biographer, Giuseppe Pecchio, who was fairly active as a writer during his period of exile, although only a few of his works written in England were actually published here.[26] Two books on Spanish politics appeared in 1823 and 1824 in London, his *Anecdotes of the Spanish and Portuguese Revolutions* and his *Journal of military and*

political events in Spain during the last 12 months. In the latter he has
little to say about Italy but the former has frequent allusions to
Italian affairs and roundly condemns the Austrian government:
'You have no doubt by this time heard how Italian liberty has
been shipwrecked, and who knows how many victims are about
to fall under the poignard of despotism.' Edward Blaquière, in
his introduction, expressed the conviction that his Italian comments 'will find sympathy in every patriotic bosom' and protested
vigorously against 'the hateful principle of the Holy Alliance'.
In the same year, 1824, Pecchio published *A letter to Henry
Brougham Esq. M.P.*, which was promptly praised by the *Edinburgh Review*. In his *Letter* Pecchio condemns the severe suppression of freedom of speech and the press in Austrian-controlled
Italy. He collected as much evidence as possible for Brougham
to use in his attacks on the Tories for their support of Austrian
policy.[17] Pecchio also contributed an article to the *Edinburgh
Review* on the political and economic situation in Austrian-
occupied territory. These and various other works aroused a good
deal of interest and sympathy in Britain, and were noticed in the
Foreign Quarterly Review, the *New Monthly Magazine*, *Fraser's
Magazine*, etc. Pecchio was therefore quite an influential figure.
His *L'anno 1826 dell'Inghilterra*, published in Lugano in 1827,
contains an illuminating analysis of the changing attitudes of
Italians towards England over the previous fifty years. He compares the eighteenth century enthusiasm for Britain with the
turn-of-the-century dislike and distrust engendered during the
Napoleonic wars: 'Abbagliato dal carro di Napoleone... sedotto
dai benefizi ch'egli largamente compartì alla mia patria, torsi gli
occhi dall'Inghilterra, ch'è pur la stella polare dei popoli che
vogliono essere liberi.' It was his own direct contact with Britain,
in exile, that brought his change of heart and a renewed faith in
free institutions.[28]

   Luigi Angeloni arrived in England in the same year as Pecchio,
1823, and like Pecchio divided his attention between teaching
Italian and preaching the cause of Italian independence.[29] He had
been a member of the tribune of the 1795 Roman republic and
he fled to Corsica and France soon after. He was involved in
various political conspiracies in Paris, and contributed to the
Italian journal published there by the exiles, *L'Esule*. Among the
books he printed in England are two long works which reveal

his Encyclopaedist education—long, wide-ranging treatises embracing politics, philosophy, literature, astronomy, and mathematics. The first of these, published in 1826, *Della forza nelle cose politiche. Ragionamenti quattro di L. Angeloni Frusinate. Dedicati all'Italica nazione*, is a revised and enlarged version of three letters previously printed in Naples, in which he criticised the decrees of the Congress of Vienna relating to Italy. He distinguishes between a government of 'forza artificiale', in which the majority obeys, and one of 'forza naturale', in which the majority commands. The effect of the former is to 'tenere in obbrobrioso servaggio venti milioni d'Italiani' and Angeloni aims to expose 'le astuzie e le frodi di che si valsero e valgonsi tuttavia i più dei governi europei per tener soggetti tanti miseri popoli, e soprattutto quello della nostra Italia'. Angeloni objects above all to the suppression of fundamental human rights: 'Si prova in diritto naturale che tutti gli uomini hanno dalla natura una libertà e una indipendenza ch'essi perder non possono, se non per assentimento loro.' Aristocratic birth was of no significance; the important thing was 'l'aristocratico naturale ottenimento d'ingegno, di acquisizione, di sapere', such as was respected in the United States of America. He attacks the Neapolitan court, on whose treachery he lays the blame for the failure of the 1820 revolution, and he insists on the military valour of the Italian troops, particularly in Spain.

Angeloni took up this theme eleven years later in another book, also printed in Italian in London, entitled *Alla valente ed animosa gioventù d'Italia. Esortazioni patrie così di prosa come di verso*, where he discusses various ethical and political concepts and establishes what he calls 'sei principali condizioni del Consorzio'; here he accepts the inequality of man, justifies private property, and insists on the duty of society to provide for the basic needs of its members. In particular he attacked Canning for a speech in Parliament in which he had spoken ironically of the 'illustrious foreign heroes' at present benefiting from British hospitality:

> London! the needy villain's general home;
> The common sink of Paris and of Rome.

In spite of their length and their language, Angeloni's works did arouse some interest in the England of his day. The *London Magazine* in 1826 called the attention of its readers to the first book with a very favourable review, and it was referred to again in 1828 by a critic of the *Storia d'Italia*, by Botta, whom Angeloni had known in Paris.

Some of the political works reviewed above have a strongly autobiographical character. Carascosa's *Mémoires*, for example, while largely concerned with political affairs, provide virtually a diary of the author's life in 1820–1; Macerone's *Memoirs* are of a similar type and relate to a wide range of interests and activities with which the author was concerned at various stages of his life: his medical studies in Italy, his invention of a steam coach in England, his naval experiences in Turkey, etc. The writings of the exiles are therefore a useful source of biographical information of considerable social and political interest. There are at least some fifteen or sixteen fairly detailed autobiographical accounts published by the Italians who came to England in the early nineteenth century, some of them written later and published abroad, but providing a vivid picture of the conditions of exile at the time. General Pepe's *Memoirs comprising the principal military and political events of modern Italy*, published in London in 1846, is a fascinating book—an outlet for his emotions, he tells us, when his love of his country forced him into exile. He was particularly eager 'to refute the calumnies that have been circulated against the South of Italy by foreigners through ignorance and by certain wretched sons of that land who defamed her in order that they might the better conceal their own errors'. But Pepe's *Memoirs* seem barely to have been noticed in Britain when they were published, and the only allusion to them which I have found in the press was in an article in *Sharpe's London Journal* in 1850 which commented on the general apathy in England about Italy's political misfortunes.[31]

Another interesting autobiography was published by Guido Sorelli in Italian and English in London in 1836, *My Confessions to Silvio Pellico*. This book is well known to Foscolo scholars because it contains a description of a strange episode in Zurich, where Sorelli states that he and Foscolo were rivals in love. Sorelli's account is painted in romantic colours and is frequently reminiscent of *Jacopo Ortis*. 'Lascia Zurigo e mi salverai—rimani e sono perduta,' his lady warns him. 'L'indipendenza dell'Italia è inevitabilmente sicura; ma non è meno certo che la base del suo trionfo, come la lotta di religioni rivali, dev'essere fondata sulle

ossa dei suoi martiri... Ma Guido, ti esorto ad evitare le fazioni.
Tu non sei nato per la guerra'. The overlap of autobiography
with romantic fiction is especially obvious here and in his senti-
mental account of his arrival in England:

> Exiled from home and from her kindly hearts
> Amid a world which like the tree imparts
> No smiling blossom from its sterile breast.[32]

The dominant note in the book, however, is its anti-Catholic
message. After his conversion to Protestantism Sorelli set about
preaching 'la superiorità della chiesa riformata su quella catto-
lica': he confesses that his autobiography 'non è altro che
un'esposizione fedele della misericordia ininterrotta di Dio verso
un peccatore—che mostra come per una serie si avvenimenti
strani, inevitabili e imprevisti... sono stato condotto dalla
Divina Provvidenza ad aprire la Bibbia e a leggerla in uno
spirito di preghiera e di umiltà'. This anti-Catholic note won
Sorelli many admirers in England, and his book was warmly
praised by the *Literary Gazette*, *Morning Post*, *Evening Register*,
Christian Advocate, etc. The *New Monthly Magazine* declared that
'the signs of a mind of unusual ability are evident throughout
this work', and most of Sorelli's other writings were favourably
reviewed in important journals precisely because of their religious
views.

A great deal of information about the activities of the Italian
exiles in Britain is contained in Carlo Beolchi's *Reminiscenze
dell'Esilio*, which was published in Italian in London in 1830.
Beolchi arrived in England in 1824 from Spain, where he had
fled to escape the reprisals for the Carbonaro risings, and he
earned his living teaching Italian in Portsmouth, London and
elsewhere. He insists that the exiles had a significant influence on
public opinion in Britain, which previous to their arrival had
been generally hostile to Italy: 'Il contatto cogli esuli cambiò
l'ingiusta opinione, e fu forse il principio di quella nazionale
simpatia che nel 1848 conduceva l'Inghilterra ad applaudire
all'Italia nella grand'opera della sua rigenerazione.'[33] Beolchi
certainly exaggerates the influence of the exiles here. The Italians
very probably as often made a bad as a good impression on their
English hosts: Foscolo certainly alienated as many Englishmen
as he won supporters, and the little band of exiles proved as

disunited abroad as they had been at home—witness the strange pamphlet published by G. Vitalevi about his dispute and threatened duel with Celeste Menotti in 1831.[34]

One of the great frustrations of the exiles was to find the English sympathetic and welcoming to them not as the revolutionaries and patriots which they really were, but as representatives of a pre-revolutionary, Arcadian culture and of the language of the eighteenth century opera libretti. They had to teach Italian so that their fair pupils could read Metastasio. Filippo Pistrucci describes in his *Libro senza titolo* the life of an exile wandering the streets of London giving lessons to English misses, and thoroughly bored with 'quella piccola raccolta Metastasiana in cui è Zenobia amante di Tiridante, Tiridante amante di Zenobia, Mandane amante di Arbace, Arbace amante di Mandane... e via discorrendo, tutti amanti, tutti che arrivano quando vi è bisogno di loro, tutti che si vogliono ammazzare...' J. de Prati similarly cursed the day he had to teach Italian: 'maledetto destino, maledetto mestiere d'insegnare le lingue'. De Prati's passion went into his political activities: he founded a Carbonaro lodge in England which maintained contacts in France, Belgium, Germany, Spain and Italy, and promoted a number of risings on the Continent.[35]

I have drawn attention here only to a limited selection of the work published by relatively little known Italian exiles in England and largely concerned with political issues. They provide a background to the state of public opinion in Britain on the subject of Italy in the early years of the Risorgimento and they also help to show the extent to which the energies of Italian intellectuals at this time were directed to social and political problems and distracted from literary and cultural interests in Italy. Foscolo is of course the outstanding example of the Italian poet and man of letters whose exile severely restricted his literary and scholarly output, but there were many others, from Berchet and Rossetti to the writers we have considered here, whose absence from their mother country constituted a considerable loss to Italy at this critical time. To the extent that these talents and passions then served to enlighten British public opionion and enrich English intellectual life, Italy's loss was England's gain; but Britain too had something to offer in return, the example of free institutions and representative government and in due course the support and encouragement of cultivated and sympathetic Englishmen and English statesmen when the Italians themselves were achieving their political goals.

Notes

[1] For the Italian exiles in England, apart from the studies on Foscolo and Rossetti by E. R. Vincent, and on Panizzi by C. Brooks, the most useful general works are: M. C. W. Wicks, *The Italian exiles in London 1816–49* (Manchester 1937); H. W. Rudman, *Italian nationalism and English Letters* (London 1940). See also R. Manzoni, *Gli esuli italiani nella Svizzera* (Milano 1922); A. Vannucci, *I Martiri della libertà italiana* (Livorno 1887). For the Spanish exiles of this period see V. Llorens Castillo, *Liberales y romanticos, una emigración española en Inglaterra 1823–4* (Mexico 1954). Further information is to be found in the article written by F. Ercole in the *Enciclopedia biografica e bibliografica italiana* (Milano 1939); M. Rosi, *Dizionario del Risorgimento italiano* (Milano 1914–37); and the two *Dizionari di Italiani all'estero*, by L. Benvenuti (Firenze 1890) and U. E. Imperatori (Genova 1956).

[2] For the state of English interest in Italian culture at this time see Miss Speight's M.Litt. thesis (Cambridge 1930) on Thomas James Mathias and her article 'An English writer of Italian verse' (*Studies in Philology*, 1946, XLIII, 70). See also R. Marshall, *Italy in English Literature 1755–1815* (New York 1936); C. P. Brand, *Italy and the English Romantics* (Cambridge 1957).

[3] For a list of these works see my article in *Italian Studies* XV (1960), 'Italians in England, 1800–1850: a bibliography of their publications'.

[4] F. C. Albites, *Della lingua italiana in Inghilterra* (Londra 1829), p. 22.

[5] For Bozzi-Granville, not mentioned by Wicks or Rudman, see *Dictionary of National Biography*. A list of his writings is to be found in his *Autobiography* (London 1874). For Italian newspapers in England see Prof. Todeas Twattlebasket (pseud.), *Note di cronaca, ossia i giornali, gli istituti e gli uomini illustri italiani a Londra durante l'era vittoriana* (Bergamo 1897); Brand, p. 263.

[6] For Macerone, briefly mentioned by Wicks, see *Memoirs of the life and adventures of Colonel Macerone* (London 1838).

[7] *Memoirs*, II, 425.

[8] B. E. O'Meara, *Napoleon in Exile* vol. II, fifth edition, London 1822, pp. 76, 92–3.

[9] See *Quarterly Review* (January 1817), p. 505; *Hansard*, XXXV, 147.

[10] See *Critical Review* (February 1817); *Quarterly Review* (April 1818); (Dec. 1818).

[11] Published in 1831. See his *Memoirs*, II, 458–68.

[12] *Orazione di un Italiano intorno alle cose d'Italia al Congresso di Aquisgrana* (Edimburgo 1819); see pp. 10, 29.

[13] *Le Morganiche ossia lettere scritte da un Italiano a Miledi Morgan sopra vari articoli relativi a Milano ed al regno d'Italia che si trovano nel tomo primo della sua 'Italia'* (Edimburgo 1824); see pp. 32, 41.

[14] See *G. Pepe*, ed. R. Moscati (Roma 1938); Wicks, Rudman; *Storia letteraria d'Italia, l'Ottocento* (ed. G. Mazzoni); Rosi, *Dizionario del Risorgimento*; L. Fassò, *Lettere di Esuli* (Torino 1923).

[15] *Op. cit.*, pp. 27, 65, 69, etc.

[16] *Ibid.*, p. 65. For Carascosa see Ercole; P. Chiarini, 'Un uomo dimenticato: il generale M. Carascosa', *Rassegna contemporanea* (1912); *Dizionario dei Siciliani Illustri*. See also Pepe, *Memoirs*, III, 255–260. For the duel see *Morning Herald* (5 March 1823).

[17] *Op. cit.*, vi, ix–x, 28, 463–464.

[18] *Ecclesiastical Review* (October 1823), p. 343. Pepe's reply was: *Deux mots de réponse du général G. Pepe aux volumineux mémoires récemment publiés par le général Carascosa* (Paris 1823).

[19] Published in Italian with an English translation by T. J. Wooler.

[20] For Pozzo see Wicks, pp. 86–89; *Dieci mesi di carteggio di F. Dal Pozzo* (Pavia 1916).

[21] *Op. cit.*, pp. vii–ix.

[22] *Morning Chronicle* (14 February 1827, 4 June 1827); *The Times* (30 June 1827); *Hansard* (10 March 1829), n.s., XX, 932, 936.

[23] *Morning Chronicle* (4 June 1827); *Foreign Quarterly Review* (April 1829), pp. 278–284.

[24] See *Foreign Quarterly Review* (May 1834), p. 340; *Westminster Review* (July 1834), p. 118.

[25] *Op. cit.*, p. 22. Anichini is not mentioned by Wicks or Rudman.

[26] For Pecchio see Rosi, *Dizionario del Risorgimento*, etc.

[27] See *Lettere ad A. Panizzi*, ed. L. Fagan (Firenze 1880), p. 75. For reviews of his work see *Edinburgh Review* (July 1824); *Foreign Quarterly Review* (January 1833); *New Monthly Magazine* (1832), xxxiv, 154; *Fraser's Magazine* (April 1845); *Foreign Quarterly Review* (May 1832).

[28] *Op. cit.*, p. 193.

[29] For Angeloni, see Ercole; C. G. Romano, *Del Risorgimento d'Italia. Studi e ricordi* (Roma 1913); Fassò, *Lettere di esuli*; W. Maturi, *Il Principe di Canosa* (Firenze 1944). He is briefly mentioned in the *Ottocento* (*Storia lett. d'Italia*), and by Wicks.

[30] *Hansard* (2 April 1824), xi, 133.

[31] *Op. cit.* (1850), XII, 177.

[32] *Op. cit.*, pp. iv, 119–137, 225.

[33] *Op. cit.* (Torino 1852), p. 200. See also *Ottocento* (Mazzoni 1934), II, 1218.

[34] G. Vitalevi, *Rendiconto degli atti originali concernenti la provocazione, il progettato duello...* (1834).

[35] See his memoirs in *Penny Satirist* (July 1838–July 1839).

T. Gwynfor Griffith

The yeast of Mazzini

In youth an admirer of Mazzini,
in age he followed Cavour—the
yeast of the one making the
bread of the other.
Thomas Jones, of Lloyd George[1]

An invitation to contribute to this collection of essays came to me just as I was starting the first volume of the *Whitehall Diary* of Thomas Jones.[2] Several reviewers of that work drew attention to the fact that the Liberal Lloyd George and the Fabian socialist whom he brought into the Cabinet secretariat at the end of 1916 were both admirers of Mazzini. That is true. But it will seem remarkable only to those whose study of Welsh Radicals is limited to what they wrote or said in English, without reference to what they said or wrote in Welsh. This gives a perspective rather like that which we should get if we studied the Italian works of humanist writers of the Quattrocento and early Cinquecento without consideration of what they wrote in Latin: certain features which in reality enjoyed continuity would seem sporadic or coincidental, and we should be in danger of drawing each other's attention, with little cries of interest, to expressions of the most obvious of their common beliefs. Mazzini's name had been a respected one among Radicals in Wales since 1848. He became an important mentor in Welsh political life in the last quarter of the nineteenth century, a period when Liberalism and nationalism walked hand in hand.[3] After 1896 they began to move in different directions. Moreover, in the twentieth century a substantial body of Welsh Radicals moved away from both to forms of socialism which abjured nationalism or to a communism that Mazzini had rejected. But for the Welsh intellectuals and politicians formed in the period of the emergence and heyday of the Young Wales movement, Mazzini's example remained a part of their basic equipment, an object of critical reverence in some, of unqualified enthusiasm in others. The purpose of these notes is simply to comment on the attitudes to him of the most important Welsh publicists and politicians of that time—those who had most influence on the opinions of their compatriots. Clearly, Mazzini's beliefs and conduct were such that he could make only a limited appeal to the patriot whose nationalism was allied to a profound conservatism, or to a Radical to whom all nationalism was abhorrent, or to an atheist or materialist. The degree of hero-worship which he inspired at different periods is thus an instructive reflection of social and religious, as well as strictly political, attitudes. The story of the Welsh Radicals' affection for him is not without interest from this point of view, and, since it really begins in Liverpool,[4] is appropriate to this volume.

Although the growth in national consciousness which transformed Welsh Radicalism after 1868 bore spectacular political results only in the last quarter of the nineteenth century, certain circumstances favourable to it had existed for a long time. Some of these, like the fact that the vast majority of the Welsh people still differed from their English contemporaries in language and culture, are so obvious as not to need elaboration. We must, however, mention one or two factors which are not now so evident, but which contributed to a climate in which nationalism could flourish and to a situation in which certain external influences (like those of Mazzini and Thomas Davis) could seem relevant to Welsh political life.[5]

One such factor, undoubtedly, was the anglicisation of the families of many Welsh landowners and the growing gap between them and their tenants. By the first half of the nineteenth century, those landlords who could speak Welsh only very inadequately (or not at all), who had imported English or Scottish agents to help manage their estates, and who remained Anglican while their tenants had become, or were increasingly becoming, Nonconformist, were almost in the position of aliens. The growth of Radicalism separated them still farther from the society around them: with a few exceptions, they were Tories, while their tenants turned into Liberals. And when some of those tenants were evicted after the 1859 and 1868 elections for failing to use their newly acquired votes in support of their landlords' candidates, feelings ran high in some areas, although personal relations between landlords and tenants remained cordial enough in others. In a great number of cases, the landlord seemed so estranged from the community that any resentment felt by the tenant for economic, social or political reasons was liable to suggest to him that the landlord was (if Welsh) a renegade or (if not Welsh) an intruder. It was a situation in which grievances could easily arouse national feelings.

In discussing the tenants and their leaders, we must bear in mind that the Methodist revival of the eighteenth century and the later growth of other Nonconformist denominations had spread the habits of reading, study and discussion.[6] Once acquired, these were apt to be applied to purposes other than the theological ones for which they had originally been inculcated, and the later nineteenth century in Wales was to see great popular interest in politics as well as in certain kinds of literature. With its aristocracy largely alienated, the Welsh-speaking community developed into a democratic society; it was impelled to become even more so by the ever-growing industrial section of it in the south-east (though that section was in time to become increasingly anglicised and to develop political interests different from those of the Liberal tenant-farmers of the Welsh countryside). From the Welsh community arose new leaders, some of them men of great native ability; it did not yet possess a system of education which creamed off the most capable and offered them at least the possibility of escape. Many of the new leaders were Nonconformist ministers. Some of these regarded their functions as almost exclusively religious. Others devoted a generous proportion of their time to the study of Welsh poetry and the pursuit of bardic glory in the competitions of the *eisteddfodau*. Many of them, particularly in the less conservative denominations, saw politics as a logical extension of their religious activity and turned to (usually Radical) journalism and (usually Liberal) electioneering.

Clearly, Welsh Liberals shared many beliefs and interests with English Liberals, and not a few of them displayed a touching confidence in Mr Gladstone. The Welsh were, however, inescapably foreign in language and culture. Moreover, one element in that culture made their political priorities different from those of English Radicals, as was shown by their fight for separate legislation on such matters as Sunday closing and Church disestablishment and by the particular nature of their concern with education. This differentiating element was the fact that the Welsh were (and, as the century progressed, increasingly became) overwhelmingly a nation of Dissenters. To a Welshman or Englishman of our generation, adherence to a particular denomination of the Christian Church does not seem an essential feature of either Welshness or Englishness. But in the nineteenth century his religious difference from the majority of the English, added to his linguistic separateness, enhanced the Welshman's consciousness of belonging to another people. One of the events which caused his nationality and his religion to be closely associated in his mind was the curious affair known as *Brad y Llyfrau Gleision*, or the Treachery of the Blue Books, the date of which is of significance to us.

If one wished to provoke a scalding resentment in a people,

with a view to later stirring its national passions, one could hardly set about it more effectively than by having its language, culture, religion and morals slighted at an appropriate moment by foreign officials of exemplary goodwill, industry and ignorance. All this was achieved in Wales in 1847. At the instance of William Williams, a Welshman who represented Coventry in Parliament, the government appointed a commission 'to enquire into the state of education in the Principality of Wales, especially into the means afforded to the labouring classes of acquiring a knowledge of the English language'. The three chief commissioners, Lingen, Symons and Vaughan Johnson, were not acquainted with the language and literature of the people whose education they accepted the task of assessing. Anglicans themselves, they were assisted by ten sub-commissioners, of whom seven were likewise Anglicans; to Welsh Nonconformists these numbers would necessarily have appeared disproportionate, even if two of the remaining three sub-commissioners had not resigned, as they did, almost immediately after appointment. The commission was diligent in collecting evidence and undoubtedly did Wales great service by clearly demonstrating the inadequacy of the provision made for education in the principality. Of the 334 witnesses it examined, however, four-fifths were Anglicans, although the population was composed mainly of Dissenters. The commissioners took the view that the Welsh language was a barrier, not only to the Welshman's commercial prosperity, but also to his moral progress. And nowhere did the commissioners' zeal seem more evident than in the collection of material tending to prove that he needed to make such progress. At this distance in time it is possible to derive not a little humble merriment from parts of the report: an instance is the commissioners' acceptance of the view that attendance at the week-night services of the Nonconformists was the occasion, if not the cause, of unchastity in Welsh countrywomen. But in 1847 and the years immediately following, the Welshman's fury at the thought that governmental action might be based on the attitudes of the commissioners tended to blunt his appreciation of the farcical elements in which their report was so rich. He was shocked by the commissioners' religious bias no less than by what we should today call their imperialist bias—the blithe assumption that a Welshman's ignorance of English implied total illiteracy on his part, an assumption apparently not accompanied by any worry as to what ignorance of Welsh implied in men who had undertaken to inquire into the state of education in Wales. Some of the writings that followed the report's publication were little better than irrational expressions of rage; others were serious attempts to compare conditions in Wales with those in rural areas in England or to place the commissioners' findings in their historical context. What concerns us here is simply that discussion of the report aroused fierce indignation and stimulated intense national feeling. It did not, of course, produce a nationalist policy in politics, but it did help to induce in a number of Welshmen a state of mind which was to be sensitive to the influence of European nationalists and eventually receptive to the analogy offered by the movement for home rule in Ireland.[7] It was at this point that they became aware of Mazzini and Kossuth.

The Welsh Radicals who sympathised with the Hungarians and Italians in 1848 did not, of course, see any exact political parallel in their own condition. Their information came from the same sources as that of English Liberals, whose enthusiasm is too well documented for me to need to elaborate on it here.[8] Mrs Marian Henry Jones, who has recently studied the strenuous support given by A. J. Johnes to the cause of Kossuth, rightly remarks that that Welsh judge was far from considering any form of separation from the British Crown; but she also points out that, in the support for Kossuth which Johnes did so much to encourage, sympathy was being expressed for the first time in the name of Wales with a nation struggling to be free.[9] When a deputation from the Hungarian Committee called upon Johnes in 1850 to thank him for his efforts on behalf of their country and to present him with a written address of thanks from Pulszky, Johnes told them of the part played in the campaign by the Welsh newspaper *Yr Amserau*, and they then proceeded to Liverpool to thank its publisher and its editor. This editor, the militant Radical Gwilym Hiraethog (William Rees, 1802–83), has a large part in our story also, for it was he who made the names of Mazzini and Garibaldi household words in Wales in the years following 1848. It is true that another eminent Radical, Samuel Roberts (1800–85), editor of *Y Cronicl*, was also sympathetic to European nationalist movements, but his pacifism caused him to have reservations about some of the exploits of their heroes (just as it led him, in his period in the United States, to refuse to condone war, even for the purpose of liberating slaves, an attitude which led to his being grossly misrepresented, in spite of his long campaign against slavery).[10] Gwilym Hiraethog, however, was to preach the gospels of Mazzini and praise the deeds of Garibaldi with apparently untroubled enthusiasm.[11]

William Rees, the son of a farmer, was born at Chwibren-isaf (at the foot of Mynydd Hiraethog, from which he took his bardic name) in Llansannan, Denbighshire. Largely self-educated, he won a prize at the Brecon *eisteddfod* in 1826 for a poem on the battle of Trafalgar and the death of Nelson. In 1828 he abandoned the Calvinistic Methodists, among whom he had been reared, for the politically more radical Independents. He became one of their ministers in Wales in 1831. It was after moving to Liverpool in 1843 that he founded (in that city and that year) the Welsh newspaper *Yr Amserau*, which was to have so great an influence on the history of Radicalism in the principality. Professor David Williams has written of Hiraethog: 'it is probable that he had a greater influence than anyone else on the formation of Welsh public opinion in the nineteenth century'.[12] This influence he exercised, not only through his voluminous writings in prose and verse, but also through his many appearances in pulpits and lecture halls. He was one of the great orators of his time, and it was a time more tolerant of lengthy discourse than ours.[13]

The revolutions of 1848 filled Hiraethog with excitement. In December of that year, when he addressed a large gathering on the subject in the Concert Hall at Liverpool, the chairman suggested after two and a half hours that they should all return the following week to hear the rest of what he had to say.[14] The gist of what he said can be read in the pages of the Welsh periodical *Y Traethodydd* for July 1849 and January 1850. He addressed many Welsh audiences on the same theme. Indeed his biographers tell us that members of the public who attended his performances in expectation of hearing his famous lecture on Pantycelyn, found that he insisted on delivering *Y Chwyldroadau* (*The Revolutions*) instead. On these occasions, he excused himself by explaining that the advertised lecture on Wales's favourite hymnist was less fresh in his mind than that on the events of 1848.[15] In spite of pressure from English friends, he did not consent to lecture in English, a language in which he did not speak as eloquently as he did in Welsh, but in order to convey his message to them he wrote *Providence and Prophecy, or God's hand fulfilling His word, more especially in the Revolutions of 1848* (Liverpool and London, 1851). This book (pp. viii + 218), like the material in *Y Traethodydd*, suggests not only that he was apt to say a great deal in the course of a lecture or two, but that now and again he allowed his enthusiasm to run away with him. A much better performance is his more famous lecture, *Garibaldi*.[16] This, too, is somewhat lengthy: beginning with Dante and the *Veltro*, it moves forward to a fairly full examination of the woes of Italy in the nineteenth century before introducing us to Mazzini and to the hero of the title. One of the most moving and eloquent passages in the lecture is the description of Mazzini's nobility of character. Hiraethog's writings and oratory rapidly contributed to making both Mazzini and Garibaldi into popular heroes among Welsh Radical Nonconformists. It is not without significance that, by the end of the decade, even a man so lacking in strong convictions as Ceiriog, Wales's most popular lyric poet of the nineteenth century, felt the need to sing of Italian freedom in his poem 'Garibaldi a Charcharor Naples' (published in *Oriau'r Hwyr*, 1860).

In Rees's support for Mazzini there was, of course, an anti-papal element. The fact that Kossuth was a Protestant and that Mazzini's views were unacceptable to the Vatican made it easier for Welshmen to sympathise with them than with the Irish, though by 1886 Michael Davitt too was to find a warm welcome in Wales. Hiraethog's fierce opposition to the Papacy and its temporal power was frequently expressed; it can be seen, for instance, not only in his accounts of Italian history in his lectures and writings on the revolutions of 1848 and on Garibaldi, but also in the poem *Ffoedigaeth y Pab yn 1848* ('The flight of the Pope in 1848'), which he included in his *Caniadau* (1860), and in the satirical letter to Pio IX which he wrote in 1851 in the popular series of dialectal letters which he contributed to *Yr Amserau*.[17] There was nothing specifically Welsh in this aspect of Rees's writing: it merely mirrored faithfully the views of English Protestants, and the words in which Derek Beales describes their attitude could serve equally well for Rees.[18]

A great deal of Hiraethog's political work, in fact, was to present the views of English Protestants and Radicals to the Welsh public. The matters he was concerned about (religious freedom, free trade, the rights of tenants, education) were also the concern of English Radicals. One does not find in him the desire, which was later discernible in Michael D. Jones or Emrys ap Iwan, to rid Wales of English influences. Indeed, in his *Providence and Prophecy* he contrasts conditions in oppressed countries in Europe with those existing at home, and, in doing so, he makes it clear that he has a high regard for the constitutional advantages enjoyed by British subjects and emphasises that the changes he deems desirable can be brought about without revolution:

It cannot be too earnestly insisted upon, that it is not the fault of the British Constitution, that so many classes in the community are excluded from the exercise of their just right to vote for Members of the House of Commons. *Constitutionally*, they inherit this privilege, since it would be in perfect harmony with the acknowledged principles of our Government, that the universal manhood of our people should be represented. That this right has not yet been decreed, must be attributed to that fertile source of mischief in the State, *class legislation*: but this is not more a wrong done to the people, than it is an offence against the spirit and letter of the Constitution. Septennial Parliaments is another evil springing from the same cause, and an equally vicious interpretation of the original principles on which our present mode of Government rests. We regard these, and similar encroachments, as temporary evils only. The foundation remains solid and sound, and the advancing intelligence of the community will ere long refute and displace those selfish politicians who maintain the interests of the few, against the just claims of the many. This praise is not only due to our Constitution, as it is described in Blackstone's Commentaries; facts exhibit its excellency in the same light. How is it that we have passed so calmly through the late terrible crisis? That the fierce contagion which raged around us, had no power to infect the minds of our people? That surrounded by the horrors of revolutionary commotion which so lately convulsed the whole of Europe, the throne of our beloved Sovereign stood secure, and even unthreatened?

The natural temper of Englishmen cannot adequately account for this stability. John Bull, however justly celebrated for forbearance, and a more than ordinary share of immobility, is fully capable of lively sympathies with the heroes of freedom on the Continent. He can discern, at the same time, that his difficulties are not precisely theirs. They need reform in root and branch, whilst their only hope of reform is in revolution. We need no repetition of the Cromwellian age, in its turbulence and radical change of dynasty . . .[19]

Mazzini met Rees, probably on a visit to Liverpool, where there was, as Professor Rebora has emphasised, quite a group of Italophiles.[20] The Italian was clearly aware of Hiraethog's influence in Wales and of his value as a propagandist. In a letter to him dated 5 February 1861, he wrote:

. . . Esteemed as you deservedly are by your countrymen, and lecturing as you do before large audiences, you can, and will, do a great deal of good to our national cause. Will you allow me, dear sir, to remind you of the high importance which a petitioning movement towards the realisation of the non-interference principle, and the consequent withdrawal of the French troops from Rome, would have for Italy? Your movement supporting ours would probably create such an expression of European opinion as would compel L[ouis] N[apoleon] to yield, and a peaceful solution of the difficulty would be thus substituted for a warlike one.[21]

In later letters to him, Mazzini gave his own interpretation of contemporary events in Italy, obviously in the hope that Rees would be influenced by them in the guidance that he would give his compatriots. In a letter on the 'reconciliation of Garibaldi and Cavour', for instance (presumably written shortly after 21 April 1861) he stated:

Did you receive from me a circular and a photograph? Your silence makes me fear that the letter has not reached. The personal influence of the King has brought on a sort of reconciliation between Garibaldi and Cavour, which will not last a fortnight. How can a Bonapartist-policy programme and a National one reconcile?[22]

These and Mazzini's other letters to him Hiraethog was to treasure until the end of his days as his most precious possession.[23]

The sentences which I have quoted from Hiraethog's works will no doubt have suggested to the reader that his interest in Continental nationalists seemed to stem more from the similarity of his views to those of English Liberals than from any Welsh nationalist tendency. Not surprisingly, however, the aspects of European history that he presented to his compatriots suggested different conclusions to other Welshmen. As Professor R. T. Jenkins put it, 'the causes of "small nations" thus popularised entered deeply into the affection of the ordinary Welshman, and he could hardly fail to draw a moral nearer home.'[24] It is interesting to note that as early as 1852, from that same Welsh community in Liverpool which had heard Hiraethog's enthusiastic praise of the revolutions of 1848, Josiah Thomas was writing to his friend John Owen Jones:

... Then there are subjects of national importance to Wales, oh there is plenty of work even independently of going to Parliament, but that must follow in the train. I want to stir up and do my best to get a Welsh association of liberal men to carry out reforms and measures for the good of Wales: they may call the movement 'Young Wales' if they like, the Italians have their 'Young Italy'; there is a 'Young Ireland', a 'Young England'. I intend writing to the *Herald* and to the *Amserau* on this subject when I can define more distinctly in my own mind the objects of the association . . .²⁵

But over thirty years were to pass before national aspirations and political confidence had grown to the stage of forming an actual organisation called Young Wales. During those years the passage of Welsh leaders from an internationalist Radicalism to a liberal nationalism owed a great deal to the attitudes and example of Michael D. Jones (1822–98).

Jones, the uncompromising son of an unyielding father, succeeded that father as principal of the Independents' college at Bala. Before doing so, however, he had laboured, as a young minister of religion in Cincinnati, among Welsh immigrants to the United States. From his knowledge of their lives he concluded that, once they lost the Welsh language, they were apt to lose their grip on their customs, morals and religion. He thereupon became a fierce opponent of anglicisation, not only among Welshmen overseas, but also among those who remained at home.²⁶ This attitude was rather like that of the Blue Book commissioners turned upside down: whereas they had believed that the Welshman's morals would have been less bad if he had been turned into an English-speaking Anglican, Michael D. Jones took the view that in fact they got worse if he did not remain a Welsh-speaking Nonconformist. But Jones was concerned, not only with his morals, but also with his culture. Since it seemed difficult for Welshmen to preserve that culture under English rule, he played a prominent part in the establishment of a Welsh settlement in Patagonia, in the Argentine, where he believed his compatriots would be free from anglicising pressures. That he drew inspiration from the deeds of Continental nationalists he himself made clear in his writings; in one of these, on self-government, he referred to Kossuth as a star in the European firmament, 'inspiring other souls with the immortal doctrine that every nation has the right to govern itself'.[27] Professor Alun Davies has also stressed his closeness to Continental nationalists in the use he made of history and in the emphasis which he laid on the belief that the main bond of a nation is its culture, which is based on its language, and that this language is more important than political bonds.[28] He reminds us that Sir Owen Edwards, a man who was for a time a professional historian and who is to have an important part in our story, said that he found in the company of Michael D. Jones what he had not found in any school or college: enlightened love of the history and language of Wales allied to an unshakeable belief 'in the powerful force labelled national'. For years Jones had sought to teach him to write the history of Wales from the standpoint of a Welshman.[29] Ideas similar to those of Michael D. Jones were propagated by E. Pan Jones (1834–1922), a graduate of Marburg University who was associated with Michael Jones in several ventures and wrote his biography (though Pan Jones is, perhaps, more widely remembered for his 'land for the people' campaign than for any-thing else), by R. J. Derfel (1824–1905), who was a nationalist before he became a Fabian socialist, and notably by Emrys ap Iwan (Robert Ambrose Jones, 1851–1906), who was a man of more marked literary ability than the others we have named.[30]

The year 1868 has long been recognised as of fundamental importance in the history of Welsh politics: as a result of the extension of the franchise which had taken place in the previous year, Wales was then able to return twenty-one Liberals and twelve Conservatives to Parliament. Widespread eviction of tenants ensued. The history of the following period is too well known to need recapitulation; Dr Kenneth Morgan, for instance, has recently given an admirable account of how between 1868 and 1886 'the ill-formed and half-expressed aspirations entertained by Welsh nonconformists in 1868 gradually became transformed into a national programme'.[31] This is not the place to go over that ground again. I merely wish to point out that when that programme crystallised in a national organisation, that organisa-tion, Young Wales or *Cymru Fydd*, was to be an echo of Young Italy and Young Ireland, and that the man to whom Wales looked for leadership in the years immediately following its institution was the most Mazzinian of her politicians: T. E. Ellis (1859–99).

Tom Ellis,[32] the son of a Merionethshire tenant farmer and nephew of one of the victims of the notorious evictions of 1859, was among the early students of the University College of Wales, Aberystwyth, from which he proceeded to Oxford, where he read history at New College. After graduation, he spent a year as tutor in a well known South Wales family, becoming simultaneously a political journalist. He then combined his journalism with the post of private secretary to (Sir) John Tomlinson Brunner, Liberal M.P. for Northwich. Ellis was himself elected to Parliament, as member for his native county, at the age of twenty-seven, and he continued to represent it until his death. At Westminster he displayed an energy and a devotion to Welsh affairs that soon established his claim to leadership of those who had a genuine concern for Welsh interests, while his sincerity and attractive personality won him an unprecedented popularity in Wales. This was shown within four years of his first election. In 1889, while visiting Egypt, he suffered a long and severe attack of typhoid: when he returned to Wales in 1890, he was offered a national testimonial. In his speech of acceptance in September of that year, he set forth his policy for Wales, which included an elected assembly for the principality. At that time, however, there was little response to this part of his programme, and he must have come to feel by 1892 that he could do more for Wales by exerting pressure inside the governing party than by jeopardising his undoubted influence in it. In that year he accepted office as junior whip in Gladstone's administration, and in 1894 he became chief government whip in Rosebery's. His part in obtaining a land commission for Wales and his work on behalf of various Welsh institutions (particularly educational institutions) is too well known to need recapitulation. What has not been adequately stressed is his Mazzinianism, in spite of his own clear statement that his teachers in politics were 'Joseph Mazzini and Thomas Davis'.[33]

First, we must not forget that *Cymru Fydd*, or Young Wales, was an organisation founded in Ellis's lodgings in London in 1886. It received a great fillip when he was elected to Parliament later in that year; he was followed two years later by D. A. Thomas (later Lord Rhondda), and they were reinforced in 1890 by the election of David Lloyd George. For a few years it was a movement of great cultural, as well as political, influence in Wales. Its subsequent history is well known; its political failure seems ultimately to have been due partly to personal considerations (e.g. D. A. Thomas's dislike of the growing power of Lloyd George), partly to opposition within Welsh Liberalism, particularly in the industrial south, to the nationalism of the leading politicians associated with *Cymru Fydd*.[34]

Secondly, we should consider some elements in the context of Ellis's life before and after the period which is generally considered to have been the most important in the final formulation of his political programme for Wales: that of the ordeal of his almost mortal illness in Egypt (December 1889–March 1890). In 1888 he paid his first visit to Italy. In a letter to D. R. Daniel he described how he and his companion (Arthur Acland, M.P.) crossed from Austria into Italy:

... The Austrian Government, early this century, constructed the magnificently engineered road over the Stelvio, in order to maintain her grip on Italy. But Mazzini was too many for Austria, and when at last, after endless zig-zag windings, we reached the top of the Pass, and stood opposite the marble which marks the boundary between Austria and free Italy, we blessed and blessed again the work and memory of Joseph Mazzini.[35]

On 11 May 1889 Ellis gave his presidential address to the Welsh Cultural Society of London. His theme was the need for greater unity in Wales. He talked of Mazzini's concern for Italian unity, and of its glorious consequences. He incidentally drew attention to the book *Tro yn yr Eidal* ('A Journey in Italy'), published in the previous year by his friend and associate Owen M. Edwards.[36] (To Sir Owen Edwards I shall come in a moment: here I shall merely note that the book contains an inspiring tribute to Mazzini.) In 1889 Ellis again visited a number of Italian cities (including Genoa) on his way to Egypt. From Naples on 30 November he wrote to Owen Edwards to express his appreciation of the help *Tro yn yr Eidal* had been to him in his journey.[37] On 13 December in Egypt he was taken ill. The first fruit of his meditation in that country was the resolution recorded in his diary on 1 March 1890. Here Ellis quotes from Shelley's *Masque of Anarchy* the following lines:

> Let a vast assembly be
> And with great solemnity
> Declare with ne'er-said words that ye
> Are, as God has made ye, free.

Let the laws of your own land
Good or ill, between ye stand,
Hand to hand, and foot to foot,
Arbiters of the dispute—.

He then proceeds in Welsh (I translate):

Thought much today of Wales. My fellow Welshmen throughout the
world proud of their Welshness and anxious to do something for Wales.
This is the year and this the St. David's Day during which I have had
most leisure to think of Wales, her needs, her hopes, the duty of her
sons and daughters. Some Welsh people think it enough to study our
history and ruins, others half believe good education to be enough.
Most of my compatriots think Disestablishment will bring all a reason-
able Welshman can expect. Even if we got the Church free from the
Government, and the schools and the land in the hands of the people,
yet that would be freedom without unity. In order to get unity, it is
necessary to have a Parliament, a University and a Temple for Wales.

This is my vow today: to work unto Death to gain Unity for Wales in
the fullest sense of the word. May God give me strength to be faithful
to this vow.

EDUCATION—FREEDOM—UNITY.[38]

It is, of course, a thoroughly Mazzinian programme. Indeed, it is
incredible that a Welsh Nonconformist of the nineteenth century
should talk of the need for unity in religion, but this is but an
echo of Mazzini's emphasis on it. From Hyères on 4 April 1890
Ellis wrote to D. R. Daniel, stating that he would be glad to have
'the Savonarola and the Mazzini of Tomos Williams'.[39] In
September of that year he delivered his celebrated Bala oration.
In October he again had to leave the country for reasons of
health, this time bound for South Africa. From the South
Atlantic he wrote to D. R. Daniel. In his letter he again mentioned *Tro yn yr Eidal* as being among the books he had been
reading (along with Ruskin, Carlyle and works on Heine and
Goethe), and he urged Daniel to undertake 'seriously and
without delay' to translate selections from Mazzini into Welsh
for one of the series edited by Owen Edwards. 'You would [I
translate from the letter] derive much pleasure from the work, it
would do good to thousands of Welshmen and to Welsh literature,
it would be a great help to the movement. . .'[40] At the same time
he wrote to Ellis Griffith to ask him to obtain an edition of

C.E.I.L. – U

Mazzini's works for Daniel and to reinforce Ellis's appeal to him. Griffith bought the books, as requested, and presented them to Daniel as a gift from himself and Ellis. Daniel, in a lengthy reply to Ellis, went into all sorts of queries about the kind of selection he should make, the length of the biographical introduction, the title, the portrait of Mazzini that the book should contain, and even alleged that, while sleeplessly considering these problems in his bed, he had visualised the volume; it is hardly surprising that he never got round to making the translation. (The Ellis Griffith who was associated with Tom Ellis in this Mazzinian enterprise was a lawyer and Fellow of Downing College, Cambridge. He was later to be for twenty-three years Liberal M.P. for Anglesey. While Parliamentary Secretary to the Home Office (1912–15), he was to play a notable part in steering through the House of Commons the Bill for the disestablishment of the Anglican Church in Wales, a measure which had been of fundamental importance in the eyes of nineteenth-century Radicals.)⁴¹

The premature death of Tom Ellis in 1899 was widely regarded as a national disaster in Wales. Thomas Jones was at the time a student at Aberystwyth, and in his reminiscences of the period he gives some idea of how it appeared to his generation:

At Bala on April 11th, 1899, the funeral took place of Tom Ellis, whose body had been brought across France from Cannes to be buried at Cefnddwysarn. He was only forty and the immense memorial gatherings at Bala, St Margaret's Westminster, and the Cory Hall, Cardiff, witnessed to his extraordinary popularity. He was Chief Whip in the Liberal Government and it is idle to speculate on the Cabinet rank he might have attained. His character was his supreme attraction: modest, gentle, moderate, no formalist, working unseen, a lover of truth and of Wales, so his mourning friends testified. Of the Welsh nationalists of that era he most of all struck the note of personal consecration as no less necessary than political reform. He and 'the Cause' were one not two—that was the secret of his remarkable influence among students. His son has preserved a sheet of House of Commons note-paper on which his father had written this passage from Mazzini:

'Let each man among you strive to incarnate his country in himself. Let each man among you regard himself as a guarantee, responsible for his fellow-countrymen, and learn so to govern his actions as to cause his country to be loved and respected through him.'⁴²

I do not here have the space to go into the background of all the important figures who were associated with *Cymru Fydd* in 1886 and shortly after that. But I think it could easily be shown that a number of them had, as a result of the work of Hiraethog and later Welsh Radicals, considerable sympathy with Mazzini and Young Italy. If we look, for example, at a recent study of the life and work of Sir Herbert Lewis we find that, in the biographical section, his daughter writes of his travel to the Continent and his interest in its politics. She continues:

> Although he was now in sounder health, he did not return to school, but was tutored by Dr Pan Jones, minister of the Independent church at Rhewl, Mostyn. Dr Pan was an enthusiastic revolutionary, and his principal heroes were Dr Michael D. Jones of Bala, Mazzini and Kossuth. Like Emrys ap Iwan, he had spent years on the continent and had taken his degree at a German university. Herbert acquired little Latin or Greek from him, but he heard fascinating accounts of events in Hungary and Italy . . .[43]

Sir Herbert must have passed on his enthusiasm to his children, for his daughter remembers that at an early age she had read a life of Mazzini and *I doveri dell'uomo*.[44] He is remembered in Wales, of course, not so much for the posts he held in successive Liberal governments as for his important role in the foundation of the intermediate schools system and in the establishment of the National Library and National Museum.

Lewis's preoccupations will serve to remind us that *Cymru Fydd* was interested not simply in political objectives but also in linguistic and cultural matters; one of its foremost members, Llewelyn Williams, who was later to do useful research on the connections between Wales and Italy in the sixteenth century, wrote that it was concerned with true politics—education, literature, music and art, with debating societies and reading rooms as well as with electioneering.[45] It is not surprising that a recent writer on the career of Sir John Morris-Jones has stressed the close relationship to it of the Oxford University Dafydd ap Gwilym Society, also founded in 1886.[46] Early members of this Welsh-speaking society (young men gathered about Sir John Rhŷs, then Jesus Professor of Celtic) were to play important parts in Young Wales, as well as in the remarkable renaissance in Welsh scholarship and Welsh literature which characterised the final years of the nineteenth century and the beginning of the twentieth. One of these young men, Owen Edwards, was a friend of Tom Ellis's and had attended the same grammar school at Bala. After studying at the University College of Wales, Aberystwyth, he spent a year at Glasgow at the feet of Edward Caird before reverting from philosophy to history at Balliol. After a brilliant undergraduate career, he spent a year on the Continent before returning to Oxford as a tutor and (from 1889) Fellow of Lincoln College.[47] He published his account of his Italian journey, under the title *Tro yn yr Eidal*, in Dolgellau in 1888. It is dedicated to Benjamin Jowett, Master of Balliol. I do not know whether Jowett could read it, but he was, of course, a man who had known and admired Mazzini.[48] *Tro yn yr Eidal* is a kind of guide-book which contains a good deal of Italian history, clearly and attractively written. It contains a very warm tribute to Mazzini in its seventh chapter ('Bedd Mazzini': 'Mazzini's tomb'). The book enjoyed considerable success. I believe that it influenced T. E. Ellis and other members of Young Wales. Edwards went on to become a voluminous and extremely popular writer in Welsh; his works are still read with pleasure. In 1890 he became joint editor, with R. H. Morgan, of *Cymru Fydd*, the organ of Young Wales. But he clearly felt that Welshmen needed to know more about their country's past and its literature, and in 1891 he began instead to edit *Cymru*, which was non-political. In fact, politics could not interest him for long; this is shown, not only in his writings, but also in his very brief parliamentary career (as Liberal M.P. for Merionethshire, 1899–1900). Sir Owen Edwards ended his life with a substantial period as Chief Inspector of Schools for Wales, and he did much for the teaching of Welsh and for the publication of popular editions of the Welsh classics, as well as of reading-matter for children.

I have already stated elsewhere that I believe that Welsh interest in Dante at the end of the nineteenth century stemmed from interest in Mazzini and the new Italy. Dante's views on the ills of Italy and the evils of the Papacy's abuse of temporal power endeared him to the Nonconformist Radical; we have seen that he was mentioned by Hiraethog by way of introduction to Mazzini and Garibaldi. But the first serious articles on him in Welsh were the work of R. H. Morgan, who had been joint editor, with Owen M. Edwards, of *Cymru Fydd*.[49] When the Welsh translation of the *Divina Commedia* appeared in 1903,[50] Mazzini's name appeared in the bibliography with the comment that his 'excellent essays' included a very valuable one on Dante's minor works. The long introduction to this translation was the work of the great Welsh poet, T. Gwynn Jones, who is remembered also for his biographies of the Radical publisher, Thomas Gee, and of the nationalist Emrys ap Iwan; it contains a warm tribute to Mazzini. The translation itself was the work of the well known Liberal journalist, Daniel Rees (1855–1931), sometime editor of *The Caernarvon and Denbigh Herald* and *Yr Herald Cymraeg*.[51] His translation was the fruit of long and devoted study of Italian and of the text of the *Comedy*, to which he gave up his leisure for several years. There is something reassuring in the thought that in 1907 there was in the Board of Trade someone with sufficient culture to appreciate that Rees's general experience and the qualities of patience, accuracy and mental agility which are so obvious in this verse translation fitted him for the post of statistician (in which he remained from that year until his retirement in 1922). It is interesting to note that the list of subscribers to the volume includes the names of many Liberal members of Parliament and prominent members of *Cymru Fydd*: Beriah Gwynfe Evans (sometime secretary of *Cymru Fydd*), William George, his brother David Lloyd George, M.P., J. Herbert Lewis, M.P., Owen M. Edwards, J. Herbert Roberts, M.P., Alfred Thomas, M.P. (later Lord Pontypridd), D. A. Thomas, M.P. (later Lord Rhondda), to mention some of them. One of these, David Lloyd George, was President of the Board of Trade from 1905 until 1908; but I do not know whether he had anything to do with Daniel Rees's statistical appointment.

Thomas Jones is known to Mazzinians as the editor of a selection of Mazzini's works for Everyman's Library and as the author of the long introduction to his work which he prefaced to those selections.[52] To the student of Welsh politics he is interesting because of the light his writing throws on the process of thought of a Welsh Mazzinian Radical who came to reject nationalism and moved to socialism, casting doubt on the validity of some of Mazzini's thinking in the process. He is a good example, for there is no doubt whatever about the fervour of his Mazzinianism in the first place or the nature of his later doubts; he has documented both for us. In his reminiscences of his life as a student at Aberystwyth, he writes:

But for my own growth much more important than my acquaintance with *Young Ireland* was my purchase and perusal of Mazzini's *Life* by Madame Venturi and *The Duties of Man*. I was not too old for hero worship and these books gripped me as no others before or since. This was due not only to the moral elevation of Mazzini's message but to the moral elevation of Mazzini's character. Something was also due to my own temperament which, as I now realize, was much given to enthusiasm.

Life was a mission, duty its law. Each of us was bound to purify his own soul as a temple; to free it from egotism; to set before himself the problems of his own life; to search out what was the most urgent need of the men by whom he was surrounded; then interrogate his own faculties and capacity, and resolutely and increasingly apply them to the satisfaction of that need. He bade us fulfil our mission whether blessed by love or visited by hate; whether strengthened by association with others, or in the sad solitude that almost always surrounds the martyrs of thought. 'The path is clear before you; you are cowards, unfaithful to your own future, if, in spite of sorrows and delusions, you do not pursue it to the end.'[53]

Later, during his period at Glasgow, Jones was even to concoct a Ruskinian–Mazzinian wedding ceremony for himself and his bride.[54] But he was eventually to move away both from the Liberalism of his boyhood and from the nationalism of *Cymru Fydd* in the 'eighties and 'nineties, and to write:

Mazzini, like the statesmen at Versailles three-quarters of a century later, failed to foresee the difficulties which have beset post-war Europe in giving effect to self-liberation and self-determination. He minimized the importance of the material or economic factor and under-estimated the degree to which the freed nations would convert a victorious nationalism into an instrument of tyranny over internal or adjacent minorities. 'Every Ireland has its Ulster.' 'Nationality,' said Lowes Dickinson, 'is apt to be a Janus, with one face looking towards freedom and the other towards domination.' All this we are now learning through blood, toil, tears and sweat. Mazzini did not foresee that industrialism and nationalism which had been partners in bringing about the unity of Germany and the unity of Italy were to become active enemies in the next half century, the one making for international economic areas, large and few, the other for sovereign and self-sufficing States, small and many . . .

But in the Wales of the 'eighties and 'nineties these difficulties were not clearly apprehended. Tom Ellis and his friends who had felt the spell of Mazzini had not thought out the full implications of the prophet's teaching. It was enough for *Young Wales* at Aberystwyth to feel the ferment of awakening nationhood and to seek such ways of giving it outward expression as were compatible with membership of the Liberal Party, all unconscious of Marx and Engels.[55]

Very many Welsh Radicals were, like Thomas Jones, converted to an internationalist socialism. Some of his compatriots, however, came to adopt different positions. They were dissatisfied with the Young Wales movement of the 'eighties and 'nineties, not because it was nationalist, but because, through being allied to English Liberalism, it did not in their view achieve enough for Wales. After the first world war and the failure of a Liberal prime minister who had been a member of *Cymru Fydd* to give Wales a parliament, they concluded that the only hope lay in a Welsh nationalist party independent of any other political group, and in the nineteen-twenties they formed such a party. In their ranks, too, were Mazzinians, like the poet, future Archdruid and influential editor of *Y Tyst*, Dyfnallt Owen, who once told me how he spent his first night in Italy sitting by Mazzini's tomb, and D. J. Williams, one of the most eminent of Welsh prose writers, who was to write the first biography of Mazzini to appear in Welsh.[56]

The reader will perceive that I have not yet dealt with David Lloyd George. It would be easy to show that he too was interested in Mazzini, for he himself spoke of the inspiration which he and Tom Ellis in their early days as members of *Cymru Fydd* had found in his writings.[57] But this would not be an adequate examination of his Mazzinianism. For he differs from all the others we have mentioned in one important respect: in his long opportunity to exercise political power in Great Britain during many years in the Cabinet (as President of the Board of Trade, 1905–8, Chancellor of the Exchequer, 1908–15, Minister of Munitions, 1915–16, Secretary of State for War, 1916, and Prime Minister, 1916–22). And the interesting question in his case is, surely, the influence of Mazzinianism on him when he was in power (and, through him, on the peace settlement, the Irish question, and so on). That is a question that I cannot begin to tackle when I have already exhausted the space available to me; it must await another time. For the moment he must get no more treatment than other members of *Cymru Fydd*. But, perhaps, he can at least be permitted to occupy, along with Thomas Jones, our final page. On 23 October 1922, Lloyd George ceased to be Prime Minister. Here is a selection from Thomas Jones's diary for that last day:

The P.M. was full of fun, chaffing Grigg and me as the two Die-Hards who had compassed his downfall. He marched up and down on the far side of the long table, declaring this was the last time he would ever be in the Cabinet room, unless, he said, stopping suddenly, I come back as the leader of a deputation to ask some favour of the new Prime Minister. He then began a mock speech to B.L. 'Mr. Prime Minister,' he began, 'I have come here with my fellow members from Wales to ask——' Mr. Bonar Law—'Pray be seated.' Mr. Lloyd George— 'I could hardly sit in the presence of Lord Curzon.' At this point I sat in what would be Bonar Law's chair and buried my face in my hands in as miserable a posture as I could command. Mr. Lloyd George, continuing— 'We have come to ask for a grant for Welsh education and we also wish to approach you on behalf of the refugees from Smyrna'—and so on until we were all in roars of laughter except Miss Stevenson who could hardly conceal her sadness at parting with No. 10. . . . I then put before him a photograph of Mazzini which he had given me and he wrote on it 'From one admirer of Mazzini to another'. We came out of the Cabinet room.[58]

Notes

[1] Thomas Jones, *Lloyd George* (Oxford 1951), p. 279.

[2] Thomas Jones, *Whitehall Diary*, ed. K. Middlemas, vol. I (Oxford 1969).

[3] For the relationship of nationalism to Liberalism in nineteenth-century Welsh politics, see Kenneth O. Morgan, *Wales in British Politics 1868–1922* (Cardiff 1963). For the general historical background, see David Williams, *A History of Modern Wales* (London 1950), and, for the first half of the century, R. T. Jenkins, *Hanes Cymru yn y Bedwaredd Ganrif ar Bymtheg, Y Gyfrol Gyntaf (1789–1843)* (Cardiff 1933).

[4] So far as I know, the only Italianist who has given attention to the beginnings of Mazzini's influence in Wales (through the activities of Gwilym Hiraethog, who then lived in Liverpool) is Professor Rebora. See P. Rebora, 'L'Italia, il paese di Galles e Liverpool (Note sulle relazioni italo-inglesi nell'Ottocento)' in *Civiltà italiana e civiltà inglese* (Florence 1936), pp. 230–258. Unfortunately, the only work of Hiraethog's with which he seems to be familiar is his most crankish, *Providence and Prophecy* (Liverpool 1851).

[5] For the growth of national consciousness in Wales, see R. T. Jenkins, 'The development of nationalism in Wales' in *The Sociological Review*, XXVII

(1935), pp. 163–182; Glanmor Williams, 'The idea of nationality in Wales' in *Cambridge Journal*, VII (1953), pp. 145–158; Gwyn A. Williams, 'Twf hanes-yddol y syniad o genedl yng Nghymru' in *Efrydiau Athronyddol*, XXIV (1961), pp. 18–30; and the volume *Seiliau Hanesyddol Cenedlaetholdeb Cymru* (Cardiff 1949). For the relationship of Welsh nationalism to Continental nationalisms, see Alun Davies, 'Cenedlaetholdeb yn Ewrop a Chymru yn y Bedwaredd Ganrif ar Bymtheg' in *Efrydiau Athronyddol*, XXVII (1964), pp. 14–23.

⁶ I do not, of course, wish to imply that the Methodist revival was a sudden burst of light which ended a period of dreadful darkness, certainly not to belittle the great educational work of Griffith Jones, the vicar of Llanddowror, and of the S.P.C.K. Indeed, Professor Glanmor Williams has argued convincingly that Methodism was so effective in Wales because the Methodists preached to people who were already religious literates. See Glanmor Williams, 'Wales and the Reformation' in the *Transactions of the Honourable Society of Cymmrodorion*, Session 1966, Part I, pp. 108–133. But the growth of Nonconformity certainly encouraged the further spread of literacy and study.

⁷ For a discussion of the effects of the Blue Books, see F. Price Jones, 'Effaith Brad y Llyfrau Gleision' in *Y Traethodydd*, CXVIII (1963), pp. 49–65.

⁸ See H. W. Rudman, *Italian Nationalism and English Letters* (London 1940), and R. Coupland, *Welsh and Scottish Nationalism* (London 1954).

⁹ M. Henry Jones, 'Wales and Hungary' in *Transactions of the Honourable Society of Cymmrodorion*, Session 1968, Part I, pp. 7–27. Mrs Jones points out that Kossuth, who enjoyed a great reputation as a Liberal in Western Europe, appeared to the non-Magyar-speaking populations of Hungary (Croats, Slovaks, Slovenes, Serbs and Roumanians) more as an assertive Magyar nationalist than as a liberal Hungarian fighting Austrian tyranny.

¹⁰ For Samuel Roberts, see Glanmor Williams, *S.R.* (Cardiff 1950); Wilbar Shepperson, *Samuel Roberts: colonizer in Civil War Tennessee* (Knoxville 1961); and I. C. Peate, *Sylfeini* (Wrexham 1938), pp. 65–72. For a fair sample of his opinions on Italian and Hungarian matters, see Samuel Roberts, *Gweithiau* (Dolgellau 1856), pp. 380, 393–395, 472–475, 574, 757.

¹¹ For Gwilym Hiraethog, see T. Roberts and D. Roberts, *Cofiant y Parch. W. Rees* (Dolgellau 1893), and E. Rees, *William Rees (Hiraethog)* (Liverpool 1915).

¹² D. Williams, *A History of Modern Wales* (London 1950), p. 252.

¹³ For an account of a performance by Hiraethog, see J. H. Jones, *Gwin y Gorffennol* (Wrexham 1938), pp. 92–96.

¹⁴ M. Henry Jones, *op. cit.*, p. 13.

¹⁵ T. Roberts and D. Roberts, *op. cit.*, pp. 340–341.

¹⁶ It can be read in his *Darlithiau* (Denbigh 1907), pp. 67–99.

¹⁷ These letters, *Llythyrau'r Hen Ffarmwr*, purporting to be the work of an old farmer, deal in simple language with political problems ranging from the land question to British foreign policy. For the text of the letter to Pio Nono, see T. Roberts and D. Roberts, *op. cit.*, pp. 280–282.

¹⁸ D. Beales, *England and Italy 1859–60* (London 1961), pp. 22–24.

¹⁹ *Providence and Prophecy*, pp. 32–34.

²⁰ P. Rebora, *op. cit.*, pp. 236–244.

[21] Mazzini's letters to Hiraethog are now in the National Library of Wales. For the text of the one quoted here, see E. Rees, *op. cit.*, pp. 148–149.

[22] *Ibid.*, pp. 149–150.

[23] T. Roberts and D. Roberts, *op. cit.*, p. 375.

[24] R. T. Jenkins, 'The development of nationalism in Wales' in *The Sociological Review*, XXVII (1935), p. 170.

[25] Quoted by Saunders Lewis, 'Owen M. Edwards' in *Triwyr Penllyn*, ed. G. Pierce (Cardiff, n.d.), pp. 28–29.

[26] For the life of Michael D. Jones, see E. Pan Jones, *Oes a gwaith y Prif Athraw y Parch. Michael Daniel Jones* (Bala 1903).

[27] Michael D. Jones, 'Ymreolaeth' in *Y Celt* (7 March 1890), quoted by D. Gwenallt Jones, 'Hanes mudiadau Cymraeg a chenedlaethol y bedwareddganrif-ar-bymtheg' in *Seiliau hanesyddol Cenedlaetholdeb Cymru* (Cardiff 1950), pp. 113–114. Mr Gwenallt Jones mentions the influence of Mazzini and Kossuth on Michael Jones but treats the influence of the latter as being the more important. This seems to me right. Michael Jones was far less Mazzinian than Tom Ellis or Thomas Jones. I include him here, not because I wish to make out that he was a Mazzinian, but because the influence of his nationalism on later Welsh Mazzinians contributed to making their attitudes much more nationalist than Hiraethog's had been.

[28] Alun Davies, 'Cenedlaetholdeb yn Ewrop a Chymru yn y bedwaredd ganrif ar bymtheg' in *Efrydiau Athronyddol*, XXVII (1964), pp. 18–19.

[29] See E. Pan Jones, *op. cit.*, 96–99.

[30] For E. Pan Jones and R. J. Derfel, see the articles in *Y Bywgraffiadur Cymreig*. For Emrys ap Iwan, see T. Gwynn Jones, *Cofiant Emrys ap Iwan* (Caernarfon 1912), and Emrys ap Iwan, *Erthyglau*, edited by D. Myrddin Lloyd, 3 vols. (Denbigh 1937–40).

[31] Kenneth O. Morgan, *Wales in British Politics 1868–1922* (Cardiff 1963). I refer in particular to the admirable second chapter, 'From Radicalism to nationalism', pp. 28–75.

[32] I wish to record my gratitude to T. I. Ellis, Esq., O.B.E., LL.D., not only for the use I have made of his life of his father (*Thomas Edward Ellis: Cofiant*, vol. I, Liverpool 1944, vol. II, Liverpool 1948), but also for drawing my attention to unpublished material in the National Library of Wales, Aberystwyth.

[33] Ellis, *op. cit.*, ii, 15. I cannot follow Mr. Gwenallt Jones in his interpretation of Ellis's career ('Tom Ellis' in *Y Fflam*, August 1949, pp. 3–8). He suggests that his meeting with Cecil Rhodes led Ellis not only to take a more favourable view than he had previously done of Rhodes's character but to 'deteriorate politically'. He seems to assume that Ellis's principles were anti-imperialist and that his friendship with Rhodes led him to betray them. But Ellis's principles were Mazzinian, and Mazzini believed (as he put it, for instance, in a letter to his mother on 7 August, 1845) that Europeans had been 'providentially called' to conquer less civilised peoples: 'Io credo che l'Europa sia provvidenzialmente chiamata a conquistare il resto del mondo all'incivilimento progressivo: quindi, comeché politicamente ingiusti, vedo con soddisfazione alcuni paesi dell'Europa nelle contrade dominate da credenze retrograde e stazionarie: i Francesi in Algeria, gl'Inglesi nella

China, i Russi in Asia se mai v'andranno, mi paiono missionari necessari all'umanità... Ammetto che, giovandosi d'un'occasione, una potenza europea occupi anche con atto violento un punto di territorio Africano, Chinese, Asiatico: poi che, da quel punto mostri, come si fa con un modello di macchina, quanto superiore è l'incivilimento europeo al loro...' (*Opere*, ed. L. Salvatorelli, Milan–Rome 1938, I, 346–7). We may regret that these were Mazzini's principles, but we cannot justly accuse Ellis of betrayal.

[34] See William George, *Cymru Fydd* (Liverpool 1945); Morgan *op. cit.*, pp. 104–106; J. Vyrnwy Morgan, *Life of Viscount Rhondda* (London 1919).

[35] Ellis, *op. cit.*, ii, 31.

[36] *Ibid.*, ii, 76–77.

[37] *Ibid.*, ii, 93.

[38] *Ibid.*, ii, 98.

[39] N.L.W. Daniel 365.

[40] N.L.W. Daniel 372.

[41] N.L.W. Ellis 391. For Ellis Griffith, see T. I. Ellis, 'Ellis Jones Griffith (Sir Ellis Jones Ellis-Griffith, Bart., 1860–1926)' in *Transactions of the Honourable Society of Cymmrodorion*, Session 1961, Part I, pp. 125–137.

[42] T. Jones, *Leeks and Daffodils* (Newtown 1942), pp. 84–85.

[43] K. Idwal Jones (ed.), *Syr Herbert Lewis 1858–1933* (Cardiff 1958), p. 8 (my translation).

[44] I am indebted to my former pupil, Mrs Ruth Facer, grand-daughter of Sir Herbert Lewis, for this information.

[45] Letter to J. E. Lloyd, 21 September 1894, quoted by K. O. Morgan, *op. cit.*, p. 105.

[46] J. E. Caerwyn Williams, 'Syr John Morris-Jones' in *Transactions of the Honourable Society of Cymmrodorion*, Session 1966, Part I, esp. pp. 26–34; and the same author's 'Cymdeithas Dafydd ap Gwilym, Mai 1886–Mehefin 1888' in *Astudiaethau Amrywiol*, ed. Thomas Jones (Cardiff 1968), pp. 138–181. Saunders Lewis has maintained that Morris-Jones's two long poems *Awdl i Famon* and *Cymru Fu: Cymru Fydd* are the most important political poetry of the nineteenth century in Wales: in the latter he expounded the national aspirations of the Young Wales movement, while in the former he interpreted its Radical and revolutionary ideals. (S. Lewis, 'Owen M. Edwards' in *Triwyr Penllyn*, ed. G. Pierce, Cardiff, n.d., p. 29.)

[47] For his early life, see W. J. Gruffydd, *Owen Morgan Edwards: Cofiant*, I (Aberystwyth 1937). See also the article on him in *Y Bywgraffiadur Cymreig*. According to Gruffydd, Edwards studied Italian at Aberystwyth under Professor Ethé 'and was one of the few pupils with whom he read Tasso' (Gruffydd, *op. cit.*, p. 185).

[48] See H. W. Rudman, *Italian Nationalism and English Letters* (London 1940), p. 158.

[49] For R. H. Morgan, see John Owen, 'Richard Humphreys Morgan' in *Y Traethodydd*, LIV (1899), pp. 284–297, and the article in *Y Bywgraffiadur Cymreig*.

[50] *Dwyfol Gân Dante* (Caernarfon 1903).

[51] For Daniel Rees, see T. Gwynn Jones, *Cymeriadau* (Wrexham 1933), pp. 117–127, and the article in *Y Bywgraffiadur Cymreig*.

⁵² Joseph Mazzini, *The Duties of Man and other Essays* (London 1907), last reprinted 1955.

⁵³ Thomas Jones, *Leeks and Daffodils* (Newtown 1942), pp. 72–73.

⁵⁴ Thomas Jones, *Welsh Broth* (London 1951), p. 61.

⁵⁵ *Leeks and Daffodils*, pp. 74–75.

⁵⁶ D. J. Williams, *Mazzini: Cenedlaetholwr, Gweledydd, Gwleidydd* (Cardiff 1954).

⁵⁷ See T. G. Griffith, 'Italy and Wales' in *Transactions of the Honourable Society of Cymmrodorion*, Session 1966, Part II, pp. 296–297.

⁵⁸ T. Jones, *Whitehall Diary*, vol. I (Oxford 1969), pp. 216–217.

Paola de Angeli

Primi contributi inglesi alla critica verghiana

L'attenzione degli inglesi fu richiamata per la prima volta alle opere del Verga da A. De Gubernatis in un suo articolo del 28 dicembre 1872 nella rivista *Athenaeum*. Il De Gubernatis collaborava regolarmente a questa rivista e ogni anno passava in rassegna l'annata letteraria italiana.[1] Dopo aver considerato gli altri generi letterari il De Gubernatis scrive:

As to romances, I may be forgiven for passing them over in silence, for the good reason that I never read them; and if I am asked why I deprive myself of such innocent pleasure, I can only reply that it is no pleasure at all to me to peruse our Italian novels, for they all resemble each other in the slovenliness of their workmanship, in the poverty of their plots, and in the entire absence of good taste. I think they are reasons sufficient. But after speaking so ill and so sincerely of the general run of our romances and novels, surely I may be believed when I make an exception in favour of 'La Storia di una Capinera' by Signor Verga, of Catania, which is both original and poetical and stands out from the mass of commonplace insipidity and rubbish calling themselves romances . . .

Le osservazioni del De Gubernatis non erano certo tali da invogliare i lettori a volgersi ai romanzi italiani contemporanei e il suo giudizio positivo sulla *Storia di una Capinera* dovette rimanere soffocato sotto il lungo esordio, se non provocò alcuna reazione critica e il romanzo non fu tradotto in inglese che nel 1882.[2]

Per quanto mi risulta, il primo scritto critico inglese sull'arte del Verga è l'articolo di Frances Eleonor Trollope del 1881.[3] Questo articolo è stato esaminato da S. B. Chandler in 'Un articolo inglese del 1881 sul Verga'.[4] Il critico è risalito a questo scritto partendo da una lettera del Verga al Rod del 7 dicembre 1881:

mi fece piacere un articolo dell'ottobre scorso della *Rivista vimensile* di Londra che entrò perfettamente nelle mie idee e nel mio processo artistico, fortuna rara per chi scrive.[5]

Appunto con riferimento a questa affermazione del Verga il Chandler ritiene che un esame dell'articolo 'ci aiuterà a capire l'interpretazione verghiana delle sue idee e del suo processo artistico.' Ma il saggio della Trollope ha anche un suo valore intrinseco, specialmente se si considera che questo è uno dei primi scritti critici sull'arte maggiore del Verga non solo in Inghilterra, ma in Europa e che non può rifarsi che a pochissimi precedenti critici. Brevemente sono qui esposti giudizi che, svolti, saranno punti fondamentali della problematica verghiana. Siamo ovviamente lontani da un compiuto discorso critico, del resto impossibile nel 1881, ma vi sono intuizioni di così acuta perspicacia da giustificare l'approvazione incondizionata dello scrittore che, senza essere un grande teorico o critico, era tuttavia cosciente dei valori originali della sua arte e sapeva individuarne i motivi più nuovi.

Il saggio si articola entro una dinamica multipla: partendo da considerazioni di carattere storico sulla provincialità della letteratura italiana, a causa della 'imperfect unification of the kingdom', e sulle limitazioni che simile situazione può comportare ('the sense of proportion is apt to be lost'), estrae da questo contesto l'opera maggiore del Verga:

Still every now and then a book appears which, by the force of singular merit, attracts the attention of the best judges in all parts of Italy.

Così pure la lingua verghiana viene considerata nel contesto storico della particolare situazione linguistica italiana, e se ne comprende l'importanza nella considerazione particolare dell'opera e se ne intuisce la complessità nella prospettiva generale del problema. A questo proposito la Trollope cita il Capuana con cui si trova in pieno accordo, aggiungendo che 'the use of a highly polished Della Cruscan phraseology in such subjects as those della *Vita dei Campi*, would produce an intolerable artistic dissonance between the manner and the matter' e che 'the mastery' con cui Verga usa lo strumento della lingua 'is not the least striking manifestation of his genius'.

La Trollope affronta quindi il problema della lingua verghiana positivamente, per quanto guidata in questo dal Capuana, mostrando una mentalità aperta e flessibile. Si distingue in questo dal più reazionario giudizio di A. Gallenga che alcuni anni dopo, nel 1887, criticherà il linguaggio verghiano,[6] seguendo i meno illuminati giudizi di gran parte della critica italiana del tempo. Ma il Gallenga, per quanto fortemente anglicizzato, era italiano e, proprio perché tale, era forse più incline a pregiudizi linguistici e fermo a posizioni ed esigenze letterarie di carattere accademico.

Nel rilevare l'indipendenza del Verga dallo Zola e dalla sua scuola affermando che 'the intrinsic differences are ... very curious and noteworthy', nel distinguere tra il Verga teorico e il Verga artista, la Trollope tocca punti che saranno di continuo interesse per i critici verghiani. Premonisce il lettore circa la differenza tra i proponimenti esposti nella prefazione ai *Malavoglia* e l'opera stessa: 'In his preface, Verga writes like a philosophical sociologist; but in his story he happily writes like an artist. The perusal of the preface might possibly repel a reader ... But let him not be discouraged. Verga's work is, as all imaginative works should be, "its own excuse for being".' In questo la Trollope può essere stata influenzata da una osservazione simile del Torraca nella sua recensione ai *Malavoglia* del 9 maggio 1881.[7]

Il saggio continua con l'esame particolare di *Rosso Malpelo*, *Jeli* e *I Malavoglia*. A commenti di carattere psicologico sui personaggi si uniscono considerazioni sull'umanità dell'autore, che traspare nella sua opera malgrado l'impersonalità apparente, su una linea simile a quella seguita poi dal Russo nella sua monografia; senza trascurare peraltro una verifica di queste caratteristiche nella pagina scritta, nel metodo stilistico e nella tecnica narrativa:

Like all writers of native force, Verga has his own manner, his own turn of phrase, his own tone of colouring. The language throughout is . . . purposely simple. The force of the epithets is proportioned, with almost unerring artist instinct, to the importance of the matter described. What a painter would call the 'values' of the picture are admirably adjusted.

E ancora:

There is no word of comment or illustration from beginning to end. Whatever light is thrown on the personages of the story springs from the course of events and their own rustic, untutored utterances, which never rise above the ordinary phraseology of their class.

Sono, come si vede, osservazioni acutissime sulla lingua e sul metodo narrativo dello scrittore. E mi sembra indubitabile che, se questo saggio fosse stato scritto in italiano e pubblicato in Italia, occuperebbe adesso un posto rilevante nella storia della prima critica verghiana.

A proposito dei *Malavoglia* la Trollope conclude il suo articolo con queste considerazioni:

The defects of the book consist chiefly in a too great lack of cohesion between the parts, and a certain vagueness in delineating, not persons, but incidents. Events are presented in the same fragmentary fashion in which they meet our observation in daily life. The coordination and assimilation—the mental digestion, in a word—of facts, which each man has to perform for himself in real life, the novelist usually does for us in his work of art. Verga gives the reader scarcely any help of this kind; not, certainly, because he could not, but because he is resolved to be true to the theories . . .

Nel giudicare questa caratteristica dei *Malavoglia* un difetto, la Trollope dimostra di essere ancora legata al pregiudizio umanistico che vede nella realtà il frammentario e nell'arte l'unità del molteplice. Proprio superando del tutto tale concezione il Verga manifesta un'originalità e una modernità notevolissime. Questo lato dell'arte verghiana, che precede lo sviluppo di tecniche narrative più proprie del romanzo del secolo ventesimo, sarà riconosciuto con acume e sicurezza di giudizio dal Lawrence. Ed è un punto che, nella complessità dei problemi ad esso inerenti e nella sua portata rivoluzionaria, mi sembra non sia stato visto dalla critica che in parte e sia stato trattato solo marginalmente. Va riconosciuto alla Trollope il merito di averlo rilevato, anche se in termini negativi.

Alcuni altri articoli apparsi in riviste inglesi nel secolo diciannovesimo sono stati oggetto di studio da parte dello stesso Chandler in un suo breve articolo del 1962: 'Verga's fortune in English Periodicals: 1881–1892'.[8] Il Chandler li considera genericamente più come documenti per uno studio sulla fortuna dello scrittore e su certi aspetti dei tempi che per il loro valore intrinseco.[9] Li esamineremo quindi per fare osservazioni di carattere più particolare e per seguire e individuare gli indirizzi di indagine più rilevanti.

Completa approvazione per la materia e l'ambiente nuovo delle opere del Verga si trova in un articolo di Linda Villari del 1883,[10] in cui l'autrice distingue tra le vicende degli umili manzoniani e quelle dei personaggi verghiani, iniziando la lunga serie di studi sui rapporti, analogie e differenze tra Manzoni e Verga: un argomento anche questo toccato dal Capuana, sia pure molto marginalmente.

Renzo and Lucia were idyllic types exalted to sublimity by extraordinary adventures and abnormal pains, and were mainly chosen for the sake of contrasting rustic virtue with the corruption of the higher classes. No one then thought of filling in the outline and calling public attention to the daily struggles of a Renzo and Lucia in their normal village life.

La Villari considera *Zeli* (sic) *il Pastore* un capolavoro, ma mostra una decisa incomprensione dell'arte dei *Malavoglia* ritenendoli troppo crudamente realistici e giudicandoli, alla luce della prefazione, un prodotto dello zolismo.[11]

Molto più interessante un'osservazione marginale sulla 'coralità' dei *Malavoglia*, dove viene individuata una caratteristica a cui il Croce, nel suo saggio del 1903, darà una più lucida e conscia formulazione e che sarà un motivo fondamentale della critica posteriore nella considerazione del romanzo:

Through the book these village gossips, the extortionate usurer Zio Crocefisso, the lame go-between nicknamed Goosefoot, the barber, the druggist, the brigadier, the priest, and a host of cackling women, form the chorus of the play.

Il valore sociale, oltre al valore artistico, dell'opera del Verga è affermato in un articolo anonimo del gennaio del 1885, intitolato 'A quartette of Italian novelists':[12] 'His studies of Sicilian life ... have not only an artistic but a social value, and may in time be quoted as what, according to a current phrase, is known as 'human documents', when the modern history of Italy is written.' E a proposito dei *Malavoglia* aggiunge: 'The modern social romance, taken out of the innermost life of a people, has here been first created for Italy.' Il rapporto della rappresentazione verghiana con la realtà della società italiana era già stato impostato dal Torraca,[13] che pure ne riconosceva il valore artistico; e sarà ripreso poi in particolare dalla corrente storicistica della critica più recente.

Inoltre nell'articolo si distingue nettamente tra una prima e una seconda maniera, fissando la svolta decisiva, sulla linea presa dal Capuana e seguita poi dal Croce e dal Russo, nel racconto *Nedda*; e mentre sono riconosciute l'intensità dello stile, la concisione e l'esclusione di artifici letterari, la natura vera e l'originalità più profonda dello stile sono fraintese: 'He has happily blended this [Tuscan] with characteristic Sicilian expressions and technical terms'. Di questo si poteva parlare a proposito di *Nedda* e forse della *Cavalleria Rusticana*, ma non certo delle novelle maggiori di *Vita dei Campi* e dei *Malavoglia*, per cui il problema va visto da un punto di vista sintattico e non lessicale, nell'assimilazione di ritmi e forme sintattiche nel tessuto della lingua italiana e non nella fusione del toscano con espressioni caratteristiche siciliane e termini tecnici. Però, nonostante che la natura vera della struttura linguistica verghiana non sia identificata, questa viene accettata e approvata, mostrando ancora una volta una mentalità critica priva di pregiudizi linguistici, quali si trovano in gran parte dei rappresentanti della critica ufficiale dell'epoca in Italia.[14]

Di scarso valore un articolo di Mary Hargrave del 1892,[15] in cui l'autrice lamenta la poca attenzione rivolta alla lingua e alla letteratura italiana da parte degli inglesi e ne trova la ragione nel fatto che il soggetto dei romanzi italiani dell'epoca sarebbe d'interesse esclusivamente nazionale. Il Verga è definito 'the most original and powerful writer of present Italy', ma che questa sia una conclusione personale è cosa molto dubbia dal momento che, dopo aver riassunto la prefazione dei *Malavoglia*, la Hargrave parla della serie 'I Vinti' come se il Verga avesse effettivamente scritto tutti e cinque i libri. Ci troviamo qui molto probabilmente davanti a un caso di giornalismo 'per sentito dire' e l'articolo non è certo all'altezza di quelli precedenti, che dimostrano piena conoscenza dei testi e serietà d'intenti, raggiungendo notevoli intuizioni critiche. È significativo che, nel secolo XIX, *The Gentleman's Magazine*, in cui l'articolo appare, non avesse, come organo letterario, la reputazione e l'autorità degli altri periodici a cui abbiamo accennato sopra, e che proprio in quest'epoca fosse in declino.

Incominciavano ad apparire in quegli anni le prime traduzioni in inglese del Verga. Nel 1888 *Nedda*, nella traduzione di Veneri Filippi, sulla rivista mensile *Italia*. Nel 1890 era apparsa a New-York la traduzione dei *Malavoglia* col titolo *The House by the Medlar Tree*, a cura di Mary Craig, con introduzione di W. D. Howells. L'anno dopo la stessa traduzione fu pubblicata a Londra da Osgood.[16] Nel 1893 uscirono *Cavalleria Rusticana and Other Tales of Sicilian Peasant Life*, tradotto da Alma Strettel (Londra, Fisher, Unwin), e *Master don Gesualdo*, tradotto da Mary Craig (Londra, Osgood and McIlvaine).[17]

Le traduzioni provocarono ovviamente un certo numero di recensioni, tra le quali forse le più interessanti, per alcune osservazioni sul metodo narrativo, sono quelle apparse in *The Bookman*. Nell'aprile del 1892 appare la recensione di *The House by the Medlar Tree* e nell'aprile dell'anno dopo quella del *Master Don Gesualdo*. Nella prima il recensore, che si firma con le iniziali G.Y., senza formulare alcun giudizio sulla qualità della traduzione—che lascia

molto a desiderare e che, lungi dal penetrare nello spirito del-
l'opera, la svisa (basti vedere il titolo) con tagli ed omissioni del
tutto arbitrarie e con l'uso di un inglese da salotto borghese—loda
il romanzo e l'arte del Verga, ritenendolo un realista, ma separan-
dolo decisamente dalla scuola francese.

He is a realist . . . because he looks on at life fearless and unashamed,
and trusts to facts to reveal their own poetry. If his point of view is not
romantic, neither does he belittle human nature nor besmirch it.

Sulla linea della Trollope, G.Y. riflette sul modo in cui è
presentata la realtà:

A superficial reading might report the book to be a chaos, without
visible arrangement at all. So far it resembles closely any patch of life
in any given place and time—all cross lights, cross purposes, tangles and
irrelevancies at first sight. Look closer and longer, and the order, the
governing impulses, the main currents are evident.

Su questo medesimo metodo di presentazione della realtà lo
stesso recensore si sofferma nell'articolo sul *Master Don Gesualdo*
dell'aprile del 1893, affermando che il Verga 'has substantially
invented a method of fiction, and till now he has had no imitators
either in English or French literature'. E aggiunge:

He [Verga] makes you stand on the level of the human beings you are
watching: you have the advantage of your own height, and eye-sight,
and hearing—nothing more. He sets you down in gossiping little
towns, in crowded village festas, in the midst of family squabbles, and
lets you gather out of the noise and the chatter and the altercations just
what you are capable of gathering. It is all very bewildering, you say.
And so is life. A great deal of it is very dull, incomplete, fragmentary.
The liker to life. . . . At first sight all is chaotic like a page of to-day's
newspaper; but there is not a flaw in the logic of events.

Le altre recensioni[18] sono sprovviste di serio contenuto critico,
e gli ultimi anni dell'Ottocento non portano altri contributi
significativi alla critica verghiana. Con l'eccezione di un articolo
del 1902 bisogna arrivare al dopoguerra per trovare in Inghilterra
una seconda ondata di interesse per lo scrittore siciliano.

Una impostazione fondamentalmente teorica è alla base del-
l'articolo anonimo apparso nel 1902 in *The Quarterly Review*,
intitolato 'The novels of Giovanni Verga'.[19] Il critico discute e
polemizza contro la teoria dell'impersonalità, affermando che l'arte

è personale, linea che prenderà decisamente l'anno dopo il Croce nel suo famoso saggio e che sarà seguita da molti altri critici. Però, avendo sostenuto l'impossibilità di una assoluta impersonalità, il critico afferma che Verga mantiene 'without faltering his mask of impartiality' in *Vita dei Campi* e nelle *Novelle Rusticane* e proprio in questa sua supposta indifferenza, caratteristica del suo totale pessimismo, starebbe il limite dell'arte verghiana:

He maintains his attitude of the passionless and uncritical reporter of the spectacle of human life, but it is none the less evident that he is moved to make his report, not by an aching sense of disagreement between the laws of things and the claims of his heart, but rather by scorn and vivid disgust. His art, strong and vivid by reason of this very pessimism, yet misses the height of strength and vividness just because this pessimism guards the mask of indifference.

È evidente che il giudizio limitativo si basa non tanto sulla maschera di indifferenza quanto sui sentimenti che dietro questa maschera si nasconderebbero: disprezzo e disgusto.

Il saggio giunge a questa conclusione dopo un esame delle opere verghiane che vengono dapprima suddivise in due categorie, opere idealistiche e opere realistiche, stabilendo in questi termini il rapporto tra l'opera giovanile e l'opera matura del Verga. Dopo una dissertazione sul rapporto tra ideale e reale—che il critico ritiene conciliabili perché 'what is the real but the ideal in the making; or the ideal if it be not the goal and consummation of the real?'—vengono considerate prima le opere maggiori, *I Malavoglia* e *Mastro don Gesualdo*, e poi le opere giovanili. Nell'esaminare *I Malavoglia* il critico dice che, pur nel suo tentativo di imparzialità, 'it is as if Verga, for all his philosophic detachment, endeavoured to contrast the essential beauty and ugliness of virtue and vice', mentre in *Mastro don Gesualdo*

we find the wonted mingling of the angel and the beast. . . . He has been studied with the sympathy of complete understanding, and wins our sympathy in turn, not indeed by any nobility of sentiment or action, but because he rises almost to the height of heroism in the hapless tenacity of his self-preservation.

E sempre parlando del carattere di Mastro don Gesualdo il critico aggiunge:

Throughout he repels, and yet overcomes repulsion. He is selfish and yet not unkind. He is human and real, not knowing what he is nor what he does. He inspires pity, nay, wins our sympathy not only for the reasons stated above, but because we know him entirely.

A questo punto il critico passa a considerare le opere così dette idealistiche, 'leaving certain questions unanswered'. Egli riconosce che il problema del rapporto tra la prima e la seconda maniera del Verga non è così semplice come potrebbe sembrare a prima vista, in quanto 'it would be tempting enough to discover in it a gradual evolution towards realism. But it is safer to say that "Eros" bears much the same date as "I Malavoglia", and that the writer of "Il Marito di Elena" plainly remembers that he is the author of "Mastro Don Gesualdo".' Qui c'è evidentemente una confusione di date, o di titoli. *Eros* fu pubblicato nel 1875 e *I Malavoglia* nel 1881, quindi non si può assolutamente parlare di contemporaneità, anche se approssimativa. Quanto al *Marito di Elena*, il romanzo fu pubblicato nel 1882 dopo *I Malavoglia*, ma prima che *Mastro don Gesualdo* fosse iniziato. Il critico, volendo stabilire i termini del problema della coesistenza dei due tipi di narrativa, avrebbe dovuto, se mai, parlare del breve distacco cronologico tra *Nedda* (non *I Malavoglia*) ed *Eros*, e dell'anteriorità dei *Malavoglia* (e non di *Mastro don Gesualdo*) rispetto al *Marito di Elena*. In ogni caso, anche senza questi errori fondamentali di date, l'impostazione del saggio sarebbe stata probabilmente la stessa, in quanto il critico si perde un'altra volta in divagazioni di carattere teorico, dandoci la sua definizione dell'artista:

The true and complete artist at once recalls us to reality and delivers us from it. He must be a realist in his knowledge, and an idealist in his interpretation of life.

E considerando il Verga afferma:

But Verga is not of the idealists who shape the world in conformity with a superior ideal. . . . Nor yet again does he belong to those artists of high, and possibly the highest, rank, who, labouring to see and report upon life as it is, and mistrusting idealism, yet recognise the ideal in the reality which is in accordance with right living; who are idealists because they subordinate sensation to sentiment, and sentiment to the ideas that lead men to unselfish action.

Avendo così definito l'artista e avendoci offerto la sua estetica, che si basa evidentemente sull'eticità dell'arte nei termini da lui espressi, il critico limita l'accezione di idealista riferita al Verga a 'analyser of passion, of that love which is selfish, illusory and devastating'. Dopo aver riassunto ed esaminato brevemente i romanzi 'idealistici', il critico giunge alla conclusione che il Verga riduce il concetto d'amore a quello di passione sensuale e che il suo idealismo 'takes the form of a pessimistic fatalism'. A questo punto il critico ritorna alle domande lasciate in sospeso e cioè: 'What was his conception, his criticism of life? What lay behind his carefully guarded method of impersonality?' L'interesse del critico è scoprire la personalità e la filosofia dell'autore e giudicare l'opera alla luce di queste. Egli ritiene di poter trovare una risposta in una terza suddivisione degli scritti verghiani, i racconti, e nelle pagine teoretiche. In ambedue trova la conferma del profondo pessimismo misantropico dell'autore e arriva alla conclusione implicita d'altra parte nella sua limitata comprensione della poesia verghiana fin dall'inizio della elaborata discussione—che l'arte del Verga non raggiunge 'the height of strength and vividness'. In *Vita dei Campi* e nelle *Novelle Rusticane* solo due personaggi rivelerebbero una scintilla di generosità e di sentimento umano, Jeli e Santo di *Pane Nero*. E anche su questi il critico ha delle riserve. Predomina nei suoi giudizi un'intonazione moraleggiante di scarso valore critico: non solo il mondo etico del Verga, non compreso, viene squalificato moralisticamente, ma non si considera se sia coerente o meno con la sua poesia. Siamo davanti a una posizione antitetica a quella del Russo, che alla base dell'arte verghiana vede un atteggiamento fondamentalmente etico e che nell'impassibilità dello scrittore vede non indifferenza, ma sublimata sofferenza. Manca in questo saggio un'analisi diretta dei testi e il problema critico non è impostato in termini validi per un'interpretazione artistica dell'opera.

Anche per quanto riguarda la lingua e la tecnica narrativa dei *Malavoglia*, sono formulate rigorose limitazioni:

Further, like the rest of his French and Italian compeers, he is unable to draw upon the happy resource of dialect; if his peasants are to be understood, he must not only translate their speech, but resume it as far as possible in indirect narration. He endeavours, here and in his short stories, to balance his loss by the careful and constant preservation of the picturesque elements of their speech; he would have the book appear as if it came from the hand of a peasant. But his labour is a manifest labour; the peasant-writer whom we presuppose, or are allowed to suppose, is, as it were, painfully conscious that he must remember the requirements of current Italian.

Simili giudizi limitativi sulla lingua del Verga erano stati espressi dallo Scarfoglio nel 1885:

Solamente in una cosa pecca il Verga, ed il peccato è grave: nella forma. Egli non pecca di sciatteria, o di lambiccatura: ma si affatica a farsi uno stile proprio semplice e colorito e vivo insieme. Però lo sforzo è così grande e così chiaro...[20]

E anche l'opinione che sarebbe stato meglio usare il dialetto è espressa dallo stesso Scarfoglio, il quale riferisce che, avendo sentito parlare il Verga in siciliano con dei marinai 'con una così facile speditezza', si disse: '—Diavolo! E perché costui non fa parlar siciliano i Siciliani delle sue novelle?—'[21]

In tutti e due questi critici c'è una incapacità di avvicinarsi all'arte verghiana positivamente, senza riserve e pregiudizi mentali: il momento rappresentativo e stilistico è veduto in sé e non è assommato al momento ideale: la forma non è vista come 'necessaria e inerente al soggetto', per usare le parole dello stesso Verga.[22]

Se si esclude l'articolo appena esaminato, l'arte del Verga sarà, nei primi due decenni del novecento, più o meno ignorata. Bisogna arrivare al 1919 per trovare un altro articolo sul Verga in Inghilterra, scritto d'altronde da un italiano nella forma di 'Lettera dall'Italia' per la rivista *Athenaeum*, quindi al di fuori del campo di interessi di questa particolare ricerca.[23] Questo articolo è del luglio del 1919; pochi mesi dopo uscirà la monografia del Russo[24] e nel 1920 si svolgeranno, in occasione dell'ottantesimo compleanno del Verga, le celebrazioni in onore dello scrittore, presiedute dal Pirandello e con l'intervento del Croce. Nel dicembre dello stesso anno lo scrittore andrà a Roma a prestare giuramento come senatore. In questo clima di celebrazioni e di riconoscimenti ufficiali, arrivava a Taormina, nel marzo del 1920, D. H. Lawrence, e del 1921 sono le prime lettere in cui egli parla in toni entusiastici del Verga. Pare quindi indubbio che la sua scoperta personale dello scrittore siciliano sia stata un diretto risultato del rinnovato interesse degli italiani per l'arte verghiana.[25]

Come è noto il Lawrence tradusse *Mastro don Gesualdo*, *Vita dei Campi* e le *Novelle Rusticane*, e rimase un fervente ammiratore del Verga per tutta la vita. Scrisse alcuni saggi a prefazione delle traduzioni, e nel suo epistolario vi sono molti accenni al Verga che racchiudono un giudizio critico. Un esame di questi scritti va condotto nel contesto del suo metodo critico, della sua estetica, della sua filosofia e delle caratteristiche del suo stile. L'argomento richiede quindi uno svolgimento più ampio, impossibile in questa sede.[26] Per la statura dello scrittore, la sua opera di traduttore e di critico delle opere verghiane segna l'acme dell'interesse inglese per Verga. Le sue traduzioni provocarono recensioni ed invitarono spunti critici,[27] ed è senz'altro al Lawrence che si deve il maggior contributo alla divulgazione delle opere del Verga in Inghilterra.

Per quanto i saggi che abbiamo considerato non tendano a ripetere giudizi già formulati e abbiano una fisionomia autonoma, che abbiamo tentato di delineare nell'analisi particolare, pure se ne possono dedurre considerazioni generali di un certo interesse. Alcune, sui criteri di valutazione e sulle idee che li governano, coincidono con quanto è stato già rilevato in studi specifici sui periodici inglesi del periodo vittoriano. I saggi vengono svolti sul piano del gusto, delle convenzioni tradizionali e dell'analisi psicologica, più che ragionati in una profonda ed ordinata costruzione critica basata su un'estetica precisa, ma entro questi limiti l'analisi è condotta con serietà, nasce da reali interessi di critica letteraria, giungendo ad osservazioni valide. R. G. Cox, in un suo saggio sulle riviste e sui periodici inglesi dell'Ottocento, scrive: 'The reviewing of fiction in Victorian periodicals shows a good deal of uncertainty about what to expect from the novel and what standards to apply. Very often the requirements do not go much beyond those mentioned by an *Edinburgh* reviewer in 1841: "We require from the novel that it shall be moral in its tendency, that it shall be amusing and it shall exhibit a true and faithful delineation of the class of society which it professes to depict." Realism must not be carried to the point of the sordid; social criticism must not become too disturbingly precise and political; and "moral in its tendency" is often narrowed into a demand for strict poetic justice and explicit moral teaching. Nevertheless, the application of general common-sense standards of taste and morality often produced useful comments and accounts of fiction benefited especially from the generous allowance of reviewing space and the opportunity to quote at length.'[28]

Si può vedere come queste osservazioni generali siano valide anche nel campo limitato della critica verghiana del periodo. Più specificamente, mentre da una parte si milita per una poetica realistica in senso lato, dall'altra si nota una polemica costante contro il realismo francese: quando i giudizi sull'arte verghiana sono positivi, ne viene stabilita l'autonomia dallo Zola, e la narrativa è lungi dall'essere presentata come un esempio vittorioso della validità dei principi della sua scuola; quando invece i giudizi sono limitativi, lo sono perchè basati sulla considerazione che il realismo del Verga, derivante da quello francese, è troppo sordido. Questo d'altra parte è un riflesso delle concezioni imperanti in quel periodo nei circoli letterari inglesi: il realismo era ormai una tradizione nazionale della letteratura inglese; da tempo numerosi scrittori avevano cercato la loro ispirazione al di fuori di una aristocrazia o borghesia convenzionale, nelle classi povere. È naturale che gli umili verghiani siano accettati senza pregiudizi contenutistici. Ma forti pregiudizi esistevano contro la scuola realistica francese, appunto perché si riteneva che concentrasse eccessivamente la sua attenzione sui lati più meschini della natura umana, degradandola.

Dal punto di vista linguistico, se manca una comprensione del carattere rivoluzionario della lingua verghiana nel contesto storico della letteratura italiana—che d'altra parte è una valutazione a cui la stessa critica italiana è giunta solo dopo incomprensioni, incertezze e dubbi—mancano anche, come abbiamo già accennato, i severi pregiudizi linguistici che si trovano in quell'epoca in Italia. Anche questo si può riportare alla diversa tradizione letteraria, sociale e linguistica. Ovviamente in Inghilterra non esisteva il 'problema della lingua' nei termini in cui era presente in Italia. Con lo Scott l'introduzione di elementi dialettali nella prosa letteraria era stata, per così dire, ufficialmente accettata, e proprio in quegli anni si pubblicavano i romanzi di Thomas Hardy, una caratteristica dei quali è proprio l'uso particolare dello strumento linguistico nel tentativo di fondere la lingua inglese e il dialetto del Wessex. Quindi esperimenti stilistici di questo tipo non erano nuovi: la struttura linguistica verghiana non poteva provocare le stesse reazioni di riprovazione e di smarrimento che provocò in alcuni critici italiani.

Entro i limiti tratteggiati ed entro i limiti imposti dall'epoca storica e dalla conseguente mancanza di prospettiva, questi primi studi inglesi sul Verga colgono punti fondamentali—ora adombrati, ora dichiarati—che sono rimasti come esigenze e premesse del pensiero critico successivo, sia pure indipendente da essi.

Se da una considerazione della comprensione dell'opera e della felicità dell'interpretazione critica si passa ad una generica considerazione della fortuna e del successo dello scrittore, si può notare che in Inghilterra la curva dell'interesse per il Verga nell'ultima parte dell'Ottocento e nei primi decenni del Novecento segue, in maniera naturalmente ridotta, quella italiana. I contributi inglesi sono, come si è visto, scarsi: i saggi esaminati in questo studio sono gli unici scritti in quel periodo degni di essere menzionati. Non si verifica qui il caso di un'arte compresa prima e valutata di più all'estero che nel paese d'origine, ma semplicemente un interesse riflesso, che dalla critica italiana riceve la spinta iniziale e dalle variazioni di questa deriva i suoi alti e bassi. Negli ultimi due decenni dell'Ottocento, nel periodo cioè di maggiore produzione del Verga, la sua arte viene considerata come novità nel campo del romanzo e del racconto italiano: prime osservazioni, prime reazioni quindi a un'arte nuova, non solo con carattere di recensione e con lo scopo di additare al pubblico opere nuove, guidandolo e stimolandone l'interesse, ma con veri intenti critici. Nei primi due decenni del Novecento l'interesse si smorza sulla linea dello svolgimento storico della critica verghiana in Italia: risorgerà solo quando, col 'ritorno al Verga' degli anni del dopoguerra, sulla sua arte sarà attratta l'attenzione di D. H. Lawrence.

Note

[1] Nel dicembre del 1873 il critico parla brevemente del romanzo *Eva* e si trovano diversi altri accenni al Verga negli anni successivi, nessuno di particolare interesse.

[2] 'The story of a Capinera', *Italia, a monthly magazine* (gennaio–marzo 1888). Traduzione anonima.

[3] F. E. Trollope, 'Italian realistic fiction', *The Fortnightly Review*, vol. 30, n.s. (1 ottobre 1881), pp. 459–477. La Trollope era cognata dello scrittore Anthony Trollope, che fu tra i fondatori della *Fortnightly Review*.

[4] S. B. Chandler, 'Un articolo inglese del 1881 sul Verga', *Giornale Storico della Letteratura Italiana* (III trimestre 1956), Comunicazioni ed appunti, pp. 479–482.

[5] G. Verga, *Lettere al suo traduttore*, a cura di Fredi Chiappelli (Firenze, Le Monnier, 1954), p. 49.

[6] A. Gallenga, *Italy, present and Future* (Londra 1887), p. 76.

[7] Ora in F. Torraca, *Scritti critici* (Napoli 1907), p. 374 sgg.

[8] S. B. Chandler, 'Verga's fortune in English periodicals: 1881–1892', *Italica*, vo. 39, no. 4, (1962), pp. 260–267.

[9] Il Chandler riassume i vari articoli e conclude: 'An examination of the above articles indicates that, while interest in the Italian classics persisted in Britain . . . fewer people were learning the Italian language and even these were not encouraged to read contemporary authors. Interest in contemporary Italian literature was confined to specialists, who tended to look upon it as local and self-centred and so of limited significance within the background of current literature in general. Though acknowledged as the leading Italian novelist of the period, Verga was usually set firmly within the limits of his own country and no British translator addressed himself to his two major novels.' In nota il Chandler cita la traduzione di Eric Mosbacher pubblicata a Londra nel 1950 (la prima edizione apparve a New-York nel 1933) e, inspiegabilmente, non fa riferimento alle traduzioni del Lawrence.

[10] Linda Villari, 'Italian peasant life', *The Cornhill Magazine*, vol. 47 (June 1883), pp. 710–716. Linda Villari, nata White, era moglie dello storico Pasquale Villari.

[11] Vedi Chandler, *op. cit.*

[12] 'A quartette of Italian novelists', *Blackwood's Magazine*, vol. 137, no. 831 (gennaio 1885), pp. 72–92. (Gli altri tre romanzieri del 'quartetto' sono il Farina, la Serao e la Colombi.) Gli articoli di molti periodici inglesi del secolo scorso non erano firmati. Si può però spesso risalire alla paternità dei vari articoli attraverso *The Wellesley Index to Victorian Periodicals, 1824–1900*, a cura di W. E. Houghton (University of Toronto Press, Routledge and Kegan Paul, 1966), vol. 1. A pagina 164 di questa opera si legge che questo articolo è di Helen Zimmern. Nel qual caso si deve notare che della stessa autrice è un articolo sul Verga del 9 aprile 1892 in *The Critic*, New-York, intitolato 'Italy's greatest living novelist', in cui, a molti dei giudizi già espressi, ne vengono aggiunti altri, tra i quali forse il più interessante, per quanto sia piuttosto vago, è quello sulla natura, un aspetto della narrativa verghiana che non è stato osservato in questi primi articoli inglesi: 'One of his strongest points is his wonderful power of giving an idea of the outward aspects of nature . . .' Anche della Zimmern è un libro apparso a Londra nel 1914, *Italy of the Italians*, in cui si parla brevemente del Verga.

[13] Torraca, *op. cit.*

[14] Vedi ad es. C. Del Balzo, E. Scarfoglio, G. Pipitone-Federico.

[15] Mary Hargrave, 'Some Italian novelists of the present day', *The Gentleman's Magazine*, vol. 273 (1892), pp. 519–529.

[16] Circa l'insuccesso economico di questa edizione inglese vedi N. Cappellani, *Vita di Giovanni Verga* (Firenze, Le Monnier, 1940), p. 340 sgg.

[17] Per le traduzioni in inglese degli anni successivi vedi G. Raya, *Un secolo di bibliografia verghiana* (Padova, Cedam, 1960).

[18] Vedi ad es.: William Sharp, *The Academy*, vol. 41 (aprile 1892), pp. 419–420. George Saintsbury, *The Academy*, vol. 43 (maggio 1893), p. 414. Jas. Stanley Little, *The Academy*, vol. 44 (settembre 1893) p. 271. *The Athenaeum*, no. 3442 (ottobre 1893), p. 520. *The Bookman*, vol. 5 (ottobre 1893), p. 26.

[19] 'The novels of Giovanni Verga', *The Quarterly Review*, vol. 195, no. 290 (1902), pp. 362–384.

[20] E. Scarfoglio, *Il libro di don Chisciotte* (Milano, Mondadori, 1925), p. 95. La prima edizione fu pubblicata a Roma nel 1885.

[21] *Ibid.*, p. 97.

[22] Lettera a C. Del Balzo (28 aprile 1881), in G. Raya, *op. cit.*, p. 19.

[23] G. De Ruggiero, 'Giovanni Verga and the realists', *The Athenaeum* (11 luglio 1919), pp. 600–601.

[24] L. Russo, *Giovanni Verga* (Napoli, Ricciardi, 1919).

[25] *Cfr.* P. Nardi, 'Ciò che Lawrence deve a Verga', *Italia Letteraria* (febbraio 1936).

[26] I rapporti Lawrence–Verga, nella loro complessità, sono argomento di uno mi studio in corso di preparazione.

[27] Vedi ad es. l'articolo di Orlo Williams, 'The art of Giovanni Verga', *Edinburgh Review*, vol. 241 (aprile 1925), pp. 301–317. Pubblicato anche in *Studi Verghiani*, vol. 1 (1929).

[00] R. G. Cox, 'The reviews and magazines', *From Dickens to Hardy* (Penguin Books, 1958), vol. 6 of *The Pelican Guide to English Literature*, pp. 200–201.

Paola Seganti

Impressioni inglesi di Italo Svevo

L e impressioni immediate che Italo Svevo, o meglio Ettore Schmitz, trasse dai suoi viaggi oltremanica sono registrate soprattutto nelle lettere quasi quotidiane mandate alla moglie durante i numerosi soggiorni in Gran Bretagna, mentre l'influenza che esse ebbero sull'opera dello scrittore appare nella successiva rielaborazione che egli ne fece qua e là in racconti, pagine di diario e saggi. Questi ultimi toccheranno anche aspetti della vita inglese che l'autore deve aver osservato da vicino, benché non ne resti traccia nell'epistolario.

Ettore andò per la prima volta in Inghilterra nel giugno del 1901, mandato dai suoceri Veneziani ad esplorare le possibilità di vendita in quel paese della loro famosa vernice per sottomarini. Poi vi ritornò quasi ogni anno, e talvolta anche più volte l'anno, quando, su suo consiglio, una fabbrica Veneziani fu installata a Charlton, un sobborgo di Londra. Le sue visite non furono fatte, perciò, in veste di letterato, ma in quella di uomo d'affari, tanto più che gli anni fra lo scorcio del secolo e la fine della prima guerra mondiale sono proprio quelli in cui Ettore ha deciso di eliminare dalla sua vita 'quella ridicola e dannosa cosa che si chiama letteratura'. Sono, però, gli stessi anni in cui egli afferma ripetutamente il bisogno di scrivere ogni giorno qualche cosa per chiarire a se stesso il proprio pensiero:

Io credo, sinceramente credo, che non c'è migliore via per arrivare a scrivere sul serio che di scribacchiare giornalmente. Si deve tentar di portare a galla dall'imo del proprio essere, ogni giorno un suono, un accento, un residuo fossile o vegetale di qualche cosa che sia o non sia il puro pensiero, che sia o non sia sentimento, ma bizzarria, rimpianto, un dolore, qualche cosa di sincero, anatomizzato e tutto e non di più. Altrimenti facilmente si cade,—il giorno in cui si crede d'esser autorizzati di prender la penna—in luoghi comuni o si travia quel luogo proprio che non fu a sufficienza disaminato. Insomma fuori della penna non c'è salvezza.[1]

E ancora:

Io voglio soltanto attraverso a queste pagine arrivare a capirmi meglio. L'abitudine mia e di tutti gli impotenti di non saper pensare che con la penna alla mano (come se il pensiero non fosse più utile e necessario al momento dell'azione) mi obbliga a questo sacrificio. Dunque ancora una volta, grezzo e rigido strumento, la penna mi aiuterà ad arrivare al fondo tanto complesso del mio essere.[2]

Rifiuto della letteratura, quindi, ma non della 'penna' che per Ettore Schmitz è sempre stato il mezzo di sentirsi Italo Svevo. Perciò anche le numerose lettere scritte alla moglie dall'Inghilterra nel periodo del ripudio letterario assumono un interesse che non può essere considerato esclusivamente umano.[3] Esse costituiscono un altro capitolo di quel monologo epistolare, inteso come chiarimento psicologico e come ironico commento delle proprie reazioni, che, cominciato con la prima lettera alla fidanzata in cui Ettore analizzava gli effetti del primo bacio, doveva concludersi con il monologo interiore di Zeno e di certi tardi racconti. Le cose inglesi sono presentate con quell'analisi acuta, quell'umorismo, quel misto di considerazioni pessimistiche e ottimistiche che sono dati caratteristici dello Svevo maggiore. Anzi, da un punto di vista letterario, c'è da rammaricarsi che la moglie lo abbia più volte raggiunto a Charlton, privandoci così, con la sua presenza sul luogo, della documentazione epistolare di tante altre acute impressioni! Come lui stesso dice: 'dacché so che probabilmente tu verrai a Londra, ho cessato di guardare la grande città che potrò visitare in compagnia tua.'[4]

Le prime impressioni furono piuttosto disastrose e i rapporti con il mondo anglosassone resi più difficili dall'ostacolo della lingua. Le prime lettere a casa sono piene di accenni, tra l'accorato e l'ironico, a tale proposito:

L'inglese va maluccio, sai. Non solo io non capisco loro, ma essi non capiscono me.[5]

La più semplice parola d'inglese che dico crea dei malintesi e dei dubbi [...] Qui anche si dà la comedia ma in inglese ed io non capisco un accidenti.[6]

Prima di tutto sono abbattuto per le difficoltà della lingua.[7]

Solo io mi trovo ad ogni passo impedito dal non comprendere, dal non farmi capire.[8]

Studio l'inglese in modo che lo parlo anche di notte ed anzi solo allora bene.[9]

Di tutto lo spettacolo che più gustai e compresi fu un cane ammaestrato. L'inglese mi fa ancora stentare. La predica di questa mattina fu per me proprio lettera morta ed è perciò che non mi sono convertito.[10]

Mi sono accorto che interpretavo delle indicazioni di pronuncia del mio dizionario in modo perfettamente erroneo. Devo cominciare da capo.[11]

Mi misi a urlare e nell'ira perdetti totalmente quel poco che so d'inglese. Parlavo o meglio urlavo italiano tedesco francese. Gli operai ci si divertirono mezzo mondo. Gli ufficiali di bordo persino uscirono a udire i suoni insoliti ed io tutto ingozzato mi tacqui.[12]

Si potrebbero citare decine di altri esempi: quelli riportati sopra sono solamente alcuni relativi al primo mese di soggiorno in Inghilterra. Ma anche più tardi l'inglese gli dà da fare. Scrive alla moglie da Charlton il 17 luglio 1908:

Con l'inglese procedo così così. Un signore allo sbarco a Dover mi domandò qualche cosa che credetti di comprendere. Risposi. Risultò che né io avevo capito lui né lui me. Ci dividemmo arrabbiati. Sai tu che voglia dire in italiano: I think saù, so? I think so, sir.[13]

Nel saggio *Uomini e cose in un distretto di Londra*, scritto nel 1913, cioè ancora in periodo di 'ripudio letterario', dirà:

Intanto la lingua Cockney di Londra[14] è una difficoltà insormontabile per chi parlò per 40 anni il triestino. Mi difendo bene in una stanza di conversazione o anche in affari quando ho il mio inglese a faccia a faccia e lo caccio in un cantuccio da cui non esce finché non m'ha inteso. Ma al telefono! Pare che il telefono inglese non trasmetta le mie sillabe. Basta che io dica nell'imbuto del telefono oh! pochissima cosa! p.e. il nome della persona con la quale voglio parlare e nasce un putiferio. Mi urlano nelle orecchie: Who are you? I beg your pardon! Whom do you want? Avvilito m'allontano e ritorno a sillabare, spelling.[15]

A venticinque anni di distanza dal suo primo viaggio in Inghilterra Italo Svevo, nel saggio *Soggiorno londinese*, ammetterà:

In Inghilterra dovetti anche studiare affannosamente la lingua inglese. Di questo studio devo confessare un certo insuccesso. Io so quella lingua ma iniziatone lo studio troppo tardi, a quarant'anni, non seppi farla mia intimamente. Così quando vado a una commedia inglese sono sempre dolorosamente sorpreso che anche il secondo atto—con un'ostinazione incredibile—sia detto in inglese, perché la fatica di intendere il primo m'esaurì.[16]

E ancora:

A Greenwich io ho settimanalmente una recita degli ottimi attori di Lena Ashwell: Shakespeare, Sheridan, Shaw, Galsworthy e così via. Io ci andai sempre. Non per amore della letteratura ma per abituarmi al suono della lingua.[17]

Vedremo poi che anche il signor Aghios di *Corto viaggio sentimentale* sarà afflitto, in Inghilterra, da difficoltà linguistiche. Ettore

Schmitz, industriale, ha trasferito nel letterato Italo Svevo, sia egli scrittore di saggi o di racconti, il suo disagio di fronte alla lingua straniera. Italo ha aggiunto una 'm' alla 'comedia' di Ettore!

Naturalmente, con l'andare del tempo, Ettore acquistò una notevole facilità di espressione, tanto da adottare l'inglese anche in varie lettere. Fra queste, la più significativa è quella mandata alla moglie nel 1909, non da Charlton o da Londra, ma da Murano. Il fatto che perfino dall'Italia scrivesse a Livia in inglese sta a testimoniare le tracce profonde lasciate in lui da questa lingua. Tanto più che la lettera diceva:

> I had a dream this night (it was a night of about ten hours). I dreamt to have been translated in English but wholly you know. I ate beef and was stiff and well educated by the intervention of the Holy Ghost, I think. By awakening I found myself re-translated in Italian but I feel it necessary to retain a little of the second nature I acquired during the dream. This is the last letter I write to you this time and it is English. You have already tried once what it signifies to be translated. You have been translated in French.[18] I tried to re-translate you in Italian and if this translation did not give you a great pleasure it was really my fault. The only one of our little family who has not been translated is our little one. We hope that she will not be worse than we have been.[19]

Attraverso le difficoltà di una lingua aliena (ma non lo era, per lui, in fondo, anche l'italiano?) e nonostante le imperfezioni, rimane evidente l'ineffabile stile di Svevo, l'ironica analisi di se stesso e di quanti lo circondano. Anche Zeno avrà un 'problema della lingua', ma lo studio introspettivo della sua coscienza non risulterà meno efficace perché espresso in un italiano riprovato dai puristi. Anzi la naturalezza ne verrà accentuata, lo stile diverrà più 'suo'. Alla stessa maniera la 'traduzione onirica' di Ettore sarà, forse, in *broken English*, ma non per questo è meno 'wholly', meno sentita. Tutto il gioco di 'traduzioni' è tipicamente sveviano.[20]

Prima di arrivare a sognare di esser stato 'tradotto' in inglese passeranno, in ogni modo, vari anni. Intanto, nel 1901, saranno, ovviamente, le differenze tra le abitudini inglesi e quelle degli altri popoli che conosce a colpirlo maggiormente. Nella seconda lettera alla moglie dall'Inghilterra[6] fa un elenco delle cose che, a prima vista, non gli sono piaciute nel nuovo paese. Tra l'altro, non gli piace la riservatezza inglese, il fatto che si porti sempre il cappello, che al bar si debba pagare prima di bere. Preferisce di gran lunga i francesi, ma già pochi giorni dopo ha cambiato opinione:

Però debbo dirti che ad onta che m'è tanto difficile se non impossibile praticare la gente, pure sono stato meglio a Chatham che a Tolone. Il militarismo inglese è certo più simpatico dell'odioso militarismo francese. Qui è libertà, vera libertà. Io lo capisco ad onta che di questa libertà posso usare tanto poco non conoscendo a sufficienza né la lingua né i costumi dal paese. Ma io confesso ch'io verrei più volontieri a stabilire una fabbrica qui che a Marsiglia. Intanto sarebbe la felicità per Titina. Se tu sapessi come vedo nella faccia di ogni miss che passa la felicità di vivere e di essere libera. Quando sono povere lavorano, ma le ore di libertà sono di vera libertà. Non dubito che ci sia sotto anche della licenza ma la libertà è una felicità e sai come la penso io sul diritto alla felicità: La felicità è il diritto di ognuno.[21]

Dunque pare che, negli inglesi, Ettore abbia trovato la realizzazione delle sue aspirazioni vagamente socialiste: l'equivalenza libertà-felicità, la felicità 'diritto di ognuno'; aspirazioni che aveva già letterariamente illustrato nel 1897 nel racconto-parabola *La tribù* e a cui accennerà di nuovo nel tardo racconto *Vino generoso*. D'altra parte la sua visione della vita non diventerà ottimistica solo perché in Inghilterra gli è sembrato di veder attuato il suo ideale di felicità. Per lui, come per Zeno, la vita è una cosa dolorosa, ma degna di esser vissuta. Non bisogna considerarla una malattia 'solo perché duole', ma ciò non significa che 'dolga' di meno. E proprio in due lettere dall'Inghilterra[22] si trovano le espressioni 'è destino che l'omo peni' e 'Dio vuole che l'uomo peni'. Anche se usate in tono semiserio, anzi, proprio per questo, esse non fanno che ribadire quanto già si sa sulle sue convinzioni a proposito del fato umano e sulla maniera di accettarlo. Per lui, come per Zeno, 'la vita non è né brutta né bella, ma è originale'.[23] E, a conferma di questo alternarsi di ottimismo e di pessimismo anche nei confronti dell'Inghilterra, dirà più tardi nel saggio *Uomini e cose in un distretto di Londra*:

Son dodici anni che mi dibatto fra questi opposti pareri. All'arrivo sento con delizia l'aria frizzante della libertà, della grande libertà; poi certe formule da cui non è possibile levarsi in quel benedetto paese mi formano d'intorno al capo una cappa di piombo che con mia grande delizia s'allevia quando tocco il sacro suolo latino.

Questa indecisione mi rende infelice perché in Inghilterra mi manca la mia Trieste e spessissimo quando sono qui rimpiango quella data cappa.[24]

Talvolta Svevo, autore, prende in prestito da Ettore, uomo, in maniera evidentissima, le sue impressioni inglesi. L'esempio più notevole è quello dell'incontro con il bambino inglese che il signor Aghios rievoca in *Corto viaggio sentimentale* e che è la rielaborazione letteraria di un episodio descritto in una lettera mandata alla moglie da Chatham più di vent'anni prima.[25]
La lettera diceva:

Non ti descrissi ancora l'avventura mia più importante di Chatham, quella che mi fece passare un intero pomeriggio lieto o almeno meno triste del solito. Era una domenica e non ne potevo più dalla noia [...] Tutt'ad un tratto sento che dietro di me sulla sedia s'arrampica qualche cosa di assai vivo ma d'assai leggero: Forse un gatto. Mi volgo e mi vedo accanto la più bella faccia rosea, fresca, paffutella che si possa imaginare. Era una faccia da baci: Il più bel ragazzo inglese che si possa immaginare. S'era messo in quella posizione per vedere più da vicino come il fumo mi veniva fuori dal naso. Fummo subito amici. Doveva avere 5 o 6 anni e parlava perfettamente l'inglese! Io non potevo muovermi finché egli era in quella posizione perché se mi fossi alzato egli sarebbe caduto indietro. Gli chiesi quanti anni avesse. Egli mi chiese se avessi una sorellina come ne aveva lui. Io gli dissi che avevo una piccola figlia, più piccola ancora di lui la quale per piccola che fosse sapeva già parlare perfettamente l'italiano e se egli non si vergognasse di non saperlo ancora. Visto che non tutto mi capiva, gli feci vedere il mio vocabolario domandandogli se sapesse leggere. Mi disse di no ma che sapeva studiare le sue lezioni. Poi mi raccontò che a Londra aveva tre cani. In quella venne il padre il quale gli borbottò qualche parola senza rivolgerla a me. Ciò—ad onta che il padre se ne andasse—mi rovinò talmente il piacere che presto congedai il piccolo Philip, stringendogli affettuosamente la piccola manina e ringraziandolo della compagnia. Adesso quando mi vede scappa. Pare lo abbiano sgridato.[26]

Ecco che cosa è diventato l'episodio nel ricordo del signor Aghios:

Aveva sofferto allora orrendamente della solitudine. C'era stata in lui un'impazienza irosa della sfiducia e dell'indifferenza da cui si sentiva circondato. Guardava con invidia e desiderio la vita intensa che lo circondava e respingeva. Una volta, nella stanza di lettura dell'albergo, s'era messo a leggere solitario quando fu avvicinato da un bel ragazzo roseo, di dieci anni circa, che gl'indirizzò delle parole ch'egli non intese affatto, perché si capisce che l'inglese dei bambini è il più difficile. Il signor Aghios si commosse a trovare finalmente un amico. Gli parlò e parve anche che il fanciullo intendesse perché rispose con molte più parole di quelle avute. Disgraziatamente tutte in inglese! E per avvicinarsi a lui, visto che la parola non serviva, il signor Aghios gli carezzò i capelli biondi. Ma allora apparve alla porta della sala un signore che parve indignato che il bambino suo avesse a che fare con uno straniero: "Philip! Come along!" esclamò e il bambino subito s'allontanò, dopo di aver gettata un'occhiata spaventata sulla persona cui aveva dimostrato fiducia e da cui certamente poteva derivargli un pericolo, visto che con tanta premura da essa lo si allontanava.²⁷

Non c'è una grande divergenza tra l'esposizione dei fatti esteriori della lettera e del racconto. Il bambino è sì un po' cresciuto, ma ha conservato perfino lo stesso nome e il colorito roseo (anche se non è più paffutello).²⁸ È mantenuto anche il particolare della comparsa inaspettata, perciò più piacevole, del bambino, e quello del superamento delle barriere linguistiche. Cambia, però, completamente l'atteggiamento di Svevo verso l'episodio. Nella lettera si trattava, in fondo, soltanto di 'un'impressione', anche se freschissima; nel racconto si è passati all'analisi. La noia di un pomeriggio domenicale è diventata la sofferenza della solitudine, 'l'impazienza irosa della sfiducia e dell'indifferenza da cui si sentiva circondato', 'l'invidia e il desiderio' della 'vita intensa che lo circondava e respingeva'. Così come l'allontanamento del piccolo Philip è diventato materia per l'analisi psicologica del bambino. Da 'adesso quando mi vede scappa. Pare lo abbiano sgridato' a 's'allontanò, dopo di aver gettata un'occhiata spaventata sulla persona cui aveva dimostrato fiducia e da cui certamente poteva derivargli un pericolo, visto che con tanta premura da essa lo si allontanava', è brevemente tratteggiato il processo dell'arte di Svevo narratore; l'evidentissimo substrato autobiografico e il 'contrasto fra l'esiguità o magari l'inconsistenza dei 'fatti' e la profondità dei sondaggi analitici'.²⁹

La rievocazione di Philip da parte del signor Aghios sembra dare il via a una serie di ricordi inglesi, almeno parzialmente autobiografici. Anche lui era andato in Inghilterra per affari e

aveva studiato questioni politiche ed economiche solo per poter aggredire il grande Impero, il quale aveva un'organizzazione quasi perfetta, ma non perfetta del tutto e non si sentiva capace del piccolo sforzo per arrivare alla perfezione.³⁰

È indubbio che anche Ettore Schmitz fosse arrivato in Gran Bretagna armato di salde cognizioni economiche e politico-economiche per vincere la sua battaglia privata all'Ammiragliato e vendere la vernice Veneziani alla Marina di Sua Maestà. 'Mi battei abbastanza bene con gli anglo-sassoni', afferma in *Soggiorno londinese*.[31] E risulta evidente dalla lettura dell'epistolario e dei saggi *Sulla teoria della pace*, *Soggiorno londinese* e *Uomini e cose in un distretto di Londra*, che stimasse molto l'ordinamento britannico, pur non trovandolo esente da qualche difetto. Abbiamo visto come apprezzasse la maniera di considerare la libertà degli inglesi, vedremo poi come lo avessero colpito la loro serietà negli affari e il loro saper vivere, ma, per esempio, si facesse gioco della loro insularità.

Il brano che segue immediatamente quello citato e racconta del trasporto di terra inglese in Italia per renderne il suolo più produttivo—visto che al signor Aghios era stato detto che Darwin 'riteneva che la roccia della Granbrettagna fosse stata convertita in terra fertile da un vermicello microscopico'—quasi certamente non è autobiografico. È, però, un esempio tipico della maniera di Svevo di rielaborare la realtà, aggiungendovi un po' di fantasia e una buona dose di umorismo. Ettore cedeva al signor Aghios un'idea bizzarra, che non è da escludere avesse attraversato la sua mente di ammiratore di Darwin, ma conservava intatta la sua ironia.[32] Del resto in una delle *Pagine sparse* non troviamo questa osservazione: 'Si capisce che una cosa immaginata con tanta precisione non abbia bisogno di succedere'?[33]

Poi il signor Aghios parla di animali:

> Persino in Inghilterra somigliano [i cani] ai nostri e ci fanno trovare in essi un pezzo di patria [...] E l'Aghios nella solitudine li amò e spiò scoprendone il carattere e le sue cause [...] Forse il gatto a noi s'accosta di più perché a noi somiglia meglio e meglio ci conosce.[34]

Sappiamo dall'epistolario[35] che la fabbrica di Charlton era 'piena di bestie': fra le altre, due cani e un gatto. Quindi non mancava a Ettore un facile terreno di osservazione. La sua attenzione si concentrava soprattutto sul gatto: 'È il mio maggiore amico... Il gatto è assolutamente una parte della mia vita', scrive alla moglie. E più specificatamente:

> Devo dire anche che somiglia molto ai gatti di Trieste e di Venezia... L'unica cosa che ci divide (e anche in questo somiglia a te) è che non può sopportare il fumo.

Le osservazioni di Aghios e di Ettore sono equivalenti e sottintendono entrambe le medesime riflessioni: 'tanta disparità tra gli uomini inglesi e quelli italiani, tanta somiglianza tra le bestie inglesi e quelle italiane! Tanto difficile comunicare con i primi, tanto facile il contatto con le seconde (nonostante i gusti diversi in fatto di fumo)!' Il che, del resto, è rilevabile anche nella lettera già citata[10] del 30 giugno 1901: 'Di tutto lo spettacolo che più gustai e compresi fu un cane ammaestrato'. L'interesse e l'amore di Svevo e delle sue creature per gli animali è troppo noto[36] (basterebbe ricordare le innumerevoli favolette di argomento zoologico in *Una burla riuscita*) per trovare strano il soffermarsi di Ettore e di Aghios sulle similitudini tra quelli in patria e quelli in terra straniera e sull'accostamento gatto-uomo. È anche sintomatico che nelle lettere di Ettore dall'Inghilterra si trovi la descrizione dettagliata di una visita al giardino zoologico di Londra,[37] sebbene non si parli quasi mai di luoghi assai più famosi. E in un'altra lettera[38] si parla di un'incubatrice per pulcini, che parrebbe anch'essa installata nella fabbrica di Charlton, visto che, secondo una lettera già citata,[35] pochi mesi dopo, questa è piena di galline. L'incubatrice è una Foster-mother. Uno spunto, forse, per il futuro racconto *La madre?*

In *Corto viaggio sentimentale* c'è anche un'altra interessante irevocazione inglese, con conseguenti riflessioni:

Perché la donna, quand'è bella, dà subito molto e in primo luogo il sentimento dell'umanità allo straniero e a tutti. Altro che il saluto scimmiesco tra sconosciuti! Bisogna trovarsi per vari mesi isolato in un paese dove si parla una lingua incomprensibile, evitati dal prossimo solo perché non vi conosce e vi sospetta perciò capace di furti e omicidii, e scoprire ad un tratto l'intimo nesso con tutti costoro, la vostra appartenenza a quel paese, il vostro innato diritto di cittadinanza nello stesso alla vista di un occhio luminoso, di un piedino nervoso, di una capigliatura dal colore e dall'assetto sorprendente. Più giovane allora, la sua prima occhiata era stata un vero e proprio inizio di una relazione sociale. Un inizio entusiastico: Era come se fosse entrato nella casa di un intimissimo amico, addobbata per farvi onore, con tanto di benvenuto stampato sulla porta. Con quell'occhiata il signor Aghios diceva: 'Ti conosco perché sei bella'. E l'inglesina rispondeva in lingua intelligibilissima, cioè con un'occhiata: 'Come sei amabile tu cui piaccio tanto. Più amabile di colui cui diedi tutto e che non sa più che farsene'. Dopo un discorso simile il signor Aghios non aveva più bisogno dell'assenzio, perché gli pareva di trovarsi nella patria ideale dove tutti s'intendono e s'amano.

Era anzi comodo che l'inglesina non sapesse altro linguaggio. Secondo il signor Aghios di allora, quand'era più giovane e perciò più virtuoso, questa era una grande comodità. Perché se alle occhiate fosse seguita la parola, si sarebbe corso il pericolo di trovarsi trasportato di colpo da quella patria ideale al bosco più pericoloso.

Egli credeva di essere rimasto sempre monogamo virtuoso che poteva sopportare lo sguardo sincero della moglie.[39]

Ovviamente niente di simile è rintracciabile nelle lettere di Ettore alla moglie. Anzi esse sono piene di frasi come: 'Certo non sono le tentazioni che mi tengono lontano'[7] o 'Tu pensi a qualche miss inglese? Figurati che attualmente il mio maestro d'inglese, colui col quale passo ogni sera due ore almeno a chiacchierare, è Mrs Clarke di 70 anni'[40] ecc. Però, in una lettera pur tra le proteste di fedeltà, egli ammette le occasioni e riflette sul rammarico che seguirebbe al tradimento:

Io qui avrei occasione ad ogni piè sospinto di tradirti e mi sento tanto puro, tanto alieno da ogni desiderio [...] Guardo le donne come le guardo a Trieste e basta. Questa notte sognai di averti tradita e ne provai un tale dolore di non poterti raccontare tutto e di capire che i nostri rapporti necessariamente dovevano mutare che in sogno ne piansi. Capirai che puoi stare tranquilla anche tu.[41]

In entrambi i casi non c'è tradimento: Aghios non avrebbe potuto affrontare lo sguardo della moglie, Ettore non avrebbe sopportato la mancanza di sincerità che ne sarebbe derivata ai loro rapporti. Queste due reazioni possono certamente essere considerate equivalenti. Rimane dubbio, invece, dove trovare la realtà e dove la letteratura. È sincero Ettore con il suo 'guardo le donne come le guardo a Trieste', cioè, presumibilmente, senza annetter loro alcuna importanza, ed è creatura di fantasia Aghios che apprezza con occhiate che dicono 'ti conosco perché sei bella'?[42]

Nel brano citato c'è un altro particolare che ritroviamo sviluppato e con tono completamente diverso nel saggio *Soggiorno londinese*. Aghios dice: '[...] il prossimo [...] non vi conosce e vi sospetta perciò capace di furti e di omicidii'. Il saggio esemplifica:

E passavo le serate a leggere alcuni giornali di Londra, specialmente i fattacci e i processi la materia grezza per la mia cara letteratura che così mi perseguitava. Ricordo che nel 1903 fu ammazzata a Clapham Junction non lontano dal mio sobborgo in un treno la signorina Money il cui cadavere fu trovato in galleria. Non se ne scoperse mai l'assassino.

Cominciò l'indagine febbrile di tutta la vita della povera signorina e di
tutti i suoi conoscenti dei luoghi ove essa aveva soggiornato e pei
quali era passata. Io vissi intensamente quella caccia e sentivo l'ansia
ora del detective ed ora dell'assassino. Un giorno si annunciava di aver
scoperto una traccia, poi un'altra, poi tutto si annullava per ricomin-
ciare l'inchiesta su un'altra via. E un giorno ne parlai con tanta vivacità
ad un inglese ch'egli per poco non corse alla vicina Police-station a
denunziarmi. Io pensai con rancore: Quella benedetta letteratura. Non
vuole lasciarmi. Finirà per condurmi alla forca.[43]

La prova del nesso tra i due brani citati sembrerebbe essere data
dall'esistenza di un terzo brano, che, pur essendo assai simile nel
contenuto al secondo, anzi, raccontando proprio lo stesso
episodio, è però classificato come *N. 5 dell'Appendice seconda al
Corto viaggio sentimentale* ed è quindi una divagazione del signor
Aghios:

E non con la sola critica egli tentò di penetrare in quella vita. Assiduo,
col vocabolario alla mano, ogni giorno egli compitava una parte del
suo giornale inglese. Nel giornale cercava le notizie più eccitanti per
avere dalla sua grande fatica il massimo frutto. In quell'epoca a Londra
si era eccitatissimi per l'assassinio di una signorina, certa Money,
effettuato in un treno mentre passava sotto una lunga galleria. I
giornali ne parlarono per mesi e mesi. E leggendone ogni giorno, il
signor Aghios, s'identificò dapprima coi detectives, di cui seguiva il
lavoro con ansia, esitante se mandare, con l'aiuto del vocabolario,
qualche suo suggerimento, poi con la povera assassinata di cui sentiva
l'angoscia nella galleria buia ed infine con l'assassino, quel disgraziato,
che certamente ogni giorno leggeva le notizie con un incapponamento
della pelle che il signor Aghios sapeva imitare perfettamente. E, per
qualche tempo, quando prendeva il giornale in mano, specie dacché
sognava lui d'essere l'assassino, egli in quel paese non era più lo
straniero. Certo anche allora dovette prendere una dose maggiore
d'assenzio per addormentare il rimorso d'esser stato capace, lui che non
aveva mai ammazzato neppure una bestia, di prendere per il collo una
povera giovinetta per impedirle di gridare, ferirla e gettarla fuori della
vettura ad agonizzare nella notte nella galleria.[44]

Qui non si ha paura di essere ritenuti assassini perché stranieri,
come nel primo caso, e neanche si ha (più o meno scherzosa-
mente) timore di essere accusati perché troppo interessati al
delitto, come nel secondo; qui Aghios fantastica addirittura di
essere lui l'assassino, anzi è proprio questo che gli dà un senso di
belonging (non più l'eloquente sorriso di una bella donna!). Il

ricordo è diventato letteratura, tipica letteratura sveviana: il processo del rimorso potrebbe essere di Zeno.

Nel saggio *Sulla teoria della pace*, scritto 'durante e subito dopo la prima guerra mondiale',[45] si trova un altro accenno al carattere inglese sospettoso di ogni cosa straniera, reso però liberale dalle leggi vigenti nel paese.

Infatti nelle sue leggi all'interno [...] era il modello della vera pace, cosa meravigliosa per chi conosca quegl'isolani che guardano lo straniero con diffidenza e disprezzo. Vi vigeva il libero scambio, il diritto di transito e cabotaggio per tutti, la facilità d'acquisto della cittadinanza e ciò senz'obbligo alla rinunzia della cittadinanza originaria, l'ospitalità più larga ai profughi. Era un paese che appariva quale il vero Commonwealth e si poteva credere che le conquiste sue fossero fatte a vantaggio di tutta l'umanità.[46]

Rimpiange che la guerra abbia cambiato tutto questo, ma conclude:

La barbarie attuale inglese non m'interessa affatto perché non è che conforme alla barbarie che regna in tutte le relazioni internazionali.[47]

Dunque, a parte le reazioni originate dalla guerra, aperte le leggi quanto chiusi gli uomini. Nel saggio *Soggiorno londinese* si ironizza sull'insularità britannica:

Tutti questi padroni delle piccole officine che circondavano la mia fabbrica mi davano un'idea abbastanza precisa della piccolissima borghesia inglese industriale, gente piccolissima che aveva viaggiato poco perché non era stata che al Canadà o in Australia dunque non fuori dell'Impero, attaccatissima al suo pezzetto di terra, alla sua casetta, al Parlamento, alla religione di solito alla setta e mai alla High Church, e in ultimo anche al suo vetusto comune di Greenwich.[48]

Da una lettera di Ettore appare come egli avesse notato perfino dal farmacista che alle orecchie inglesi 'straniero' suona sinonimo di 'strano':

Tchaperoff venne di sera a trovarmi e mi consigliò di non dare a Nicoletto quella medicina ma invece di dargli una forte dose di chinino. Andammo da Wigg [il farmacista] il quale si meravigliò della potente dose che si domandava. 'Oh!' disse Tchap. 'it is for Continental people'. Il farmacista parve molto convinto e diede la dose domandata. Difatti oggi Nic. sta meglio [...] L'obbligai a prendere questa mane un'altra di quelle pillole ad onta ch'egli, essendo di Murano, non è affatto continentale.[49]

Del resto ancheall' Ammiragliato i signori ammiragli non avevano guardato affascinati le sue mani 'che pareva ballassero per la stanza'?[50] Eppure ciò non gli aveva impedito di fare buoni affari proprio con loro. Perché gli inglesi, in campo commerciale, non guardano alle apparenze, ma alla sostanza. Umberto Saba nel suo *Italo Svevo all'Ammiragliato britannico* riporta la scena della conclusione dell'affare, come pare la raccontasse Ettore stesso:

Lo fecero entrare subito in una stanzetta squallida e disadorna, piuttosto sgabuzzino che ufficio. Come, là dentro, gli appariva povera l'Inghilterra! Dopo pochi minuti, gli si presentò un giovanotto, vestito in borghese, che lo invitò ad accomodarsi nell'unica sedia disponibile. L'ufficiale, per conto suo, sedette sulla tavola, che formava, con la sedia, tutto l'arredamento del luogo. Accavallò le lunghe gambe, offerse ed accese per sé e per l'ospite una sigaretta molto profumata, si mostrò informato sulla questione, fece due o tre domande, disse che tutto andava bene e che l'affare era virtualmente concluso. Italo Svevo credeva di sognare. Si era preparato ad una lunga trafila di pratiche, una più noiosa dell'altra; ad una serie interminabile di discussioni. Ed erano bastati cinque minuti perché la sua cara pittura sottomarina fosse adottata dalla più potente marina da guerra del mondo. In Italia—commentava—o anche in Francia, sarebbero occorsi cinque anni.[51]

Può essere che questo racconto sia un po' romanzato, ma rimane il fatto inconfutabile che, pochi giorni dopo essere arrivato in Inghilterra, Ettore scriveva alla moglie:

Oggi fu veramente giornata campale. L'essenziale per noi è che assolutamente pretendono la fabbrica in Inghilterra. All'Ammiragliato sono stato accolto magnificamente; tutto va bene ma bisogna fare la fabbrica![52]

Degli inglesi lo colpì anche la 'grande necessità di attività ideale', come dice in *Soggiorno londinese*:

Gl'inglesi non c'è dubbio hanno una grande necessità di attività ideale. La dedicano alla politica, alla legge e chi non arriva a queste due altissime attività la dedica alla sua Hobby, collezioni disinteressate, musica e soprattutto religione. Io credo che la massima parte di loro quando sono lasciati a se stessi pensano alla religione. E visto che hanno bisogno di una vera attività, in religione si fanno facilmente aggressivi e diventano dei riformatori. La mia fabbrica è posta su una via maestra che conduce al Tamigi vicinissimo. Nei primi anni ero visitato ogni giorno da una quantità di viaggiatori di commercio che m'offrivano gli articoli più svariati. Li accoglievo benissimo e offrivo loro anche una tazza di tè perché mi portavano a domicilio la vera pronunzia inglese. Tutti mi parlavano di religione. Ne conobbi di quelli che s'erano convertiti varie volte.[53]

Nelle lettere appaiono vari di questi tipi, anche se non necessariamente viaggiatori di commercio. C'è per esempio, l'incontro in treno:

Subito alla sbarco trovai una vecchia signora che voleva mi convertissi e continuai fino a Londra la mia vita di russamento interrotto, in un salone di prima classe con la mia vecchia profetessa accanto e 14 altre persone che ridacchiavano standola a sentire e sentendo anche le mie risposte.[54]

C'è l'ispettore dell'Ammiragliato che viene a visitare la fabbrica:

Corsi a comperare una bottiglia di vino, biscotti e sigari (7s 6d) Saranno pagati dalla casa ma mangerò, beverò e fumerò io perché egli è teetotaler e non accettò niente. Un uomo gentilissimo che mi prescrisse di mangiare molti aranci quando prendo freddo, di non leggere più il *Morning Leader* ma il *Daily Mail* (di cui mi regalò una copia) di non credere al bluff delle varie sette religiose ma di tenermi alla chiesa unita che sia d'Inghilterra d'Austria o d'Italia. Non sapendo con chi avevo da fare non volli confessare che tutte le mie simpatie erano per i Whigs; egli è un Whig puro sangue e cercò di convincermi che l'Inghilterra non poteva imporre dazii. Per ultimo mi consigliò di far bollire l'acqua di Londra prima di berla perché è troppo calcarea. I reumi provengono non dal caldo e dal freddo ma dalla calce [...] Si fermò e disse: 'Voi come straniero non dovreste leggere sempre lo stesso giornale ogni giorno... ecc. ecc.'[55]

In altri non è proprio la 'grande necessità di attività ideale', che egli trova. Come nei due marinai che gli spacciano per zibellino un manicotto e un collo di nessun valore,[56] o nel signor Wickland che gli rivolge la parola solo quando ha bevuto e allora lo chiama 'suo old man'.[4] Ma tutti descrive con il solito umorismo, con la vivacità del suo stile parlato, con ironico più o meno sottinteso commento, anche quando quest'ultimo è fatto a sue spese. Dei marinai dice, per esempio: 'Cominciai a chiacchierare con loro per aver gratis la mia solita lezione d'inglese' e conclude la narrazione dell'episodio alla moglie con: 'Porterò i due cosi mostruosi il manicotto a Trieste e li metteremo nel tesoro di famiglia'. Con lo stesso spirito tratteggia anche altri compagni della *boarding-house* di Londra[57] e dà un vivissimo quadro degli alberghetti della provincia.[58] Per questo ironico commento anche le lettere che si fermano alla descrizione senza approfondirsi nell'introspezione o nell'analisi non sono mai (o quasi mai) 'quadretti di maniera', ma impressioni fresche e spontanee, che, nella loro immediatezza e nell'assenza stessa di preoccupazioni letterarie, rivelano una vena tutta personale, capace di essere risvegliata anche da avvenimenti banali.

In moltissime lettere di Ettore dall'Inghilterra appaiono altri motivi non strettamente inglesi, ma da Svevo resi 'letterariamente' famosi, quali l'ultima sigaretta, il violino, i sogni, la morte, la gelosia. Proprio a proposito di quest'ultima è interessante notare che, in una lettera alla moglie, egli scrive:

Bisogna rassegnarsi, cara Livia; io resterò sempre uguale e può anche avvenire che quando morrò vedendoti guardare ansiosamente il mio medico anziché pensare di dare l'ultimo fiato alle ultime disposizioni, io ti dica: 'Non civettare!'[59]

Non ha mantenuto lo stesso carattere anche Zeno che fugge dalla casa di cura in cui era entrato per liberarsi del vizio del fumo perché teme che, nel frattempo, Augusta lo tradisca col suo dottore? E non aveva già Emilio domandato a Angiolina: 'Perché civetti'?[60]

Qui, però, sono le impressioni 'inglesi' di Ettore Schmitz che ci interessano,[61] e la somma definitiva dell'esperienza anglosassone dell'uomo e dello scrittore ce la dà lui stesso in non incerte parole nella breve dichiarazione contenuta nel saggio *Soggiorno londinese*:

Io dicevo sempre che gli anglo-sassoni mi avevano ringiovanito. Sarei stato più esatto dicendo che mi avevano rasserenato.[62]

e più specificamente in una pagina del *Profilo autobiografico*:

Dal 1902 in poi fino al 1912, per i suoi doveri professionali, lo Svevo soggiornava annualmente per qualche mese in un sobborgo di Londra. Anche tale soggiorno gli alleviò il suo destino [di scrittore misconosciuto] e lo fortificò nelle sue risoluzioni. In complesso gli parve che nel paese delle grandi avventure l'avventura fosse più che altrove respinta. Ognuno in quel sobborgo lavorava tranquillo al proprio posto inserito nella propria classe in cui s'adagiava più o meno attivo ma poco incline a ribellioni o ad avventure. E credette di scoprire che la forza di un paese fosse dovuta piuttosto a tali elementi e che anzi le intraprese di un Lord Clive, o di un Rhodes o di un Nelson non potessero produrre tanta ricchezza se l'avventura non fosse nella nazione un fatto eccezionale, un innesto che nobiliti il vecchio tronco di un'attività giornaliera, tranquilla, regolata. L'avventura letteraria ch'egli aveva tentata non era una diminuzione della sua forza quale cittadino comune e utile? Certamente la vita nella fabbrica inglese fu una cura, un tonico per lo Svevo, e la sua rassegnazione si fece anche più lieta.[63]

La vita inglese, dunque, era stata un'altra conferma che la mediocrità vale almeno tanto, se non di più, dell'eroismo. Svevo sarebbe sì ritornato alla letteratura, ma con Zeno, l'antieroe per antonomasia.

Note

Tutte le citazioni di Italo Svevo sono tratte da: Italo Svevo, *Opera Omnia* in quattro volumi, ed. Dall'Oglio, a cura di Bruno Maier (Milano 1966–9).

[1] *Op. cit.*, vol. III, *Pagine di diario e sparse*, p. 816.

[2] *Ibid.*, p. 818.

[3] Il Maier parla, a proposito dell'opera di Svevo, di osmosi lettera-letteratura. (*Op. cit.* vol. I, Introd. p. 19.)

[4] *Op. cit.*, vol. I, lettera del 7 luglio 1901, p. 300.

[5] *Ibid.*, vol. I, lettera del 13 giugno 1901, p. 270.

[6] *Ibid.*, vol. I, lettera del 13 giugno 1901, pp. 271–272.

[7] *Ibid.*, vol. I, lettera del 14 giugno 1901, p. 274.

[8] *Ibid.*, vol. I, lettera del 15 giugno 1901, p. 275.

[9] *Ibid.*, vol. I, lettera del 16 giugno 1901, p. 278.

[10] *Ibid.*, vol. I, lettera del 30 giugno 1901, p. 295.

[11] *Ibid.*, vol. I, lettera del 14 luglio 1901, p. 315.

[12] *Ibid.*, vol. I, lettera del 17 luglio 1901, p. 317.

[13] *Ibid.*, vol. I, lettera del 17 luglio 1908, pp. 486–487.

[14] In realtà qui Svevo non si riferisce alla lingua cockney, che è tutt'altra cosa, ma all'accento londinese.

[15] *Op. cit.*, vol. III, *Uomini e cose in un distretto di Londra*, p. 701.

[16] *Ibid.*, *Soggiorno londinese*, p. 689.

[17] *Ibid.*, p. 695.

[18] Allude al fatto che Livia, come tutte le signorine di buona famiglia triestina dell'epoca, aveva ricevuto un'educazione francese e parlava e scriveva preferibilmente in tale lingua.

[19] *Op. cit.*, vol. I, lettera del 27 ?, 1909, p. 533.

[20] Questa lettera rivela, fra l'altro, anche l'accentuarsi dell'interesse di Ettore per i sogni. Non è forse una coincidenza che risalga circa a questo periodo la lettura di Freud.

[21] *Ibid.*, vol. I, lettera del 19 giugno 1901, pp. 283–284.

[22] *Ibid.*, vol. I, lettere del 6 aprile 1906, p. 439, e dell'11 settembre 1906, p. 453.

[23] *Op. cit.*, vol. II, *La Coscienza di Zeno*, p. 869.

[24] *Ibid.*, vol. III, *Uomini e cose in un distretto di Londra*, p. 701.

[25] *Cfr.* nota di B. Maier in *op. cit.*, vol. III, *Corto viaggio sentimentale*, p. 146.

[26] *Op. cit.*, vol. I, lettera del 17 giugno 1901, pp. 281–282.

[27] *Ibid.*, vol. III, *Corto viaggio sentimentale*, pp. 145–146.

[28] La descrizione di Philip fatta da Ettore ha un precedente letterario molto simile. Nella lettera del 1 novembre 1797 Jacopo Ortis, descrivendo la sorellina di Teresa dice: 'guancie pari alle rose, fresca, candida, paffutella, pare una Grazia di quattr'anni'. Si tratta forse per Ettore di una inconscia reminiscenza foscoliana che diventa conscia quando dalla lettera passa alla letteratura, tanto da indurlo a sopprimere il 'paffutella' e ad aumentare l'età del piccolo Philip?

[29] B. Maier, introduzione a *op. cit.*, vol. III, p. 12.

[30] *Op. cit.*, vol. III, *Corto viaggio sentimentale*, p. 146.

[31] *Ibid.*, *Soggiorno londinese*, p. 689.

[32] Altri esempi del trattamento ironico delle teorie darwiniane sono nel saggio *L'uomo e la teoria darwiniana* e nel racconto *La buonissima madre*.

[33] *Op. cit.*, vol. III, *Pagine di diario e sparse*, p. 836.

[34] *Op. cit.*, vol. III, *Corto viaggio sentimentale*, p. 148.

[35] *Ibid.*, vol. I, lettera del 15 settembre 1906, p. 458.

[36] Unica vistosa eccezione quella di Zeno che, col suo gusto del paradosso, sosterrà di odiare tutto il popolo britannico a causa del graffio ricevuto da un gatto inglese.

[37] *Ibid.*, vol. I, lettera del 23 giugno, 1901, p. 288.

[38] *Ibid.*, vol. I, lettera del 26 marzo 1906, p. 426.

[39] *Ibid.*, vol. III, *Corto viaggio sentimentale*, pp. 157–158.

[40] *Ibid.*, vol. I, lettera del 6 luglio 1901, p. 298.

[41] *Ibid.*, vol. I, lettera del 9 o 10 luglio 1901, p. 305.

[42] È vero, però, che anche Zeno amava 'la donna... a pezzi'.

[43] *Op. cit.*, vol. III, *Soggiorno londinese*, p. 690.

[44] Ibid., *Appendice seconda al Cortio viaggio sentimentale*, p. 500.

[45] B. Maier, *La personalità e l'opera di I.S.* (Milano 1961), p. 163.

[46] *Op. cit.*, vol. III, *Sulla teoria della pace*, p. 655.

[47] *Ibid.*, p. 656.

[48] *Ibid.*, vol. III, *Soggiorno londinese*, p. 691.

[49] *Ibid.*, vol. I, lettera del 30 marzo 1906, p. 430–431.

[50] *Ibid.*, vol. I, lettera del 7 luglio 1901, p. 301.

[51] Vedi *Opere di Umberto Saba* (Milano 1964), vol. I, p. 153. 'Italo Svevo all'Ammiragliato britannico'.

[52] *Op. cit.*, vol. I, lettera del 21 guigno 1901, p. 285.

[53] *Op. cit.*, vol. III, *Soggiorno londinese*, p. 694.

[54] *Ibid.*, vol. I, lettera del 5 settembre 1906, p. 446.

[55] *Ibid.*, vol. I, lettera del 4 aprile 1906, pp. 434–435.

[56] *Ibid.*, vol. I, lettera del 5 aprile 1906, pp. 436–437.

[57] *Ibid.*, vol. I, lettere del 29 giugno 1901, pp. 292–293 e del 6 luglio 1901, p. 298.

[58] *Ibid.*, vol. I, lettera del 10 luglio 1901, pp. 307–308.

[59] *Ibid.*, vol. I, lettera del 1 dicembre 1903, p. 370.

⁶⁰ *Ibid.*, vol. II, *Senilità*, p. 459.

⁶¹ Non mancano anche 'impressioni' della cucina e, naturalmente, del tempo inglesi. Della prima non pensa troppo male, anche se trova 'imbevibile' il caffé (*op. cit.*, vol. I, lettera del 10 luglio 1901, p. 296). A parte questo, soltanto una volta (*op. cit.*, vol. I, lettera del 29 novembre 1903, p. 368) esprime un giudizio decisamente negativo. Invitato a pranzo a casa di amici ('feci ridere molto le signore', proprio come Zeno in casa Malfenti), trova 'un mondo di vasellame con dentro delle cose complicatissime a base di colla di pesce, o di barbare patate in acqua'. Gli apprezzamenti non certo lusinghieri sul tempo si ripentono, invece, quasi in ogni lettera. Molto espressivo: 'Il sole qui è circa la metà del nostro; ha un aspetto di ammalato di qualche malattia della pelle' (*op. cit.*, vol. I, lettera del 26 novembre 1903, p. 364). Interessante l'altro: 'È un freddo terribile accompagnato da una nebbia giallognola sporca che cambia il giorno in notte. È strano parlare con qualcuno nella nebbia e vederlo da vicino. La sua fisonomia assume un'importanza incredibile; ogni suo tratto acquista fierezza e forza. Io credo tuttavia che la nebbia avuto una grande importanza nella pittura inglese. Quelle facce deliziose di fanciulle inglesi ideali e superbe devono esser state viste attraverso la nebbia.' (*op. cit.*, vol. I, lettera del 6 dicembre 1903, p. 378.) Un'eco forse di 'nel paesaggio umido e grigio imperò la biondezza di Angelina' (*op. cit.*, vol. II, *Senilità*, p. 529)?

⁶² *Op. cit.*, vol. III, *Soggiorno londinese*, p. 693.

⁶³ *Ibid.*, *Profilo autobiografico*, pp. 807–808.

Subscribers

Howard A. Abbott, 1 Lynmouth Drive, Gilmorton, Rugby, Warwickshire
Adele Beghe, 39 Montrose Place, London SW1
Olga Benotti, Via Schina 15, Turin
Trudie Berger, University of York Language Teaching Centre, Heslington, York
Brunero Bernardini, Via S. Antonio 4, Pisa
Anna Ramorino Bertacchi, Viale Bernardo Segni 11, Florence
Umberto Bosco, Piazza Minzoni 9, Rome
C. P. Brand, Department of Italian, University of Edinburgh
G. L. Brook, Department of English, University of Manchester
Stella Brook, 26 Chandos Road South, Manchester
L. Brooke, Healey House, Huddersfield
Miss R. I. Brookes, 27 Sherlock Close, Cambridge
Miss A. M. Burnet, 26 Green Lane, Ford, Salisbury, Wiltshire
Mabel Burdess, 2 Roe's Cottages, Weston, Hitchin, Hertfordshire
Charlotte Burton, Department of English, Riverside City College, California
Howard Burton, Department of English, Riverside City College, California
Christopher Cairns, Department of Italian, University of Southampton
Lanfranco Caretti, University of Florence
Toni Cerutti, Via Millefonti 39/6, Turin
S. B. Chandler, Department of Italian and Hispanic Studies, University of Toronto
Sir William Mansfield Cooper, Fieldgate Cottage, 9 Station Road, Meldreth, Royston, Hertfordshire
Beatrice Corrigan, Department of Italian and Hispanic Studies, University of Toronto
R. G. Cox, Department of English, University of Manchester
J. A. Cremona, Trinity Hall, Cambridge
Mrs May Cristea, 45 North Side, Clapham Common, London SW4
Carlo Dall'olio, Via Cosmè Tura 39, Ferrara
R. M. Davie, Department of Italian, University of Reading
Carlo Dionisotti, 44 West Heath Drive, London, NW11
Filippo Donini, 39 Belgrave Square, London SW1

Diane Dyer, Department of Romance Languages, McMaster University, Hamilton, Ontario
Conor Fahy, 25 Graham Road, Ipswich
Giulia Fermi, Piazzale Porta al Prato 21, Florence
Mrs F. M. Firth, 101 Reedley Road, Stoke Bishop, Bristol
Kenelm Foster, Blackfriars, Cambridge
Peter J. Fuller, Department of Italian, University of Leeds
Catherine A. Galbraith, 30 Francis Avenue, Cambridge, Massachusetts
Rachel Giese, 5825 Marine Drive, West Vancouver, B.C., Canada
Creighton Gilbert, Department of Art, Queen's College, City University of New York
G. P. Giorgetti, 74 Linden Way, Southgate, London N14
Ida L. Gordon, The Crook, Ulpha, Broughton in Furness
Lewis Hall Gordon, Brown University, Providence, Rhode Island
Ian Greenlees, Via Santo Spirito 15, Florence
T. Gwynfor Griffith, Department of Italian, University of Hull
Gerald B. Gybbon-Monypenny, 15 Mabfield Road, Manchester
R. D. Hawkes, 62 Belgrave Avenue, Gidea Park, Romford, Essex
Miss C. M. Hill, Department of French, University of Manchester
T. E. Hope, Department of French, University of Leeds
P. R. Horne, 19 Lathbury Road, Oxford
Elsie M. Horrox, 10 Portland Gardens, Marlow, Buckinghamshire
J. K. Hyde, 'Walbrook', 110 Andrew Lane, High Lane, Stockport, Cheshire
F. J. Jones, Department of Italian, University College, Cardiff
T. L. Jones, 4 The Beeches, West Didsbury, Manchester
J. D. Jump, 3 Belfield House, West Road, Bowdon, Altrincham, Cheshire
R. E. Keller, Department of German, University of Manchester
A. C. Keys, Department of Romance Languages, University of Auckland, New Zealand
Margaret Lally, 24 Parsonage Road, Withington, Manchester
Eleanor Lancelot, 11 Arundel Road, Southport, Lancashire
Delia Lennie, Piazza Ennio 11, Rome
A. L. Lepschy, University College, London
C. Salvadori Lonergan, Department of Italian, Trinity College, Dublin
Jennifer Lorch, School of Italian, University of Warwick
C. A. McCormick, Department of Italian, University of Sydney
Philip McNair, 213 Huntingdon Road, Cambridge
Ronald Marshall, 23 Hillside Crescent, Belfast
Christopher Martin, Bassingbourne Mill, Bassingbourne, Royston, Hertfordshire
Sadie Martin, The King's Mill, Great Shelford, Cambridge

Frederick May, Department of Italian, University of Sydney
M. F. M. Meiklejohn, Department of Italian, University of Glasgow
Ian Michael, Department of Spanish, University of Southampton
Eileen A. Millar, Department of Italian, University of Glasgow
B. Moloney, Department of Italian, University of Leeds
Phyllis A. Moore, Teachers' College, Peterborough, Ontario
Mrs Geraldine Noll, 8 Cavendish House, Eastgate Gardens, Guildford, Surrey
Mrs M. A. Ormerod, 62 Walton Road, Chesterfield, Derbyshire
T. O'Neill, Department of Romance Languages, Queen's College, City University of New York
Sybille Pantazzi, Art Gallery of Ontario, Dundas Street, Toronto, Ontario
J. H. Parker, School of Graduate Studies, University of Toronto
Vincenzo Pernicone, Università Degli Studi di Genova, Genoa
Christopher Pirie-Gordon, Via Palestro 3, Florence
Giovanni Pozzi, 235 rue de Morat, Fribourg
Olga Ragusa, Department of Italian, Columbia University
Paul Renucci, Grand Palais Perron Alexandre III, Cours la Reine, Paris
Barbara Reynolds, University of Nottingham
Christina Roaf, Somerville College, Oxford
Camilla Roatta, Via dei Renai 23, Florence
Daisy Dina Ronco, University Hall, Bangor, Caernarvonshire
Jacky Sanoff, Via Masaccio 107, Florence
F. W. Saunders, Department of French, University of Manchester
John A. Scott, Department of Italian, University of Reading
Mrs. Lilian Speight, 821 Chelham Way, Santa Barbara, California
Geoffrey Stagg, Department of Italian and Hispanic Studies, University of Toronto
Frau Helene Stieve, Kühlerhof, Doveren, Krs. Erkelenz, Düsseldorf, Germany
Antonia Stott, 34 Leadervale Road, Edinburgh
F. E. Sutcliffe, Department of French, University of Manchester
Mrs Ruth Tait (Mrs M. D. C. Tait), 125 Farnham Avenue, Toronto, Ontario
Walter J. Temelini, Department of Hispanic and Italian Studies, University of Windsor, Ontario
R. M. C. Thresh, Lloyds Bank Europe, 43 boulevard des Capucines, Paris
Michael Ukas, Department of Italian and Hispanic Studies, University of Toronto
Maria Valgimigli, Brunswick Cottage, 1 Hale Road, Altrincham, Cheshire

Pamela Waley, Westfield College, London NW3
Donald W. T. Watson, Department of Education, University of Manchester
D. M. White, University of Leeds
Frederick Whitehead, 25 St Hilda's Road, Northenden, Manchester
John H. Whitfield, 2 Woodbourne Road, Edgbaston, Birmingham
Miss M. P. Wigley, 18 Manchester Street, London W1
Andrew Wilkin, University of Strathclyde
J. R. Woodhouse, Department of Italian, University of Hull
Kathleen M. G. Wooldridge, 54 Elvina Gardens, Toronto, Ontario
Lucrezia A. Zaina, Department of Italian, University of Liverpool
Mrs S. Zoll, 176 Christopher Street, New York, N.Y.

Libraries

Aarhus, Statsbiblioteket
Belfast, Queen's University, Main Library
Birmingham University Library
California University, Department of Italian
Canterbury, University of Kent Library
Cardiff, University College Library
Connecticut University, Wilbur Cross Library
Dublin, University College Library
Florence, British Institute of Florence
Glasgow University Library
Kansas University Library
London
    Birkbeck College
    Italian Institute
    Royal Holloway College
    Warburg Institute
Manchester, John Rylands Library
North Carolina University Library
Padua University, Instituto di Filologia Neolatine
Pretoria, University of South Africa Library
St Andrew's University Library
Stanford University Libraries
Sussex University Library
Sydney University, Fisher Library
Toronto University Library
Warwick University Library